The Civil War Letters of

Colonel Charles F. Johnson

Invalid Corps

The Civil War Letters of
Colonel Charles F. Johnson
Invalid Corps

Edited with an introduction by
Fred Pelka

University of Massachusetts Press
Amherst and Boston

Printed in the United States of America

LC 2004013505
ISBN 1-55849-451-0 (library cloth ed.); 460-x (paper)

Designed by Dennis Anderson
Set in New Baskerville by Graphic Composition, Inc.
Printed and bound by The Maple-Vail Book Manufacturing Group

Library of Congress Cataloging-in-Publication Data

Johnson, Charles F. (Charles Francis), 1827–1867.
The Civil War letters of Colonel Charles F. Johnson, Invalid Corps / edited with an introduction by Fred Pelka.
p. cm.
Includes bibliographical references and index.
ISBN 1-55849-451-0 (library cloth : alk. paper) — ISBN 1-55849-460-x (pbk. : alk. paper)
1. Johnson, Charles F. (Charles Francis), 1827–1867—Correspondence. 2. Disabled veterans—United States—Correspondence. 3. United States. Army. Invalid Corps—Biography. 4. United States. Army. Veteran Reserve Corps. Regiment, 18th (1864–1865)—Biography. 5. United States—History—Civil War, 1861–1865—Personal narratives. 6. United States. Army—Military life—History—19th century. 7. United States—History—Civil War, 1861–1865—Campaigns. 8. Disabled veterans—United States—History—19th century. I. Pelka, Fred, 1954– II. Title.
E493.1.V58J64 2004
973.7'41'087—dc22

2004013505

British Library Cataloguing in Publication data are available.

Frontispiece: Colonel Charles F. Johnson. Courtesy of Mrs. Grace Johnson Lynch.

to Denise Anne Karuth

Contents

Editorial Method and Acknowledgments

Most of the war-time letters of Colonel Charles F. Johnson are collected as photocopies at the U.S. Army Military History Institute Archives in Carlisle, Pennsylvania. This is where I first encountered them in fall 1998. The copies had been deposited there more than ten years earlier by Mrs. Grace Johnson Lynch, great-granddaughter of the colonel. A first reading required two trips to Pennsylvania—four full days—after which I contacted Mrs. Lynch to ask if she would allow me to edit and publish the correspondence. She very graciously shipped the original letters from her home in Minnesota to my home in Massachusetts, where I began the process of rereading, transcribing, selecting, and annotating the collection for publication.

What Mrs. Lynch sent me in two carefully wrapped boxes was a total of 206 handwritten letters or portions of letters, including many not in the Carlisle collection, as well as other original documents, such as children's report cards, a map of a homestead claim, various government documents, and several photographs. Along with these were photocopies of twenty-five additional letters, the originals of which were not in Mrs. Lynch's possession; two typed transcripts of complete letters unavailable as originals or as photocopies; and transcribed fragments of four other letters, which also lacked corresponding originals and photocopies.

Almost a year after Mrs. Lynch's death in 2002, I learned of another branch of the extended Johnson family, the Sicard/Becker family in El Mirage/Adilanto, California. It was this portion of the family that had possession of many of Johnson's letters of 1861 and 1862, including the originals of the photocopies and transcriptions Mrs. Lynch had made available to me. Together with the letters in Mrs. Lynch's possession, these most likely constitute the total of the extant letters of Colonel Charles F. Johnson.

Some 143 of these letters are included in this volume. These chronicle Johnson's time as lieutenant colonel and then colonel of the Eighty-first Pennsylvania Volunteer Infantry, as well as his involvement in the history of the Invalid Corps. Also included are the bulk of Johnson's travelogues through Missouri. The letters I excluded are either entirely redundant or else deal only with such mundane matters as the location of a particular paper in his desk, lists of items he wanted his wife Mary to bring when she visited him at camp, discussion of the weather, and so on.

The letters were transcribed as close to the original as possible, with all of Johnson's spellings and punctuation retained. Now and then I have added a period where Johnson neglected to use one at the end of a sentence, or a word or a letter where one had obviously been omitted. All of these additions are set off in brackets. Johnson remarked once that his daughter Clara was "death on periods"; Johnson himself was a strong believer in the dash, using it enthusiastically, often in place of all other punctuation. The dashes have been retained as have Johnson's frequent underlining of words, rendered here as italics, and use of quotation marks for emphasis. Like many nineteenth-century writers, Johnson also often used the abbreviations "inst." and "ult." when referring to previous letters. "Inst." is the abbreviation for "Instant," meaning the present or current month. "Ult." is the abbreviation for "ultimate" or "ultimo," meaning the last or previous month. Thus, a letter written on May 20 referring to "your letter of the 10th inst." would mean "your letter of May 10th," while a reference to "your letter of the 10th ult." would mean "your letter of April 10th."

Johnson's handwriting, though usually fairly legible, was sometimes difficult to make out, particularly when he was writing in haste or in the field. Occasionally I was unable to decipher a word or phrase, and some of the letters are torn or blotted. In these instances I have indicated, also in brackets, either my thought as to what a word might be or a question mark to indicate my unwillingness to venture a guess. Last, I have noted when Johnson's letters are written on military letterhead or on that of a hotel where he was staying.

Annotations generally occur whenever Johnson first mentions a name. Sometimes these are more or less well-known military and political figures, more often they are personal friends and associates. Like many educated men of the time, Johnson liberally sprinkles his letters with literary quotations. Here too I have tried to identify the reference. On a few occasions I was not able to locate anything noteworthy about the person mentioned or the phrase quoted and so remain silent. Typically, I annotate those portions of the letters that I feel make significant allusions to developments in the Invalid Corps, the status of people with disabilities, or other issues on which I want to elaborate.

There are always many people to thank in a project such as this. I most especially thank Jill Abraham, Charles W. Johnson (no apparent relation to the colonel), and Dennis Edelin, archives specialists at the National Archives and Records Administration, who were always willing to steer me in the right direction as I worked my way through the records of the Invalid Corps and the Provost Marshal General's Office in Washington, D.C. I also thank Steven L. Zerbe for his research at the Philadelphia Free Library, and Shirley Evans,

Linda Cope, and Amy Snyder for their assistance at the Camden County Historical Society, and Linda Knaack, Elise Feeley, Elise Dennis, and Lu Knox, the reference librarians at the Forbes Library in Northampton, Massachusetts. Another great help was Ted Dombroski, historian at Company K, Eighty-first Pennsylvania Volunteer Infantry (reenactors), who eagerly responded to my many requests for information on Johnson's original unit. His comments on the manuscript were also quite helpful, as were those of Susan O'Hara and Mary Lou Breslin, advisers to the Oral History Project on Disability Rights and Independent Living at the Regional Oral History Office, Bancroft Library, University of California at Berkeley. My thanks also go to Joanne Graves, who helped with finding the photographs and posters used to illustrate the book. I also owe much to Paul K. Longmore, professor of history at San Francisco State University, who encouraged me to undertake the project and agreed to read and comment on the manuscript.

Mrs. Lynch and her son John were exceedingly gracious, first and foremost in allowing me access to the colonel's letters but also in sharing their family history. I regret that I was not able to complete the book before Mrs. Lynch's death in May 2002. I am also grateful to Shawnette Becker and to Mr. and Mrs. Richard and Lucille Sicard for sharing with me Colonel Johnson's letters of late spring and autumn 1862 and their photographs of the Johnson family. My thanks also go to Clark Dougan, senior editor at the University of Massachusetts Press, whose enthusiasm for this project was evident from the start.

Justin and Yoshiko Dart have been mentors to several generations of disability rights activists and scholars. Justin is widely identified as "the father of the Americans with Disabilities Act," but what is less known is that he was also a Civil War historian. In the months before his death in June 2002, he and I had several long talks about this project. Justin and Yoshiko also kindly provided me with a place to stay (and many delicious dinners) during my trips to Washington to do research at the National Archives. There was an outpouring of sympathy and sadness at Justin's passing, and I often thought of him as I did my work.

Finally, I thank the person to whom this book is dedicated. Denise Anne Karuth has been my best friend and partner for three decades, supporting me in my various odd (and some of them have been *very* odd) projects. I cannot express all that this has meant to me, except to say that this book would not have been possible without her support, her insight and intelligence, and her unfailing love.

The Civil War Letters of

Colonel Charles F. Johnson

Invalid Corps

Introduction

Among the personal effects of Charles F. Johnson (1827–1867) was a postcard-sized scrap of paper with the following inscription:

> Steamer Miantinami Nov. 15th 1855
> Written by Samuel Gessbury
> a man born without arms
> written for C. F. Johnson
> with my left foot.[1]

One can imagine Johnson on the *Miantinami,* crossing from his home in Camden, New Jersey, to Philadelphia or traveling to some other point on the Delaware River. There he meets Gessbury, who drafts this memento of their encounter. Did the two men know each other? Were they friends or neighbors? Or was this a trick Gessbury performed for passing strangers, a way for him to earn his living, perhaps?[2] Whatever the case, the note was enough of a curiosity to have been carefully preserved by Johnson's family, along with his commissions in the Union army, a subpoena to appear before a congressional select committee, and several hundred letters written to his wife Mary during the Civil War.

There is also the report of an army surgeon, dated November 12, 1862, declaring the likelihood of Colonel Johnson's recovery from gunshot wounds to his legs and testicles in June of that year to be "distant and uncertain." Like Samuel Gessbury, Johnson would spend the rest of his life living with his disabilities. For most of that time, this former commander of the Eighty-first Pennsylvania Volunteer Infantry would serve as an officer in the Invalid Corps.

The Invalid Corps was a unique military organization, and it played an important role in the Union victory. Organized in May 1863 and later renamed the Veteran Reserve Corps, it consisted primarily of veterans with disabilities, like Johnson. With twenty-four regiments and many detached companies, the corps was at one point twice as numerous as the entire prewar U.S. Army. Its soldiers enforced the draft, patrolled the streets as provost marshals, guarded prisoners and supplies, fought to protect the nation's capitol from Confederate raiders, and served as the honor guard for Lincoln's funeral. After the war, its officers formed the nucleus of the Bureau of Refugees,

Freedmen, and Abandoned Lands. Johnson himself, from spring 1866 until his death in 1867, would serve as a subcommissioner with the Freedmen's Bureau, attempting to provide assistance and enforce some measure of justice for newly emancipated slaves.

Despite all this, the Invalid Corps has been largely overlooked by historians, as enigmatic in its import as Sam Gessbury's note. "Disability," writes Douglas C. Baynton, "is everywhere in history, once you begin looking for it, but conspicuously absent in the histories we write."[3]

Certainly, disability was everywhere in the American Civil War. Never before had so many Americans been injured or sickened in so short a time. A nurse at Columbia Hospital in Washington, D.C., described how an order came, midway through the conflict, "to make ready to accommodate *one thousand wounded patients:* and as we look over to Carver Hospital, the work of putting up more tents is going on, so as to accommodate fourteen hundred more. . . . on our right, they are making the same preparation."[4] Stewart Brooks, in his *Civil War Medicine,* notes how "when [Confederate General Robert E.] Lee and [Major General George B.] McClellan clashed along Antietam Creek the water under Burnside's Bridge actually ran red, and at the end of the bloodiest day in American history there were 10,000 Federals and 4,500 Confederates crying for help. To this staggering number of tortured men can be added another 3,000 at nearby Frederick, Maryland, who had been cut down three days before at South Mountain."[5] After the battle of Gettysburg, the line of ambulances required to remove the Confederate wounded stretched seventeen miles, even though the most severely injured were left behind for treatment in the field.[6] The three days of that battle left nearly 30,000 men injured, a high proportion of whom would no doubt survive with significant disabilities.[7]

As staggering as these numbers are, they represent only a fraction of the war's casualties. For every soldier killed in combat, two more died of disease, the most common cause of death being chronic diarrhea.[8] Malaria, dysentery, tuberculosis, typhoid, scurvy, and other diseases also rendered hundreds of thousands of men disabled or debilitated, in a total U.S. population of roughly thirty-two million.[9] Countless others were left with psychological scars, the constellation of emotional disabilities which medical professionals today call post-traumatic stress disorder but which in the less clinical language of the 1860s was termed "soldier's heart."[10] Twenty years after the end of the war, close to a quarter million Union veterans were collecting disability pensions, Confederate soldiers being ineligible for federal benefits.[11] The vast majority of these had been young men in the full flush of health and ability when they became ill or injured.

As prevalent as disability was, Baynton's observation rings true: disability remains a largely unexplored topic of Civil War history. Of the more than fifty thousand books written about the conflict to date, few if any focus explicitly on disability.[12] And although hundreds of the war's participants wrote and published their memoirs in the years after Appomattox, disability, when mentioned at all, was generally used only to illustrate the horror of the struggle and the depth of sacrifice required. Even those writers who were themselves disabled seemed reticent to discuss the subject. General O. O. Howard, who lost an arm in the Peninsula campaign of 1862 (and later became director of the Freedmen's Bureau), mentions his disability on no more than 20 of the 1,207 pages of his autobiography; similarly, Joseph Crowell, in his best-selling memoir published in 1906, ends his story just before he enters the Invalid Corps.[13]

This relative silence is no accident. It arises from an ancient and enduring ambivalence about disabilities and the people who have them. Disability, as one poet has observed, is like a magic wand, effecting "a profound metamorphosis" in those around her.[14] The nature of this change reflects the attitudes and prejudices that accompany disability, what historians Paul Longmore and Lauri Umansky have described as "'the existential anxiety' that disability often evokes."[15] Rosemarie Thomson, in her study of the role disability has played in American culture, describes how "constructed as the embodiment of corporeal insufficiency and deviance, the physically disabled body becomes a repository for social anxieties about such troubling concerns as vulnerability, control, and identity."[16]

Throughout most of recorded history, disability has been considered a manifestation of moral and spiritual failure, its impact on the individual inextricably linked to prevailing social attitudes about physical and psychological difference. From biblical injunctions that hold them to be ritually unclean and thus unfit to enter the temple to New Age pronouncements that disability is the result of bad karma, people with disabilities have been shunned, stigmatized, segregated into asylums and institutions, at times even murdered, simply because of their physical or mental differences.[17] The body that is physically disabled exists, then, "as a cultural text that is interpreted, inscribed with meaning—indeed made—within social relations," and "disability" has become "another culture-bound, physically justified difference to consider along with gender, class, ethnicity, and sexuality." Modern disability rights activists use the term *ableism* as shorthand for this complex spectrum of reactions, ranging from pity to suspicion to outright hatred, which they believe to be the greatest obstacle to the achievement of their full civil and human rights.[18]

This stigmatizing of people with disabilities often occurs as a part of the "just world" theory elucidated by Melvin Lerner and applied to disability by Rosemarie Thomson. Simply put, the theory holds that bad things happen only to bad people. To suffer a disabling injury or illness or, worse yet, to be "born without arms" or with some other serious disability is therefore a sign of divine or cosmic retribution for a sin or shortcoming, known or unknown, conscious or not. This doctrine "provides a psychological safeguard against the intolerable randomness of experience," but it also "results in victim-blaming and scapegoating of those who are different."[19]

"Ableism" and "victim-blaming" certainly colored the way contemporaries perceived the Invalid Corps. Its members were ridiculed as the "Condemned Yanks" and the "Cripple Brigade." Historians have hardly been more kind. Bruce Catton describes the Eighteenth Regiment of the Veteran Reserve Corps, which Johnson commanded, as "a strange little detachment of hopelessly crippled men who did not seem to think that mere physical disability need keep a man out of the army."[20] Byron Stinson, noting the lack of published material on the corps, concludes: "Surely, something was wrong with an outfit which mustered 60,000 men and merited scarcely a kind word outside of the *Official Records,* and the written record of its last commander."[21]

That what was "wrong" with the outfit might have had less to do with the men than with societal attitudes is an insight we owe to the relatively new field of disability studies and to the disability rights movement from which it originated. Just as the civil rights movement and the women's movement brought a new sophistication and inclusivity to the writing of American history, so has the disability rights movement of the past three decades begun to illumine the lives of people such as Samuel Gessbury and Charles F. Johnson. As with race and gender, disability can now be seen as "not simply located in the bodies of individuals," but as "a socially and culturally constructed identity" well worth the investigative and analytical efforts of social historians.[22]

Johnson's letters, together with the other documents he left behind—his official reports, the affidavits he collected, and his letters to his superiors and subordinates—constitute perhaps the most complete record to date of the Invalid Corps, as seen from the perspective of one of its members and organizers. Moreover, they offer us a unique opportunity to begin to examine the "magic wand" of disability in the context of the most violent and transforming period in American history.

CHARLES FRANCIS JOHNSON was born in Philadelphia, Pennsylvania, on September 22, 1827, the fifth child of Henry Johnson and Mariah Hufty

Johnson. Henry had been born around the turn of the century, Mariah in 1803 or 1804 in Camden, New Jersey. Henry died on October 2, 1836, when Charles was barely nine years old; Mariah never remarried. She was listed in the Camden City Directory of 1863–1864 as living at 327 Mickle Street, "widow, cupper and Leeching," earning her living by bleeding patients.[23]

Before the war Johnson worked as a clerk and an engraver. By 1856, his participation in a committee investigating the causes of a ferry boat disaster on the Delaware River earned the attention of the local press.[24] This was not the last time Johnson would appear in the press, and his investigative skills would be used often in the years ahead. That Johnson's financial means at the start of the war were substantial, if precarious, can be seen in the fact that the Johnsons apparently employed domestic help and sent their children (the boys at any rate) to a private school. Further evidence of Johnson's status is his being awarded a commission as a lieutenant colonel in an era when officers were often appointed more for their political, social, and financial standing than any military acumen.

Johnson's wife Mary came from what seems to have been a financially secure but geographically scattered family. Mary Ann Davis was born on October 28, 1827, in Smyra, Kent County, Delaware. Her father, Aaron Davis, was described as "a very high class bootmaker, having a shop which catered to the high class in Philadelphia," and "a new Jersey shoe manufacturer." A "trader's note," dated May 5, 1845, was made out to Davis enabling him to operate a shoe store in Baltimore. Mary had four brothers, three older and one younger. At the outbreak of the war Mary's older brother William Blackiston Davis lived in southern Maryland, not far from Washington, D.C.[25]

Charles and Mary were married on January 27, 1850, in Spring Garden, Pennsylvania, the Reverend Joseph Kennard presiding. Their first children, twin boys, were born on November 7 of the same year. The eldest by forty minutes, Joseph Hufty Johnson was evidently more rebellious than his brother, William Ewing Wiley Johnson. Joseph was a bright child, and earned good grades at school. At age nine or ten he was caught sipping the dregs of liquor glasses left at table by adults. Both he and his brother were considered cute and mischievous. A daughter, Clara Adelia, was born on September 24, 1858.[26]

Perhaps it was his family that kept Charles Johnson from enlisting in the first rush of patriotism that followed the Confederate bombardment of Fort Sumter in April 1861. Not until three months later, after the stunning federal reversal at the First Battle of Bull Run, did Johnson join the next great wave of Union volunteers. Unlike his relatives the Huftys, Johnson did not join a New Jersey regiment. Instead, he received his commission from Pennsylvania

Governor Andrew Curtin on September 17, 1861. That month the Eighty-first Pennsylvania rendezvoused at Camp Washington near Easton, where the new soldiers adjusted to camp life and the beginnings of army discipline.[27]

Johnson's first letters to Mary provide an officer's eye view of this process. He describes "a Court Martial for three offenders, which will be held to morrow—I suppose that the result will be reducing two men from non-commissioned officers to the ranks and depriving a private of one month's pay—all for violating orders." Military discipline—an entirely new experience for most of these "citizen soldiers"—also provided the occasion for Johnson's first reference to African Americans in what would, in one year almost to the day, become a war of emancipation: "To-night I turned both of Cap't Alexander's Negro cooks out of camp for abusive language to officers—so you see that we are down to strict military life."[28]

It was during this period of waiting for the real war to begin that Johnson acquired a black servant. "To give you some idea of the non-sense that will come in the heads of men," he writes in a postscript to his letter of October 19, "the enclosed paper was presented to me at my marque by a committee of officers with the Nigger, whom I duely christened in his new name, after a long exhortation, which he received in earnest."[29] The "enclosed paper" does not survive, but it perhaps resembled another "certificate" Johnson would send home more than a year later, giving him a liquor jug "to hold in trust for the use, benefit, and pleasure of the occupants" of the boarding-house where he lived.[30] That he had the right to own a black man, to "exhort" him, and to change his name to Abraham, no doubt in honor of the president, seems to have gone without saying for Johnson.

There is nothing else in Johnson's surviving papers to indicate his or Mary's feelings about slavery, but this lost "title" to Abraham is perhaps a good clue. At least one of Mary's forebears—Lewis Blackiston—was a slave holder.[31] The Johnsons' feelings toward black people are not recorded in their prewar correspondence, though in several letters during the war Johnson would give vent to the crudest racism: "I tell you Mary, a nigger is a nigger and the *best* of them is not worth a God damn!"[32]

Similarly, though he loved his wife and doted on his daughter Clara, Johnson shared the standard mid-nineteenth-century, middle-class American view of the place of women, even while he gave Mary considerable latitude in her management of the family finances: "In reference to the sewing machine, you can do as you deem proper—provided—provided always—that you do not undertake to get work out side of the family to do—I mean your *own* family—I know you so well that if you take a notion some fine day, you would be over in town in a hurry for work, and I would not like *that,* while I live and have a possission."[33]

ON OCTOBER 10, 1861, the Eighty-first broke camp for Washington and was issued arms after arriving at its new post on Kendell Green. The regiment then became a part of the Army of the Potomac, drilling and parading through fall and winter, as its organizer and commander, Major General George B. McClellan, weighed his plans. Boredom and drunkenness seem to have been problems, though desertion less so because the Eighty-first was stationed so far from home. The regiment was sent out on patrols or scouting forays, and in November 1861 it went into Maryland for several days to protect Union men going to the polls in the local elections. Through it all, Johnson seemed to relish the military life and shared many of the details of the camp's routine with Mary.

On April 4, 1862, the Eighty-first Pennsylvania was marched to the docks at Alexandria, Virginia, and loaded onto the transport steamer USS *Spaulding.* The regiment arrived the next morning at Union-held Fort Monroe, at the tip of the Virginia Peninsula. From there it marched to Ship Point, where the Eighty-first was put to work, as Johnson wrote, "un-loading the stores from the numerous vessels (of all sizes & kinds) that are constantly arriving."[34] After several days of this, the regiment was moved up toward Yorktown to join the rest of the army as McClellan cautiously prepared his assault.

"I could write you some very interesting accounts of the movements of the army in this section," Johnson told Mary, "but you will be compelled to receive *all* your information from the papers, as it would not do for an *officer* especially to violate 'orders'—even with his family. I for one feel that the trust is to important and *honourable* to violate—so *my* 'war news' will be very meager."[35] Johnson seems to a great extent to have obeyed these orders, but he did provide Mary with details of the regiment's daily life while on the Peninsula. The Eighty-first Pennsylvania, together with the rest of the First Brigade, "built corduroy roads, besieged Yorktown, and built two bridges, the most famous of the two being Sumner Bridge, across the Chickahominy River within eight miles of Richmond. These bridges helped provide the link between [the two wings of McClellan's] army, now divided by the river."[36]

The brigade was on the north side of the river when Confederate General Joseph Johnston launched his attack May 30. The Eighty-first arrived on the scene the next day for what was alternately described as the battle of Fair Oaks or Seven Pines. Casualties in the Eighty-first were heavy, with eight men and officers killed, thirty-two wounded, and fifty-one captured. Among those killed was Colonel James Miller, the Mexican War veteran who had organized the regiment in Philadelphia. With Colonel Miller dead on the field, Lieutenant Colonel Charles F. Johnson took charge of the regiment on June 1, 1862.[37] Among those wounded on the Confederate side was General Joseph Johnston, the command of what would soon be called the Army of Northern Virginia therefore falling to General Robert E. Lee. During the next weeks McClellan slowly advanced on Richmond, while Lee prepared his new command for an offensive he hoped would defeat or even destroy the federal army.

Lee's trap for McClellan was sprung on June 25, the start of what would become known as the Seven Days' Battles. Initially, the Eighty-first was held in reserve but was then ordered to a position just south of the White Oak Swamp. On June 30, the First Brigade was attacked by troops under the command of Major General Thomas J. "Stonewall" Jackson. It was during this engagement, at Charles City Crossroads, that Charles F. Johnson, now a full colonel, was shot four times, twice in the right thigh, once in the left, and once in his testicles. Command of the Eighty-first once again changed hands.[38]

Within forty-eight hours Johnson was moved, first to Fort Monroe, then to the hospital ship *John Brooks,* a side-wheel steamer chartered by the U.S. Army. Johnson was a passenger/patient on the *Brooks* from July 2 to July 4, when he was admitted to the U.S. Army General Hospital in Annapolis, Maryland. He spent at least a day at the hospital but was listed as being "on furlough" from July 5 to August 5. A surgeon's note dated July 5 recorded that Johnson's wounds were "supperating" from "the left thigh and testicle," meaning that they had become infected. On August 1 Johnson wrote from his home in Camden, asking for an extension of his leave "on account of wounds." An affidavit from a doctor accompanied this request and reported that his wounds "are not yet healed, and I further certify that it is my belief that it will require about sixty days before he will be able to travell and join his regiment."[39]

Johnson apparently returned to the Eighty-first before the end of August. In his letter to Secretary of War Edwin M. Stanton of August 13, 1866, Johnson wrote that he "was present" at the battles of Second Bull Run, South Mountain, and Antietam.[40] Even so, his wounds obviously continued to trouble him. He applied for a twenty-day leave of absence on September 28, which was granted the same day. At its expiration Johnson briefly rejoined the regiment. Exhausted and ill, Johnson was granted a medical discharge on November 24, 1862.[41]

He returned to Camden, where he evidently remained until early May

1863. The Camden city directory of 1863–64 lists Johnson's address as Hamilton Street but gives no occupation.[42] On discharge he had received $957 as payment for his service from July 1 to November 24, 1862.[43] This was a substantial amount of money, but evidently much of it went to pay the debts Mary had accumulated while he was in the service. Johnson was eligible for a disability pension, but there is no evidence that he applied for one.

On May 26, 1863, Johnson wrote a letter to the War Department in Washington: "Having been honorably discharged from the service of the United States on account of wounds received in action at Charles City Cross Roads . . . I respectfully solicit a position in the Invalid Corps."[44] On June 10, 1863, Johnson was ordered to "at once report to Col. E. A. Parrott, 1st Ohio Infantry A. A. Provost Marshal Gen.l at Columbus, Ohio for duty in the Invalid Corps." Carrying a provisional commission as major, he set out immediately, arriving at Columbus three days later to resume his military career.[45]

THE INVALID CORPS of 1863–65, in the words of Captain J. W. De Forest, its last commander, sprang "from a national necessity," but it was created in a series of administrative half steps.[46] By summer 1862, it was obvious to the high command that not enough men were enlisting in the Union army to replace its casualties or to meet its escalating needs. The Confederacy faced the same problem and responded by extending all volunteer enlistments to the end of the war and imposing a draft.[47] The North likewise, in mid-1863, began to draft those unwilling to volunteer and also took the highly controversial step of enlisting black troops. Even so, the manpower shortage continued, and Union leaders groped for ways to use more fully the men already available.

A first step was made on April 7, 1862—almost three months before Johnson was wounded—with a War Department directive authorizing the chief medical officer at each military command to employ as nurses, cooks, and hospital attendants "any convalescent wounded or feeble men who could perform such duties, instead of giving them a discharge," as had been the general practice. These men would take the place of fit soldiers, who could then be sent to the front. A convalescent man would be retained for such duties just so long as he was unsuited for regular service; on recovery he was expected to return to his original regiment.[48]

Although promising, this arrangement, proved ineffective. Often the men were permanently lost to their commands, remaining at their hospital assignments long after they had recovered from wounds or illness. Even worse, they were retained on the rolls of their original regiments, inflating their unit's paper strength and cutting into each state's federally assigned quota of "able-bodied men" required for military service. Meanwhile, front-line regiments continued to be filled with men who were only marginally able to tolerate, or entirely unfit for, the rigors of field and combat.

The military problem of what to do with men too disabled to march or to fight but not too disabled for other service was not a new one. As early as 1690, soldiers with disabilities had been used by the French army in "detached companies" to garrison military camps at Saumur, Augers, and Fort Ecluse. During the American Revolution, a congressional resolution on August 26, 1776, called for the creation of an Invalid Corps of disabled officers and soldiers capable of doing guard or garrison duty. The following year, some eight companies of roughly one hundred men each were formed into a single regiment. "Men having only one arm or one leg each were deemed proper recruits" for this new unit headquartered in Philadelphia and commanded by Colonel Lewis Nicola.[49]

This first American Invalid Corps was disbanded at the end of the revolution. The most severely disabled veterans were provided with a pension,[50] and a network of hospitals and asylums was established for those who could provide a "surgeon's certificate [stating] that the candidate [was] unable to support himself by manual labor, and also that he was disabled in the line of his duty." A resident of such an asylum, for example the Naval Asylum in Philadelphia, was generally required to forgo a pension in return for room and board. By the 1860s, the average population of the Philadelphia asylum was 125 men.[51]

While the military was turning to disabled soldiers as a way to alleviate its manpower shortage, civilian leaders were grappling with what to do with the thousands of newly disabled men being discharged from the army. There was a call to expand the asylum system and a realization that the federal government, overwhelmed as it was by the insurrection, would not be able to deal with the issue anytime soon: "For the present, then, the discharged invalid soldier and sailor must depend upon private munificence, upon the aid of his friends, upon that of towns, and such openings as he may find in the old United States hospitals." Private philanthropy was mobilized to found the Home for Discharged Soldiers in Boston, which by April 1863 had provided services to some 628 disabled veterans; a second home was established in Weston, a suburb of Boston, to handle the overflow. The issue was popular with both philanthropists and the general public, leading to a series of fairs and fundraisers at which the plight of the disabled veteran was often highlighted. A correspondent for the *United States Service Magazine* noted how "the sympathy now existing for those who have served their country is greater than for any other class of sufferers. Charitable societies that assist or instruct them take precedence of all others in the public estimation."[52]

The reference to the "instruction" of disabled veterans is revealing. Although disability may have inspired added sympathy, sympathy by no means displaced or diminished society's "existential anxiety" toward people with disabilities. One reason for establishing the new soldiers' home in Weston, rather than in Boston itself, was that "being three miles from any rail-road station or village, [it] is free from most city temptations and from too ready access to the same." Discharged from the military and theoretically free and equal citizens, disabled veterans were still subjected to close scrutiny. It was thought prudent to forbid residents of the new institutions to leave them "except for reasons of urgent necessity," and that they be supervised with "strict discipline."[53] The implication seems to be that once disabled, a man needed to be closely supervised lest he slip into idleness or something worse.

Philanthropists in Boston founded new soldiers' homes and carefully regulated the lives of their residents, but the Union League of Philadelphia considered the issue in a different light. Originally founded to counter what were reputed to be the pro-secession sympathies of Philadelphia high society, this association of business and civic leaders engaged in a variety of projects meant to support the federal and loyal state governments. Among these was a committee established to explore ways of "providing employment for disabled soldiers who have been honorably discharged from United States service."[54] The committee held its first meeting on April 8, 1863, and soon concluded "that large numbers of meritorious men [disabled in the war] are now seeking employment or means of supporting their families, and this class must be constantly increasing from the exposures and casualties of war." On May 5, the league sent a petition to President Lincoln, signed by 115 prominent Philadelphians, urging that "a corps of 'National Invalids'" be organized "to absorb 12,200 men." Lincoln forwarded the petition to the War Department on May 12, along with a note stating that "the within is . . . a very praiseworthy object" and asking "the best attention that can be consistently given it."[55]

Neither the Union League nor the president seemed to be aware that General Order 105, issued by the adjutant general's office and approved by the secretary of war on April 28, 1863, had already authorized "the organization of an Invalid Corps." The new unit would consist of three battalions, each organized according to the severity of disability: "Those who were able to bear a musket and do garrison duty were recommended for the First, those who had lost an arm or hand, or who were otherwise so severely injured as to be fit only for hospital guards and attendants, for the Second, while the severest and most hopeless cases of disability were assigned to the Third."[56]

Candidates for the new service were to come from three sources: "First, men in the field who had been disabled by wounds or by disease contracted in the line of duty; second, men absent from their colors in hospitals or convalescent camps, or otherwise under the control of medical officers; third, men who had been discharged for injuries received through honorable service. . . . A circular was issued on May 22, inviting officers who thought they might qualify to apply to the Provost-Marshal-General's office in Washington, where the next day Colonel Richard H. Rush, formerly of the Sixth Pennsylvania Cavalry, was appointed head of the new command."[57] Johnson was, no doubt, replying to this circular in his letter of May 26.

In its first six months, the Invalid Corps expanded from Colonel Rush and four clerks working at their office in Washington to more than 200 companies scattered across almost every northern and several southern states, for a total of 17,764 enlisted men and 491 officers. The vast majority of the new command's enlisted men had been transferred from "armies in the field, hospitals, and convalescent camps, to serve their unexpired terms of enlistment." In addition, some 1,431 were disabled veterans who had already left the army but decided to reenlist specifically as members of the Invalid Corps. Most officers seem to have been retired veterans. Ranks ranged from second lieutenant to colonel, of which sixteen had been appointed by October 31, 1863.[58] An officer was rarely able to reenter the service with his original rank; Colonel Johnson, for example, started his career in the Invalid Corps as a major.

By the end of 1863, the Invalid Corps had been organized into sixteen regiments of ten companies each, with forty or so companies remaining "detached." Each regiment consisted of six companies of First Battalion men and four companies of Second Battalion men: "The First Battalion is armed with muskets and is designed to perform duty in large cities and towns as provost guards, and to make short marches, in case of necessity; to convey drafted men; to guard prisoners and convey prisoners to their destination and, if need be, to man fortifications. . . . The Second Battalion is armed with swords and revolvers, and is designed to do duty in hospitals, offices, store-houses, and depots of supplies. This battalion is composed of men who have lost a leg or an arm, or whose physical disability . . . renders them unable to perform duty in the First Battalion." Efforts to organize a Third Battalion were abandoned during this period, and soldiers enlisted as Third Battalion men were folded into the Second Battalion.[59]

Candidates for the battalions appeared before one of five evaluating boards appointed in May and June 1863, which traveled to the hospitals and convalescent camps in the various military commands. At the same time, "depot camps of rendezvous" were established at St. Louis, New York, Harrisburg, "and other suitable points," where men were sent to await assignment to a company and regiment. Officers were reviewed as well, though initially this typically occurred after their appointment, which meant their commissions were "provisional"—a source of some irritation to Charles Johnson and no doubt many others.

The notes of one of these boards provide a good overview of the candidates under consideration. On January 26, 1864, the board saw twenty-three men, mostly officers. In one case, the candidate's paperwork was deemed incomplete so no examination was made. Of the remaining twenty-two, fourteen were disabled due to gunshot wounds. Three were disabled by illness, including chronic diarrhea and rheumatism, two by hernia, and two by artillery fire, with the board unable to determine the cause of the final man's disability. The list of disabilities included three amputations (including one of the left arm at the shoulder joint), the impaired use of hands or legs (ten cases), and one man whose wound by cannon fire had caused the removal of a substantial portion of his face and jaw. Of the twenty men determined to be "unfit for field service," eleven were assigned to the First Battalion and eight to the Second Battalion of the Invalid Corps. One soldier, a private whose gunshot wound to the right hand was still infected, was sent back to the hospital. Two officers were rejected because their disabilities were deemed "not sufficient to entitle" them to positions in the corps.[60]

This sample, by all indications a typical day's work, would seem to demonstrate that the men who entered the corps were indeed disabled and that their disabilities were due to honorable military service. And yet, from its inception, the Invalid Corps was the object of jokes and sneers, open contempt, even violence. Some of this ill will no doubt resulted from the inevitable resentment frontline soldiers bore toward an organization whose express purpose was to keep its members away from the fighting, no matter the reason. (Those in the ranks of the Army of the Potomac expressed a similar disdain for "the heavies"—those members of the "heavy artillery" regiments assigned to garrison the forts around Washington.) This "bitter prejudice of [the] field troops . . ." as Captain J. W. De Forest wrote, "found scope in a multitude of sarcasms and jeers which made the title of Invalid Corps a burden."[61] De Forest's final report of November 1865 both summarizes the corps' history and makes the case for its value to the Union war effort, providing the "kind word" described by Byron Stinson.

The very name of the new unit was a problem. De Forest in the same report wrote how "men frequently begged to be sent back to their old regiments in the field rather than remain in garrison at the price of being called invalids." This is a remarkable statement, considering the mortality rate of many of these frontline regiments.[62] That the initials of the Invalid Corps, I.C., were the same as the military designation for anything substandard or spoiled did not help matters. Rotten meat, moldy ammunition, defective rifles, worn-out shoes were all stamped "I.C." for "Inspected, Condemned." Members of the Invalid Corps soon had to put up with being dubbed the "Inspecteds" or the "Condemned Yanks"—along with other sobriquets such as the "Cripple Brigade."[63] To make matters worse, hospitals and convalescent camps, and by extension the Invalid Corps itself, were commonly viewed by the rest of the army as "asylums for shirks and cowards."[64]

The first verse of a popular song of 1864 seems to sum up the attitude:

> I wanted much to go to war
> and went to be examined;
> the surgeon looked me o'er and o'er
> my back and chest he hammered.
> Said he, "You're not the man for me,
> Your lungs are much affected,
> And likewise both your eyes are cock'd
> And otherwise defected."

And then the chorus:

> "So now I'm with the invalids,
> and cannot go and fight sir,
> The doctor told me so, you know,
> And so it must be right, sir!"[65]

The narrator is not an amputee who has lost a limb in battle, nor is he a man whose face and jaw have been shot off by a cannonball. Rather, he has the notably less martial disabilities of being cross-eyed and "affected." Subsequent verses also demonstrate him to be a drunkard. How the members of the real Invalid Corps felt when they heard tunes such as this can well be imagined.

The army compounded the problem by attempting to issue to the new command its own distinctive uniform. Indeed, on the first page of five hefty volumes of official correspondence of the Invalid Corps at the National Archives is a note dated May 13, 1863, from Provost Marshal James B. Fry to the secretary of war (and marked "approved, Edwin M. Stanton"), which recommends that the uniform for enlisted men of the Invalid Corps be a "jacket of sky blue . . . with dark blue trimmings, cut like a cavalry jacket, to come well down on the abdomen," as opposed to the dark blue uniform of the regular and volunteer armies. Officers were also to be distinguishable from their former comrades on sight. A follow-up letter of May 28 contains an order for twenty thousand of the new uniforms.[66]

The new uniform was immediately resented and resisted. It "was becoming, but has never been popular. The men do not like to be distinguished from their comrades of the active service by a peculiar costume. . . . This feeling was aggravated by the inevitable jealousy between field and garrison regiments, which ripened into something like bitterness between soldiers of the Invalid Corps and the ranks in which they had so lately marched and fought."[67] Johnson noted this resentment in a letter of early June 1864, when he took command of a "provisional brigade" made up of regiments of both the Invalid Corps and units of the mainstream army: "Some of the Colonels &c. did not like the idea at first of 'coming into the field to be Commanded by an invalid,' they did not like the *light blue*."[68] The uniform's light color also made it nearly impossible to keep neat in the field, which, despite the best intentions of the War Department, was where many of the Invalid Corps regiments were sent. And however "becoming" the new outfit might have been, the men forced to wear it concluded that the army for which they had suffered and bled now deemed them unworthy of its standard uniform.

Last, some believed that the new organization was less a military command than a form of charity. The signers of the Union League of Philadelphia petition certainly held this view, linking the formation of the corps less to military necessity than to the fact that thousands of "meritorious" men were unable to find work in civilian life.[69] That at least some members of the Invalid Corps agreed with this assessment can be seen in a petition sent to Secretary of War Stanton at the end of August 1863 by former cavalrymen who had been "sent to the Hospital at Pilot Knob [Missouri] and afterwards transferred into the 'Invalid Corps'" in St. Louis: "We remonstrated at this Transfer . . . [in] that we have so understood that the Invalid Corps was intended for those who were more or less dependent on the United States in consequence of having been broken down in health &c. in the service, not for those who like ourselves are more than able to maintain our families." The men asked that they be discharged and sent home rather than suffer disgrace by being assigned to the Invalid Corps.[70]

But if some felt demeaned by their association with the corps, others saw it as a way to salvage their self-esteem. One of the earliest applications for entry came from George Masson, "an old Soldier of the U.S. Service who has served four enlistments in the U.S. Army, and has been six and one half years at the Soldiers Home. . . . he says that many . . . are fit for some of the duties of the Invalid Corps. He seems to be much ashamed of his present position, desires to render more service and get better rewarded, considers himself in the light of an inmate of a Poor House, or House of Correction, takes great exception to the organization of the Soldiers Home, its system of rewards and the rules for its government."[71] Masson also protested the low pay given to those residents who kept the grounds and did other labor at the asylum, in a regimen that anticipated the exploitative "sheltered workshops" and "state schools" of the twentieth century. Disabled veterans outside of the soldiers' asylums also looked to the corps as a way to improve their condition, having experienced "the existential anxiety" of a society unwilling to accommodate them. "Young volunteer" Joseph Crowell was given the option of being sent home with a medical discharge or joining the Invalid Corps' Second Battalion, "composed of men who had lost a leg or arm." Most men given this choice, Crowell reported, "selected the service, for they began to appreciate the fact that a man minus one of the more important members of his body was lucky if he could get anything to do to earn a living."[72]

Apparently faced with this reality himself, and hoping also for a chance at a commission, Crowell, like Johnson, chose to enter the Invalid Corps.

JOHNSON SPENT a little more than two months in Ohio, as "the Senior Officer and hence 'Commander of the Post,'" in charge of mustering the forwarded recruits into their new units: "In the office we term them the '*Infidel* Corps' and me the 'Infidel Major' . . ."[73] At the beginning of August Johnson was ordered to St. Louis, where he began his assignment as inspector general for Missouri.[74]

Johnson's principal task work was traveling (generally in civilian clothes) to inspect the various military posts in the state and reporting back to Colonel Edmund Burke Alexander, acting assistant provost marshall for Missouri. Alexander was "regular army." He had entered West Point in 1818 and been brevetted a major and then a lieutenant colonel for "gallantry and meritorious conduct" during the Mexican War.[75] The two men got on well, despite Johnson's initial prejudice against "regular army" officers.

Union control of much of Missouri was tenuous, and rebel guerrillas were always a threat to federal outposts or any unit much smaller than a company. A bitter internecine conflict had started in neighboring Kansas five years before Sumter, and it would simmer in both Kansas and Missouri during the decade after Appomattax. By mid-1863 the struggle had degenerated into a series of raids and counterraids, atrocities and counteratrocities, with rebel "bushwackers" and "Secret Joes" attacking Unionist civilians and straggling soldiers. Federal troops and local militia launched an equally brutal counterinsurgency campaign that included forced resettlements and the incarceration of families of rebel sympathizers.[76] The conflict intensified further that summer when the federal government attempted to implement the draft.

Johnson's reports to Alexander reflect a man scrupulous in his duty, with an eye for detail and an ability to understand the broader picture. Given his commitment to the Union cause and his openly expressed hatred for the enemy, Johnson was surprisingly even-handed in these accounts, as when he blames the ill will of the populace in one county on the local federal commander's "hasty and ill judged acts" in arresting suspected Confederate sympathizers without evidence or charge. At least one of these, according to Johnson, was in fact a Unionist refugee from Arkansas.[77] In other reports he describes how, despite a conscientious and capable, local commander, the enrollment of white male citizens for the draft "is progressing slowly on account of a number of the Counties being infested with guerilla bands."[78] On August 29, he tells Alexander that conditions in the area around Lexington are such that in "two of the Counties (Jackson & LaFayette) no enrollment has been made except in villages occupied by our troops. . . . [D]uring the time I remained in the district (48 hours) . . . I passed five trains of families 'gone north,' having been drove from their homes by these armed bands." Here too, Johnson was "of the opinion that Capt. Comingo is doing all in his power to remidy the evil but that it is impossible to perform the duties of his office thoroughly unless a large military force is sent into a great part of the 6th District."[79]

Johnson, in his letters home, was more explicit and emotional about what he had seen, reporting in one instance the massacre of thirty blacks taken off a river boat by one guerrilla band and the murder of a teenage boy and the gang-rape of a teenage girl by another. "Mary, this is war in Missouri . . . my God! if I was only able to stand the constant use of the saddle and had a few good men, how I would cut down the sons of bitches—the cry has gone forth through all Missouri—'ask no quarters—give no quarters' and it will be lived up to and extermination is the cry—the Militia is now ordered (after the 9th of Sept.) to hang *every man* who does not enroll himself at that date to hunt Guerillas—to remove his family south and destroy his houses and crops . . . [I] assure you Mary that the Militia will execute *that* order, for nearly all have felt the effects of the 'Secreat Joe.'"[80]

A Union officer traveling alone through Missouri put himself in considerable danger, and this was another reality Johnson shared with his wife. Still, his letters are filled with humor and wordplay, alliteration and comic exaggeration: "Hot-hot-hot—then stop for breath and say—Hot-Hot-Hot and if the perspiration does not wet your shirt through, you have no idea what is *Hot.*"[81] "[H]ot no!! . . . first *boiling* and then after there is no more greace to come out then commenced the scorching and roasting . . . hot travelling [on a train], yes, fat woman felt fussy and fumed furiously, lean woman leaned languidly back (like withered lilies on a lake), shabby slipshod servants sat silently and sadly on the shady side of the cars, yea! babies bawled bravely . . . cinders crept into your clothes . . . varily, it *was* hot!"[82]

An admirer of Byron, Thomas Moore, and other Romantic writers, Johnson often quoted poetry to emphasize a point. One of his favorite poets was Martin Farquar Tupper (1810–89), and he evidently had a copy of Tupper's *Proverbial Philosophy: A Book of Thoughts and Arguments Originally Treated* or his *Complete Poetical Works,* both published in 1851, nearby while writing. Johnson was also a reader of Shakespeare, and though he preferred to quote *Hamlet* and *Othello,* his observations more often take after the wry comments of a Shakespearean clown. Dismissing the great west as a "great humbug," he describes the outback of Missouri as "the land of corn-cakes and log-houses," "where men thought nothing of [going] to *church* with Bowie-knife and pistol."[83] An unabashed patriot, Johnson could also write mockingly, "[O]h! it is sweet to *live* for ones country—I believe the text is to *die* for ones country but I prefer the other version."[84] He could be as scatological as Chaucer and as iconoclastic as Twain. When Mary recounts the rumors she's heard about Lee's foray into Pennsylvania (which would culminate in the battle of Gettysburg), Johnson admonishes her not to pay attention to "every fart that sails upon the wind."[85] He delights in sharing with her his observations on everything from the function of napkin rings to the Missouri way of "shitting (bah! you dirty fellow! never mind Mary, 'a dirty subject requires dirty words.')"[86] "[D]amn them!" he explodes in a paragraph condemning the hypocrisy of churches and churchgoers, "if ever the Almighty forgives me for having visited such places in years gone bye, I promise him *never* to do so again."[87]

In other letters Johnson shares the exhilaration of being lifted entirely out of his old life in ways he could not have imagined before the war. On one of his tours of inspection through Missouri, he was forced to take the reins of a stagecoach after the driver had become too ill to drive: "I tried it *very* delicately at first, then got bolder and finaly used the whip—hurrah! here is Charly Johnson the Engraver, the Chestnut Street clerk, *Colonel* Johnson driving a four horse coach across the Prairies of Missouri." He ends the story with a dig at the "skin-flint" coach company agent, who refused to pay "a half days wages for driving his infurnal old coach."[88]

Such playful banter does not mean that life during war time was easy for either Charles or Mary, and the correspondence recounts several family and personal crises. In one, we learn that the twin boys were evidently sexually abused by "that damn scound[r]el Reed"—the custodian at a Camden school.[89] In another, Mary apparently describes what seems to be a severe depression and discusses making arrangements for the care of the children in the event of her death.[90] There also were arguments, as when Charles berates Mary for socializing with a married couple while he is away, particularly when this leads to the husband taking what Charles considers improper liberties with Mary.[91] Generally, Charles is respectful of his wife, often admiring her intelligence and independence. "I am glad that you can get along without me . . ." "Decide for yourself . . . I have an abiding faith in your good common sense . . ." "I do not want to know what you do with the money . . . some times I want to know what you *have on hand* and then I *ask*—but [for you to feel obligated] to render an account of expenditures—pshaw!"[92]

Johnson's matter-of-fact style is evident when he discusses his disabilities, reporting how they keep him from riding or walking any distance. Certainly, he does not seem to have defined himself by them, and it is difficult to imagine him ever signing a paper, in the style of Samuel Gessbury, as "Charles Johnson, a man disabled in combat." His most explicit regret is contained in his reply to Mary's desire for another "dear darling duck of a baby": "[A]h! Mary that thing is 'played out'—or more properly . . . speaking '*I* am played out'—I am sorry (for your sake) that I can not accomidate *you*." Johnson seemed to take this change in their married life philosophically: "[A]s for my self I rather like it, for I am clear of . . . 'a world of trouble.'"[93]

Through it all, Johnson yearns to be closer to his family, and the thread that runs through his entire Invalid Corps correspondence is his desire to obtain a transfer back east. For a time it seemed he was a likely candidate for command of the Sixteenth Regiment of the Invalid Corps, which was headquartered at the Harrisburg depot. Instead, in early 1864 Johnson received orders that placed him in charge of the Eighteenth Regiment in Indianapolis.

"Here goes for a Barrack's life"—he laments in his letter of January 19, 1864, "fare well to Citizens dress—henceforth it is uniform—uniform—Reveille—Tattoo—drill &c. the same old thing, except being *shot at*."[94] Johnson was correct about having to wear a uniform at his new post. As it turned out, however, he would not long be expected to wear "the Light Blue" of the Invalid Corps, for by late spring the army would relent and allow its officers to wear, unofficially at least, standard army garb. He was incorrect, though, about not "being shot at." Despite every promise and the army's best intentions, within six months of assuming his command Colonel Charles F. Johnson would once again find himself in harm's way.

IN LATE 1864, the commander of each Invalid Corps regiment—Colonel Johnson among them—was ordered to provide an accounting of the services performed by his command; these were then summarized in De Forest's final report.[95] "The services performed," De Forest concluded, "have been so varied in nature that it is impossible to state them in a compendious exhibit. Where one regiment has escorted thousands of prisoners, convalescents, recruits, and conscripts, whose numbers can be given with accuracy, another has simply guarded important posts and vast stores of public property, thus performing duty which cannot be expressed statistically."[96]

The First Regiment, to pick one at random, seems typical in its mix of duties. It was stationed principally at Elmira, New York, with companies detached for duty at Rochester and elsewhere. Elmira was the site of a major prisoner-of-war camp. De Forest reports how "Up to the close of the war the prisoners constantly in camp averaged between 10,000 and 12,000; frequent attempts to escape and one prisoner recorded as escaped; duty of guarding them very severe. Squads of convalescents, recruits, conscripts, &c., generally 80 or 100 strong, escorted to the front or to other posts; no record of a single escape. Many volunteer troops disbanded at this station; at one time 15,000 present; various disturbances resulted; order restored by this regiment. Two companies on duty at Rochester, N.Y., repressing disorders committed by disbanding regiments."[97]

Harrison Gardner was a twenty-three-year-old farmer from Illinois and a private in Company F of the Twelfth Regiment, also stationed in upstate New York. His diary entry of February 25, 1864, records how the camp "had quite a riot . . . between the 1st Michigan Cavalry and the patrol guard in which one soldier was killed instantly and another has since died from the effect of the bayonet wound made by one of the guard. One officer was wounded and all of the military that had arms were called out to quell the disturbance. One young fellow from the 16th Reg't I.C. [Invalid Corps] on patrol guard was shot through the wrist and his arm had to be amputated. The disturbance was quelled before any serious demonstrations."[98] Given this description, one cannot help but wonder what Gardner would have considered a "serious demonstration."

Alfred Bellard, a private originally in the Fifth New Jersey Volunteers, was wounded in the leg at Chancellorsville in May 1863. He was transferred to the Invalid Corps in October. Bellard's account of his military career, published in 1975, is one of the few that dwells in any depth on time served in the Invalid Corps. Among Bellard's first duties was escorting prisoners, both Federal and Confederate: "Our [northern] prisoners were a hard lot, being for the most part deserters and bounty jumpers, who were on their way to a government fort for punishment."[99] To prevent accidental shootings—a not uncommon occurrence—Bellard's unit at first traveled with their rifles unloaded, using only bayonets to control their charges. This changed, however, after his company was stationed in Washington D.C. A relatively sleepy town before the war, by early 1864 the population of the capitol had grown to several times its prewar size. Union soldiers, sutlers and other merchants, escaped slaves, southern refugees, and an assortment of con artists, pickpockets, and prostitutes all converged on Washington. Adding to the tension was the fact that much of the native population was pro-southern and regarded Union troops as little more than an army of occupation. The crime rate soared, and streets and alleyways were filled with soldiers absent without leave, sometimes armed, often intoxicated.[100]

Bellard devotes an entire chapter to the "Duties, Pleasures and Dangers at Provost Marshal's Guard and Patrol" in the capitol. His duties included guarding the Old Capitol Prison (where other guards would be assigned from Johnson's 18th Regiment), where political prisoners and suspected spies were kept. The pleasures included (unofficial) visits to the city's bars and brothels. As for the dangers, Bellard recounts how, "On the night of the 4th [of June 1864] one of our squads had a little shooting scrape on 11th Street. Lieut. Tyrell of our company was on duty at the theatre, when an officer came along drunk and refused to show his pass. . . . The Sergt. was ordered to take him to the guard house. When the guard had got a short distance with him (Lieut. Tyrell being close in the rear) the officer pulled out a revolver, and turning round fired a shot a[t] Tyrell and put a ball in his neck . . . but the Lieut. [Tyrell] coming up fired 5 shots, 3 of which took effect." The gun battle incensed residents of the street, who came out "in full force, for the purpose of cleaning out the patrol," but after an angry confrontation the crowd dispersed. The upshot of all this, Bellard reports, was that the drunken officer died of his wounds, and Tyrell recovered and was promoted.[101]

Other Invalid Corps regiments had to deal with more organized threats to the government's authority, from both inside and outside the army. In fall 1863, the Third Regiment was sent to Burlington, Vermont, where "a violent outbreak in a volunteer brigade was quelled by seventy men of the Third, two of the rioters being shot, some ironed, and many arrested."[102] The Sixteenth Regiment was sent out to "the mountains of Pennsylvania" to contend with an uprising that was a confluence of anti-war sentiment and labor unrest: "This regiment . . . carried on a campaign of several months . . . where deputy provost-marshals and enrolling officers had been killed and wounded by disloyal persons engaged in resisting the draft. Treasonable organizations 500 or 600 strong were broken up. The expeditions were made through a wooded and mountainous country in winter. . . . Hundreds of deserters and recusants were arrested; some were killed in skirmishes; one man of the regiment killed."[103]

There were times when "simply guarding important outposts and vast stores of public property" could also be dangerous, as Colonel Johnson and his men would discover. The American Civil War was the first major conflict in which railroads played a significant role, and at any one time tens of thousands of Union troops were detailed to protect the railroad stations, yards, and tracks needed to supply the armies. Among these troops were the members of the Twenty-third Regiment, who saw duty in Wisconsin, Minnesota, Missouri, Kentucky, and Iowa. Company B spent most of its time escorting prisoners and recruits but was also called on to defend the railroad from Louisville to Lebanon, Kentucky. In one engagement, the company killed the commander of a group of rebel raiders, wounded others, and captured ten horses. Two Invalid Corpsmen were wounded in this engagement; in another skirmish twenty-three soldiers of the company reportedly held off a band of forty-eight guerrillas, killing and wounding twenty-three.[104]

But it was in enforcing the draft that the Invalid Corps proved most valuable in its first year of existence, and it is no coincidence that its rapid expansion came during the months of the worst antidraft (and antiblack) violence. In addition to riots in New York City, where more than 105 people were killed, there were outbreaks from New England to Chicago, with some 98 federal marshals murdered.[105] Provost Marshal General James B. Fry responded by sending contingents of the First Battalion of the Invalid Corps as far north as Montpelier, Vermont, to arrest outspoken opponents of the draft. Desertion was also a problem, and here too the Invalid Corps was pressed into service. "We have orders to hunt up a deserter today by the name of Charles Frost, 2nd Vermont Vols.," Gardner noted in his journal of April 17, 1864, after the Twelfth was transferred to northern Virginia. "[D]eserted from General Hospital at Alexandria, Va., yesterday, but we have not been successful yet."[106]

The Eighteenth Regiment had barely been organized when Colonel Johnson arrived at its headquarters in Indianapolis in February 1864.[107] Companies were scattered across southern Indiana and northern Kentucky as guards at various hospitals, at the prisoner exchange camp at Louisville, and as provost guards at Jeffersonville, Indiana.[108] By far the regiment's greatest responsibilities were to oversee the Burnside Barracks, a rendezvous for draftees and volunteers, and nearby Camp Morton, one of the Union's largest prisoner-of-war camps. The five companies (some five hundred men and officers) stationed there had responsibility for "over 3500 Rebel Prisoners."[109] Johnson dove into the details of managing his own command, "endevouring to bring the 18th Regiment 'up to the mark' and make it compete with the 5th regiment and some older ones here."[110]

A page chosen at random from the regiment's descriptive lists names twenty-nine privates, from Pennsylvania, Massachusetts, Connecticut, Ohio, Maryland, New York, Michigan, and Vermont. There were also members born in France, Austria, Prussia, Ireland, and Great Britain. The greatest number of men (nine) were farmers before the war, but there were also two bricklayers, two blacksmiths, two carpenters, two wheelwrights, a clerk, a paper manufacturer, a mechanic, a cigar maker, a peddler, a boatman, a harnessmaker, and a teacher. Two men are listed as "laborers"; the remaining two men have no listed occupation. The men ranged in age from 18 to 54, with most (twelve) in their twenties.[111]

Among the officers sharing the post with Johnson was Samuel A. Craig, originally a captain with Company B of the 105th Pennsylvania Volunteers. He had been wounded once in the face and neck, also on the Virginia Peninsula, the day before Johnson, and like Johnson had recovered well enough for a time to return to his regiment. "By fixing a wax plate over the hole in the roof of my mouth," Craig wrote years later, "I was enabled to talk and drink soup."[112] Wounded again at the end of August 1862, this time in the wrist, Craig returned once more to the front but was finally forced to take a medical discharge on May 19, 1863. He immediately applied for duty in the Invalid Corps and received his captain's commission on August 1. After commanding two companies of First Battalion men in Louisville, he was transferred to Indianapolis on October 15, where he took command of Company A, 17th Regiment Invalid Corps.[113] Like Johnson, Craig would also serve in the Freedmen's Bureau after the war.

Camp Morton, according to Craig, "was constructed as barracks or large sheds 100 feet by 20, bunks two story on each side, a passage way thru the center, in which at intervals were large six plate stoves for the burning of wood or coal as fuel. . . . 'A high fence of boards and heavy posts surrounded the camp, on the outside of which, about two and a half feet from the top, was a walk or platform, so that the guards could walk on it, head, arms and shoulders extending above the fence, giving a good view of all prisoners and their movements." The winter of 1863–64, he wrote, "was extremely cold, and when as Officer of the Guard I saw prisoners sometimes massed close about the stoves, and even with plenty of wood, they seemed cold."[114]

Craig's duties "kept [him] pretty busy." Even so, he managed to attend classes at nearby Northwestern University, studying German and chemistry.[115] Amid all this, he noticed the tensions between the Invalid Corps soldiers and those in the mainstream army who passed through on their way to and from the front. "Some of the soldiers did not understand that we were all disabled and thought we were in soft jobs and featherbed places. Many unkind remarks were heard and in some reports it was said that we were shirking our duties." For their part, the men in the Seventeenth Regiment obviously resented these calumnies: "Owing to the bad blood no doubt stirred up by these remarks, a Regiment [of the Corps] while at dinner, suddenly rushed out and secured their arms. It looked serious for a while, but Colonel Warner, a tall slender, crippled pock faced man, climbed on a box and with his cane waving talked to them in a firible manner so that they again stacked arms and finished their meal."[116]

Responding to such incidents and to the general protests of its members, the army finally decided to abandon the Invalid Corps name. On March 18, 1864, General Order 111 of the Adjutant-General's Office introduced the Veteran Reserve Corps (VRC).[117] The powers that be justified this change with the hope that "[a] Veteran Reserve Corps might accept classes of men which an Invalid Corps could not," the idea being that men who had already served the length of their three years might consider reenlisting if they were assured the relative safety of provost or garrison duty. In fact, the hoped-for reenlistments did not materialize, because such men generally preferred re-upping with their old comrades. Even so, according to De Forest, and "[n]otwithstanding the absurdity of the prejudice against the word invalid, the new nomenclature was no doubt a benefit, inasmuch as it removed, at least in part, an obstacle to that esprit de corps which is so essential to the well-being and efficiency of a military organization."[118] Gardner recorded the event in his diary, remarking, "I don't know whether the uniform will be changed or not."[119]

Other problems with the fledgling organization were not so easily fixed. De Forest lamented how "It was soon found that unsuitable officers were sometimes nominated for the organization by [field] corps commander[s]. . . . It seemed to be considered a proper receptacle for persons who were useless or noxious at the front, but whose offenses were still not flagrant enough to warrant dismissal from the service."[120] As a result, direct transfers from the various corps in the mainstream army were stopped, and all officers had to apply through the already established examining boards.

Johnson, even though he had been serving for months, was also required to appear before one of the boards. The board's undated report lists his education as "Good," his intelligence and discipline as "Fair," his knowledge of army regulations and the articles of war and his attention to duty as "Indifferent," and his industry as "bad."[121] Johnson was perhaps aware of his poor showing, writing to Mary in response to a query from his brother Harry that "the whole thing is put[?] in a political shape—officers are passing and not passing in accordance with the pressure that they bear on the Sec. of War."[122] This may have been a case of premature sour grapes, for Johnson's commission was confirmed despite the report.

The organization was also sifted for "useless" and "noxious" enlisted men who had been foisted on the corps by their original commanders. "There is a general order from the War Dept. authorizing Commanders of Companies and also Commanders of Regiments of the Invalid Corps, [to] send back to their respective regiments all men who get drunk and become unruly and all those that behave themselves in a disrespectful manner," Gardner wrote on February 5, 1864; "My idea of the order is, very good."[123]

Finally, in spring 1864, the army quietly abandoned its effort to force soldiers with disabilities to wear its special, "becoming" uniforms. "We are informed (unofficially) . . ." Johnson wrote home, "that our uniform coat will be *dark blue* and advise all of us who require new uniforms to purchase the dark blue." It was either that or toss half the corps into the guardhouse for insubordination.[124] This was a remarkable concession made by a military establishment in wartime to assuage the sensitivities of its soldiers and an indication of just how determined and widespread the opposition to the light blue uniforms had become.

"News paper rumors, Camp Rumors and other rumors are so rife here as to what they intend to do with the Corps," Johnson wrote in this same letter, "that some of the officers are getting frightened out of their faculties." Nine days later, the official word came down: "I am ordered to report to Brig. Gen. Briggs as Draft Rendezvous at that infernal *hole* Alexandria, V*a* where six companies await me."[125] This was only a temporary assignment, however: "I write at 1 o'clock in the morning [of May 12]—I have just received 'orders'—damn their orders—to move my regiment (entire) . . . to Belle Plains with 3 days rations and 200 rounds of ammunition per man."[126]

THE MOVE of the Eighteenth Regiment, east from Indianapolis and then south from Alexandria, was a very small part of the Union's massive spring offensive. For the first time in the war, federal armies, now all under the command of Lieutenant General Ulysses S. Grant, were simultaneously to converge on what was left of the Confederacy from virtually every point on the compass. In the west, Major General William T. Sherman was to move southeast from Tennessee and into Georgia, while an army in Louisiana under Major General Nathaniel P. Banks was to march southwest into Texas. On the Virginia front, the Army of the Potomac under Major General George Gordon Meade was to march south against the main rebel force under Lee, while smaller armies under Major General Benjamin Butler and Major General Franz Sigel came in from the east and the west. As Lincoln put it, after Grant had explained the plan, "Those not skinning can hold a leg."[127]

In order to bring overwhelming force against the rebels, Grant pulled into the fighting corps every soldier to whom he had access. Quartermasters and cooks, ambulance drivers and headquarters guards on "detached duty," all were given rifles and sent back to their regiments as Grant prepared for what he hoped would be the last campaign of the war. Not stopping there, the lieutenant general denuded the army's depots and supply wagons of their guards and escorts, stripping even the fortifications around Washington of their "heavy artillery" regiments. "The 1st Corp H. Artillery left for the seat of war," wrote Harrison Gardner on May 12, "and the V.R. Corps [is] left to take their places in the fortifications."[128]

De Forest recounted how, "As General Grant advanced toward Petersburg, it became necessary to move the base of supplies southward, and on the 23rd of May a medical examination was made of the Eighteenth to decide what men could go to Port Royal, a distance of about twenty-five miles by land. The surgeons reported that of the 474 present 166 could march without knapsacks, and that the rest were not able to march at all. The officers all refused to be examined. . . . While the mass of the regiment, 308 men, were put on a transport and sent by water to their destination, Colonel Johnson with his select band . . . set out as part of the marching column. The first field night of this forlorn hope of invalids was passed in a furious storm of rain and hail, without tents or other cover, the men wrapping themselves in their wet blankets and finding what shelter they could in the corners of the rail-fences."[129]

Johnson described the regiment's travails to Mary in his letter of May 26: "Here we are ('invalids') in the rain without any tents &c.—we left Belle Plains on the afternoon of the 24 and arrived here last night. . . . to say that we are a 'used up party' is but a slight expression of the condition of all of us. . . . [I]t is, to use the lightest word—a damn outrage and in direct opposition to *all* the pledges of the Government in reference to the Corps. . . . [I]f Grant continues to throw his left around—*our* next front will in all probibility be at the White House [Landing] or West Point on the Peninsula once more."[130]

At Port Royal the Eighteenth resumed its usual duties—guarding prisoners and the supplies stockpiled for Grant's ongoing offensive. Johnson's prediction that "*our* next front will . . . be at the White House," meaning the Pamunkey River Landing, turned out to be accurate. At the landing, he was placed in command of a "provisional" brigade consisting of his own regiment and a collection of miscellaneous companies, a total of some fifteen hundred soldiers.

Among the army high command, there seems to have been little concern that it was sending Johnson and his "invalids" into any danger. White House Landing was close to the front but still behind the lines. Stockpiled at the landing were supplies intended for forces under the command of Generals David Hunter and Philip Sheridan, among them "150,000 rations in waggons that with the ambulances would strech out five miles."[131] In anticipation of these troops arriving at the landing, most of the station's garrison had been ordered to the front as part of the effort against Petersburg. But then, Sheridan and Hunter failed to arrive. Federal control of this part of Virginia was tenuous at best, with rebel guerrillas, so-called Secret Joes, waiting to pick off any target of opportunity. And so the men settled down to wait, not daring to leave the perimeter for fear of being, as Johnson put it, "gobbled up."

Despite the precarious situation, Johnson told Mary, "I hate to hear that firing [at the front line] and not have a 'finger in the pie.'" Whether this was out of bravado, frustration, or sheer boredom he doesn't say. Perhaps there was a part of him eager to prove his continued courage and competence, despite being a member of "the Light Blue" or, to put a more Freudian cast to it, to assert his "manhood" despite his loss of sexual function. To hear the sound of distant fighting, he wrote, "makes my blood warm to fever heat—if we could *march* I suppose that they would have us out there before this, but we *can't* and that settles the hash."[132]

Two weeks after writing those lines, Johnson got his chance to put "his finger in the pie." On June 20, 1864, Confederate General Wade Hampton made his attempt "to get at" the supplies stockpiled at White House Landing. De Forest includes an account of what followed as the dramatic highlight of his final report on the VRC: "Several of the men had been discharged and were on transports about to sail for the North; they returned to the camp, borrowed arms and accouterments, and begged to go into line of battle with their old comrades. Twice during the engagement an aide [from Johnson's commander, Brigadier General John J. Abercrombie] rode up to Colonel Johnson with the question, 'Will your invalids stand?'" "'Tell the general,' was the answer, 'that my men are cripples, and they can't run.'"[133]

The moment is vintage Johnson, yet Johnson does not mention it in the account he sent Mary two days after the battle, nor is it recounted in his official history of the Eighteenth Regiment, written on September 30, 1864. In it, he simply states that the regiment, while at White House Landing, was "stationed in the Rifle Pits and remained there (participating in the defense of the works June 20) until June 22, 1864, when the Regiment was ordered to report to the 'proper authority at Washington.'" Johnson made good use of the report to stress again (but "respectfully") that "the above duties were performed while four fifths of the entire Regiment was 'entirely unfitted for field service or fatigue duty such as they have been called upon to perform since having been attached to this command,' as per report of the Medical Board."[134]

The high command seems to have realized this, even before Hampton's raid. An order of June 20, 1864, to Major General Meade, signed by Lieutenant General Ulysses S. Grant, instructed Meade to "Direct the commanding officer at White House to break up that post and send his Veteran Reserve troops back to Washington."[135] Once in Washington, Johnson wrote Mary how, "My action at the fight at the White House is beginning to attract some attention. . . . [W]e (the 18th) are termed among the Corps here 'the war torn veterans' and I have been introduced to scores of officers as the 'Hero of the White House'—'the Man that saved Sheridan' &c. &c. . . . they appear to be tickled at the idea that 2000 men *under an 'Invalid'* should repulse between 5 and 6000 picked troops under such leaders as [General Wade] Hampton and [General] Fitz Hugh Lee."[136]

The Eighteenth was sent to Cliffburne Barracks to recuperate after its efforts in May and June. Its men performed no duty until July 1, when two companies were ordered to report to "Maj. General [Christopher Columbus] Augur commanding Department of Washington for the purpose of relieving two companies of the 6th Regt. Veteran Reserve Corps now guarding the Baltimore and Ohio Rail Road."[137] On that date, Colonel Johnson had available to him a total of six companies, consisting of 474 officers and enlisted men, of whom 112 were still on the sick list.[138]

By this time in the war, the federal high command was relying on the VRC for much of the provost and garrison duty at Washington and its environs. A good example of this would be the Ninth Regiment, stationed at the capitol since November 1863. On July 1, 1864, its commander, Colonel George Gile, had available to him, as present for duty, a total of 447 officers and men.[139]

"We performed our usual routine of guard duty until [July 10]," wrote the Ninth's lieutenant colonel, R. E. Johnston, "when we received orders to be ready to march at a moments notice."[140] The occasion for this order was the defeat of federal forces the day before at the Monocacy River, Maryland, by rebel forces under the command of Lieutenant General Jubal Early. The

Eighteenth Regiment also was told to expect trouble. Johnson wrote Mary how, "there is a great scare here and all the Malitia are called out to fill the place of the Vet. Res. Corp. who will follow me towards the 'front' i.e. Baltimore (some what changed is that '*front*')."[141]

Johnson was wrong about the "front" being at Baltimore. Early's purpose was to incite panic in the Union rear, hoping this might distract Grant from his stranglehold on Petersburg. Early came within hours of succeeding beyond his wildest dreams. A combination of poor judgment and bad luck had left Washington vulnerable to rebel attack. At the time, Washington, D.C., was probably the most heavily fortified city on earth, but its miles of forts and rifle pits were useless without soldiers to man them. Finally recognizing the danger, the War Department cabled Grant to send reinforcements, but this would take time. In the interim, it was frantically calling out the militia, arming clerks and civilians, and drawing on the only organized military force within reach—the VRC. Everywhere in Washington, nervous unionists asked essentially what General Abercrombie had asked Johnson at White House Landing: "Will your invalids stand?"

At least two of the eyewitness accounts of the action that followed were written by members of the VRC. Private Alfred Bellard remembered how "[o]n Sunday the 10th orders came to move, so with 35 rounds of blue pills [minié balls] in our cartridge boxes, and our knapsacks on our backs, we left camp at seven o'clock p.m. and forming the brigade on Pen. Ave. we marched through Georgetown and Tennallytown with bands playing and colors flying. The streets being thronged with people to see us off.

"Reaching Fort Reno soon after, we halted, and the brigade was deployed out as skirmishers (about 3 feet between each man) in the rifle pits. Orders were given to keep awake and have an eye on the supposed rebels in front. We remained there all night, but as for keeping awake, I for one did not, for I had several cat naps during the night. Had the rebs made an attack on Was. that night, nothing could have saved it, as their was no troops round the city but our brigade, and we were supposed to be unfit for active service."[142]

The next day, July 11, found the Ninth VRC still in line around Fort Stevens, a strong point in the Union defenses. "About 4 o'clock, P.M.," according to Lieutenant Colonel Johnston, "the enemy advanced a heavy line of skirmishers and drove our skirmish line some distance back and took up their position so close to Fort Stevens, that they became quite annoying to the gunners, killing and wounding a number in the fort."[143] Those in the fort at this point included not only gunners and other soldiers but also visiting dignitaries there to watch the fight, Abraham Lincoln among them. Lincoln stood for several minutes at the top of the parapet, until the nervous commander implored the president to take cover. The fighting here would be the only combat personally witnessed by the president during the entire four-year struggle. (Lincoln came back the next day, and an irate Captain Oliver Wendell Holmes Jr., obviously forgetting himself, called out to him, "Get down, you fool!" Holmes was instantly mortified at his lapse, but Lincoln reportedly chuckled and again took cover.) "The regiment was ordered to advance and relieve the 25th N.Y. Cavalry (dismounted),[144] and if possible, to dislodge the enemy from the position they had taken up. The regiment was at once moved forward from the line of rifle pits and ordered to advance." The Ninth VRC advanced, and Early's skirmishers fell back. Losses for the Ninth were one killed, four mortally wounded, and seven severely wounded.[145]

Early's raid on Washington marked the low point of northern morale that summer but perhaps the high point of strategic usefulness for the VRC. When reinforcements finally arrived from the Army of the Potomac, the rebels had no option but to retreat. By the end of the summer, the capture of Mobile and Atlanta and then Sheridan's victories in the Shenandoah Valley had secured Lincoln's reelection and the Union's ultimate triumph.[146]

Johnson did not participate in this climactic battle, and he and the Eighteenth Regiment spent the rest of the war guarding the railroads, patrolling their assigned area in southwestern Maryland, and doing provost duty in Washington. "The Discipline," Johnson wrote in a report September 30, 1864, "is not such as should be desired or required," and the regimental books of the Eighteenth VRC from this period until the end of the war are filled with the reports of courts-martial for various infractions.[147]

The VRC performed one other notable service when the war was all but finished. An order of April 20, 1865, signed by Colonel Charles F. Johnson, detailed three men from the Eighteenth Regiment "to escort the remains of the late President of the United States to Springfield Illinois."[148] Among those who stood honor guard over Lincoln's body was Samuel A. Craig, who accompanied the president's remains from the railroad station to the Pennsylvania state capitol, where Lincoln lay in state. "I could look directly into the cold dead face of the President, during my tour," Craig remembered, "His face looked natural."[149]

Regrettably, little survives of Johnson's correspondence with Mary after December 1864, only a letter written two years later, the last included in this collection. Much of that gap can be explained by the fact that Mary and the children came to live with Johnson in Washington, a happy circumstance for them but an unfortunate one for historians. Nevertheless, there were clearly times—such as when Johnson worked for the Freedmen's Bureau in

Tennessee and Kentucky—when they were separated, and his last letter refers to others he had written. For reasons unknown, these were not preserved; in any event, neither Mrs. Grace Johnson Lynch, Johnson's great-granddaughter and the keeper of most of his letters, nor Mr. and Mrs. Richard Sicard, who hold the remainder of the letters as well as photographs and other memorabilia, were able to provide them.

THOUGH ITS members were selected to be among Lincoln's honor guard, "the Veteran Reserve Corps did not participate" in the Grand Review, the army's two-day victory parade through the streets of Washington on May 23 and May 24, 1865.[150] This was perhaps the earliest indication that the post-war era would consign "the Condemned Veterans" to oblivion. The unit at this time was just short of its peak strength. Its roster of May 31 included 762 commissioned officers and 29,852 enlisted men. Most of its enlisted men were mustered out by the end of 1865, but in March 1866 some 621 of its officers were still in federal service.[151]

There was some discussion of continuing the VRC as part of the regular army, a notion no doubt driven by the continued need for a federal police force, particularly in the occupied South. On December 13, 1865, a resolution passed the House of Representatives "requesting the President to suspend any order mustering out the officers of the Veteran Reserve corps until Congress shall take some legislative action in regard to the corps."[152] Colonel Johnson followed this discussion closely: a copy of the House debate of March 26, 1866, was among the papers he felt important enough to keep.[153] In July the VRC was officially terminated, however, and its last commander, Captain De Forest, and his remaining half dozen clerks were transferred to the Bureau of Refugees, Freedmen, and Abandoned Lands, popularly known as the Freedmen's Bureau.[154] The official end of the Eighteenth Regiment had come earlier, in December 1865. Colonel Johnson, among the many retained officers, then "awaited orders" until April 1866, when he was assigned to duty in the Freedmen's Bureau.[155] Johnson was one of several hundred former Invalid Corps officers (including Samuel Craig) so assigned, all of whom came under the direction of Johnson's old brigade commander, General O. O. Howard.

Among the final pages of the official correspondence of the corps are answers to Howard's repeated requests for lists of "officers of the Veteran Reserve Corps suitable for assignment to duty in the Bureau."[156] By March 1866, some 295 VRC officers were on duty in the Freedmen's Bureau, representing close to 40 percent of the wartime peak of commissioned officers in the corps and roughly 15 percent of the early staff of the bureau.[157] Others, already discharged from the VRC, also hoped to gain a position with the bureau. A typical example would be Capt. H. Horton, "late of the 23rd regiment VRC . . . on account of loss of left arm" who wrote to Provost Major General Clinton B. Fisk from his home in Chicago.[158]

As in the Invalid Corps, Johnson's first role in the bureau was as an investigator and reporter. In mid-May 1866, he was in western Tennessee, "in accordance with the instructions" of the bureau and the "confidential instructions" of General Howard, to conduct "an investigation of the late riots in Memphis," one of the worst outbreaks of racial violence in American history. His report, coauthored with Major T. W. Gilbraith, General Fisk's aide-de-camp (Fisk was assistant commissioner of the Bureau in Kentucky and Tennessee), recounts the story of what could perhaps best be described as an anti-black pogrom. A white mob, driven on and then assisted by municipal authorities, undertook a reign of terror during the first week of May. Forty-six black men, women, and children were killed, at least five black women were raped, and the commercial center of the black district of Memphis was largely burned to the ground. Two white men also died, one of a self-inflicted wound, the other killed by white man in the confusion of the violence.[159]

Johnson explained his method of preparing this report to the Congressional Select Committee on the Memphis Riots, which traveled to that city at the end of May to conduct its own investigation (it was this select committee that issued the congressional subpoena contained in Johnson's papers): "Not having the power to enforce the attendance of witnesses, we were under the necessity of getting our evidence voluntarily. We have examined two hundred and fifty witnesses, white and black." Asked the ratio of whites interviewed to blacks, Johnson replied, "one white out of five." Asked why this disparity, Johnson responded, "The colored ones were the sufferers—they had complaints to make. The whites were the aggressors, and, of course, did not volunteer to come before me."[160]

The Johnson/Gilbraith report, together with the affidavits they collected, conveys a stark picture of race relations in a Southern city immediately following the Civil War. They quote, for example, a Memphis civic leader exhorting a white crowd to "go get arms, organize, and go through the negro districts" with the purpose of "killing every God damned nigger." The result, Johnson and Gilbraith maintain, was that the mob "seemed to act as though vested with full authority to kill, burn, and plunder at will." Indeed, the investigation revealed that members of the Memphis police and fire departments were among the worst offenders: "Instead of protecting the rights of persons and property as is their duty, they were chiefly concerned as murderers, incendiaries, and robbers."[161] Johnson, who had in the past written that "a nigger is a nigger and the *best* of them is not worth a God damn!" was now cast as a witness to racial oppression.[162]

After finishing this report and several others of a more mundane nature, Johnson was appointed chief superintendent of the southern subdistrict of Kentucky, headquartered in Bowling Green, where he supervised a staff of present and former Union officers, occupation troops, Southern Unionists, and Northern missionaries. He reported on the progress of the newly founded Freedmen's schools, tried to mediate labor disputes between blacks and whites, and provided emergency rations for refugees and freedmen. Through it all, Johnson had to navigate the often brutal intricacies of American racial politics, personally intervening in situations a "Chestnut Street clerk" could hardly have imagined before the war. "If you have any record of a girl named *Marrilia Fairbanks*," he wrote on October 1, 1866, to the trustee of the Shaker Society of South Union, "who was about 5 years old when she was left at your establishment by a white woman about the year 1850 or 1851 and who left your society about two years since, you will oblige me by giving information on . . . her history (as far as you have any knowledge) previous to her entrance into your society. . . . She claims to be the child of a Mulatto woman (Father unknown) and has married a Mulatto man, but being white in both Color and features she is threatened with prosecution under the state law prohibiting the intermarriage of Whites and Blacks. She cannot establish the fact of being of Colored extraction unless through your Agency. Please answer at your earliest convenience."[163]

The letter illustrates both the transformations wrought by civil war and the limits of those changes. Here a Union officer, an official of the federal government (who himself has experienced prejudice because of his disability), was empowered to take direct action on behalf of a "mulatto woman" who five years earlier would have been beneath his notice, except perhaps, like his servant "Abraham," as little more than property. At the same time, it is clear that, despite the war and emancipation, the American legal system, most especially in Southern and border states, was still steeped in the distinctions of race.[164]

Indeed, many Southern whites refused to let emancipation end their political and economic hegemony, and this recalcitrance took a wide variety of forms. In some instances, black children were retained in virtual bondage by their former masters, who refused to allow them to join their parents. Johnson became particularly involved in one such case: "The Gray family claim that the [Berger] Children are indentured to them if so the indenture is illegal as the boy is 12 years of age and the girl between 9 & 10 years old and the parents have not given their consent."[165] One of Johnson's last acts with the bureau was to order a contingent of Union soldiers, on March 18, 1867, "to proceed to Butler County Ky and procure the children of Coffer Berger (colored)."[166]

Johnson also documented instances of widespread violence against blacks and white Unionists throughout his jurisdiction.[167] He forwarded numerous reports of "an apparent armed organization . . . to resist the orders of the Government" of "Regulators" and "Night riders."[168] He issued arrest orders for those perpetrators whom he could identify. "It is necessary," he wrote to the commander of one such arresting detail, "that you take great caution so as to not alarm the above named parties before the arrest, and that the arrests be made simultaneous, and also that they leave your locality *immediately* after the arrest to prevent the local courts issuing a Habeas Corpus and thereby take the prisoners out of our hands."[169] Johnson already had considerable experience with Southern courts, learning, for example, that despite emancipation they still "refuse to admit the evidence of colored persons where the whites are defendants," so as to render any white perpetrator of violence against a freedman or woman entirely immune from prosecution.[170]

On March 21, 1867, Johnson asked for a twenty-day leave of absence during the month of June "to visit Iowa on private business and also to recruit my health." What business Johnson might have had in Iowa is unknown, but Mary was to live there in future years, so it may have been that the family had already resettled there from Camden. (Among the items in Johnson's papers is a hand-drawn map of what appears to be a plan for a federal homestead, with plots assigned to several VRC officers, Johnson among them.) On June 30, he wrote to the bureau office in Louisville, requesting that three local employees be terminated and forwarding his "monthly return" of expenses incurred by his office.[171]

Charles Johnson died less than one month later on July 28, 1867, at age 39. The cause of death was "chronic diarrhea," but his wounds "doubtless shortened his career on earth." A meeting of "the officers and ex-officers of the U.S. Army" held in Bowling Green on August 8, 1867, passed a resolution mourning the loss of "a kind and affectionate husband," "a kind father," "a worthy citizen," and "an active and efficient officer."[172]

THE INVALID CORPS was gone, but the hundreds of thousands of men disabled by the war remained. As before the conflict, pensions and soldiers' institutions were the standard societal response. The efforts of veterans' organizations, in particular the Grand Army of the Republic (GAR), were crucial to the expansion of these services. Initially, individual GAR chapters attempted to provide relief to their members with disabilities but in most instances found that they lacked sufficient resources. Veterans' groups therefore became active in lobbying for the admission of their most severely disabled members to the newly founded state and federal institutions, which in turn often appointed GAR members to their boards of directors.[173] By 1919, the individual states were managing more than thirty such "soldiers' homes," with a total population of approximately 11,000, which included, in some states, a small number of their family members as well as the veterans themselves. In addition, the federal government expanded its network of asylums, where the number of residents from 1865 to 1919 peaked at 30,000.[174]

The vast majority of veterans, however, preferred receiving a pension to virtual incarceration in an institution. Legislation approved by Congress in 1862 had provided for a monthly stipend for disabled veterans and for the widows and minor children of those killed while in the service or whose death could be demonstrated to be "the immediate or ultimate result of his performance of military duty." Disability pensions ranged from eight dollars a month to thirty, and were determined based on a soldier's rank and the severity of his disability. The ratings were increased several times, and in 1890 the system was expanded to include all disabled civil war veterans, regardless of cause of disability. The civil war disability pension system was thus the federal government's largest disability compensation program until Social Security Disability Insurance (SSDI) was introduced in 1956.[175]

The pension system was highly controversial and the subject of partisan politics. Conservative critics denounced it as "demoralizing and pernicious" in that it lowered "the tone of American independence and patriotism."[176] Anecdotes of abuse by undeserving slackers filled the popular press, the perception of the system as being irredeemably corrupt extending even to those most obviously disabled advocates who were instrumental in expanding it. The GAR's most visible and articulate advocate for disability pensions was James Tanner, a double amputee who was appointed U.S. government commissioner of pensions in 1889. Accused of corruption, he was eventually forced to resign and was then held up as representative of all that was wrong with the system.[177]

Parallels can be drawn between the attacks on the Pension Act of 1890, particularly the repeated references to unscrupulous attorneys advocating for undeserving clients, and criticisms of the Americans with Disabilities Act (ADA) of a century later. Peter David Blanck and Chen Song note how, "In the area of disability advocacy . . . many ADA claimants today are cast as undeserved, frivolous, and motivated by fee-driven attorneys," and go on to describe how nineteenth-century editorial writers similarly cast many of those who applied for civil war disability pensions, as well as the attorneys who represented them, as "Staining a Nation's Honor-Roll with Pretense and Fraud."[178] Theda Skocpol describes the civil war pension system both as a precursor to Social Security and as one reason why Americans in the early twentieth century never enacted the "European-style old age pensions and social insurance" typical of the rest of the western world. The massive civil war program ameliorated the need for such programs, while at the same time its perceived flaws alienated progressive supporters and energized conservative skeptics of any form of civilian social security.[179]

It can be argued that ableism also played a critical role in undermining support for the pension system. Social unease often increases as people with disabilities assert their rights to just treatment and inclusion. And if, as the "just world" theory suggests, there is indeed a tendency to attribute disability to individual failure, then the sudden reality of tens of thousands of obviously disabled war veterans would have been socially unsettling to the extreme. For far from being a deserving victim of God's wrath or his own moral laxity and unworthiness, a legless or armless "war cripple" was in fact a courageous warrior, a man of patriotism and self-sacrifice. And yet this same man, in his disabled state, had lost his "independence" and thus his "manliness." He was now dependent on others, particularly women, whose traditional role it was to provide comfort and assistance.

"Yes sir, it is inconvenient" noted one navy veteran, whose arms had been amputated above the elbows. "Now . . . if I want a drink through the day or the night, or a bite of bread and meat at any time, somebody must put it into my mouth. The women-folks about are always willing to help a fellow in this way; but, you see, there's undressing to turn into bed at night, and dressing to turn out of a morning, and washing, and other things, have to be done at odd times, which can't be safely trusted to the chance-help a fellow situated as I am may always get from his women friends for the asking."[180]

What was one to make of such a composite of hero and cripple, warrior and dependent? His very existence was a rebuke to any belief in a "just world," where disability, poverty, and dependence were the punishment for cowardice and sloth. Similarly, what was one to do with all those women who had gone to the hospitals and battlefields and done a job (nursing) that many men either could not or would not do? How could one reconcile the existence of such women with the Victorian notion of "proper" women as weak, demure, and dependent?

These questions were asked, more or less explicitly, within the context of a struggle over how American society would remember its civil war. At the very heart of this controversy, as Johnson might have gathered during his work with the Freedman's Bureau, was the issue of race. David Blight describes how an "emancipationist" vision of the war, in which the conflict was seen foremost as a struggle against the evil of slavery, was superseded by the "reconciliationist" view, in which both sides were glorious defenders of their own truth and morality. White Northerners and Southerners eventually united in a shared, sentimentalized version of civil war history, taking American memory from Lincoln's "new birth of freedom" to D. W. Griffith's *The Birth of a Nation*. This version all but expunged the struggle of African Americans for freedom and civil rights, and erased their crucial contributions as Union soldiers and sailors. The cataclysm of the 1860s was thus transformed into a regrettable misunderstanding over states' rights, tariffs, and economic competition. Slavery and the ongoing existence of racism and white supremacy became taboo topics unless romanticized (and often justified) in melodramas such as *Gone with the Wind*.[181]

This "reconciliationist" view could not accommodate the memory of the massacre of blacks (as recounted, for example, in Johnson's letters), the grim absurdities of battle (as described in De Forest's 1867 novel *Miss Ravenal's Conversion*), or the abuse of prisoners at Andersonville and other prison camps. Similarly, severely disabled veterans, who served as physical reminders of the consequences of war, were removed as far from the mainstream as possible. The connection between disabled veterans and the survivors of the prisoner-of-war camps is especially visceral and not merely because of the role played by the VRC in guarding Northern camps. An interesting juxtaposition might be made between photographs of Andersonville survivors and of such late nineteenth-century "medical curiosities" as "Living Skeletons" J. W. Coffey and Rosa Lee Plemons, who were portrayed as marginally human "freaks" of nature.[182] Some way had to be found then, if the "reconciliationist" version of civil war history was to prevail, of repressing or at least mediating the most disturbing artifacts of the national trauma—be they explicit accounts of its barbarity or the actual bodies of severely wounded veterans.

And so it was probably no coincidence, as Rosemarie Thomson points out, that the post–civil war era saw the carnival "freak show" grow to be perhaps *the* major form of American popular entertainment.[183] "Can those be men?" Walt Whitman asked, when confronted with Northern prisoners repatriated from a southern prisoner-of-war camp. Spectators at a "freak show," where attractions were billed as "half man, half beast," were encouraged to ask precisely that question, because it is the very humanity of people with disabilities, the inevitability of disability as part of the human condition, and thus their own vulnerability to disability that the "temporarily able-bodied" generally find most disturbing.[184] Along with freak shows came the rise of the eugenics movement, with its emphasis on providing "scientific" evidence of the "links" between heredity, disability, and criminality, and the construction of massive state institutions to house—and isolate—people with such obvious and disturbing disabilities as cerebral palsy, epilepsy, mental retardation, and mental illness. The "just world" theory was recast as social Darwinism, and disabled veterans portrayed as greedy and conniving, not so heroic after all.

In any event, the history of the Veteran Reserve Corps was lost to popular memory. In part this was because regimental histories written after the war were most often prepared or commissioned by private veterans' groups, as opposed to being compiled as official records of the federal or even the state governments. Such veterans' groups were generally organized by members of the same social sphere as the civic and business leaders who had pulled the volunteer regiments together in the first place. Because the VRC was purely the creation of the federal military establishment (which itself was almost entirely dismantled when the war ended), there was apparently no group vested in recounting or preserving the memory of its exploits.[185]

Another factor was the way that disabled veterans tended to identify with their regiments of origin, rather than with the VRC, perhaps perceiving their service with the Invalid Corps to be less legitimate, even less honorable. Likewise, disabled veterans made no particular efforts to organize themselves after the war. As Peter Blanck and Michael Millender point out, though tens of thousands of disabled veterans may have applied for pensions, "their consciousness as disabled persons rarely prompted them to identify with other disabled veterans, let alone disabled persons who had not shared their experience of war-time service."[186]

This was in direct contrast to later post-war periods, which saw the emergence of such grassroots organizations as Disabled American Veterans (DAV; following World War I) and the Paralyzed Veterans of America (PVA; following World War II). These groups advocated for improvements in medical care and the expansion of rehabilitation services, at first only for veterans but then increasingly for *all* people with disabilities. The PVA, for example, went on to press for wheelchair access at American colleges and universities, and was instrumental in fostering the organization of civilian groups such as the National Spinal Cord Injury Foundation and the National Wheelchair Basketball Association. Educated and accustomed to living in the mainstream, twentieth-century disabled veterans had a leavening effect on the general disability community and were often in the vanguard of the emerging disability rights movement. They provided new ideas, fresh leadership, and perhaps most important a sense of entitlement, derived from the sacrifices they had made for their country, often lacking among disabled civilians.[187]

None of this happened in the decades following the civil war, and so disabled civilians such as Samuel Gessbury probably found little if any relief from the prejudice they faced, despite the dramatic increase in the prevalence of disability in American society. It would remain for subsequent generations of veterans, and their disabled allies in civilian life, to confront finally the notion of a "just world" that stigmatizes the various forms of disability and oppresses those people who, for whatever reason, happen to have them.

MARY JOHNSON moved to Iowa after the war, and following her husband's death, she married, divorced, and then married again. She died in Des Moines on March 7, 1906.[188]

The twins were not quite seventeen when their father died. Joseph Hufty Johnson married in Des Moines in 1872 and then moved to Minnesota. He became an engraver like his father, and worked for a time at the *St. Paul Dispatch.* He took out a homestead at Fawn Lake, Minnesota, north of the Deer River, which he farmed with his mother-in-law, wife, and three children. He died there on May 15, 1913.[189]

William Ewing Wiley Johnson married Harriet Stites Sewel Deal, the daughter of Charles Johnson's friend George (often mentioned in his letters). Their first child, Norma Avenel Johnson, was born in Philadelphia in 1878. According to her adopted brother, Arthur Levon Allen, "Norma was born lame. Her right leg was [put] in a steel cast and all of her childhood pictures were taken with her leg concealed. . . . Imagine a girl growing up all through the teen years with such a handicap."[100] William worked for a meatpacking firm in Philadelphia, but by 1888 had relocated to Chicago. He became a successful real estate broker, until a partner with the firm absconded with its funds, leaving Johnson to pay the debts. He died in Chicago in 1921.

Clara Adelia Johnson married Solon Radolphus Mower in May 1875, also in Des Moines. She had three children and died on February 21, 1928, in Canyon County, Idaho.[191]

It was Charles Johnson's disabled granddaughter Norma who preserved his letters, along with most of the other family papers that survive, leaving them to Arthur Allen when she died in 1964. Allen, in turn, bequeathed them to Mrs. Grace Johnson Lynch, Johnson's great granddaughter, who donated copies of the letters to the U.S. Army Military History Institute and made the originals available to me for this book. Mrs. Lynch died on May 4, 2002, in Hibbing, Minnesota. It was her wish that her great grandfather's papers be preserved and made available to future historians. And so I have, with her family's permission, placed them at the Bancroft Library at the University of California at Berkeley, where they are now part of an expanding archive on the history of disability and disability rights. Another portion of the letters as well as Johnson's field diary and kit were passed down to Richard and Lucille Sicard, descendants of the Colonel's son Joseph Huffy Johnson. This material remains with the Sicard family in California.

Many questions about the disability experience of the middle and late nineteenth century remain to be explored by social historians. How did the most destructive of all wars fought on American soil affect the day-to-day lives of people with disabilities? What was the war's lasting impact on the social history of disability? And, likewise, what role did disability play in how the Civil War has been passed down in history and in the struggle, still unresolved, over its legacy? What did the sudden disabling of hundreds of thousands of young men do to the nation's political, social, economic, and spiritual life?

There is no doubt that disability altered the lives of Charles F. Johnson, Samuel Gessbury, and millions of others during that period. Yet, disability, and the struggle over its meaning, is common to all societies in all eras. Disability is an inevitable part of life and an integral facet of human diversity. It thus offers a vital tool to social historians, a ubiquitous standard, like gender and race, class and sexual expression, existing everywhere and at all times.

Remove disability from the picture, then, and we severely limit our ability to understand the past and gauge the realities of our present time and place. Exclude people with disabilities from the social mainstream, and we fatally compromise any "just world" we might ever hope to build.

1

"Down to a strict military life"

September 19, 1861–December 27, 1861

Recruiting for the Eighty-first Pennsylvania Volunteer Infantry began in August 1861 after the Federal disaster at First Bull Run. The thousand or so recruits, mostly from Philadelphia and its environs, gathered at Camp Washington in Easton, Pennsylvania, where they tried to prepare themselves for what would become the world's first industrialized war.

1

Camp Washington[1]
Sept. 19/61

Dear Mary,

I take my pen in hand to night at 11 o'clock, after a horse back ride of ten or twelve miles over the mountains, in company with Dr. Dixon,[2] viewing the unparralled beauties of the LeHigh River by moonlight—such sceanes I never imagined to have existed out of Switzland—one in particular, as we rode up to the top of a mountain, the road turned sharply around, revealing the river with its sides studed with shrubry and high bluff of rocks at least a half a mile below us, the sound of the horns from the canal boats and the ringing of the locomotive bell, (as the long coal trains wound like serpents at the base of the mountain) mingled together as they reached us in our high location—it was a sceane that will never be effaced from my memory.

Last night, (the first of my camp life, for I am sleeping on my bed at "quarters"), last night I remained awake for hours thinking of you and the little ones at home, of Clara and the boys (God bless them) and how you all were getting on; I however at last went to sleep with the sound of the feet of the sturdy sentinal as he paced up and down before my quarters humming in my ears and mixed you, the children, him (the sentinal) and I believe every thing else in my dream.[3]

But, stop! it strikes me that I am getting prosey and sentimental, and yet how could I remember any thing else but you, as Moore says

"Remember thee? Yes, while there's life in this heart,
It shall never forget thee, all lorn as thou art;
More dear in thy sorrow, thy gloom, and thy showers,
Than the rest of the world in their sunniest hours."[4]

The Col.[5] just arrived and desired a Court Martial for three offenders, which will be held to morrow—I suppose that the result will be reducing two men from non-commissioned officers to the ranks and depriving a private of one months pay—all for violating orders—to-night I turned both of Cap't Alexander's[6] Negro cooks out of camp for abusive language to officers—so you see that we are down to strict military life. There is a great amount of work yet to be done, but with calmness, perserverance and a just determination to carry out that which is right, I hope to succeed to the fullest extent in retaining the confidence of *all* the officers and men, which confidence they all tell me I have at the present time.

There is not much prospects of our moving immediately from here—but I will be able to speake more advisedly in my next. In the mean time let me hear from you; direct to Lieut. Col. Chas. F. Johnson Camp Washington, Easton, P*a*.

Give my love to the Boys and a kiss to little Clara for me.

Your
Charley

P.S. George Deal[7] appears to get along first rate with his department and has made many friend[s] among the new men here[.]

2

Camp Washington
Sept. 22/61

Dear Mary,

I take up my pen again to write to you upon this my birth-day.[8]

Since writing my last (the 19th inst.) I have passed the time in a very business like manner; the Col. being absent yet. To give you some idea of how we pass the time, I will give you the Drum Call for each day.

I am called at my request, by the Sergeant of the Guard at 15 minutes of 5 o'clock in the morning

At 5 o'clock the Reveille beats for all hands to "turn out" and rolls called
at 5½—squad drills for 1½ hours
at 7—Breakfast

at 8—Guard Mounting
at 9—Company drills for 2 hours
at 12—Dinner and rolls called
—2—Regimental drills
—4—Company drills for 1½ hours with guns
—5½—Dress parade
—6—Supper
—9—Tattoo and rolls called
and 9¼—lights out[.]

then add to that the writing necessary for a camp, and you can see that I have not much spare time on my hands unless I quietly walk off; which I did on Friday morning at the break of day and mounted my horse, and rode near twenty miles before breakfast. We took the rout of the Delaware River, and visited places whose beauties are far beyond the power of my pen to describe.

I expected a letter from you yesterday but "nary one" came, and I certainly feel desirous of hearing from you and the *little ones*—do not delay from day to day or you will never write.

Is everything goin on all right at home? that is the question that constantly comes to my mind at every spare moment; more particulary when I retire at night. I do not think that I have closed my eyes since I have been here, but what *home* has been the last thought that flitted o'er my mind—in the morning I am too busy to think of any thing but the camp. Yet I think that it is the very thing for me—the exercise, the open air and regular habits make me eat like a glutton, I am the first down and the last up from the table[.]

George[9] sends a letter by the same mail as this, he appears to get along *all right*[.]

There is at least a dozen men waiting for me, for all sorts of purposes (I suppose) so I must close—remember me to the children always[.]

Yours[,]
Charley

P.S. 11 o'clock P.M. I have just returned from another moonlight ride, over the same route that I took yesterday morning—or rather we attempted to take the same route and lost our way and, as Dutton[10] would have said also lost our geography: for we had to stop and knock at a cottage door and enquire where we were—in New Jersey or Pennsylvania—what do you think of that; a set of men not knowing their native state. But as it happened we were in both states, for we were first in Phillipsburg, N.J. and then had crossed the Delaware into Pennsylvania and up the river, along a road built on the side of the mountains, high up, above the tops of the tallest trees on the banks of the stream—it is truely delightfull to dash along at the full speed of your horse, now in the broad light of the quiet moon, and then in the darkness of the thick woods, then suddenly out in the moonlight again as you turn a sharp angle of the mountain path, with the ripling river (for it is but a broad creek with a pebble bottom here) dancing in the moon. We visited the Pink Rocks, a place noted for its Pic Nicks in this section—the Blue Rocks, also another place of summer resort, and five miles further on there is a rock in the river called the Alegator Rock, on account of its close resemblance to a huge monster of that name, dashing on we came to the Wigat (supposed to mean "wind gap") a place where the Delaware squeezes itself between two mountains, one of which is clothed with tall trees—the other a perpendicular mass of rocks high in the air, around which the road winds itself—we then turned into the rural districts and the whole face of the country changed—all was a quite scean of country life, with highly cultivated fields, pushing on we reached the Bushkill Creek, at the foot of the Chestnut Mountains, and here was the most perfect representation of the *wissahicken*[11] that I ever saw (even the old worn out mill was there) persuing our way we reached the brow of a hill which gave us a birds-eye view of Easton, through which we passed to our Camp.

3

Camp Washington
Easton, Pa.
Sept. 27/61

Dear Mary,

I sit down at my quarters to-night in the midst of one of the most violent storms of wind and rain that I have experienced for a long time. I have just ordered the guards to be drawn in, for it storms to much for any man to undertake to leave the camp and walk to Easton, even if he felt disposed to run away at any other time—I went in person, for I thought it would please the boys to see their officer sharing their troubles with them.[12]

The Col. arrived here last night and left this morning for Philad- and thence to either Harrisburg or New York according to circumstances, so I will be obliged to remain until next week, when I think it more than probable that I will give you a flying visit.

Yesterday I gave the boys a Regimental Drill—my first attempt in commanding entirely alone—they were so well pleased with it that the Col. (from their representation) suggested me to continue it in his absence.

I have had a hard time of it, to keep the boys from leaving the camp in a body, on account of the government not being able to furnish them their clothing—not a blanket or over-coat[13]—the Col. said that he expected to see a regular stamped[e] when he returned (and if *he* had been here there would have been) for the men said openly that it was the Lieut. Col's kindness that kept them—I could not blame them much if they had have goin, but as it was I have not lost more than twenty out of seven hundred—this nights storm will try them and I will have an other "*oiley*" speech to make in the morning.

Give the children a squeeze for me and bless you all, I have just been having a mental conversation with your deguereotype spread out on my desk—I quite forgot that I was not at home again—it is one of the greatest pleasures of experience—to look at your pictures just before going to bed and then lay and think until I fall asleep.

Expecting to see you again in a short time I am

your
Charley

[Wri]te in the mean time[.]

4

Camp Washington
Midnight Oct 9/61

Dear Mary,

I have just returned from a long walk over the fields and through the woods, hunting for men who took French leave of camp and feel pretty well used up, but could not neglect to write to you, as to-morrow will be a very busy day with me, for we have received our orders to march on Friday morning at 8 o'clock to Washington, via Harrisburg and Baltimore, so I will not have an opportunity to write to you again until I get "down in Dixie," which I shall do on the first chance after I arrive there.[14]

I would have liked to get home once more, before I went, but our orders did not come until to-night and it is "*impossable*" for me to come—however I guess it is as well as it is, for even if I had an opportunity to go, and *did* go, the desire would still be in existance to see you even then again.

You need not write to me here as I will have left before an answer could be received, I will inform you in my next *where* to address me, which will be in a few days, three or four [portion missing] from Friday next.

If you should get short of money borrow some from Geo. Hufty,[15] or any one else you chooce; as I intend as soon as my month is up to draw up my pay roll and get it cashed at a small discount and will send you the funds as early as possable.

I received Joe's letter from George (who arrived safe) and it did me considerable good—press the boys to your brest for me and give *that* little one a few kisses[.] Trusting that divine Providence may guide you and them until we meet again in our happy little family circle.

I remain ever

Charley

P.S. I am compeled to make this rather shorter than usual, as I want to "turn in" as *all* the officers will be up the entire night to-morrow, and I want enough sleep to-night to enable me to do so without feeling it to any extent—you see I am *very* considerate of my health, which is better than it ever was before—but I *must* stop—good night—
Did [smudge] a letter from me through the mail this week?

5

Camp Scitz
Kendell Green[16]
Washington City
Oct. 17/61

Dear Mary,

Your brief, concise, and very welcome letter came to hand via[?] Lieut. Wilson[17] this day, and I find that you are out of funds which of course I expected, and I have been informed that the government will not pay until after the 1st of Nov. Can you live on tick until that time? If not I will hypothicate my pay at any discount asked, for you and the children (all that I love in this world) *must* and *shall* be comfortable if I can make it so—speak out and let me know.

We received our arms from [the] Government to-day, and last night was the first that I slept in my marque; having been compelled to sleep where ever I could get a place; two nights I slept in what is called a one horse ambulance—a waggon used to pull the wounded from the battlefield to the hospital, it holds two persons, and the Major and myself, "froze on to it."—all hands (field & staff) had to ruff it, but it has done me good, for I weighed myself to day and I have gained 4½ pounds since I left home—if I continue I shall be a Dan.l Lambert[.][18] I can not button the top of my gray pants and my full dress one (which I could not keep up without suspenders) are tight—in fact the men all say that they can see me grow.

Our Mess Chest has not come yet, and you would have been amused to see me getting broke to private's fare yesterday morning, I looked at the breakfast—"old joe" (stale bacon) coffee with out milk, hard army crackers fried in bacon fat—was the "bill of fare" I looked at it and walked away, got hungery, went back, looked again, and—walked off—in about an hour, got infernal hungery, went back and began at it, (the officers all laughing) and eat about a pound and a half, six crackers and emptied two tin cups full of coffee—I think that I have "crossed the Rubicon" and can eat "old hoss" if requisite. We fare better, however, now, having systemized the affair, and appointed a market man to go to Washington and purchase our grubb.

The Colonel has made inquiry at the Department, and been informed that the government will allow the Field & Staff officers pay from the date of the acceptance of the Regiment, that will give me two months *more pay;* making three months due me on next pay day, which will enable me to settle for my horse, wipe out my debt at the store, and pay the money that I have been compelled to borrow for here and four days board at Easton, and enable me to give you a much better start than I did before—in fact I will be compleatly on my feet again, which I have not been for some years.[19]

We are now enjoying the luxery of a north-east storm, all out of doors is wet, mudy, dark and dreary to night and the rain patters on the top of the tent, like the sound upon a roof, in side it is as comfortable as in a house, except that I have not any carpet, but the men have offered to crib (a soldier *never* steals) some lumber and floor my marque, which they have not offered to any of the other officers, in fact they remarked when pitching the tents—"this is the Lieut. Col's, boys, put it up right, if it takes all day" and they did, for they took it down twice and put it up again before they were satisfied with it, notwithstanding I insisted that it would answer; it makes me feel proud of having their good will.

I am writing this upon the top of my trunk, but will have a camp stool and table to-morrow, there is a man goin from one camp to another with them for sale; the table folds up into a very small space and is only one dollar, cheap for this section of the country where they charge you five cents for the privalage of farting—the Philad- Inquirer is brought to camp every morning after the day of its issue for five cents each, a good price for a paper one day old.

Your letter was so brief to-day that you did not say any thing about the children or yourself, say something about them in your next, for I love to read their names in *your letters,* it does me more good than a thousand verbal messages.

As I am getting at the bottom of the sheet I must close, though I could write for an hour yet.

If you do not get any letters regular you must not be disappointed, for the trains from here does not run upon any thing like time, every thing must give away for the trains with military—there is at least two hundred thousand men along the Potomac River and four or five trains loaded passes our camp each day,

Your Charley

6

Camp Scitz
Kendell Green
Washington City
Oct 25/61

Dear Mary,

Yours dated 22 inst. received yesterday and I had written to you the 23rd and forwarded by John M. Dutton, who will pass through Philad- on his way to Harrisburg & Easton to finish up his business—he promised to send you $20.00 when he sent the letter to Camden, he not having time to call himself.

Night before last was about the coldest that I experienced this season, it had been raining all day and cleared up, with a rushing north-west wind, which actualy pulled the long tent pins out of the ground. It was so infernal cold that I went to bed at 7 o'clock and slept like a dog[?] with only a piece of canvas (the side of the marque) between me and the wind—a frail wall for such weather.

The next day (yesterday) was more mild but cold again at night, and this morning a frost at least an inch thick covered every thing—we thought it had snowed in the night, every thing was so white[.] I have an extra blanket and put on my under shirt and feel more comfortable, except about the legs—*if* Dutton sends you the $20.00 I would like you to get me two pair of wove or net drawers, I do not care for colour so that they are *thick* [underlined twice]—the heavyest and *thickest* that you can purchase, also a pair of *thick gloves for* [?].

Now while writing in the tent (for we have not any fire, of course) I am compelled to lay down my pen occasionaly and hold the bowl of the pipe in my hands to warm my fingers so that I can guide my pen,—I shall go out as soon as I finish this, and take a drill with the men on a "double quick" which warms us all up.

Yesterday our Regiment attended the funeral of Col. Baker,[20] with side arms, as mourners we had a long tramp (some of the officers being mounted)

from here to the place of starting and thence to the Congressional [?] Grounds and we under took to make a short cut for home across the fields and were compelled to wade & jump quite a number of ditches for our pains—which was done by the men in the best of humours.

You ask for "war news"! why bless your soul! we do not know any thing about that, except what we read in the New York and Philad. papers that is received in Camp—even the Washington papers copy from them.

I actualy can not tell you half as much as you know yourself. After we begin to move I may be better posted and shall not fail to give you any and all such information as may intrest you, but you can read more in one day in the papers than I *now* could give you in a week.

In reference to your visit to William[21] I would say that when we are on our feet I will endevour to arrange that for you.

Joe Parker paid me a visit this morning and appeared quite glad to see me here in this possition; I know quite a number of the men in his regiment, several members of Coaganock Lodge are there, some of them Past Grands[.]

We have been informed (in an indirect manner) that the future number of the regiment will be the 81st Penn. but direct your letters as usual (the 36th) until I notify you of the formal change.

An Irish woman just this moment looked into my marque to know if I wanted to buy some good *mince pies,* so you see that we do not want for the delights of life if we choose to *pay* for them, at Washington prices—we have had an offer to serve us with oysters every day at a dollar pr gallon.

I must close as Col. Miller just informed me that he was leaving camp and I must attend to the Company drills.

Your
Charley

P.S. Saturday morning—

Last night I received information that our men had been in the habit of selling thier clothing for rum at a place on the suburbs of the city—after investigating the case I ordered a Sergeant & six men there, and acccompanied them myself—we found a lot of our clothing and I ordered all the liquor emptied into the street which was done accordingly.

Last night the Col. ordered the Long Roll beaten at midnight and the whole regiment formed in line of battle in fourteen minutes ready for action. Not a one of us had any information of the event to take place—some of the men appeared half dressed. I was the fourth man on the field, and I always strip myself except shirt & drawers—the other officers sleep in their clothes—I am goin to Virginia this morning[.]

7

Camp Good Hope
Some County—some where
Oct 30/61

Dear Mary,

We are at last encamped at the above place, exactly *where* I cannot tell you yet, as I have not had time to look around me; the Col. having ordered me (as usual) to supervise instead the laying out of the camp [grounds?]. He says that I go to work at it like a regular, and can scarcely believe that I never had any experience at it before.

We have pitched our tents upon a mountainous tract of land, having upon the front a clear and long view of most miserable, Godly-forsaken farms, owned by the degenerated sons of old settlers, who are too lazey to keep the lice off their sacred bodies[22]—[in] the rear we have a wild, dense woods, that look as though mortal man never trod through its deep under brush—down a deep ravine of which, the men are busy building a dam around a spring for water—if you was here, you could indulge your romance to its fullest extent—that is if you did not know that you was within a mile or so of the outside pickets. We are in the midst of a secession neighborhood and last night was the first since I left home that I have slept with all my clothes on, prepared for any emergency; and yet I felt more like an officer than I have since I left home; it looked like work and I felt the responsibility. Genl. Sickles[23] is just behind us in order to keep the rebels from crossing in force from Aqua Creek and we are expected to co-opperate with him.

We arrived here yesterday morning—the whole Brigade was ordered to move (the balance *up* to Bladensburg, our regiment down) at the same time, we had the revellie sounded at 2 o'clock in the morning, ate some breakfast at 3 o'clock, pitched tents and just at the break of day began to move with 33 waggons loaded—the rest of the brigade was asleep yet and did not move until nearly noon; the Brig. Gen. (Howard)[24] was surprised and so well pleased[?] with our promptness that he went himself to the department and insisted upon our overcoats and every thing else that we wanted and we got them. I wish you could have seen us—the 900 men busy rolling up tents, loading waggons each with 4 & 6 mules strung along and around[?] the camp, the officers (mounted) dashing here and there giving and receiving orders, the red glare of the huge camp fires (lighting up every thing around) contrasting with the white frosty ground a warm sight not often seen by many and never by me before.

I received last night two papers from you and then three from some one else who I do not know—they were acceptable nevertheless; also one for George—who was mustered into the service last Sunday morning—he became very much dissatisified before, but is now better contented, I believe however you need not say any thing of *that*—you know.

I have upon my table a pile of Chestnuts and two cups of Parsimmons brought me by different parties of our scouts, who gathered them while out last night and this morning. I like these little attentions, they speak well for the feeling of the men, particulary as I am the only officer that they do so with—I hope it will always be so; not with the officers but with me.

How is the little ones coming along? All well and right I hope—I was too tired and used up last night to write, from being up and at work from 2 o'clock in the morning until 9½ o'clock at night the first time I stop[p]ed except to eat my supper, my dinner I ate while moving about—I was too tired to write, but not too tired to look at your deguerrotypes and fell asleep with them on the bed.

I have just been informed that I am appointed the "Brigade Officer of the Day" for to-morrow, so I will be compelled to ride between 30 & 40 miles to visit each encampment and Regiment in the brigade during the day, rather more work than honour, however it brings me into notice and gives me the advantage of the experience and I become acquainted with quite a number of officers, which goes to compensate for the labour.

Direct your letters as before, there is no post office here and we must send to Washington each day for letters, so direct Lieut. Col. Chas. F. Johnson

36st Reg. Pa. Vol.[25]
Col. Jas. Miller
Washington City

Your
Charley

8

Camp Good Hope
Nov 8/61

Dear Mary,

I have at last arrived at home (as we call it) and received two letters from you besides quite a number of papers. We have had a long and continuous tramp the whole week and to the regret of *every* one *no fight.* We did not leave the camp until 5½ o'clock p.m. on Sunday last on account of some delay in the Quartermasters department at head quarters; and arrived at Centerville at 9 o'clock that night; as we left without camp equipage we of course bunked in the woods, and I for the first time wraped my blanket around me and spread myself on the ground, at the same tree that my horse was tied at, using the saddle for a pillow, Abram sleeping at the next tree,—he assured me on the rout down, by his constant and deturmaned endevours to be near me; as also George, who sholdered a gun and remarked that where the Lieut. Col. was, there he would be. We left Centerville before day light and arrived at Marlboro at 9 o'clock, on the morning of the 4th inst. where our instructions was waiting for us—which was to protect all the Polls, as the simpathizers with the Rebels had threatened to kill every Union man that made his appearance that day—the Col. gave me charge of three of them, one at Piscataway, 18 miles off; at Nottingham, 16 miles off, and at Horsehead 19 miles off.[26] I fell asleep in the woods, arrainging my plans, and started the next morning at an hour before day, with my command of 600 men and 40 rounds of cartrage per man; I took the longest point as my head-quarters, that is Horse Head, where I arrived in the afternoon, and took possession of the town, fixed my guards and moved my two companies (I have divided them in two companies for each Poll) out to a field and, we having built a fire, rolled ourselves up in our blankets to sleep, prepared for any emergancy the next day—during the night several Union men called and insisted that I should sleep on their plantations, but I refused and continued to ruff it all through with the men. I was aroused in the morning with the rain splashing in my face—it had been raining for an hour and some of the guard had fixed a seder tree, while I was asleep, over me, to protect me as much as possable—we left the town at the break of day on the 7th and arrived at Marlboro in the afternoon, where all our Regiment assembled during the day and evening—we left at 3½ o'clock on this day for Good Hope and arrived in perfect condition. I must confess that I am tired and shall be glad when night comes to enjoy a good sleep—I have not even had my spurs off for 6 days & nights, much less any clothing. One of the men at Nottingham shot a member of his company through the head, killing him instantly, we brought his body to camp where it now lies in a pine board box, we will take it to Washington—the man who shot him has been sent to the Provost Marshall for examination—what will be the result I do not know, we also sent a prisoner to the Marshall who had the hardyhood to propose three cheers for Jef. Davis, at the Polls—there is an immense number of *quiet* traitors in this state, but by the military protecting the Union men and making all that were suspected, sware allegiance, we have carried the entire state by a rousing majority.

There is one thing that I remarked that all the middling class are true, nearly all the wealthy ones are in favour of the south, but we made them all publicly proclaim to the contrary, that was a kind of spite opperation, which was all we could do, as those against whom we had *evidence,* had fled to Virginia.

When I returned to camp and entered my marque the first thing that I saw was the poor faded flowers that you sent me with my things—they lie before me now and I shall keep them there until they compleatly dry up.

In answer to yours of the 3rd inst. I would say that I regret extreamly to hear of the continued illness of your mother but hope that she may be spared, at least until I return home, for if she steped out before, you would indeed feel lonely, but let us hope for the best and look upon the sunny side of life and not upon the side you appeared to be gaizing at when you penned that letter. In reference to the box, why, "never mind it"—I do not much care for "schlek" (is *that* the way to spell it) and would much rather receive a cheerful, hearty and lively letter from you than a thousand boxes of "stuff"—but if it will give you any satisfaction to send one, do so and I will certanly eat the contents,—and box too—if it would please you: *if* you do send, direct to me the same as the letters, and send by Adams express and I will have the Commissary Sergeant (who goes to town every day or so) to call at their office—notify me by mail[.]

In reply to your letter of the 4th inst—I would say give that old skunk (Dougherty) perfect fits. Damn him, if I had him here I would shake the puddings out of him. I gave George a raking down about his not writing home frequently. I did not know anything of it until I received your letter—the fact is that his department and mine are so different that we never get togeather, unless one of the other starts right off to visit, which we of-course do to have a talk at times.

Tell the Boys that I expect to hear of their promotion as soon as the examination is through. It will make me feel proud of them and myself too for being their Father, but, if they are not promoted *this* time, pick it up again and do so the next.

Tell Clare that I will "come home" "safter a while"—bless her little heart, I must get her (and all) dagarreotypes out of my trunk to night, I have not seen them for a week—the result of the orders "no baggage" in our forced march.

I am pleased to see mother's name in the list of the goodly women of Camden, I suppose the old lady (you need not show her that word), I suppose she *must* get at something and that is about the best, most creditable, and deserving of any—for the government is *rather* short of such articles.

There, I think that I might as well close *this* letter—if I have not written for a week, I certainly have made up for it to day. The fact is that this out-doors work (including the sleeping) has made me feel like a Giant, I *never* felt better than I do at present, excepting being tired and (a fact which I forgot in the previous part of my letter) that I have a sore leg, resulting from a kick by one of the team horses—I happened to be mounted on Cruger at the time or my leg would have been broken—as it is it nearly took a piece out of my leg—I have to-day put some of Mother's cure-all plaster on it—it happened while we were on the march and I did not look at it until we came home—three days after—and I had a jolly time of soaking the stocking and drawers loose from it, but it is fixed and I "feel like a new man"[.]

Col. Miller has received a letter from home dated the 1st inst desiring his presence as his mother was dying—he sent a tellegraph to know the condition of affairs and if she still lives, he will in all probabilities go home, if he can reach there before she dies, if not he will not go.

Your
Charley

P.S. Dutton is sitting opposite to me, reading *that* Despatch—he takes it quite phylosephicaly[27]

9

Camp Good Hope
Nov. 15/61

Dear Mary,

I this day forwarded to you by Capt. Foster, Company K of Eckley, Luzeme Co.,[28] a package containing two hundred dollars, which I suppose he will hand to you in person, use him to the best of your abilities and if possable invite him to dine or sup (if he arrives near the time) as he mearly passes through Philad. for the Lehigh Valley[.]

To-morrow will be another busy day for me, as I have just received an order to report myself at Bladensburg by 8 o'clock (10 miles) to attend the "Grand Guard Mounting" as Brigade Officer of the Day—another ride of thirty-five or forty miles, over roads two inches (at least) deep with mud, for it rained here for this last two days.

I have from what I consider good authority the information that the Examining Committee will give four and perhaps five officers leave to resign, viz. Capt.s Hacker & Robbins (perhaps Stiles) and Lieuts. Pickett & Booker of Co. A.[29] Sharp work that,—all that were before them.

On Wednesday last we had a thorough review and inspection by the Brig. Gen.l when the Col. gave me the command, he went to Washington; I do not know, but, it struck me that he intended it as an opportunity for the Gen.l to see what *I* was made of—if he did, it did not hurt me any, for I passed through it and a long regimental drill without a single error and so satisfactory to Gen.l Howard, that he formaly remarked (before the entire line) that I had the men in the best shape and drill of any regiment in the brigade, which so pleased the boys, that as soon as he left the ground they gave me three cheers.

The Col. speaks of sending me to the Lehigh Valley to arrainge some accounting business (to fill the vacancys caused by the board) for the regiment, *if* he does I surely will avail myself of the opportunity to run to Camden, if I possably can, even if I travell all night there and back. However, you need not set your mind too strongly upon it as several contingencies are depending upon my goin, but if so, I will inform you of the fact. *Keep the cause of my coming,* if I should, *to yourself* as it is an inside opperation to be unknown to the rest of the regiment and their friends as the men or rather officers do not like the idea of strangers coming in on what they consider their places—but we want and *must have* more men, and they can only be had by offering offices to those that have men under them.

If I come at all it will be at the last of this or the first of the next month—I should not have mentioned this to you until it was certain, but I could not resist the temptation.

Give my love to the boys and kiss Clara for me and tell them to send me more papers; I do not know if you send them regular but, I do not see a paper but about once in ten days, do you send them more often or not?

Your
Charley

10

Camp Good Hope
Nov. 21/61

Dear Mary,

I have just returned from a march of eighteen miles (to Bladensberg or near it, and back) and a brigade drill of three hours. To begin the story properly I should state that yesterday Gen.l Howard drilled the regiment on our drill grounds (between two & three miles from camp) in the presence of the Colonels of the other regiments in the brigade—one of them rather sneered at some of our movements, which rather riled us field officers, and we challenged a regular brigade drill of all the regiments and offered to go to their grounds to do it, they of course could not but accept, and we went—the consequence was that the General was so highly pleased—both at our promptness in getting there an hour before time and our proficiency—that he publicly, in the presence of the *entire* command, expressed his astonishment at our exactness of execution of the various movements and informed us that a Maj. Gen.l in the regular army who witnessed the drill remarked to him, that the most of our movements "excelled any thing that he had ever seen done by a regiment of regulars"—those who sneered the most acknowledged themselves entirely beaten—and we were satisfied—the 5th New Hampshire regiment insisted upon playing the part of the host, and each company conducted its corresponding company of ours to their quarters—thus company A of the N.H. took our company A and their Co. B. took our company B. and so on, their staff took ours and Col. Miller & myself dined with Col. Cross[30] and his Lieut. Col. and all togeather we had a very plesant day of it—the Gen.l sent the Col. & myself an invitation to dine with him, but, we were compelled to refuse, having accepted Col. Cross' first.

I am now writing with a boquet of flowers before me, sent with the request that I would "not forget the one whose fingers tied it togeather"—now stop!—do not anathamize some fair "*she*"—the black cook had been promised a pass to go out of camp by me—and he sent it as a reminder—the white roses are made out of *turnips,* the red ones of *beets* and the chrysanthems of carrotts, the green leaves of parsely, the whole stuck on pieces of sticks for stems—it looks so natural that every one mistakes them at first sight—I would send it to you, if I could without getting it broke—I also have on my table one of the prettiest bird's nests I ever saw, given to me by Lieut. Smith of Company E.,[31] who found it to day and brought it to my quarters.

Dr. Gardiner will be ordered into arrest for charges brought by the "Surgeon General of the Army of the Potomac," Dr. Triple,[32] in whose presence he went in a beastly state of intoxication—he undoubtably will be court Martialed and sent home in disgrace—but of this do not speak, until I inform you farther in regard to the matter.

Your Dispatch & Transcript came to hand on Tuesday, in reference to the letter in it (the Dispatch) I can only say that the examining committee has ceased to look like a "bug-a-boo" to me—I *think* that I can satisfy them of my compitancy for my position—at least, those who *should* be the judges, give me credit for the rapidity in which I always have instructed the officers (as well as the men) in the various batallion movements—Col. Miller has threatened several times to give me the entire charge of regimental drills—if *he* is satisfied—God knows *any* one else *should* be—for nothing but the most extreem exactness of movements pleases him, and he has said in the presence of the Line officers, that he believed I could get along faster with them than he could—so let the committee "come on"[33]

My leg itches me intorably, *if* that is any sign of getting *well*—it should be improving rapidly—I do not know how it looks for the plaster has not been off since I first put it on.

I have been compelled to purchase a new cap—the old one having turned a perfect claret—I took the Bugle off and George sewed it on the new one—so the whole thing cost but two dollars—"econcing in wealth"—

Nov 22/61

Yours of the 21st inst (post mark) received to-day containing express receipt, the freight I find you have paid—why did you not leave that to me? I am not entirely out of money yet.

I have not received any communication from Shields yet—and of course do not know in what I can assist him—if any thing that he requires is in my power, I certainly will do so.

Will you get Sam.l Hufty to write to me, making an offer of his company, stating the number of men, actualy mustered in or if not any; the number he posatively can bring—there *will* be vacancys and I think that I can fix affairs to answer him.

The tenor of my resent communications in reference to *that* committee, I think should give Scout some confidence in my examination, for he knows that I am not given to any considerable amount of boasting.

I have written a letter to Mother to-day, which I shall mail to-morrow morning in which I have accepted Bill's brandy—of course you will see the letter, so no more on that score[.]

I am doubely glad now that I did send you the ballance, or nearly so of my funds or that matter of the Lodge could not have been settled without farther inconvenience to you—I believe that if it is square there will not be anything to pay, as long as I remain in the army—my impression is that a resolution to that effect was passed in both the Lodge & Tribe.

I will write an order on you for that parcle belonging to the Great Council of N. Jersey, in all probility in favour of Chas H. Willets of Burlington, who is the Great Chief of Records.[34]

I have just purchased from the Suttler an Indian rubber Haverlock for the cap, an Indian Rubber cloak and Indian Rubber Legings and now can defy the cold north east storm that is gathering around us, which threatens to burst upon us at a hours notice—the suit cost $8.25 and that made me hesitate for these three weeks, but I at last came to the conclusion that my health was of more importance than the money and when this storm began to-day to gather I "let her went."—

I have just been informed by our Teamster (who has charge of our express business) that it is *always* several days before the things can be had from

Adam's Express, as they are not allowed but one car per each train for *any* packages; if it had been directed in care of some one in Washington I would have received it sooner we will know better next time, and inform you to whom to direct your packages if we decide upon any more.

I shall write as soon as I receive it, in the mean time let me hear from you, and how poor Joes eye is getting along—tell him to keep a "stiff uper lip." I suppose it worried Willie considerable—hug that little thing for me—write soon, for you can not imagine what comfort I derive from the receipt of a letter from you—it is like meeting a long absent friend.

Your
Charley

P.S. that note of mine is in the State Bank at Camden—do not forget it—when you pay it lock the note up as it is the same as a receipt in account[.]

11

Camp California
Dec 2/61

Dear Mary,

This morning I left camp with Meeves at day light and visited all the Pickets and out posts of this Division, to Clotts Mills, Edson Hill, Munson's Mills and other places of intrest, and of course had that which I never had before, an opportunity to become familiar with the details and routeen, practly—of Picket and out-post life. Meeves appeared about as well pleased to see me, as I was to see him, and we had quite an old fashion time of it—their regiment is encamped about a mile behind us—which makes us *near* neighbors.

I find that the Washington papers circulate a report that, at the affair at Springfield "the 36th Reg. was cut to pieces excepting two companies which were taken prisoners, with Gen.l Howard"—I do not know weither the Phila. papers copied or not, but I can only say, if you should hereafter read any thing of the kind, *let it go bye*—for *if* we should be engaged I certainly will write to you as early afterwards as I possably can—and *if* I am not able to write there are others who will do so for me—so always *hereafter,* no matter *what* you see in the papers, *wait! wait!! wait!!!* for a letter—I am reminded of that from the fact that there are *many* men in camp who feel anxious about those at home, whose hearts will bleed if they should see any such things in the paper. I felt easy from the fact that I *had* mailed my letter before I heard of the papers.

To-day['s] report says that 15 of our men (Meeve and I met them goin out this morning) have been captured by the enemy at Annandale, about 5 miles from our camp—since we have crossed into "dixie" it looks more like what a soldiers life *should* be, and if there is an engagement our regiment will be there—I say this from one little circumstance—there was likely to be an occasion for the use of a regiment to perform a certain duty (which I can not state at present) that required men who could be relied upon under the most trying difficulties, and Gen.l Sumner ordered Gen.l Howard to pick out the regiment that he had the most confidence in, and he immediately selected us, a compliment we will make good when the time comes.[35]

The part in bracket [all of the previous paragraph] keep to yourself for no one but Col. Miller and myself know of it—I mearly mention it, to show that we gain the confidence of all officers that we are connected with.

I neglected in my last to state that while at Alexandria I visited the Marshall House and having borrowed a hatchet, I cut a piece of the joice (the floor was gone) that supported the floor on which Col. Ellsworth fell, and also a piece of the door frame against which Jackson stood when he fired, I have them in my trunk for George Chambers, who I promised for his collection of "curio" as he calls it.[36]

Tuesday night Dec. 3*rd*

Mary, I again take up the pen to porrtray a few rambling thoughts—this morning was the coldest that we have experienced since I left home; there was almost an inch of hard frozen snow on the ground that grated and cracked under the feet like an old fashioned winter at the north, the water in the bucket in my marque was frozen a half inch thick—the men made a rush for the suttler's for gloves, mittens, or any thing else to cover the hands, for drilling at day-break with cold iron is not very comfortable in such weather—the gloves you sent was so acceptable that you was even in my mind during the entire exercise—the question frequently asked "Col. where did you get your gloves" yielded a kind of pleasure and pride when answered, "my *wife* sent them."

The report of the affair mentioned above at Anndale, was incorrect, for we lost but *one* man, while we killed one and captured two.

One invoice of tripe & oysters was consumed by George and myself to-day with considerable satisfaction and quite a long discussion of "the girls we left behind us," and I intend when I finish this to eat the balance of the mince pie, which is warming on the stove now.

I had for the first time since I left home some indications of one of my old-fashioned bilious attacks, but a dose of compound carthartic Pills soon settled that hash and to-night I feel that "Richard's himself again"—in the army every one and every thing must *work* and I suppose they intended that their medicine should do the same, for this morning I enjoyed the extream fecility of runing (between 2 o'clock & day-light) over the frozen ground about 400 yards, down a hill, over a ditch, into the woods, some 4 or 5 times, to *let them work*—army rules, you know, every thing must *work*—and I being a superior officer could not violate the rules and of course consented, reluctingly no doubt—but still consented and they accordingly *did* work—however as this is rather a dirty story on the *latter end* of a letter, we will *wipe* the subject *off.*

I shall not mail this until to-morrow as I expect an answer from you, to mine of the 30th inst.

Now for the pie[.]

12

Camp California
near Fort Worth, Va.
Sunday Dec 8/61

Dear Mary,

Another and another day has passed and "no letter for you Col." is still the postman's reply to my eager inquirary, *what* is the matter?

I have just this moment received a visit from an *old* member of the Mechanics Library[37] who is a sargeant in the New York 61st Reg—I did not recognize him, but by relating a few incidents of our former days, I soon placed him—we had a good old fashioned talk of rare old time, about the Library and Bill Simpsons and old associates who turned[?] before us as we rattled on—*he* recognized me as I rode through their camp and immediately followed me to my quarters—it is astonishing at what queer and unexpected places and times one meets old friends.

We have received a formal notice from Gov. Curtin that hereafter our number is the 81st Reg. and that our colours will be here in a few days[.]

The 5th New Hampshire Reg. has left on Picket duty for 4 days, each regiment is to take its turn. Last night they raised a false alarm by sending word that the rebels was in sight (in force) of their own post, and the entire regiment was ordered to be ready to march at a moment's notice,—the boys jumped when the order was given, as though they were invited to a feast—we remained a half hour under arms with our horses saddled and then ordered, to our extreem regret, to our quarters—it would have been a splendid time for a fight, just warm enough for work and a beautiful moon-light night.

To-day the suttler presented me with a *what*—ah! *what* do you think?—a pair of white kid gloves, *gauntlets* at that!—I think of that ye gods and weep—white Kid gauntlet glove for dress parade on Sundays—oh! My eye!!—of course I took them—a soldier takes any thing offered—and expressed my obligations for the—the—the white k-k-k-kids.

Speaking of Dress Parades reminds me that we have a Brigade dress parade each day of the entire command—after which we close in mass and the chaplains of each regiment stands at the head of the column and after a short prayer, just as the sun sinks towards the edge of the horizon, the bands strike up "Old Hundred" and between 3000 & 4000 voices catch up the air and sing it—although I am decidely opposed to this *prayer* business, yet I would not miss the "Old Hundred" for something—it has to me, a peculiarly impressive appearance to see such a mass of men, in regular military order with heads uncovered, leaning upon their muskets, and uniting in that old fashioned song, with the sinking sun shining full upon the bright uniforms and equipments—the effect is truly grand.

I am Brig. Officer of the Day again and while in my quarters resting I thought that I would write a little—here I must stop and put "times up"—

Sunday Night

As I am waiting for 12 o'clock to make my "grand rounds" I thought that I might as well finish this sheet—

I received a visit from Grapewine (you remember him, who lived back of us) he is a Lieut in the Jersey 4th and four other Jersey officers.[38]

Meeves expects to go home on recruiting service in a few days from this—I will give him a letter for you when he goes. Col. Miller wants to get off for the time allowed, 4 days, some time next week, and I am to go, so as *to be home on Christmas* if it is possable, we are endevouring to arrange it—four days is *all* that is allowed, if I get off, I will endevour to start so as to be home half a day before Christmas and leave the middle of the day after—

I want an answer to *this* letter certain, or else I will be compelled to come to the conclusion that it is perfectly indiferent as to my presence or not.

Your
Charley

P.S. do not forget to direct, *if* you *do*—to the 81st Reg, P. Vo. Alexandria, Va. I should have mentioned that Stickney and Meeves passed the evening with me, last night.

13

Camp California
Saturday Dec 14/61

Dear Mary,

I have just returned to camp, after an absence of four day[s] on Pickett duty and hasten (as usual) to communicate with you. Yours of the 9th & 10th inst. was placed in my hands at Edsell's Hill, that of the 11th came to hand to-night, since my return. George's idea of the contest being ended by Congress is certainly a new move to all hands in this direction, it look to me to be the contrary, to use a phrase in vogue here, "I can't see it in that light"—I have not any recolection of the pipe for the Christmas Garden being broken, the small piece, I think is some that I had over, when you come to put it in its place you will find it (the large piece) to fit all right.

In reply to yours of the 10th inst.—do not set too much store upon the certainty of my being at home at Christmas—for we have a tough customer in Gen.l Sumner, who think[s] that an officer especialy has no right to be any where else than with his command; the Col. leaves here to-morrow for 4 days, *he* failed to get his leave of absence himself, and I (considering his goin as a precedent for my demanding mine) went to work and got it through for him—it was hard scratching, but I succeeded—he remarked to-night, at supper—that if I did not get home it would not be because *he* would not move heaven and earth for me. You appear to think that my former letters implied that I had an idea that you was begining to get indifferent in regard to your letter[s]—if mine conveyed such an impression, for God's sake remove it at once, for I certainly did not intend such—why, God bless you, such a thought never entered my head. I mearly became impatient, as 10 days had elapsed since I heard from you, then I got two in one day, which (had they come regular) accounted for "the milk in the coconut." You speak of having some conversation with *Mrs.* Pelouse in reference to Shields—for heavens sake—for *my* sake—do not get intimate with that double, trebled-face woman—if you do you will assuredly have cause to regret it, as many have done before you. Dr. Gardiner has not gone home, yet, and perhaps will *not,* as he is doing "first rate" at present and there are certain reasons *why* we will endevour if possable to keep him, which reasons are so lengthy that I prefer *telling* you than writing. Dr. Dixon is home temporary on account of sickness, we expect him here in a short time. The blunder in those orders, was not in giving them, I do not think, but was in countermanding them, for we could have held that post (Springfield)[39] in spite of the rebels, and we might as well have remained there; my impression is that in less than 10 days we will be ordered there again—I know we would, if *I* had the power. In reply to yours of the 11th inst, I would say—in reference to the apparent feeling of desolation that occasionly overcomes you—

> "Yea, though the breath of disappointment should chill the sanguine heart,
> Speedly gloweth it again, warmed by the live embers of hope
> Though the black and heavy surge close above the head for a moment,
> Yet the happy buoyancy of Confidence riseth superior to Despair."
> "Cease to anticipate misfortune,—there are still many chances of escape;
> But if it come, be courageous; face it, and conquer thy calamity."[40]

You speak of a "change that has come over me"—in liking a shifting of sceans—now if you could see the inside of my marque you would find it precisely as it was when I first "pitched" it—the only change is the desire of moving to any location—and *that* would cease if I had my family with me, but I find that whenever I am long in one place—long enough for the novelty of the surrounding scean to ware off, I begin to feel as though a certain *something* was wanting—then the excitement of a moving army—the numerous details attending it occupys the mind and I feel contented (as it is possable)—for the time—I know that it is the feeling generaly in an army—with those whose whole heart, feeling, sympathy and existance is with those who are absent—the mind *must* be occupied or a soldiers life would be a curse, but with that occupancy of the mind, you have not any time to think of your situation—hence, the shifting of our sceans, that I mentioned—adds a novelty to a soldiers life.

As for Joe, I scarce know what is best to recommend—my feelings at present is to purchase a whip—such as they drive niggers with—and when I come home, give him the damnedest whipping he ever had—tell him for me that if I hear any more such reports of him, that I will cut him until the blood flows down his hide, I will make my coming home one of the sorest jobs for him that he ever experienced—inform me if there is no improvement, and I will make him [page torn]. Tell Willie that I am pleased to hear of his good behavior and his enjoying himself—let him continue, and if I get home on Christmas, he shall not regret it.

Now, having answered your various letters, I will give you a short sketch of how we passed the last four days in our new position as Picketts—we left camp on the 10th and bivouacked in the open air on Edsell's Hill, and threw out our pickets from the New Jersey's left until we reached Gen.l Seidwig's[41] right—across the country for three and a half miles—the first night Capt. Schafles[42] (who had the extreme left) reported having seen about 80 caverly of the enemy a short distance out side of the lines at a certain house—the next night I got permission from Col. Miller to take a Company and watch it, which I did—at about 10 o'clock at night we arrived there and I posted the men under the fences and in the woods and waited for them; the weather was so cold that the waters actualy froze in the mens canteens, so after waiting until 12 o'clock, I came to the conclusion that we might as well work our way farther down and wait until morning, which we did—but no enemy came that night; we reached camp at day-light. The night was so cold that I was compelled to take a hatchet and break the ice in the bucket to get a drink, and yet—I lied down on the ground with nothing but some ceder branches over me, my blanket of course, and slept as sound as if I was at home in bed; the next day was passed by the major and myself exploring the by-roads in the various woods &c. and on the following day, the Col. gave us permission to select 100 of the best men in the regiment and scour the country—we did not want but 25, but he would not let us go without we consented to take 100 men—we left Edsell's Hill (who by the way is a Jerseyman) about 2 o'clock in the afternoon and struck through the woods to Springfield, from there to Bertes Station where we ate our supper (which we carried in our haversacks) and hearing that some of their caverly was at Anondall (the place were the last scirmish took place) we cut across the country—keeping off the highways all the time—to that place, and reached a point about 2 miles below it—just in time to see a house in flames that they had set fire to, and left towards Fairfax Court House, after a consultation, the officers came to the conclusion that I should push on and attack their pickets, which we found to be one mile this side of that place (Fairfax) but, as some of the men (50 at least) had been up on picket duty all night before and was consequently not as fresh as desired I over ruled them and ordered a march back to the hill—having been six miles out side our lines and travelled a space of seven miles along the face of them, from Siedwig's Division on our left, passed over, passed the Jersey and into Blanken's (New York) Division,[43] we reached the Hill at 2 o'clock in the morning—the boys although tired out, said that if I said so, they would "follow me to the gates of hell." I was on foot all the time and they thought, if I could stand it they could, and now are all high up for me to get permission for a day or two tramp—the Col. made a statement to Genl. Summers of my scouting and a rough map of the by-roads through the woods that I made; the Gen.l was pleased with the opperation but gave the Col. a setting down for acting without authority—the Col. told him that he could trust me in any position that he (the Gen.l) choose to put me, and explained to him my mode of opperating, when the Gen.l paid me the compliment of saying that "it was as well done as he could have done it himself"—which pleased the Col. quite as much as it did me, for he has mentioned it to several officers since.

I want you to tell John Whitney to send me *by mail immediately* [*immediately* underlined twice] a pocket map of Virginia, the best he can get, with all the roads on it—do this at once Mary—I will pay for it, when I come home.[44]

Give that little one another kiss for me and I will take them all back when I once get a hold of her.

As the Col. will be away for 4 days I of course will be busy—busy all day drilling and busy at evenings teaching the officers, for we are ordered to have an officers school *every* night to be instructed by the Col. but as *he* will be absent I will have to take his place.

Do not forget my *map*[.]

Trusting to soon have the substance in my arms (as I have constantly the shadow in my eye) of your faithful self, I shall close[,]

Your
Charley

14

Camp California
Dec 17/61

Dear Mary,

I wrote to you last Saturday evening and gave it to Col. Miller, who was to have left it in Camden on his way through on Sunday, which I suppose you duely received[.]

I received a letter from Mother and the Despatch from you to-day—I perceive that Picket-Duty has (I suppose) prevented "Alma" from communicating with it last week.[45]

I have my hands perfectly full at present—the Col. absent, the Major detailed more than half the time on other duties, and added to which (since the Col. left) we have "Evolutions of the line," with the entire Brigade four hours each day—and I have been ordered to have an Officers School *every* night, to instruct the Capts & Lieuts in the Batallion movements, so between acting Col., Lieut. Col., Major, and school master, I have scarce time to answer the call of nature[.]

Dr. Dixon arrived at camp last night but not fully recovered in health.

Four of the officers have had to leave to go home by the Examing Board, viz. Capts. Hacker of Co. E. Robbins of Co. D & Lieuts. Prickett and Brooker of Co. A & Stiles who was before the board passed *his* examination.[46] There is an other board just organized for our Division and Gen.l Howard requested me to send him with such names as I desired to be examined, but I of course refused to act in the Cols. absence.

I am happy to hear that Anna is recovering from her severe indisposition and trust that Mothers expectation of her convalesence may be realized. She tells me that Harry has been spitting blood,—God help! his little ones if they should be thrown upon the cold charity of this world.[47]

Abram (to add to all my other labours and anxiety) has taken such a severe cold that he can hardly stir—he came to the conclusion, while out on picket, that he could sleep better and warmer near the fire than under the cedar boughs, and did so, but the fire burned out and he consequently suffered for it—and as he has such an eversion to medicine that he would not do any thing for it until he was brought down, and consequently now lies rolled in his blanket unable to do any thing—and as if to carry out the old saying "trouble comes in legions" my horse has an attack of some damn thing or another that has laid *him* up—so we go, from one thing to another—I am compelled to borrow a horse now when ever I am forced to ride, which I do not unless compelled.

In my letter of last Saturday, I wrote for a map—do not forget it Mary, for I am much in want of it to assist me in the locations and geography of the surrounding country.

To-morrow I am "Brigade Officer of the Day" again, how in the devil Gen.l Howard expects me to get through with all my business I can not perceive—but I have made up my mind that it *shall* go through all right, and it *shall.*

As it is now mid-night I feel as though I had better close this letter—but having a few moments to spare, I could not resist the temptation to write, well known that

> "a letter, timely writ, is a rivet to the chain of affection"[48]
> even if it is as this one, full of any thing but pleasing thoughts and expectations.

I can not say any thing definate in reference to my being home yet, and will not be able to do so until the Col. returns, until which time I live in hopes—Gen.l Sumner was thrown from his horse a day or so ago and is not able to transact any business and Gen.l Howard is "acting Major Gen.l" if Sumner does not recover sufficiently to be about by the time I want to leave, I will be able to come certain for we can get almost any thing from Howard that we ask—if he does get better it will be a tight squeese.

Capt. Meeves passed the entire day with me last Sunday, and we had a good old time of it—his only regret was that Shields was away—for then we could have the usual Euchre parties this winter.

How is Joe getting along now—is Willie still improving and does that little fary still prattle as much as ever?

Do not forget the *map* and oblige

Charley

15

Camp California
Dec 20/61

Dear Mary,

Yours of the 18th inst came to hand to day, and it could not have come in a more propitious time, for I was in the position of being out of temper—the first time since I left home—and its happy and cheerful strain made me laugh and feel good humoured in spite of my self although I could have bit a ten penny nail in half a moment before—the fact is that since Col. Miller has been absent we have had the most intricate movements to perform in our brigade drills and our regiment under me have been the "first in the field"—so much so that the General and the Field Officers of the other regiments in our brigade have given me the credit of being the *best drilled* Lieut. Col. on the ground, and I felt the importance of keeping up my reputation, and have accordingly studied with a will, to prevent *any* officer from getting ahead of me—but, to-day the fates appeared to be against us, for the Gen.l in throwing out his lines on the very first move brought our end of the line over a high fence, through a garden and against a house—and I ordered the men (who went over the fence like cats) that if they could not walk *over* the house, to go *through* it, and they did so—which was all right, but some what broke our line, the next move brought us in a deep marsh up to our knees—I plunged in to the horses belley and the men with a shout followed, but I was getting mad, for I thought that he should have moved the lines up, so as to have avoided it, but our blood was up and we were determined to go through the gates of Pluto's dominions, if his orders brought us there—although my lines was becoming more and more irregular—just at that moment he rode up and asked, "Col. Johnson what does this mean" and I was just in that humour that I did not hesitate to tell him what I thought, and he left us—the next move, or rather the next command given was not in the *book,* or more properly speaking could not be done—so I quietly sat upon the horse (mad as the devil) and did not move—he called out that he wanted me to do thus and so—and I very improperly asked him *why* he did not say so in his commands—which made *him* mad—and so we had it—and I just came in from the drill when I found your letter on the table and it had a most softening effect upon my temper which was still farther increased by the Gen.l calling in my quarters and acknowledging (before a number of officers) that it was carelessness on *his* part in keeping us in the unplesant predicament we were in, and that his commands were wrong on the reason refered to, and that "Col. Johnson did perfectly right in remaining still and not moving at the time"—so between the two (the letter and the Generals equinimity) I feel to-night quite "burcome[?]" and the men sware that they knew that I *must* be right, for "Col. Johnson is *never* wrong," which expression I frequently heard; for the affair is the subject of camp conversation.

However I feel all right now, and if home could enjoy one of the Mince Pies that I did not get into while being made.

I am afraid that you are making my visit too much of a certainty—do not for the Lord's sake build to high upon it—for as I told you at first it will be hard squeesing to get it, and just as like as not will be refused and I would not have the cloud of desponding sorrow hanging upon your brow for that which neither of us could help—*if* I do not get home on Christmas (having made up my mind to come) I shall certainly be there soon after, for I feel every day, more and more like coming—and *will* come, *some hour* or another, in the meantime I can only repeat my motto:

"*Never* give up! it is wiser and better
Always to hope, than once to despair;
Fling off the load of Doubt's cankering fetter,
And break the dark spell of tyrannical care;
Never give up! or the burthen may sink you,—
Providence has kindly mingled the cup,
And in all the trials or troubles, bethink you,
The watchword of life must be, *never* give up!"[49]

Let those tiny hands and arms encircle *your* neck until I come and I will relieve them with full intrest—

I expect Col. Miller here to-morrow some time, when I shall know my fate as early as possable there-after, until then, we will look upon the sunny side of the picture, even if there *is* a storm upon the reverse.

Your
Charley

16

Camp California
Dec 27/61

Dear Mary,

I arrived at camp about 10½ o'clock this morning and feel pretty well wore out—having no sleep last night and been three hours on Brigade Drill this afternoon, beside having *walked* from Alexandria to camp this morning—it is excessing cold here to-night so much so that I can not feel the stove three feet off more than if it was out of doors; beside a perfect hurrican blowing from the north-west which is constantly tarring the cords from the pins and makes the flies flap like roring thunder—I am writing this with my great over-coat on, and must stop (even with these few lines) to warm my fingers.

I was received by the men (officers included) in the most gratifying manner, but the individual most pleased was Abram—who was coming up behind the tent with a load of wood when he heard my voice he droped wood, axe and all right where he stood and cried "He!! gor ah mighty—dar is de boss his self" and ran into the tent, bursting off a hook in his anxiety to get in—he says that "'tis mighty lonesome, kinder while you is away."

I sent him immediately over with Mrs. Meeve's letter—tell Mrs. Wilson that *her* Willie is now "*Captain* [underlined twice] Wilson of Company E 81st Reg. Pa. Vol."—the Col. appointed him at my earnest request—he (the Capt.) does not know any thing about my instrumentality in his appointment and I did not tell him.[50]

The Col. and Gen.l Howard has had a glorious fight since I was away—three of the Gen.l pets (as we call them, the 5th N.H.) having insulted the Col. on our own grounds and they was immediately knocked down and then draged to the guard house—the Col. of thier regiment by consent of the Gen.l had them removed from there immediately—when the Col. gave Howard one of the plainest talkings imaginable—and immediately prefered charges against the men to have them Court Marshaled—which he would not have done if the Gen.l had not interfered—the Gen.l says that there will be trouble if he (the Col.) pushes it, and the Col. says that he *will*—in contra distinction to *that*—the Gen.l sent his Brother to my quarters to invite me to his, for the purpose of having a friendly chat—remarking that he "felt as well pleased to see me, as if I was an old friend[.]"[51] Dr. Dixon's would be sucessor left camp to-day and said that if [the] government did not transfer him, he would never come back—not an officer has spoken to him since he has been on the grounds—which has been since Monday.[52]

Mr. Scitz[53] of Easton sent us a cooked Turkey—a monster—which they kept until I returned and we ate it to-day—or rather ate *at* it—for it will last two or three days[.]

I have just been warming my fingers again and will finish—I do not know when ever I left home with as heavy a heart as I did last night—I felt as though I would choke every now an again—and I stoped in Sam.l Miller's (Chestnut St. House) to get a drink when his little boy in bidding me "good bye" said—"may dod bless you Col."—I felt considerably renewed when I thought that I was leaving with even the prayers of the children for me—I hope that the seperation has worn off some—for I feel like any thing else than laughing—the adjutant asked me several times to day if I felt well—for he had never seen me so solemn and sober since he knew me and I could not shake it off when ever I thought of [page torn]

Give my love to the boys and tell them that I sat in the cars until broad daylight thinking of them and that little darling Clara—I hope that they will be the best of boys now and give you all the pleasure that they can—to compensate as much as possable for my absence.

My fingers are stiff and feet frozen so I will stop—write soon and I hope it will be (without disemination) a hopeful and joyous letter—keep a plesant thought always in your mind and persistantly look on the sunny side of the picture—God bless you is ever the prayer of

Charley

2

"It was a sorrowful sight"

January 1, 1862–June 22, 1862

THE twelve months of 1862 would be among the most traumatic and significant in the nation's history, encompassing the Peninsula campaign of the Army of the Potomac, the battles of Second Bull Run and Antietam, and Lincoln's Preliminary Emancipation Proclamation. For Charles Johnson these months would bring illness, promotion, and then disabling wounds on the battlefield.

17

Camp California
Jany 1st 1862

Dear Mary,

Yours of the 29th ult. came to hand to-day and found me in the best possable humour imaginable for we have received a "New Years Gift" in the shape of a compliment from the Gen.l that we are the best kept regiment in the Brigade—that the camp, arms, accoutrements are in the best of order and the drill and discipline of the regiment is such (coupled with the other) that he is "*more than pleased*"—we of course feel as proud as Turkey-Cocks—and immediately requested his influence to get us the new and improved arms—which request he readily promised to comply with—they *will* come, if they are to be had.

We have had a perfect spring—I may say a *summer* day—for it was so warm that over-coats and every thing else was thrown off—but to-night the change is sudden the other way—it is blowing great guns. The Major, Adjutant and myself visited (for the first time since we have been here) the various encampments in the neighborhood—I saw Bald. Hufty—who is perfectly well—Capt. Pelouse and nearly all my New Jersey friends or acquaintances as well as some strangers, among whom was Libbie Lizie (or whatever her name is) Remlot's[?] brother who introduced himself to me. Capt. Pelouse *expects* to leave about Monday on a ten days furlough, if he lets me know in time I will send a letter by him—Capt. Meeves left early this morning on a six months recruiting service, I did not see him before he went. The most joyful one that I met was George McGloughlin, who fairly jumped when he first set eyes upon me.

I regret to hear of your mothers continual illness, but hope that she may be spared many days yet.

How is Mother Johnson and the rest of the family?

The delivering up of Mason & Slidell is all right under the circumstances surrounding the *manner* (and the *causes*) in which it was done—I have read at length the documents in the case and believe that it could not have been done otherwise—it certainly was done so that we as a nation did not loose one iota of *dignity*. The demand of England was only a request for us to examine the subject—and the delivery was made without an *apologe* and at the same time *not* blaming the officers who made the arrest—but was done upon purely *American grounds*—and at the same time has deprived Secessa of its greatest hopes in receiving assistance from abroad—the *question* is a political policy for us, can be resumed at any time that we feel prepared for it—and that time I think will be as soon as *this* war is over—it could not have been managed better.[1]

I shall be compelled to give you a short letter to-night—I intended a long one—but the wind is blowing such a gale that my candle flickers so much I can scarce see how or what I write—I do it between the puffs of wind.

How are the boys getting along? Give my love to them and hugg that little one for me[.]

Your
Charley

P.S We have a report here in camp that Gen.l McCall's division advanced to day some eight miles—if that is true—we hope it is so—we all expect that the entire column will move in a short time[.]

I gave Abram a new cap to-day as a new years gift and he now considers himself "some"—the horse is still improving with his cold—other wise he is in *better* condition than he *ever* was—he is so full of life that Abram is forced to use a bridle, instead of the halter, when he takes him out to water or exercise—I do not use him yet and will not if I can help it, until he is perfectly well; by that time I expect he will be able to clear a five railed fence[.]

Capt. Alexander expects to leave here soon on a six months recruiting service, when he does I will send my gray jacket and other clothes to you by him[.]

So! a new fear has taken possession of you—

"a change come o'er the spirit of my (your) dreams,"
and you exclaim
"strange footsteps are hear'd ever and anon"—
and I suppose that the next thing will be terrable sights
"That will make thy two eyes start like stars
From their spheres; thy knotted and combined locks
Part, and each particular hair stand on end,
Like quills upon the fretfull porcupine"[2]

Oh Mary! Mary! what a state of feverish excitement you must be in—all because some *petty thief* while proweling around the yards of the neighboring house happened to steal a tin wash basin—a worn-out senilt[?] brush—a dish rag—a wash rag—a "hunk" of soap or some such thing—why bless your soul! a *burgerler* does does not prowel around houses so that he could be identified or a description given of him in case the house is robbed "of course not," but a petty thief, who would not have the courage to enter a house at night does. However you have a rattle there and if needs be a pistol—if you have the nerve to use it get Harry or some one else to load if for you. I carried one around the house several times of nights (when the folks heard "strange sounds") when I was no older than the boys.

You want me to "secure you with chains and bolts" when I come home—if it will make you any easier why not do it *now* and not waite for me?

Give my love to Willie (Joe if he deserves it—I think not) and many kisses to Clara[.]

Yr[.]
Charley

18

Camp California
Jan. 4/62

Dear Mary,

Yours of the 1st inst. is in hand—do not purchase a Gold pen if one of those in the green Box (it was there when I left) will answer you, try them—I mean those with the silver cases.

It makes me feel proud to read of the up-rising of your patriotism on the "English Question"—believe me, Mary, there is no emotion that will sustain the mental and physical body through the vicissitudes of this life, like that of a pure patriotic love of country and her institutions.

You speak of George's gaining eight pounds, I never have seen him look better in my life, than he does at present—I weighed myself on the 1st inst. and weighed 143½ pounds; some differance between that and 128 pounds—my old weight.

Yesterday Sam. Hufty called to see me while out on Brigade Drill—he spoke but a moment—I promised to call on him at the 3rd Jersey regiment—but could not as I filled Major Conner's place as Officer of the Day, he having some business he was compelled to attend to. The 4th R.I. Reg. has left the brigade to join Gen.l Burnsides expidition,[3] leaving one sick man behind, who has since died—and Gen.l Howard has detailed us to perform the usual ceremonies over him, we will do so, and I have started the idea among the men to place a board with the proper inscription on it, over his remains—they say that it shall be done.

Have you heard any thing of the Olden Legion? Some of our Officers visited them to assertain if any deserters of ours were there, and they report that they have only about 300 to 400 men, and they in the most compleat state of insubordination—do you know any thing of them?[4]

We have one Lieut. from the LeHigh Valley who has exhibited signes of insanity of late—he has taken the notion that all the officers are "down on him" and does nothing but sigh and look dispressed—he will not accept of a sick leave as that will be positive evidence that we want to be clear of him. The other night or rather morning at 2 o'clock while returning from my Grand Rounds, I saw a light in his tent and went there—and there he was, having got up, lit his candle, made a fire, and sat brooding over his case and trying to remember whenever he gave any officer cause for such treatment—I went in and talked for an hour or more with him, endevouring to convince him that he was mistaken—but could not, and left with the promise that I would make them tell *me* why they done so—poor fellow! it made me feel very bad—we will be compelled to send him to the Hospital by some subterfuge.[5]

Last night it hailed and froze as fast as it came down and this morning it snowed about ⅛ of an inch on it—and I had a jumper made of long poles, got a team horse, put him in it (harnessed him with ropes &c.) and went a "sleighing in Dixie." the old horse would not go—so Capt. Conner ran along side with a whip and Capt. Harkness and myself sat on the—the—hem!!—the *sleigh*—we visited, in that manner, all the camps in the division, creating considerable fun—scarce any one knew us, as we all had on privates uniforms—and we all felt like "boys again"—it was "the *first sleigh* of the season" in this section of the country—and we laid it up, for another spit of snow—about 1/16 of an inch will answer.[6]

It is excessively cold here to day—in fact has been since the night of the 1st inst.—the men can scarse handle their pieces when on drill—blue noses and red cheeks is all the raige with us.

Sunday night 5 = Jan

I left this open until to-night as we have not any mail delivery on Sunday—It is now hailing, snowing, raining and freezing—but it is *not* blowing—so we can be quite content to *hear* the storm without, with the full conviction that we will have ice roofs on our quarters in the morning.

We buried the member of the R.I. Reg. this morning on the hill, by the fort and did as creditable as if he belonged to us.

We have flying rumors of an advance being made in 5 or 6 days—they appear to base their conclusions upon three facts—first, that *all* passes are refused by *all* of the commanders of the different divisions next, that officers having furloughs have been ordered to report immediately to their quarters, even if their furloughs have *not* expired and 3rd Gen.l Howard told us to-day, while the guard was complaining of the cold, to "never mind, you will not be required to stand guard *here* again," I give you all the causes for our rumors, that may know *how much* grounds we have for our conclusions and also to show how sharply we watch every thing that has *any* indication of a movement.

We are under Gen.l Heintzleman temporarly,[7] until Sumner is well, but if we *do* move, Sumner says that he *will* command, if he is "compelled to go in a buggy" and I believe he will, for a more thorough firm man I never have seen—a perfect locomotive.

John Dutton came to camp to-day he is still very sick, but being three days behind his time, he thought it best to come to save difficulties—and he did right, for there are men here that would jump at the chance to throw him—Col. Miller among the number.[8] I believe that I have given you all the news and events since my last so will close.

Give my love to the boys and tell me how they are getting along, and do not forget the usual amount of kisses to that little farey.

We have all been mustered for pay and will probably receive it by the 13th of the month—I suppose that you are compleatly out of funds,—if you cannot hold on to that time write and I will send you some[.]

Your
Charley

19

Camp California
Jan. 8/62

Dear Mary,

Yours of the 4th inst. came to hand yesterday with the Despatch.

In reference to that huggin of or by a Dentist; I can only say that I hope you will not be compelled to have any teeth extracted during my absense; for it would be rather hard if another man received (voluntary) that which circumstances deprives me of enjoying—however if you are again to hugg, or be hugged, I suppose a Dentist may do it as well as any one else.

While I feel pleased with the contents of your letter in reference to the favourable report of the boys, it is some what dampened by that of yourself—do not over-exert your self Mary, for my sake, for a report of your sickness would fill me with the deepest gloom, more particulary as it would be out of my power to see or be with you, if ever there was a "hell on earth," that would be one.[9]

Last Sunday night (directly after writing my letter to you) it commenced snowing, and the following morning, we had the sleigh (I wish you could see the magnificent out-fit) out and horses harnessed "tandem" (i.e. one before the other) and the Col. [,] Maj. Adj. [,] and myself started for Alexandria, but about a mile and a half from camp we could not find any snow, so we had to turn back—the horses having never been harnessed that way before, cut some high-dutch and just as we turned began kicking, the Col. and Maj. rolled off in the road and just then the horses started and the adj. and I came to the conclusion not to stop them and we went in, leaving the Col. and Maj. to walk back, which they *did*, much to *our* amusement but not to *thier* satisfaction—they sware that they will be even with us—if they do, they will be compelled to be up early.

John Cunningham called to see me yesterday and remained for an hour or so, he looks the same "old thing" and is in high glee at being "down in dixie" once more.[10]

Ex.-Captain Hacker and Ex.-Lieut. Brooker arrived in camp again yesterday—Hacker left this morning, but Brooker remained, and talks of opening a boarding house (to follow the regiment) for the officers—it is singular what a strong feeling men have to return to their old associates—particularly while they remain togeather in the field—the feelings and friendship engendered between men, while isolated (as it were) from other objects and interests must be strong, for not a man has left us but has either returned to see, or written to assertain if there could not be *some* position that they could occupy in the regiment.[11]

The 64th New York regiment (Col. Parker) has arrived to fill the vacancy of the R.I. Reg.

I have a door—yes a regular door made to my tent—a door; hinges, latch and all and a door plate (getting proud) that is I have nailed the canvass which you saw at home

"Quarter of
Lieut. Colonel"

on the door, the boys say that I must have a "knocker" on, and I should not be surprised if some morning I should find a thundering big log of wood fastened there in place of one—for no specie of devilment that could be thought of, or invented but what is immediately put in practice.

We have "put the ball in motion" to have the regiment transfered to another Brigade, as Gen.l Howard's favoritism for Yankees and dislike for us is more and more apparent every day—but thank God! we are equal to him; for we do our duty to the very letter and in spite of all his watching, can not be caught napping—we have told him that "we ask no favours, and shrink from no responsibilities"—he does not dream of our desires of or intention to be removed or he would not sleep, for when the R.I. Reg, left, he told certain parties that them and ourselves were the only ones that he would rely upon if called early into the field for action, and as we alone are left it will be a thunderbolt to him if we succeed—keep this to yourself—do not tell any one for none but the Field officer know anything of the movements yet and will *not* if we fail.[12]

The very minutia of Military law, rules and discipline is exacted of us, but as we came prepared to perform our duty—our *whole* duty, we can laugh at his abortive attempts to spite us, and it at the same time makes us better soldiers and is a benefit to us, for while we know and feel that all our actions are watched we are doubly careful to live up to the exact marke of a soldier—it has improved the Officers and the men becoming imbibed with the spirit it has improved *them,* so we as a regiment feel the advantage of it: so much that (although I say it myself) we can beat the lazy backside off of all the brigade and would not hesitate to accept a challenge for drill from any regiment that has been in the field the same length of time as ourselves—we have offered many but none has accepted—vive! Gen.l Howard!!

Dr. Gardiner has "went off" on one of his old drunks this two day—the first since we left Good Hope and to crown all the old charges of Dr. Tripler (the Surgeon Gen.l of the Army of the Potomac) has arrived and been refered to a Court Martial—what the consequences will be, I can not divine—either being "cashiered" or being "suspended" for a time—I hope the latter for we would not like to loose him, but it would serve the d——n fool (he makes me so infurnal mad) just right, but either case it would be a detriment to the regiment for his abilities is not to be found on this side of the Atlantic Ocean.

Gen.l Howard has started the plan of requiring the Cols. and Lt. Cols. to drill the Brigade in turn—Cols. Cross & Miller have had theirs and mine will come soon.

I have deturmaned that if hard study and close application will accomplish any thing that I will not be *behind any* [*any* underlined twice] Field Officer in the command—I would do so for my own credit and that of the regiment if none other, but *now* am doubly deturmaned that he *shall* acknowledge that we are the best under him.

Lieut. Davis (who went home with the spine disease from Good Hope) reported himself to-day for duty and brought me a kind of woolen slipper to put on the feet at night while sleeping to keep them warm—I of course accepted them but will not use them, as I am deturmaned to not make my self any more tender than I can help.[13]

The Adjutant (who is a single man) also informed me to-night that a "lady friend" of his, had nitted a couple of woolen arrangements for the ears (similar to the furs that I was telling you about) and that he intended one of them for me.

The many little acts of kindness that I have received from the men (strangers as it were) who surround me, has placed them so indellably upon the tablets of my memory, that no time, no trials, no vicissitudes of life can ever efface.

Give my love to the boys and tell them that I feel highly pleased with the good report that you have made in regard to them; they feel doubly dear to me when I know that they are doing their duty to you[.]

Give our little one the usual kisses for me—if she has not already received them—if she *has* why—repeat the dose for me—bless her, I would like to feel her tiney arms encircling my neck to-night.

Take good care of yourself, and may God in [H]is infinite wisdom keep you from *all* bodily ills, is ever the prayer of your

Charley

20

Camp California
Jan 10/62

Dear Mary,

Yours of the 8th inst. came to hand to-day while I was giving my clothing a general over-hauling—it being a rainy one, I had not any thing else to do—Abram says that I can do any thing as if I was brought up to it, but sewing and "dat you cant do"—and I believe that he is right on the sewing question; but if I do *not* sew "naturaly," I *do* sew *strong*—there is no doubting *that*—for the way I stick buttons on is death to the material and total annialation to thread.

In reference to the sewing machine, you can do as you deem proper—provided—provided always—that you do not undertake to get work out side of the family to do—I mean your *own* family—I know you so well that if you take a notion some fine day, you would be over in town in a hurry for work, and I would not like *that*, while I live and have a possission.[14]

As for the Boys schooling—you will be compelled to manage some way, if they are forced to leave—if I was out of debt I would say, send them to pay school—and I think we had better, as soon as that time arrives—until then you (I have no doubt) will manage as well as "any business man of the house" could[.]

As you report them to be doing so admirably well and being such good boys of late I certainly feel like humoring them in all that is right and proper and if they continue so, you can assure them that I will not forget them, whenever an opportunity occurs to express and show my aprobation.

Your report of Little Clare (God! bless her!) reminds me that I was with you *all* last night and remained there until the sound of Revillie reached my unwilling ears.

> "It is a happy thing to dream,
> when rosey thoughts and visions bright
> Pour on the soul a golden stream
> Of rich luxurious delight"—[15]

The Court Marshal to try Dr. Gardiner will start to-morrow and from the evidence and feeling in the case I think he will be "permitted to go home."[16]

We have had a continual rain since I wrote my last and to-day has added a fog, (so heavy that you can not see the tent next to you) by way of an "extra"—and if you would like a sample of what *is* mud you would have it here—I have not been away from my tent, except to the Suttlers for my meals, and I have waided in five inches of clear mud, and on the top of the hill at that.

They tell us that this some-what (not quite) aproximates to the condition of the country during the last of February and all of March. If it is so, there will be plenty of idle times and a corrosponding amount of sickness; however I think we will be away—that is if our endevours (recited in my last) are crowned with any success[.]

I was over to the Jersey boys yesterday and seen Bald. Hufty, he received his commission as 2nd Lieut. the day before and felt quite elated—he is a good boy, that, Mary, and if ever an opportunity occurs will prove himself worthy of his post.

You appear to "draw a few more easy breaths" because we are not on one of the expiditions, now you should serve me like you do the boys, wait and see—see first *where* the expidition (if I should be on one) goes to, and then wait until you hear of its fighting—for it does not follow that there is any certainty of a fight on them than there is here—two already have left and there been *no* fight—it might be so with half of them.

I certainly would like to be on one of them, for I dislike to remain so long in one location, but Col. Miller does not appear to fancy it, and I do not think that he will be very likely to press the regiment upon the powers that be, for that purpose—so you may "breath on" Mary[.]

Give my love to Mother Johnson and all inquiring friends. And do not forget (even if she lets you) my kisses for Clara.

Take good care of yourself Mary and [?] [?] do not indulge again, so suddenly or continue at it so that your system may become inured to the hardships of high living—either way—so you continue well[.]

Your
Charley

21

Camp California
Jan 15/62

Dr Mary,

I believed that I informed you that while writing my last letter that it was raining, hailing & freezing—but it did not continue so long for when I turned out in the morning just before day, at revellie, the snow was from four to six inches deep and as a natural consequence there was numerous officers who claimed to be my *particular friends,* and droped sundery hints about *that* turnout—viz. sled—hem! excuse me—*sleigh*!!!!

After breakfast I had the nags (yay nags) yay *even if* they were worn out—old team horses, harnessed up; and as the Col. had business at Washington, the Maj. on Court Martial, the Adjutant sick; I took three of the line officers with me, and we accomplished that, which we had made several attempts to do before, namely; sleigh to Alexandria and back. You should have seen the people start and stare at us as we "went it" with a "ya lang!" in true Broadway style. Having taken a "turn" around that antiquated, infurnal old City, where we could have hired out for $1.00 per square, we started for camp and just as we left it—chuck! went the establishment against a large stone; kur-r-r-up! whack! crack! went one of the runners, and our magnificient "get up" was a pile of lumber—but perserverance and that necessity which is "the mother of invention" soon "fixed the thing" and we were "once more on deck"—but I am forced to admit that we went into camp with *one* shaft, *one* runner and the sleigh as perfect a diamond shape as could well be made; but we "went it" and *sleighing* at that, and *that* was all we desired. A new pole cut, a few wooden pins, and a few pieces of ropes is all that is required to make it "as good as new."

Last night it commenced to rain and froze as fast as it came down and continues to do so today, but as *all* the teams are busy hauling wood, we can not "hitch up" but are repairing damages and are now all ready for the next fly[.]

Our Flag (from the state of Penn.) is here, they (the authorities) offered to send Congressman Grow to present it, and the officers decided that I was to receive it on behalf of the regiment, but the Col. having brought it with him from Washington, has already cut-off all the ceremony.[17] However, I suppose it is "all for the best," for, probaly I could not do full justice to the occasion and thereby might disappoint my friends[.]

Yours of the 12th came to hand last night—the writer in the Despatch is unknown to us, nor do we think it worth wile to bother ourselves about it or any other correspondent for the papers, say *what* they may.[18]

I should have liked to have been in a corner and seen poor Meeves; I laughed as my mind pictured him in his delemia.

Tell the boys that I feel highly pleased to receive their letter and would feel happy to hear from [them] often—Mary, encourage them to write frequently—not that their information is all that is desired, but, that it may improve them in that most of all desirable accomplishments—letter writing.

Hugg to your heart that little piece of perfection (at least so to me) of ours, and say that I sent it[.]

In closed you will find the letter from the Transcript—I send it for fear that you could not purchase one so late in the week—I also inclose another extract on the same subject that about fairly represents the affairs in the army[.][19]

There is a delegation of six gentlemen from the LeHigh valley here tonight—friends of the regiment and we intend to have a grand jolification on the strength of it in the Maj. quarters, and as they have sent repeatedly for me and are now waiting I will close[.]

Yr[.]
Charley

P.S. the rain has sceased and if it gets cold enough to-night to freeze, I have promised to take the "Chunkers" out sleighing in the morning—if I do and there is not an up set or break down it will not be my fault[.]

22

Camp California
Jan 16/62

Dear Mary,

I forwarded, this morning a bundle in care of John Stockten (Sutler), containing my gray jacket & pants and my old blue pants—also a staple from the slave pen at Alexandria, a specimen of petrified wood, and the two pieces of cedar from the grave of Washington and two pieces of wild Grape vine (tied out side) from the *top of the grave*—put them in water Mary and try to cultivate them.

The Staple, wood and one piece of cedar is for George Chambers—will you send them to the store for him with the inclosed letter.[20]

Yours of the 14th inst. just came to hand. I would like to comply with your request to visit William at Washington, but can not at *present* for all leaves of absence from camp is cut off—no furloughs of any kind are granted—as there is a prospect of a movement some time within ten days and we do not know *when* the order may come—if it does not come in that time, the prospects are that we will not move for some time to come, and *then* I will go to see him, *if* it can be done in one day, and if I do not get there before you visit him, I will certainly come *when you are there;*—if any amount of work and exertions will accomplish it.[21]

My Horse is well, or rather *has* been, but is rather under the weather, with his old cough, which has returned; I am in rather of a box for on Sunday next we go out on picket and I *must* have horse, so I will be compelled to use him and then I fear that he will be worse again—by George! the first sechess horse that falls in my way, I will "mitton on"[.]

George sends his respects and obligations for your papers which he receives regularly[.]

The famous Miss Dix paid us a visit to-day with sundry little nick-nacks for the Hospital[.][22]

The delegation from the LeHigh Valley (mentioned in my last) left here this morning highly pleased with their visit—I have promised that when we are mustered out to visit that section of the state—invitation[s] (from one day to one month) sufficient to last for half the year—one in particular Mr. John McClain (who owns the Summitt Hill Coal Works) insists that I shall remain with him two or three weeks.

They appeared to have come here prejudiced so much in my favour that they would not move without me, the Col. said that "one would suppose that they had called especialy to visit the Lieut. Col."—though I had never seen one of them before—they were all heavy coal opperators and mine owners except one Doctor: two of them wanted to stay a week, but the others would not consent[.]

I mailed a letter to you this morning before I knew of Stockten's contemplated visit.

I am pleased with the Boys partiality for music, it is an agreeable past-time and will have a tendency to keep them out of the street—encourage it. Give (God bless her little soul) give Clara the usual amount of kisses for me.

Yr[.]
Charley

[first two paragraphs in brackets:] P.S. the Charges against Col. Miller has been presented and were forwarded by Gen.l Howard to take the usual course, weither the Division Gen.l will approve and order a trial is of course not known.

We expect the Col. (as is usual) to be placed under arrest every moment—if so, I will be in command of the regiment until the trial is over[.]

Keep this to your self for "an evell report travelleth fast" and I would not like to be the means of spreading the information, at least until after the court martial is formaly ordered—then it is public property[.]

23

Camp California
Jan. 18/62

Dear Mary,

Genl. Howard having been desirious of reconoiting the country with a force, had the Illinois Caverly assined to him for that purpose, and he invited me to go with (the *only* officer in the Brigade) him and take charge of the "advance guard"—of course I jumped at the offer and have just returned, having been in the saddle from 4 o'clock a.m. until 6½ o'clock this evening, not even dismounting to eat or feed the horse, and I assure you that I feel rather "used up" to-night. As we go out on picket to-morrow morning and I will not have an opportunity to write for nearly a week, I intended to give you a long letter, but I shall be compelled to "cave"—however as I have done pretty well this week, I feel my conscience some what eased with this ones shortness[.]

Continue to write as usual, for I will receive yours as regular as if in camp, although (not having any thing with me except what is on my back) I cannot answer them until I return to camp.

The weather is warm and rainey and the mud is at least five and six inches deep—I am not exagerating—for last night in goin[g] my Grand Rounds I frequently waded (by actual measurement) seven inches deep in this red and yellow clay and water—it becomes like our snow storm after a rain upon it—it is a *fine prospect* to lay out on picket—but I suppose, like all *other* exposures will "make me *fat*," so farewell untill I return to camp[.]

your
Charley

P.S. Since writing the above Abram has placed in my hand yours of the 16th inst which he received while I was absent to-day.

Your disposition of the Holly leaf to Mother was a good idea—it never occured to me—however "two heads is better &c. &c. &c."

You suppose that I am "pleased at the prospect of picket duty," from what I have written above in regard to the weather and the soil—"the sacred *soil* of Virginia"—you will perceive that I do not meet *this* trip with "all the ardour of my soul," but we *may* enjoy ourselves for all, as well as if it was more plesant—the old adage "sufficient for the day is the evil thereof" is our maxam, when ever we anticipate any rubs in the way of service.

Give my love to the boys and tell them that I feel highly gratified at the continued good report that I hear from them. Give Clara a kiss for me—that is when she has not the pot in her hand, for at that moment it would not be very classical.[23] And *do not burn your self with the flat iron* [*your self* and *flat iron* underlined twice]—as for me—long rides, hard day's work in the open air, and a hard bed renders it entirely unnecessary for such an appendage being attached to my body—the cooler I keep *that*, the more convenient it is for me—

I stop[p]ed writing at the request of a committee who requested me to visit one of the tents, I did so and found that they had organized a society called the "Sumner Legion" for the purpose of sending the dead bodies of its members home, when practicable and when not practicable to bury them with markers so as to identify them at some future time, and they elected the following officers;

President Col. Miller
vice—Maj. Conner
Recording Sec.y—Adj. McKeen
Corresponding—Qr Mast. Dutton
Treasurer—Lt. Col. Johnson[24]

Get to-days Inquirer, if you have not seen it, and you will find a letter from the "Chippewa Reg." in the 1st column, 2nd page; it was written (I think) by a Mauch Chunker, I think so from the fact that the Philadelphians *never* use the term "Chippewa"—[25]

I find that I have written a letter at last, even *after* appologizing for a short one, it is astonishing, that when I take up my pen to write to you I never know *when* to stop[.]

Good night, Mary, good night.

24

Camp California
Jan. 24/62

Dear Mary,

I have just returned from picket duty of four days, and *such* days, we went out on Sunday and it rained as though it never intended to stop—on Monday it became warm and so fogy that the guards could not see each other—on Tuesday it rained—on Wednesday it rained, snowed and frozed and today it rained again—so you see that we had a *happy* time of it so far as the weather and its concommitant *mud,* is concerned and all this exposure without tents or any covering than cedar brush will make—and yet we returned with but *three* added to the sick list—I never felt better in my life—it appears to me that the *more* I am forced to expose myself, the better I feel[.]

Yours of the 18th and 20th inst. came to hand while out on picket.

In reply to the former, I would say that the Sec.y of War, resigning *will* destroy *all* prospects of our back pay—damn it![26] I wish he had held on a little while longer—but let it go—there is (I know) a discount on Treasury Notes, but there is no necessity for it as the government is able and in fact *is* meeting *all* and every demand upon her—the discount business will not last long—you *can* retain the piece of petrified wood and cedar if you wish—you may send him [George Chambers] the piece I took home, *or not* just as you desire, but I *do* want him to have the *Old Staple*—if you send them to him burn the note accompanying them—if you read it, you will see that it will not answer—*send me word what you want him to have* and I will send another note to him through you, so that you can send it with them[.]

I regret to hear of Harry's accident but hope that it will soon resume it[s] former shape and activity—I think that it is the wisest conclusion that you could arrive at in reference to Mrs. Cunningham "let her slide"—The charges against Col. Miler is "conduct unbecoming an officer and a gentleman"—the specifications are that he usurped and prevented the Chaplain from performing his duties, treating the Asst. Surgeon (Kimball) in an unofficer like manner—using disrespectful language towards the Gov. of Penn.a—seizing a man violently by the throat and choaking him—advising two privates to go out side of camp and fight their revenge for each other out &c. &c. &c. I do not think that any thing will come of it—as the powers that be do not appear to think that the charges are serious enough to trouble a Court Marshall with.

You must know that the officers are as a general rule obliged to stand by their "Brother Officers" and there must be a decided *neglect of duty* on the part of one to induce the other to give him any trouble and hence I do not think that any thing will come of it.

I sent you, by Sergent Curtis of Co. C. the brick[?] thorn that I cut from the top of Washington's grave—lay it away carefully and I will have a cane made of it.

Give my love to the Boys and the kisses to that little prattler of ours[.]

Yr[.]
Charley

P.S. Inclosed you will find Twenty dollars ($20.00) which I got from a friend—the Pay Master says that he will be here at Camp on Monday or Tuesday next, when I will of course send you more immediately[.]
[in brackets:] Private—Dutton wants to resign if possable and George is in great trebulation—but the Col. refuses to receive his resignation[.]

25

Camp California
Feb 11/62

Dear Mary,

In accordance with my promise, I sit down to write to you before "turning in" tonight.

I arrived safe and sound in the midst of a snow-storm, which has every prospects of ending in that most-desirable-greatly-required-change-of-weather-*rain;* which will of course considerable improve the roads.

[The next paragraph is in brackets, the word *private* written in the margin:]

Maj. Conner returned returned to-night (on account of the storm) and in all probability not go out again for two or three days; when I am to take charge of the party; it will then be increased to four or five companies and a squadron of cavelery.

I gave [the] Col. one of my photographs (in fact he *took* it, and the Major the other, both considered it excellent likeness and were highly gratified to possess them.

Abram was disappointed because he did not see "Madam Lieut. Col."—for he entertained the idea that you would surley accompany me to camp—but he has found solice in a *watch* that he purchased in Alexandria this morning and is the proudest nigger in camp to-night—he has it under his head and says he is "ferd dat he wont be able to sleep dis night, on account of de ticking of dis thing"—but he *is* asleep never-the-less and to-morrow morning I will insist that it kept him awake all-night[.]

There has been a "high old time" here since I left—between the Gen.l and the Col. and some pretty sharp correspondence passed between them—it appears that one of our men (who was detailed as hosler for the Gen.l) stole a dog from another of our men, the Col. sent for him and he refused to come, as he was under the Gen.l direct and the Col. sent a file of men and *brought* him, the Gen.l thought that it was treating *him* (the Gen.l) with disrespect and sent one of his aid-de-camps to demand an explanation, but he did it in such a haughty and defiant manner that the Col. refused to give any and the Gen.l *then* opened his "paper balls" on the Col. in the way of "orders" in writing and that produced a reply from Miller and they continued and are continuing it, with a pile of documents before them; in the meantime the Col. placed the man in the Guard House and swares that he *shall* remain there until *he* is ready to take him out—so far as the *legality* of the question I think that the Col. has the advantage—as to the *policy* of the act I do not think that is all "O.K."—however *that* is *his* lookout—I shall not have any thing to do with it.[27]

I shall be compelled to give you a short letter to-night as I feel rather tired with my ride for the roads on this end of the line were so rough that I was forced to *trot* the entire distance, from a couple of miles the other side of Washington to Camp, and *that* kind of riding is not exactly like a rocking chair—it is astonishing how much longer the road was returning than goin—there was no bright anticipation to shorten the distance—but they say that "pain follows pleasure" and I suppose that I must have my share of it as the world turns—however I am *here* now and will relaps into my former active life and take it philosophicaly.

Yr[.]
Charley

How does the little darling take the departure! I do not think that she quite understood it this morning.

I will write to the boys to-morrow afternoon or evening[.]

26

Camp California
Feb 19/62

Dear Sons,

Your letter of the 16- inst. duely came to hand and I was very much pleased with its contents, more particularly in the reported improvement that you are making at school and the fact that you have remembered your sister while she is absent.

I have just returned to-night from another visit to your Mother: as I had business in Washington that detained me over night; I mounted my horse and rode out to your Uncle William's and arrived there (quite unexpected to them all) some time after they had all been in bed, but they were soon out, Clare and all, when they heard my voice out-side. I remained there all night and left early this morning: as your Uncle William lives 18 miles from Washington and our Camp is 11 miles the other side of the city, making 29 miles from one place to the other and the same distance back, making 58 miles that I travelled on horse-back for the pleasure of being *one* evening with them and I of course feel rather tired to-night, and so is the horse, for nearly the entire distance the roads are from 5 to 8 inches deep with mud and it is hard travelling.

One of the Captains in the regiment has presented me with a Dog, he is the same kind of a dog as "old Watch" was, only a little larger and black and white spotted; I call him "Dixie" and he is now sitting with his nose on my knee as I write—I intend to send him home the first opportunity that presents itself to me, and I want you both (when he *does* get home) to take the best care possable of him—he is very sharp and will not let any one enter my tent while I am out and I would like very much to keep him with me all through the war, but as I am afraid that I might loose him, I will place him in your charge[.]

I suppose that your Mother has informed you that Clare has the Measles—

she is getting better and calls it the "Weasles" and does not like any one to tell her that she has them.

Give my love to Grandmothers Johnson and Davis and answer this letter and when you do so, I want you both to endevour to improve your writing, I shall keep this one that I received to-day to compare with it—so now let me see how much you can improve[.]

Your affectionate
Father[,]
Chas. F. Johnson

27

Camp California
Feb. 19/62

Dear Mary,

I arrived safe and sound at Camp today at 4 o'clock and assertained that we have not received any posative orders in reference to our future movements: although all are in anxious expectation from the Gen.l down to the drummer boys—there appears to be a movement on foot somewhere, for today (amidst all the rain) five regiments crossed to this side of the Potomac and four *left*, for parts unknown to us.

Your letters of the 15th & 17th—one from the boys and the Transcript awaited my perusal. "Alma" is out again in the Despatch—he calls upon the Lieut-Col. "who is as humane, as he is brave" to rectify an evil complained off in the management of the Hospital, and gives the Col. (of course) an other "blast"[.][28]

Joe says that the Teacher told him that if he continued as he is now doing that he "will soon be at the head of his class." Willie "thinks that Mother writes very short letters" and "wishes that she would write longer ones" so you see that you must improve upon your communications, if you desire to remain in the good graces of your "folks at home." They have both sent Valentines to Clara, extracts of which they both have sent me, and I must say that (if it is of their *own* selection) it desplays considerable taste.

As it is pouring down to-night, I shall defer until Morning to see Doctor Gardiner[.]

Your
Charley

P.S. I have answered the boys' letter and gave them three pages to read so look out for your laurels[.]

Dr. Gardiner thinks that it would not be advisable for Clara to be exposed under at *least* two week from the time that the diseas first appeared and then *every thing* should be favourable—i.e. disease and weather[.][29]

28

Camp California
Feb 22nd/62

Dear Mary,

This (Washington's birthday) has been one of excitement with us at Camp—the impression appeared to prevail at headquarters that we would be engaged in a fight some time during the day, and consequently we received orders last night to have prepared one ration for each man, and this morning it was ordered to be put in their haversacks and fourty rounds of buck and ball cartrages in each box and to hold ourselves in readiness to march in ten minutes notice—then commenced that eager and anxious, yet *restrained* excitement, such as known only to an army that has been encamped for months expecting and "spiling for a fight," which was not, I assure you allaid when the guards reported that three regiments of infantry and one of Cavelry had quietly passed the camp during the night—swords were examined, pisols recaped, horses saddled, trunks packed and every thing ready and waiting for the long looked for and ardently-hoped-for commands "forward, march!"—moments were hours and hours were days—about 10 o'clock a pack of artillery dashed pell mell passed the camp as fast as eight horses could carry each gun through the mud and water—then was the anxious inquiry "when will the orders come to march?" passed from lip to lip, each appeared afraid that the fight *might* be over before they "had a chance."[30]

At 11 o'clock the entire brigade was ordered out to hear the "Farwell address of Geo. Washington" read by Gen.l Howard, and then back to our quarters with the strict injunction to hold our men at their various posts to move on a double quick at the sound of the beaugle, and so we remained until night and then dismissed—bad luck to it, and "no fight"[.]

I wished you could have seen us while listening to the "address" amist the pelting rain, not a man moving during the entire two hours—first a prayer by one of the Chaplains, then Hail Columbia by our Band, then the "address" followed by the Star Spangled Banner by the 64 N.Y. Band, then a prayer followed by "America" by the 5th N.H. Band and the entire Brigade singing the song—I will endevour to give you some idea of our arrangements—imagine the spot where Gen.l stood to be upon the extreme top of a high hill and the regiments on the sloping sides

[drawing of the arrangement]

the above rough sketch will give you a feint idea of our possission, supposing Gen.l Howard to be facing to-wards you and the artillery behind him and all parties facing inwards[.]

I see by the papers to-day that Jim Hufty and Henry Little are among the exchanged Prisoners and in all probability are in Philad- by to-night there will be great rejoycing in some homes this day.[31]

I have been anxiously expecting an answer to my letter to you of last Tuesday night—what is the matter—is Clara worse, or have you so little time to spare that you cannot write—you should have received my letter by Thursday night and if you mailed the answer on Friday morning I should have received it to-day—however I must waite patiently, now until Monday's afternoon mail—

I will keep this open until to-morrow (Sunday) night and mail it Monday morning[.]

Sunday night 23rd

I have had a visitor today in the shape of Capt. Meeves, who remained with me the greatest part of the day—he says that Shields did not get that possission in New York that he expected and is now at home without any [thing] to do yet[.]

I had two likeness taken to-day of myself on horse-back, in full uniform with sword drawn, both of which are *good;* but the gem of all pictures is one with Abram holding Couger by the bridle—the glossy hair of the *black* horse and the shiney skin of the *blackest* of *black* men is taken truely lifelike; I will retain them and endevour to bring them to you if we do not move and I can trump up some excuse to get into Washington before you leave—if not I will endevour to *send* them by *some person,* for I have them cased and it will cost almost as much as the pictures to send them by mail[.]

We are to have an inspection by either Gen.l McClellan or his Staff to-morrow and have been all day (Sunday as it was) preparing for it, with the determination to excell any regiment in the whole Division; and I think that to-night there is not a man in the entire regiment, but would be fit to visit a ball room[.]

I have not received any letter from the boys this week and none from you, which is the first *week* since I left home that such a thing has occured.

Did you get my letter of last Tuesday night?

How is Clara?

Your
Charley

29

Camp California
Feb 27/62

Dear Mary,

I reached camp (in due time) to find them in a great state of excitement, as they had orders to be ready to march at 4 o'clock this morning, but at 3 o'clock it was countermanded.

The Adj. kindly had placed parties on the road to notify me of it, so that the Genl. would not ketch me in the rear—I shall remember him for it!

We are ordered to have our muster for pay ready to-morrow at any trouble no matter what, and the impression is, that we march immediately there after—and the officers are to "reduce their baggage to a carpet bag and no more." So I was compelled to mount another horse (mine was used up, for I was compelled to ride from Washington to Alexandria) and go to Alexandria to purchase one, which made 10 miles extra riding for me to-day, and I feel pretty well used up, I assure you—but must finish packing it to-night before I "roll myself up in the blankets"—my trunk, bed, and bed stead I shall send home by express[.] My sword, and it is a beauty (the Col. says far superior to his) was presented to me to-night in the presence of the entire regiment, with a speech by Capt. Lee[32] to which I responded—*what* I said exactly I cannot tell—it was something about my inability to thank them—requiring a speech, the golden harvest that follows the flowering of thought—a glorious burst of winged words, bounding from the tongue—&c. &c. to express the feelings that reighn triumphant within me at the present moment—then something about—when the trumpet shall awake this slumbering mass of armed men, and flashing eyes and bristling hands shall catch the murmers that coming hoursly on the wind, swelling until the very sphere is filled with the echo of *Forward!!* that this blade shall leap from its scabard in defence of *our country* and its *Constitution*—I shall endevour that no act of mine will bring the blush of disgrace to either the givers or the recipitant—if it shall please the Great Omnipitance! (very patheticaly—yes raised) that I should expire upon the battle field, I ask for no greater boon than my last grasp shall be upon the hilt of this naked blade, &c. &c. &c. how much more I do not know—however *it* pleased the boys—*I* got the sword and *all* hands were pleased—I shall have it boxed and sent home, as soon as the men have a chance to see it—keep it as you would the apple of your eye.[33]

Friday night Feb. 28/62

I have packed my valice, which is one of those that open in the centre, and I find that I can carry in one side of it, my good uniform, so I have packed it in—there is several articles such as books &c. that I would like to take with me, but as far as *absolutely necessary* things I think that I have all that is requisite,—the dugerrotypes I return, for I would not have them broken for any thing.

I have packed my good cloak in the bottom of the trunk and rolled my bed up in the top and I will only have the two articles to send viz: trunk and bed-stead, which you can put up in this manner [drawing here] open the feet as wide as they will go—then place No. 1 (on each side in the *upper* holes in the side of the feet—then open the ends and put the pieces No. 2 in the *lower* holes—blow up the gum pillow (in the case) and you will have my bed compleat.

As I do not expect you to get this letter *before* Tuesday or Wednesday next, I will direct my next to you at home—and that will be *when* we move, provided we move *soon,* if not, of course I will write by the time you reach there.

The trunk &c. I will not send until just before we leave here—there will be *two* blankets and my shabrack on the top—my saddle valice you will find inside as I have prefered dispencing with it, so as to take two (instead of *one*) blanket with me, on my saddle—which I could not do, with it there also.

Give my little darling any amount of kisses for me and my love to the boys when you get home—this writing is miserable, but the fact is that my stove smokes so much that I was compelled to put the fire out—and it is infurnal cold setting in a canvass house with this stinging wind blowing clear through, and attempt any thing like penmanship—I hope to date from Fairfax or Centreville, the latter prefered[.]

30

Camp on
Alexandria & Orange
Rail Road
March 5/62

Dear Mary,

I now write this sitting saylor fashion and by the light of a bivouck fire in the midst of a dense woods with the heavens for a roof—tall cealen this—

We left Camp California yesterday morning at day-light and took the cars—platform ones, such as they use for wood, timber &c.—the engine in the rear, running very slow so as to repair the road as we went—the front men on each car, sitting with their feet hanging over the next rank kneeling and the remainder standing, and ready loaded and prepared for action, my self on the front car, the adjutant on the second, the Col. in the centre and the Maj. on the rear—thus we went for three miles beyond our picket line, when we was stopped by a bridge being burnt, when we landed and are here yet; the 64 N.Y. followed us about 3 hours after, with the Illinois cavalry.

As soon as we landed, I was despatched 2 miles farther ahead with 400 picked men to take and hold a station that far in advance, while the Maj. was to take a small party and follow the road to assertain the damage done the road and fall back on me in case of difficulty—we returned to the regiment at night and to-day I was sent out again to the same spot, while the Maj. (who is a rail road engineer) was detailed to build the bridge and the Col. to excavate the embankments that they (the rebels) has slid into the road—we have finished both jobs to-night and if the government sends rails to us to-morrow we will have the road open to Fairfax station by noon[.]

Abram and the other servants brought the horses around by the by-roads and were taken prisoners by our own party, and were considerably frightened there-at, but, are now safe along side of me; the dog (Dixie) laying along side of the fire as contented and happy as though he was perfectly at home—

Give my love to the Boys and the usual kisses to Clara—

this writing on ones knees is rather tedious work.

I have enjoyed the luxory of marching with my sword, pistols cartrage[s] and 3 days grub straped on my back and that in stepping from sleeper to sleeper on a rail road, well if I can not sleep at night I do not know who should.

We have had a sight of the rebel videts and I hope soon to get much closer, so as to take the color of their eyes—

The road that we are on is that which runs to Richmond via Mannassas so I expect some work ahead—

I will write as often as possable you direct as usual to the Regiment near Alexandria and I will get it, for we have made arrangements to have the mail to follow us.

I shall roll myself up in the blankets and enjoy "tired nature's sweet restorer, balmy sleep.["]

Yr[.]
Charley

P.S. Did you receive my things in good condition viz, sword, trunk & bedstead—how did you get home[,] did the key arrive[.]

31

Camp California
March 9/62

Dear Mary,

We have returned again to our old grounds as the heading of the letter indicates.

Last Thursday (after I had mailed my letter to you, of Wednesday night) I was ordered to proceed to Berks Station again, with my little command, which I did, and at noon I received a note from the Gen.l to hold the place at all hazards until he arrived, in the afternoon, the enemy had then advanced their lines to within a half mile of mine, we could see each other quite plane; the Gen.l came up with the Brigade at about 4 o'clock and ordered me to take four companies out as an advance guard.

We proceeded quietly (the rebels retiring before we arrived near thier posts) and took possession of Fairfax Station, and just beyond was several rebel vidette posts; our little party skirmished through the woods until we were within range of them (Delaney Guards, I believe they are called) when one of the men, in his haste to get a shot, fired his piece, thus preventing me from getting their rear and capturing the whole party, and in an instant every man rushed forward, when they put spurrs to their horses and over fences they went, and we (like so many devils) after them, but they being mounted and having the advantage of the roads and by-paths, escaped, thus we drove in one post after the other and had the whole place clear before the balance of the regiment arrived—we slept there that night and returned to Berks the next morning; having been 24 hours without any thing to eat from the Col. down—the balance of the Brigade remained at Berks and its neighborhood—we slept at Berks on Friday night and were relieved by the 1st New Jersey Brigade, when we immediately returned to camp, arriving there at noon Saturday, having been absent a week—we did not expect to ever return to camp again, when we left it, but such is the uncertanty of war, "here to day—and gone to-morrow[.]"

I should have mentioned, that on Friday night our Picket post (near Fairfax Station) shot Chas. Dillon of the 4th Mississippi Reg., the noted rebel spy—the authorities have been for the last two months endevouring to find him, they knew that he was about but could never lay their hands upon him—he endevoured to force by one of our picket posts and they fired, the ball entering his brain killing him instantly—upon his person was found some valuable papers that he was conveying to the rebels—the Gen.l feels quite proud as he was an extreamly slipery costumer.

We are ordered to have two days rations ready and expect to move again at short notice probably as soon as the men recruit, for they have had a hard week, having built the bridges, laid the rails, and excavated the road and done the picket duty of the entire Division for six consective day, one of which we were *short* of rations and another we had none at all, the other regiments in the brigade being in the rear about 3 miles all the time—but the boys would have done twice as much rather than be put out of the "*advance* guard," such is the spirit of emulation in the volunteer service[.]

I did not get to see Meeves when they arrived at Berks Station, as we moved out immediately, but I inquired of young Test (the druggest's son) who reported him "all well[.]" I would have liked to have seen the little Dutchman, for I think that our course will be in another direction when we move again.

I have not received any tidings of you or *any* of the family for 11 days now and I begin to feel quite anxious to hear from you all—as to how you got home (*if there at all*) and if my sword, trunk & bed stead arrived safe—if I do not hear from you *before* we leave again I shall feel quite uneasy about you—*do* write, if you *can not,* just tellegraph "*all well*" and I will thank you—it is a damn unpleasant feeling to be constantly crawling over you, as to the state of the family and *if* any thing *could* have happened to prevent the writing—did she get home or not? if so did she get there safe? &c. &c.

I have mailed you a letter on Tuesday, on Thursday and will mail this tomorrow (Monday) making *three* within a week—have you got them?

If we move in a day or so I will write again the night before if I know it, or at the moment, if not.

Give my love to the boys and kisses to Clara, and may God bless you is ever the prayer of your

Charley

P.S. I see that the Philad. Evening Journal of last Friday gives me quite a fuss with my sword, some of Jones work I guess[.]

32

Union Mills
Bull's Run
Battle Ground
March 12/62

Dear Mary,

I write this by the light of a bivouac fire on the old battle ground at Bull's Run and *no enemy* in sight—nay more—with the full knowledge that they have run from this strong hold Manassass and in such haste that they have not had time to take any thing with them, even their officer baggage, which they piled up and set fire to—in fact they are in full retreat—burning and destroying *every thing* (friends or foes) as they leave.

I wrote you on Sunday night—on Monday we marched to Brimstone Hills (16 miles) through a pelting rain and five inches of mud, expecting to meet the enemy, but they had left—we slept in the open fields and started the next morning at day light for Sangster's Station on the Alex. & Orange R.R. and they had left again—here we received information that they had become panic stricken and was leaving Manassas—but as we had pushed through with only two crackers per man and *no meat,* we were compelled to stop for supplies and did not reach this place until near mid-night—it is now near 1 o'clock and we are sleeping in the rebel rifle pits and thier masked batterys.[34]

Mary, the back-bone of rebellion is broken—they are whipped and not a blow struck—thanks to the well laid plans of McClellan—we fear now that we will not see a fight, but it will be one continual chase—we *may* be mistaken but things all look that way[.]

I received your letter of the 5th inst. while on the road to-day—(we being detached to guard the artillery, the rest of the division, 10,000 strong having goin by the rail road) and was rather surprised to find that you had not started for home—I have directed the last three or four letters there to you, however I suppose that you are there by this time.

I received a letter from Mother at the same time dated the 9th inst. informing me of the safe arrival of my sword, trunk &c.

I shall be compelled to make this short as it is getting late and we may be off again at day light—for (we think) Manassas and hence due south, we all hope so—as our grubb is here and the boys are willing and anxious to march until they get a sight of the infurnal scound[r]els.

I neglected to mention that I had a little sorrell mare, that can run and jump like a deer—a four rail fence is no obsticle—but she is rather too light and young (only four years old) for my heavy work, but will make a splendid horse in time—I could sell her for $125 or $150 dollars if I was north with her—if I had stable room home I would ship her at the first opportunity—however, as long as we *march,* Abram can lead her and we get along pretty well, dog and all.

I also received a letter to-day from Whitney—it never rains but it pours—this is the first letters I received for 13 days.

Give my love to the boys—tell them that I have a poney for them—to Mother and others, and that little darling—of whom I think daily and dream nightly.

The Chaplain who overtook us to-day with the mails, will leave in the morning with this and as I do not know *where* we mite be next, you had better address to me, thus

Lieut. Col. Chas J. Johnson
81st Reg. Pa. Vol.
Howard's Brigade
Sumner's Division
via Alexandria
Va[.]

Your
Charley

33

Head Quarters of the
5th Alabama Reg.
Manassas, Va
March 19/62

Dear Mary,

I wrote you last from Union Mills, (Bulls' Run) on the 12th inst. where we laid until the 16th inst. (Sunday) when we received orders to march to Fairfax Court House, there to wait for Gen. Banks Division,[35] and then to return to Alexandria to ship for Yorktown, so off we started through the pelting rain and mud—the men had not slept the previous night on account of the rain (having no shelter) and reached Fairfax C.H. at noon—at dusk the "long Roll" beat and we marched back to the Mills—making twenty miles through the mud, with one meal, and no sleep for 36 hours—we experienced *what* a soldiers life was—the next morning we marched to this place and now await for—I do not know *what*—wether we will advance in this direction or return to camp and ship, is a matter for future consideration—

Yours of the 12th came to hand on the 16th inst.

You do not mention wether you received the letter containing the key of my Trunk or not—and wether the two blanketts & Shabrack was in it or not—in fact you appear to be too crazey to mention any thing—I suppose by this time that you are settled—have subsided.

You had better *oil* the *blade* of the sword[.]

The Pay Master will not visit us until the first of the month—I have not seen a quarter for near a month—inclosed you will find an order on Geo. Chambers—if you stand in need—and I suppose you do—of money—*he* will give it to you[.]

If we ship for Yorktown I think that I can not take my poney with as we will be restricted as much as possable—so I will either send it home or send it to William for him to put out at pasture until my return to Washington—which of the two I will do will depend on circumstances—when I return to Alexandria.[36]

I have a picture of *Washington* (a very fine one) which I took from the Head Quarters of Genl. Beauregard—I will send it home as soon as possable. it is quite a trophy—to-geather with quite a number of little articles—if we had the means of carrying them we could get bushels of articles of interest[.][37]

Geo. Deal arrived here last night and goes to Alexandria to-day so I will send this with him—it is the first sheet of paper and pen that I have seen for a week—my valice, with plenty of writing materials—I have not seen for some time—I believe it is at Fairfax or *some where* on the road—we having been on light marching orders all the time, the mens knapsacks having been left on the road (under a guard) until we could transport them—our mess business is knocked into a cocked hat for the present—the cook and his utensils being *droped* on the road until we could send for him—hard crackers and salt pork is the only fare we have had (officers and all) for four day—I can eat it now three inches thick with fat—and smack my lips at that Ye! Gods!!

Twice within a week we have been on one meal per day—a screw loose some where in the commissary department—our horses were without any thing *one* day and then we came to the conclusion that the enemy *must* feed them—and they *have*, for we do not hesitate to enter *any* barn and feed the horses as we go on—the Genl. told me that he did not like it—but I informed him that if his Brigade Quartermaster did not furnish feed, the state of Virginia *must*—he walked away and that was the last of it—and we continue to feed[.]

In closed you will find a due bill on Geo. Chambers—get the money from him—for it may be a month before we see the Pay Master—I would send it to you in preference—but there is *not* ten dollars in the entire Regiment.

Direct as per my last to me with this exception that it is Richardson Division—Genl. Sumner having been appointed commander of a "Corps de Armee[.]"

Direct now to me as follows

Lieut Col. Chas. J. Johnson
(Howard's Brigade
Richardson's Division)
via Alexandria,
Va

that will likely reach me, if we should move befor you write—I will write at the first opportunity, but you must not expect letters as regular as usual now, for the prospect is that we will move constantly and the opportunities *may* be slim, but you shall have them whenever I can.

Give my love to the Boys and kisses to Clara[.]

Your
Charley

P.S. Our men are now in comfortable log houses formaly used by the 5th Alabama Reg. and we (the Field officer[s]) are in the quarters of their colonel[.]

34

Camp Manassas
March 24/62

Dear Mary,

I last wrote you from Washington City on the 22nd inst., and as I did not receive any tellegraph from the Col. I came to the conclusion to take the mare to William's myself and arrived there at about four o'clock, took supper and reached Washington at 2 o'clock in the morning—the horse having cast a shoe and I was forced to walk all the way to Grieve's (near Washington) until I arrived at a blacksmith shop, there I routed nearly every one up until I at last found the smith and had the shoe fixed, but that delay brought me into the City at the above hour and there was not a single bed in the whole place, so I returned to the stable and slept in the Hay Mow and was up again at 6 o'clock and off for this place, reaching here at 8 o'clock at night (near 40 miles) and I realy believe that horse and rider both slept as they went along—it was about 3 of the stiffest days work that I have had for some time—the horse actualy went asleep eating his dinner and I had to stand and hit him on the nose to keep him awake—I shall not use him for a day or two if I can help it. By-the-way on my road to Centreville I attempted to forge Bulls Run and had to swim the horse and as a consequence was wet to the waist and had to ride 13 miles (to Fairfax C.H.) before I found my valice to change my clothing—it is astonishing *what* a man can get through with and not feel any effects from it—at home the opperations of Friday, Saturday & Sunday would have laid me up for a week and *now* it only had the effect of making me eat (if possable) more than usual.

During my absence the Col. (thinking to confer a favour) shipped my picture of Washington, through the store—it was not pack[ed] as I intend[ed] it to be and I am afraid it will get damaged—if it does arrive safe you had better get it framed (*when* in funds)—it is torn a little on the side and at the corners but not enough to hurt when under a glass—I intended to have written (before I sent it home) in the corner "Taken from the Head Quarters of Genl. Beauregard, Manassas, March 17th 1862"—and will do so when I get home[.]

Your letter of the 15th & 18th inst. was here when I returned and I regret very much to hear of our little darlings sickness[.] God grant! that it may not be serious. I shall feel very anxious until I receive your next and live in hopes and prayers for its good tidings[.]

You say "They are taxing every thing from a hooped skirt *up*" now I would like to know *what* are the rates of tax on *all* that is *up* the hooped skirt—they would not tax *that* article here in this locality, I assure you[.]

The watch of Shields is cheep at $60.00 and if I had funds I would not mind purchasing it, for I want a good one—that is a valuable one[.]

As to *where* we will get when we move from here, the Lord only knows, but it is perfectly immaterial to me, *what* direction we take—there is a certain amount of work to be done by each division of the army and I expect that ours will have its portion—it is just as easy to do your duty as a soldier in one state as another and no more dangerous at that—for I hold most emphaticaly and seriously that no man dies until his alloted time has ran its course—so do not get uneasy on that score, for if the Lord wills that my days are near an end, saltpetre will not save me, and on the other hand if *he* decrees that I should live for years to come, all the balls in secceshindom can not carry me off before *he* is ready[.]

Give my love to the Boys and tell them that poor "Dixie" (the dog) is lost—some one has *found* him as I did—however I will raise another before many days[.]

Yr[.]
Charly

35

Warrington Junction
March 28/62

Dear Mary,

As the Paper Carrier is about returning to Alexandria for his morning edition of paper (for he follows us regulary) and will carry our letters I hastly write this, while the Brigade is under arms ready to march—

We arrived at this place with about 20,000 men yesterday afternoon and drove in the Rebel pickets—the rear guard of Gen.l Stewarts cavelry who was covering thier retreat from Manassas.[38]

I feel quite anxious to hear from you all, especialy in regard to Clara's sickness—I have not received any word from you since (I think) the 17th inst. when I returned to Manassas from Washington; although I suppose that there are several on the road somewhere, but we are so constantly on the move that the letters might follow us for several days before they reach us.

Has my picture of Washington arrived safe? Did you draw on Geo. Chambers for funds? Did you get my last from Mannassas?

Be particular to answer this weather we ever return to Alexandria or not, it is of course impossable for me to say as the powers that be very properly keep it to themselves[.]

I must close as the carrier is waiting for this[.]

Give love to all and write as directed[.]

Yr[.]
Charly

36

Warrington Junction
March 31/62

Dear Mary,

To-day being clear at last and we having a day of rest, I have seized my pen and written (or intend to write) this letter, with out any knowledge as to *when* I mite have an opportunity to forward it[.]

I wrote you on the 28th inst and sent by the paper carrier, just as we were under arms to leave here, which we did with the Brigade, the Illinois Cavelry and two Batteries of artillery and made a "reconnaissance in force" driving the Rebels before us for 13 miles; when they crossed the Rappahannock River and burned the Bridge, thus preventing farther pursuit. When we met their vidette posts (one mile from here) thier force (2 brigades) were about one hour in advance of us, and we stepped out pretty briskly I assure you, but the cowardly scound[r]els burned *every* bridge as they passed over (and there were quite a number) which compelled us to ford the streams, most of them up to the armpits, and also to build temporary bridges for our artillery, yet so anxious were the boys to overtake them, that when they (the Rebels) crossed the Rappahannock, they were but 20 minutes ahead of us—there they considered themselves safe, and having cannon planted they opened fire upon us, to which we replied with our artillery which was kept up by each side until dark, when we retired out of the range of their guns and bivaoced for the night, and returned to this place the next morning.

We took several prisoners who represented their force as 8000 strong (under Genl. Stewart), if that is so, they were an infurnal set of cowards, for *our* force did not exceed 3800 men all told (the remainder having remained at this place) [.]

It was the first time that I stood before thier fire—heretofore they did not return ours—and it was amusing as well as singuler to watch its effects upon the men—at the first shot, the ball of which tore up the ground a few yards from our regiment, the men were *all* serious, at the second they were courious, the third interested, and at the fourth defiant and indifferant and I suppose that it is usually the effect in *all* engagements.

I have not received any letter from you since my return to Manassas from Washington, about the 17th or 19th inst. in which you informed me of the illness of Clara, and I feel quite anxious I assure you to receive *some* information on the subject—oh! that I had a satisfactory letter to read to-day!—it is the only drawback to this constant movement in the field—if our chaplain was worth a continental damn, he would have displayed more energy than he has in getting our mails to us—damn him when I *do* see him, he will hear from me—my anxiety to hear from home has become a mania by day and dreams by night—there is *so much* that I want to know—

I suppose that you have seen in the papers that there is *no pay* yet and *if* you have not drawn on Chambers, do so at once for God only knows *when* we will get any—the discount is from 8 to 10 per. cent (nearly $40.00) on mine, which I do not like to loose, unless it *must* be done—let me know candidly how you stand in regard to the funds.

It is three weeks to-day since we left Camp California and have been but one day at one place, so you see that we have moved *some* if not more since then—most of the time it has rained and we have not had a shelter over us, most of the time not even cedar brush, and it is beginning to tell on the health of the men—although *I* personaly never felt better in my life—what will be the *next* move I cannot tell, for we small fry are justly in the dark, we get under arms and march, and never know *where* we are until we stop.

I shall now close and take a tramp through the grounds to find some one to mail this—

Give my love to the boys, God bless them! and many kisses to Clara, and may God be the ever protector to you, is the wishes and prayers of your

Charley

4 o'clock A.M.

I have just received yours of the 23rd & 25th inst. and feel as joyous as the birds on the opening of spring although they did not bring news *quite* as satisfactory as desired—yet it was news from *home*[.]

In reference to Joe, I feel justified in reiterating my advice on a former occasion use the lash! use the lash!! use the lash!!! you *must* crush that rebelious spirit of his, and make him stand in bodily fear of you—that is the only way to curb *him.*

I did not know anything about the disaster of Saml. Hufty.

I feel relieved in reference to the funds: call on him again if you should desire more[.] Do not send me any box or any thing that you value until I inform you *where* to send it—for in these sudden moves we do not know where to find ourselves even much less any thing else—

The sun is shining once more and soldier like we have (in an hour) forgot all the trials and troubles of the last four days—every one is singing or whistling—even myself, for your letters has raised me mountain high and I could fight today with a joyous spirit and a merry heart.

"N-never rains but it pours" for after an absence of 14 days we have received *all* the mails at one time, nearly a barrell full and the men were like children at a show each fearing that he would not get all that he was entitled to.

You must excuse the style of writing for I am *squating* on my hams and writing on my cap top[.]

Continue to direct as usual, but do not put the Division before the brigade it is Howards Brigade,

Richardsons Division[.]

Your
Charley

37

Camp Manassas
April 2/62

Dear Mary,

Here we are again in our old quarters, with (thank God!) a roof over our heads again—I thank God—because it is raining, blowing and as cold as midwinter and would have been an awful night to bivouac out as we have done for the last fifteen days, without *any* covering but the canopy of high heavens, and last night without even a *blanket*—for we put them all in the waggons when we left Warrington Junction and did not see them until an hour ago.

The remainder of the Division have left for Alexandria in the cars and we expect to do the same to-morrow morning—our destination will be (so supposed) to Fortress Munroe, *when* we will embark I do not know, nor do I even know that we will go even there, for the programe is changing constantly and I would not be surprised when we reached Alexandria to be ordered back or to be ordered even to remain here and see the others return—so we go—[39]

You had better hereafter direct your letters to Howard's Brigade, Richardson's Division, *Washington City D.C.* and then *if* we *do* leave for "*away down* in Dixie" they will reach us whenever the mails are carried.

There is a prospect of our being paid when we arrive at Alex. if so I will send by Adam's Express and add a P.S. to this—Did you get the Picture? inclosed is a likeness of Lieut. Booker Co. D place it with the remainder.[40]

As I intend to enjoy the luxery of a *wash* and clean under clothes (availing myself of a roof) I will bid you a good night[.]

Your
Charly

38

Alexandria
April 4/62 6 o'clock a.m.

Dear Mary,

We arrived at this place at midnight and expect to embark immediately—the remainder of the Division are now anchored in the stream—no Paymaster here yet—if you want more funds call on George Chambers—expect letters at longer intervals although will write as often as possable you continue to write frequently also. I do not know what effect new law in reference to stopping soldiers letters will have on me—but—"*there is a will there is a way*"—wrote this on a board pile at the depot[.]

Give my love to all and kisses to Clara—kind respect to Mother Johnson & Davis[.]

Yr[.]
Charley

39

Shippen Point, Va.
April 8/62

Dear Mary,

In accordance with my previous intentions I sit down to write to you on every opportunity—we are at the above place yet having been engaged since our arrival in un-loading the stores from the numerous vessels (of all sizes & kinds) that are constantly arriving.

To night I have received an order to move the regiment up the road towards Yorktown, while Col. Miller remains behind, with two companies to superintend the unloading—the move, although generaly desired, is not relished just at this time, as we have had and are continuing to have, one of those infurnal northeast storms, with plenty of rain and a cold, cutting wind from the face of the bay, and we feel entirely too comfortable in our spacious quarters to desire a change until the storm is over; but, the "orders have arrived" and the word is *move,* and move it is.

I have not seen, nor heard any thing of either, Abram or the horse since the 4th inst. when I put them aboard of the Steamer Croton at Alexandria, I *suppose* that they have put into some place for safety until the storm is over;—the horses of our entire field & staff are aboard of the same boat, and all without shelter—God knows weather they will be worth any thing or not if this storm continues—we begin to feel very anxious about them and are constantly upon the ramparts, with glass in hand, watching for their appearance, and as the sea, ever and anon dashes with renewed violance at our feet, scattering the spray high in the air, the ejaculation is—"*what* in the devil *has* become of the horses!"

I mailed a letter to you the day after I arrival here, which I suppose you will receive *some* time—it may be a week or more in reaching you, as I understand that it goes via Fortress Munroe, we have not received any here yet.

I would like you to mail the Inquirer (also a Sunday paper) as frequently as convenient for we are *now* out of the road of its delivery; and if you mail them often, we *may* get them *occasionaly* and "half a loaf is better than none"—we have neither seen or heard any thing from the north for a week and feel as though we were shut out entirely from "all the rest of mankind[.]" After this storm is over we expect some fine weather, as the shrubery is all out and the Peach trees are in full blossom—which indicates that the full spring time is coming.

I have not met a single union man, no, nor woman either in this section of the state; all appear to be intensely "secessesh"—so much so, that they will neither give nor *sell* any thing to the officers of the army—when you bring them out (it is not often that you can) but, when you *do*—they are as bitter as wormwood and heap imprications mountain high upon our heads, in which they are comparitively safe, for the "orders" are very explicit in forbiding any of us from touching either them or their property—other wise God help them! for *thier* course has made *us* more bitter (if possable) than ever, and every man feels that when the time *does* come, they will be paid with interest.[41]

I could write you some very interesting accounts of the movements of the army in this section, but you will be compelled to receive *all* your information from the papers, as it would not do for an *officer* especialy to violate "orders"—even with his family. I for one feel that the trust is to important and *honourable* to violate—so *my* "war news" will be very meager—any thing that I can consistantly communicate will be done as early as proper.

Give my love to the Boys—I hope that Joe still continues subdued—watch him and do not let him get the *first* step forward.

Kiss Clara (bless her little soul) for me and give my best wishes to all others.

How is Mother Johnson & Davis getting? Continue to direct to me as per my instructions and I suppose that I will get them sooner or later—they will be duely appreciated and eagerly perused *when* they arrive.

Yr[.]
Charley

P.S. That box business you may as well dismiss for some time to come—

Did you get the parcle that I sent per express to you on the 4th inst?

40

Opposite Shippen Point
April 11/62

Dear Mary,

We are now bivaocing on a penninsula opposite to the place of our first landing—the moon is over and we have the most beautiful of spring weather and can fully appreciate our location, as the waters dance and sparkle in the glowing sun, around the entire regiment; for with the exception of about 100 yards we are surrounded by salt water and use the canues to go from place to place instead of horses; which by-the-way have made their appearance at last; they were landed at Fortress Monroe and had to make their way (27 miles) here by land—both horses and men nearly starved to death.

The principle amusement of the men are gunning for wild Ducks, digging for Clams, raking for Oysters and fishing for Trout; and like true soldiers, a few days of clear weather and a little recreation fully compensates for nearly two months privations—the misery of yesterday is buried in the pleasures of to-day—it is fortunate for our happiness that it is so, or we would be a miserable set of devils, the sugar plum soothes the smarting of the whiped child.

I am now in command of the regiment; Col. Miller being detached to the Quartermasters Department (much to his regret) to superintend the unloading of stores, it may be but a temporary affair or it may last for months.

The 6th & 7th New Jersey regiment are encamped (they have tents) on a point opposite to us, and I received a visit from Cap. Moore, Serg. Carles, Figner[42] and a host of others yesterday, and as we sat (in the bright sun) upon the beach discussing old times and recalling old sceans; the birds chirpping in the very joyousness of their hearts; I felt more contented than *any* time since I left home, and *if* I only had *you* hear I could be the most contented of mortals, but as that cannot be, I sit, and love to sit and live in the memory of the past and speculate upon the future.

We have not received any mails from home yet, nor have we any facilities to do so—last night I induced Gen.l Howard to appoint a Brigade Letter Carrier, whose duty will be to travell between us and Fortress Monroe and *now* we may expect an occasional mail, it will necessary be occasional as we must avail ourselves of the return of transports as there is no other way.

I must hastly close as a boat is just goin off—my love to all[.]

Yr[.]
Charly

41

[Lynch transcription]

Camp Winfield Scott
near Yorktown, Va
April 26/62

We are quietly lying here waiting for the ball to open—our division is located near the centre of the lines and are held in reserve to march either to the right or the left as the case may require—we are to support any place along the entire line that may be hotly pressed—when the fight *does* commence it will be such an affair as is seen but once in a century or two—they have 500 cannon and 100 to 120,000 men—so they say—we have about as many guns as they are [and?] 100,000 men—and when all (1000) of the "dogs of war" open their mouths together it will make noise sufficient to reach the high heavens itself—to which add the clatter of 100,000 rifles and muskets and you may conceive some faint idea of sound on an extensive scale.[43]

Our line of Fortifications are fast being compleated and are within (almost) speaking distance of theirs—one singular part of the affair is, that they suffer us to continue building with but slight interruptions, *we* [w]ould have blown *them* to atoms had the case been reversed.

George intends to send some money home in an envelope inclosed in mine[.]

Saturday morning at day break

Mary, this is one of the most lovely mornings that I have ever seen—it was warm all night but just as the sun rose above the horizon a mild breese [came] out and a thousand birds all lovely of plumage and vocal powers commenced to make the place echo with their warbling—the air is filled with the fragrance of wild flowers—all nature appears in a calm enjoyment of the blessings of the Almighty and yet this day the "Dogs of War" are ready and man stands prepared to commit a "legalized murder[.]"

42

Camp Winfield Scott
near Yorktown, Va.
Sunday, May 4/62

Dear Mary,

Yesterday I ship[p]ed per Adams Express a package directed to you containing $170.00 and mailed a letter also and upon my return I found yours of the 27th & 29th enclosed in one envelope; which I hasten to reply. You mention not having received any letter since the 21st. (Monday) that is not correct as there is not a week but I have written from three to four letters—but *if* they do *not* come—it is not necessary that you should picture a "grave-yard" in your minds-eye—come—come—Mary! you are certainly right, it is "nonsence"—no matter how great is the desire to receive information from the absent, it is not necessary that the worst possible view of the picture should be taken *if* it should not come[.]

You "have been complaining, but are very *near* all right again" do you have medical attendance or not? I am afraid that you neglect yourself.

The papers come "spasmimodicaly," "easy by jerks"; as there is a paper stand five miles from our quarters and as yours do not come regular, and when they do come they are four or five days behind those that we purchase I think that you had better *not send any more*—we get them 24 hours after they are issued, or nearly so, as we receive at 2 o'clock P.M. the issue of the day before—and yours do not come under five days—so do not send any more until I desire it, which I certanly will do, if we move and the paper carriers do not follow.

I regret to say—and I do so in confidence—that George was taken very ill yesterday with the Typhoid Fever—it promises to be a very bad case—*do not mention it to Harriet* as it will only worry her and certainly *can not help* him. He has a great aversion to goin into the Hospital, and long since made me promise that if possable he should never be sent there if he ever was sick; yesterday (after the fever abated) he recalled the promise—he is foolish as he could be better cared for there than any where else as the Medical department *always* has the best quarters on the ground—but I have made arrangements for the Hospital Stuart to take him in his quarters and as the Stewart and George are great friends I suppose it is all correct, I shall move him today.[44] I have given the department instructions to spare no pains or *expense* and I will foot the bill, to get any thing (no matter *what* it costs) that the government does not furnish—Dr. Gardiner says that it will be a severe case—during his rational moments to-day I will inquire if he desires his wife to know it, if so I will write, but do not mention it until I tell you.

Give my love to the boys and tell them I feel quite proud of their continual good behaviour; give any amount of kisses to Clara and regards to all others[.]

Your
Charley

P.S. George is easier this morning—he has consented to go to the Stewarts quarters—as the call is "breakfast gentlemen" I will close[.]

43

Yorktown, Va.
May 8/62

Dear Mary,

We are again at the above place and are or were waiting for transports to convey us to West Point, but as the telegraph has just informed us that "Norfolk is ours" it may change the moves on the chessboard of war, at any rate it has kept us here "awaiting farther orders."[45]

We arrived here yesterday at 10 o'clock, (I mailed a letter at 6 O'Clock A.M.) by an entire new road and we looked more like a "may party" or Picknick, for we nearly all had boquets of blossoms and wild flowers, and if it was not for the presence of the usual concommitants of war, no one would have supposed that the "gay and happy" throng were "legalized murder[er]s."

Willie Dutton arrived a few hours after with the photograph &c. and I will in all candor say that I do not like it—you have not the least bit of your usual (or I may say *old*) expression, although I have no doubt that it is "a good likeness."

You say that "Mrs. Deal gets two letters to my one"—he must write *very* often—your[s] notices the receipt of mine of the 20th ult.—since then I have written on the 21st, 24th, 26th, & 28th ult. and the 3rd, 5th, & 7th inst.—Seven letters in fourteen days. I presume that by this time Mr. North is satisfied with the "book"—You are correct in regard to Josephine—money is not, nor will not be too plenty—if we are disbanded it will be necessary to have a little on hand until "some thing turns up."

Your "favorer[?]" in reference to a probability of my being wounded "in the coming engagement," I suppose is "null and void" *now,* as there is no one to inflict "the deadly blow." Seriously, Mary, I have made ample provisions to meet any and every conceivable causiality that may happen to me and you need not make yourself uneasy in regard to it, *that* has been attended to long ago between the Col.[,] Maj.[,] Adj. & myself each for the other, and as George will not be in any engagement but always near the spot, it will be well attended to, so far as I am conserned.

I have sent a messenger to see George to-day, who has just reported him improving so rapidly as to be "out and moving about." I expect that he will be with us in a few days.

This morning I visited the battle field at Williamsburg and am sorry to find some of our Camden boys killed & wounded—I saw Capt. Jackson, young Radclift—Capt. Moore was at the hospital attending to his wounded—I did not see him; Capt. Lee has been "missing" since the battle, supposed to be a prisoner.[46]

It was a sorrowful sight to see them hunting for and burying their dead companions, but still more sorrowful was the sight of four or five slowly carrying a wounded companion along to the hospital—they appear to be well taken cair of—the "Medical Department" is well represented by *volunteer surgeons.*[47]

I have some tropheys for Chambers, viz. two canister shot from the "water batteries," and a Pike head from Yorktown; a sechesh bayonet from the Williamsburg battlefield—I also have a canvass bag—termed "sand bag" for you—from the "water batteries" at Yorktown—I shall abide my chances to forward them home—bye-the-bye—my two Flying Squirls are dead, having been smothered in their transportation.

Have you heard from William lately—I would like to send him ten dollars on account of expenses of the Poney, but the damn Mails are so uncertain that I am afraid to trust them.

Give any quantity of kisses for me to that "sunney cool" scholar and my love to the boys, as you have omited them in your last one or two letters, I suppose that they are "all right."[48]

I will write again to-morrow, if we move, but *always* direct as usual[.]

Charley

P.S. Your medicine stoped the "back-door-trots" on the Col. with one dose—great stuff that[.]

44

Camp near
Yorktown, Va
May 10/62

Dear Mary,

Yours of the 4th inst. came to hand yesterday just as we were packing up to move camp to a location about a mile from Yorktown—we are now "spread out" in a Peach orchard of some thousand trees—and as cross a[s] bears with sore heads—for this change to "a better location" looks like a longer stay than we desired, the men grumbled, the officers swore, and the Brig. Gen.l "protested" against this halting in the rear; damn it, we do not appear to have any chance to see *what* we *are* made of.

You are right about corse living, I would give this day two dollars for one good meal and walk five miles for it, at that, even as hot as it is to-day and it is *hot*! *hotter*!! *hottest*!!!

Campion[49] returned to camp yesterday, he did not call at the time appointed because he was confined to the house sick and when he got well he started off without thinking of it.

He has brought us (the Field [Officers]) each, that which I suppose will please you, viz: a "bullit proof vest" and we intend this afternoon to test them with muskets, rifles & Pistols—the only objection that I have to them is that they are so confounded heavy for this season of the year—what? carry a pound or two of steel around you (in connection with *all* the other paraphanalia that you *must* carry) with the sun pouring down on you, and *all* mearly to protect a few square inches of the body, in case a shot *might* accidently hit you in that precise spot—I think that they are a *humbug*! *humbug*!!

2 o'clock P.M.—the committee have just returned with the great, mighty, powerful "*bullit proof* vest" and the result is that a common musket put a ball clear through it at 50 yards, through, yes, and carried some four or five inches of the stuff with it—which would have killed the devil himself if it *all*

had entered his body—they "won't do" no! no!! Mary, the best way is to fully and freely place your trust in *him* who ruleth all and *face your foe* fearlessly and let him do his worst—when the order comes "pitch in" and take your chances without *skulking* behind a *"bullit proof vest"* that is not worth a continental curse at that.

As it is very hot and as the mail will be in to night I will lay over until then[.]

Yr[.]
Charley

P.S. Evening as there is "no mails to day" I will close—

George arrived here this morning and is improving rapidly though rather weak yet—has he informed Harriet—if not, for God's sake do not you do it.

I received from our cook the list of prices asked by the Sutlers and other *Sharks*, viz: Butter 60 @ 75 cts per lb. Bread (two & three weeks old) 15 @ 25 cts per loaf—the size of your fist. Eggs 62 @ 75 cts per doz (stale) Pickles, 75 cts per bottle (15 in it) and every thing else in proportion; why it would take our whole pay to live any thing like deceant—oh! yes! Ham 26 @ 30 cts per lb (if you take a *whole one*.)

Give that "whoping toof" girl her usual kisses and the Boys my love—

As the Col. &c. are waiting for me to take a hand at "Euchre" I will close[.]

Your
Charly

P.P.S. I am out of letter paper and have but four Envelopes—the Gen.l intends to send me to Fortress Monroe to-morrow to hurry up the statinary for the Brigade[.]

P.P.P.S. yours of the 7th just came to hand and I am glad that you received the money all right—we expect to receive our last pay this month and then you will be easier in money matters and I will be eas[i]er in my mind about it—the night is splendid, the moon superb, how I would like to sit with you under these trees[.]

45

Cumberland, Va
May 16/62

Dear Mary,

Yesterday at 4 o'clock A.M. we "pulled up stakes" and marched amidst an incessent rain to this point; it being some 18 miles by water and 12 miles by land to the north-west of our location, from whence I last wrote to you, the 13th inst. Yesterday was the day for me to write to you, but as we started before day-break and reached here at 10 o'clock and then had to stand leaning against a tree to let the water run off as fast as it poured on, until 5 o'clock in the afternoon for the waggons to come up; it was *rather* inconvenient and I omitted it.

We are *now* no nearer to the concentrated point of our ambition, Richmond, than we were three days ago, so far as *miles* are concerned, but are concentrating a large force at this point and will in all doubt make a decisive strike in "a few days" as our Gun Boats proceeding up the Chicakahomania River[50] have cut off some 20 odd thousand of the Rebels that we have been driving before us, while the remainder (who crossed the Chicahomania below, near Williamsburg) are held off by the same boats, so that we have them in *rather* an uneasy possition—but what is the use of my writing for the papers will have showed up the whole case long before this reaches you.

It is now raining to-day and such infurnal roads as these will be again, I suppose can or could be seen in *no* state under the universe except in "the Old Dominion" or "the sacred state" pshaw! Mud! Mud!! Mud!!! Mud to walk in, mud to stand in, mud to sit in, mud to *lay* in, mud to eat in, and nothing but mud to *drink*—why! do you know that [there are] not ten men in the entire army that can say they "had a natural stool to-day," I have not (for color and consistancy) had one since I left Alexandria the 4th of last month, and all because it is utterly impossable to get a glass of water free from *mud*!; if the male population of the north are not troubled in *future* with the "gravell" from drinking this infurnal "sacred soil," it will be because their blad[d]ers were so antagnistical to the "southern soil" as to not be able to hold the "infurnal stuff."

I have had, but am *now* perfectly well, an attack of the Jaundice—"yaller jandis"—and such a figure—you should have seen it—no! you should not either—for you would have got out of conceit of it, if you had—yellow hands—yellow face, yellow nails, yellow eyes, and (as the dye is wearing off the whiskers) yellow beard, *every thing* yellow except my *hair*—the Doctor said the "liver did not work," well if it did not, I don[']t want it to, for it worked the bile so eturnaly over my system that I thought I was *all liver*—but after some ten days physicing—bah! old school—rhubarb, calomell, jalap, castor oil &c. &c. &c. bah!—I at last got it under and *now* it has disappered except a slight shade in the eyes—however as I continued "at my post" I did not think anything more of it than a "sevear cold." We have had several cases of the Jaundice among the officers of the Regiment—Gardiner informs me that it is quite previlent with the bilious cases of the army—the diet, exposure, and hot sun all contributing to stay the activity of the liver.[51]

The Leader of the Band has just arrived from Washington with an entire set of new musical instruments ($635.00) presented, or rather purchased by the Regiment—he also brought a light felt hat for us (the field) caps are at a discount and will continue as long as it is so hot—we now sport low crowned, broad brim[m]ed felt hats with black and gold cord and acorns dangling over the edge—Lord help them *when* we go out, if the rain does not make sad havoc with the *gold* then I am mistaken.

Give our darling her usual kisses and the boys my love also to the two mothers[.]

yr
Charley

46

June 14/62
Camp Victory
Fair Oaks, Va.

Dear Mary,

The mail to-day brought yours of the 4th inst. I can not conceive where it could have goin to in the mean time, as yours of the 8th came two days since, which I answered on the 12th inst. You appear to have firmly made up your mind that you "can not hear if any thing should happen"—why, Mary, I have assured you time and again that I have made every and ample arraingements for your information in case of the same occuring.

Endevour to school your nerves to keep steady and look *always* upon the bright picture of Hope and *never* let one desponding thought cloud your joys for a moment—it is time enough to despair when the blow is struck—it is useless to pass hours of agony and dread of events that have not and never may take place—tens, aye! hundreds of thousands of men that are in the army will return again to their family, and why should I not be of that number? No! No!! Mary, to use a homley phrase "never hollor *before* you are hurt."

Yesterday we had a visit from the "great little man"—"our George"—McClellan[.] he looked as fresh as if this immence army was but part time to handle—cool, collected, mild and plesant to all—speaking to every one whom he thought wanted to speak to him, I tell you he gets through a great deal of work in a very little time—and away he goes, you think that he has been about such a short time that he could not have done any thing, yet when you begin to look over *what* he has done you ask yourself *how—when* did he do it?—so smoothly and quietly and rapidly does every thing glide from beneath his fingers.

I was rather astonished yesterday afternoon to see the familiar physiog of George Mulick approaching my tent—I do not know that I have met any one, since I have been out with half as much pleasure, those plesant sunday afternoons and those cosey sunday suppers loomed up as we clasped hands, and I felt like meeting one of the family. He is in Baxter's Zuoaves,[52] and says that he several times within the last month endevoured to get to me, but could not, I certanly did not expect to see him here. I felt sorry that I could not ask him to remain to dinner—but this rank—rank—knocks many a social tie to pieces—

I am gradualy and quietly eradicating some of the preduces and partialitys of Col. Miller, old favorites who held nominal posts so as to exempt them from duty gradualy find those posts abolished—officers who never worked except they feel liked it find that an order means *all,* without an exception—there is frequently an expression of surprise upon the countinance of some of them—which soon passes away as they see that the commands are general and *all* must obey—most of these parties of course are from the Country, but there were a few from the City, and to avoid any charges I scraped off the city ones first, *that* satisfied officers and men—they say that they believe "that Col. Johnson won[']t know any man when work is to be done"[53]—I have not had occasion to speak one harsh word since the Col.['s] death, nor had occasion to punish a single man—before, scarce a day passed without some one having a log or sand bag on his shoulder,[54] and a constant yelling whenever in line—now I can almost give my commands in a whisper and be heard. My discipline is much more severe, but as they think I do it for thier good (and it is) and they have confidence sufficient to do it without one word of complaint[.]

The flowers from Uncle Joe's[55] grave recalled many sceans—it was like opening the casket of Memory and turning over the few but bright gems treasured there—it made an

"hour when memory wakes
 visions of joy that could not last;
an hour when fancy takes
 a survey of the past—

The few we liked, the one we loved—
 a sacred band! came steeling on,
and many a form, far hence removed,
 and many a pleasure gone.["]

Give our darling her kisses for me and my love to the boys respects to the folks generaly and Maria in particular.

Yr
Charley

47

Camp Lincoln
Fair Oaks, Va.
June 17/62

Dear Mary,

Having waited for the mail of to-day and as "no letter for you Col." was the answer I came to the conclusion to write nevertheless.

Our Brigade is now on the 1st line and protecting the men who are working in the trenches. We expect to remain here (our present position) for three days yet—we have been here three—and then *perhaps* be relieved. Of course I am not able to judge of what the Gen.l's plans are, but it looks to me as though that battle, spoken of by him, would not take place for two or three weeks yet. We are within hearing distance of each other (a dense woods prevents our seeing each other) and although their sharp-shooters do not fire at our men, yet when ever an officer pops up his head or pokes out his nose—crack! goes their rifles—whis! goes the ball in rather closer proximity to his phyz than is agreeable[.]

The day before yesterday Capt. Sam.l Shurlock was killed instantly by a ball from a Reb. sharp shooter, while out on Picket—he was a Chunker and appointed by Col. Miller as Capt. in a Philad. company (D).[56] I regret very much to loose him as he was a splendid officer *in a fight* although not worth the grub he ate at any other time. As if the fates were against us or providence was deturmined that the injustice done Philad. in the regiment should be set right—our Quarter Master was on a train of cars goin to the White House [Landing, in Virginia], when a band of Guerrillas fired into it, and he received five balls—he now lies at the "Floating Hospital," and will proceed home at the first opportunity—it is not known yet *what* may be the result of his wounds. There was one thing that happened in connection with the above that I did not like and that will in all probibility alter my actions in future with George, if the Q.M. *should* die,—this I want you to keep to your self—as soon as I heard of the affair (he was reported dead at first) I sent for Geo. and told him that I wanted him to take charge of the establishment, when he *refused* unless I "*ordered it*" and "I will not take the responsibility of any mans office again—I never got paid for the work that I did before"—I turned on my heels and detailed Lieut. Smith[57] as "Acting Quarter Master"—now Geo. knew as well as I did, that *I* and *I alone* am responsable for the regiment being supplied with the necessary stores, that is if they are *not* supplied the government condemns me for not seeing to it—and I thought that no matter *what* he might think of the treatment he received previously

I certainly could not help it then, and again, I seized the opportunity to put him in the post so that he would be *there* and have things to his liken, if Brelsford should die. He came later in the day with an attempt to explain away his emphatic refusal—I listened to him—made no comments or reply and thought that if *he* would not help himself (at the same time helping me) that there was no absolute obligation on *my* part to help him. The Medical Dept. some time since ordered a half a gill of "medicinal whiskey" (i.e. whiskey & quinine) to be given each officer and man in the army morning and night, and I think that Geo. (who is handy to it) imbibes it so as to keep himself more or less stupified nearly all the time.

You may ease the minds of my "envious friends" Shields &c. by informing them that I have my Commission from the Governor for Colonel, "duely signed, sealed, and delivered"—I take the rank from the day of the battle (June 1st) so *if* they were *afraid* that I would *not* get it, they can ease thier minds on that score.

You need not forward me any more envelopes as I have received my quarters stationary from the government and now have a good stock on hand.

Give my kisses to Clara and my love to the boys[.]

Charly

48

Camp Lincoln
Fair Oaks, Va.
Sunday, June 22/62

Dear Mary,

Yours and the boys of the 18th inst. came to hand to-day—I was truely astonished to hear of the position of Bill Seymore, not that I do not believe that "the way of the transgressor is hard" but astonished because I always considered that he had talent sufficient to carry *some* rascaly scheam through, but he appears to have went down like a "spent ball" flattening himself as he struck.

You are not more impatient for a "on the Richmond" move than we all are here, but so unbounded is the confidence in "our George" that we would patiently waite a month for the order "up and at them" and think nothing of it—of one thing you may rest assured that when the time *does* come, victory will certainly perch upon our banners—the entire army have made up their minds to *that* and each man feels deturmaned that so far as in him lies the power, the next shall be the last great fight that they (the Rebs) shall make.

There is one thing that I should mention, that is, that the roses sent in the letters, although pressed are yet very fragrant and every one in the quarters stands ready for a smell when ever I open the letters—it reminds us all as forcably of *home* as any little thing possably could.

I am truely glad to hear that Clara is goin to make a singer, for it certainly is an accomplishment that sits well upon any girl no matter *what* her sphear of life—I was goin to say cultivate it, but that is not necessary for I know you will do that with out any sugestions.

Yesterday I had the pleasure of witnessing a short battle without being engaged in it—the enemy made a sallie upon Hooker's[58] Brigade, which is on our left, in an instant all hands were in arms, and as the fighting was about a ½ mile distant, I mounted the parripetts and viewed the whole engagement—the Rebs left the woods and rushed across the open field to take a redoubt that mounted three guns, when they [Hooker's soldiers] opened Grape and cannister[59] on them cutting wholes through their ranks, but regiment followed regiment and it came to close musket range, when our (Richardson's) guns let drive the shells, which exploded in their [the rebels] midst scattering them in all directions. [T]hey started to give three cheers—they gave one—two—when our shells fell among them and they forgot the third—they hesitated—another volley of shells and they turned and ran, then we piled shell on shell in front of thier retreating column while Hooker pitched into their rear, such a scampering you never saw—for two miles we pitched the shells into them—Gen.l Richardson (the "Old Farmer"—"fighting Isreal" as the boys calls him)[60] called out "Col. give three cheers to help them along" and we gave it with a will—it looked at one time as though the whole line would be engaged—we were ready and eager for it—it is a singular sensation for armed men to stand quietly by and see their comrads fighting—they chafe like unbroken horses, it is more exciting than being actualy engaged in it—I do not think that they will try *that* point again very soon. Three days ago they drove in the Pickets in front of our redoubt (we supposed at the time for the same purpose) but we were so quick on them with our Grape that we killed a whole company before they had time to form—they have not been near *us* since—they have now tried nearly every point on our lines with the same result—we have been ready for them every time, and no wonder that we are, for scarce a night passes but we are in line two or five times and always in line from half past 2 o'clock in the morning until 8 o'clock (one half eating their breakfast at a time) and one half of the regiment sleeping at their stack of arms all night—so you may see that *we* too do not care how soon this fight comes off, for until it does "there is no rest for the wicked" at least we who are in the "1st Line."

Geo. McLaughlin[61] was to see me yesterday and I expect Bald. Hufty here this afternoon, they are about a mile in the rear of us—I would like to go and see them all (Meeves &c.) but can not leave the regiment for 5 minutes so uncertain are the events that surround us.

Give my kisses to our little warbler and love to the boys[.]

Your
Charly

P.S. The Paymaster—blast him! has not made his appearance yet—inclosed you will find $5.00 give the boys whatever you deem proper for Fire Crackers—Fire works &c. let them have the “Glorious 4th” as usual, I may spend mine under arms but they at least can be “gay and happy” upon that day[.]

3

"My indignation is great"

August 28, 1862–November 22, 1862

IN FACT, Johnson did not spend the Fourth of July "under arms" but rather recovering from wounds he received at the battle of Charles River Crossroads on the last day of June 1862. He was evacuated to the U.S. Army General Hospital in Annapolis, granted a medical furlough, and returned home to Camden to be nursed by his wife. He returned to the regiment before the end of the summer but apparently still suffered from the effects of his wounds and of the various illnesses he'd contracted while on the Peninsula.

The Eighty-first did not participate in the Battle of Second Bull Run, but it did fight at Antietam at the Sunken Road, or "Bloody Lane." During the battle, Colonel Johnson was listed as "absent, sick," presumably still suffering from either his wounds, his illness, or both. He rejoined the regiment for its move to Harpers Ferry. The Eighty-first left this post on October 29, 1862, marching first to Charles Town, Virginia, then to Warrenton.[1] In the meantime, Johnson's hero General George B. McClellan was relieved of his command and replaced by General Ambrose E. Burnside. The army's morale plunged, desertions climbed, and Charles Johnson himself seemed greatly depressed.

49

Washington City
Aug. 28/62

Dear Mary,

I did not leave Philad. until 12 P.M. (a screw loose on the road some where) and consequently we missed the connection at Baltimore and did not arrive here until 10 o'clock instead of 6 o'clock. Harry, Jim, Campion, Dutton, Cap. Wilson and a host of others were at the depot to start me off.

Capt. Cunningham is now sitting near me (I met him on the street here) he is well.

I meet Maxwell, Capt. Ware and a number of others here that I am acquainted with—it was almost like goin into Camden, there were so many "familiar faces" scattered "around loose."

The War Department can not give me any information as to the where abouts of the regiment, but, say that McCellan & staff were at Alexander last night, so I shall go down there immediately. I rather expect that the 81st is at Alexandria.[2]

I will write at the next point—how did you pass the night? God bless! you all; I did not sleep a moment for thinking of you all, however I expect that I will to-night as I feel tired out; it is so infurnal hot that the water is dropping down on the table from my face while I write.

Give my love to all, the boys especialy and kiss that little prattler for me—I can feel her tender little arms around my neck yet.

Excuse the brevity (as well as the writing, for my hand shakes) of this and I will make up for it at some future time.

Yours
Charley

50

Bivouac on the
Frederick City Road
Sept = 10/62

Dear Mary,

I sit down at sun rise to write to you trusting to circumstances to get it mailed. I would like to write as regular as formaly but I can not and if I could it would be impossable for me to send it; however, I shall not omit an opportunity to communicate with you.

Yours of the 5th inst. came to hand a day or two since—I am glad that you made inquiry in reference to the furniture, for the man that would chizle his father would stick a friend—you are mistaken as to the cause of the loss of the Desk and Regimental papers at Centreville, it was not on account of the "hurry," but for want of transportation. The facts are these; we left Arlington Hights in light marching order and proceeded direct to Centreville, in the mean time the Ambulance train was loaded at Camp California to proceed to Arlington Hights, but when they arrived at Alexandria they were by *some one* ordered direct to Centreville and there dumped our baggage down, and when we were ordered to "skedaddle" there were no wagons to take it back and of course we were compelled to leave it behind—at the time the retreat was ordered our regiment was in the woods on the front line and half a mile from our baggage, and we would have lost all if I had not assumed the responsibility and sent for the officers baggage before I moved—had I been near the spot I would have contrived some plan to have saved *all* my papers—we secured a spare horse and put one of the pack saddles (that I got at Manassas) on him and now carry the majors and my valice on him—all the Quarter Masters papers were left behind also, which has saved George considerable trouble as *that* effectualy "squares his accounts."[3]

I slept one night within seven miles of Williams, but our supreme Mogule (Gen.l Caldwell)[4] refused me permission to go out of camp, for which I have twice remembered him by refusing *him* favours—we have it now "pull Dick, pull Devil"—darn [h]is infurnal cowardly soul, I will pay him in full with interest before I have done with him.

I suppose the *cause* of his refusal was because I raised "old Ned" with him on account of the men not being as well cared for as in the other Brigades—we have no transportation (not a single wagon) and it is nothing unusual for the men to go a day and a day and a half *with out bread,* and that within 20 miles of Washington City, and I would not stand it—*after* I had raised a row the other Colonels *followed* suit.

Mr. McLuster was here last night and if he calls here to-day I will send this by him—I forwarded a letter to you on the 8th inst. to be mailed by Tom. McKeen at Washington, which I suppose you received.[5]

The Major and I intend to purchase a light wagon to carry our traps in and then the department may go to thunder, as it is now we have to ruff it to the full extent, and these morning fogs and night dews are any thing but plesant, perticulary with a scorching mid-day sun—I have had an attack of the Neuralgia—I would not have mentioned it, but you were deturmined to know how I am *all* the time—however it has not returned and I suppose *that* is the last of it.

Tell Capt. Wilson that I can not get his recall at present as the Department will not go to the trouble to square his accounts and a few weeks after square that of his successor, so he will be compelled to abide his time.

Give my love to the boys (how is Joe? and does Willie have any better opinion of his Pop than he had when I left?) and my kisses to Clara.

Yr[.]
Charly

P.S. Tell Lees that *now* is the time for the sutlers as we move constantly and they are the only dependence and *they* are not half the [time] here, a good active one with the proper kind of goods can and does sell out a wagon load in half a day at his own prices.

[P.]P.S. Yours of the 8th just received—"cheer up" the next blow will settle the war in Maryland, we are waiting for them to get all over the Potomac that they like—they will not get back in a hurry—William is *not* near the point of attack and is getting farther off every day, as we are marching from his locality to Frederick City—he is safe[.][6]

51

Bolivar Hights
Oct. 22/62

Dear Mary,

We have just returned from our advance guard and as the General remarked that I was "destined to commence it rough," for it rained the entire night and blowed!—Jeruselem! it was out of the question to keep a blanket around one—however we got through with it and are back again with the prospects of a fine night except—cold—cold—cold—this will be a glorious spot to freeze salt mackrel this winter; if the present is any criterion.

I have any quantity of work before me, as both Gen.ls Hancock and Caldwell have entered complaints of the condition of the regiment as to the state of their arms, desipline &c. &c. &c. &c. &c. Gods! a long string—&c &c. &c &c. hem! &c. &c. &c. again and over again—it certanly does not speak *very* well for "our Harry's"[7] ability as a commander—it was my first introduction to Gen.l Hancock[8] and not a very pleasing one, although he complimented me *personaly* upon my reputation as an officer and my reputed ability to make "things all right again[.]"

The 1st assistant Surgeon (Beshler)[9] is charged with neglecting the sick and I have received orders to night to place him under arrest; which I have done[.]

Capt. Harkness and his brother-in-law (Lieut. Morton) and Lieut. Rieber have presented thier resignations—cause—the appointment of Capt. Lee to the Majority; although they assined other reasons for it—the Gen.l intends to return them "not accepted."[10] Capt. Alexander also presented his resignation, but his is valid as he has the dropsie and is swolen to such an extent that he can not ware his cloths or get his shoes on.[11]

By a recient order of the Sec.y of War, volunteers in Infantry can be transfered to the regular service in Artillery, and during my absence some twenty-five or thirty of my men have went in to it, and as they accept none but the most able bodied men the loss is great.

So you see taken it all in all we are a "happy family" and I have a happy time ahead of me—God forgive me if I should do any extra amount of "cussing," but it is enough to make Job himself abjure his faith. Thank God! that I have a disposition calculated to meet obsticles, for what would make most men sit down in dispair only moves me to greater action, and I have quietly yet emphaticaly notified the company commanders of my determination to set every thing right from a "shoe string up" and that the first one that fails to co-opperate with me I will Court Martial him immediately—to-day I put all hands through such a "course of sprouts" that they came to the conclusion that it was "look out boys the Colonel has his dander up and means some thing certain[.]"

The men are counting the *hours* as to when the Sutler may be expected; in fact they have lost sight of the absence of the Paymaster in the anxious expectation of the Sutler[.]

"Chunk" appears to think that her days are numbered as all the regimental positions are being filled by Philadelphians—I think so too[.][12]

George has subsided (from all apperance) in a deturmination to quietly await his fate[.]

As this letter will be neither pleasing or interesting to you, and as I have not any thing to write except in the above strain I think that I had best close.

To-morrow we are to have a review of our Brigade by Gen.l Hancock and I shall retire to-night with the full expectation of catching "little perticular h—hem! from him again—I wish that he had decided to let it remain for a few days yet until I had an opportunity to fix things up—well! "let her come[.]"

Give my kisses to our little darling and my love to the boys—do not forget to inform me as to how they get along with their drawing. That your slumbers may be light and your dreams happy is the wish of your

Charley

P.S. I wrote to you on Monday night the 20th inst[.]

52

Bolivar Hights
Oct. 28/62

Dear Mary,

Tuesday night—mail in—and "no letter for you Colonel," well patience—Job had it and as he was not such great "shakes" I do not see why I can not have it to—so patience—patience, say I.

We are held here from day to day by first one rumor of moving, next of another of staying—each with just sufficient apparent authority that we remain in perfect "status quo" and suffer the numerous inconveniences constantly arising from improper quarters &c. &c. what! they intend to do with us, I do not know, but sincearly wish that they would decide upon some thing or else we will have the melancholy pleasure of filling the Bolivar Cemi[t]ary, for it is no unusual thing to see four and five graves opened at once—the low solemn beat of the music and quick report of musketry (as they bury one after the other) is sounding from sun-rise until sun-set. It could not be other wise when men (by thousands) sleep upon the frozen ground with a single blanket and no other shelter than a piece of canvass open at both ends; the rain of the last two days sweeping through from end to end as though an entry; even the officers not having any shelter except a few old, tattered and worn tents that they picked up from time to time, and they so crowded that they have not room to move from one side to another to avoid the water that flows in the various holes. Yesterday we had an inspection of camp equipage which resulted in a return of two—*two* servisable tents in the *entire* regiment.

We are all anxiously waiting for "some thing to turn up"—when once located for the winter we can *build* ourselves comfortable quarters. The men have volunteered to build me a perfect log house—now there is the Lieut. Col. Adj., myself and regimental office (four quarters) in one old tent without any fly, two holes in the topp and a half of a door or front—no fire or place for it—for two days Harry and Swain[13] have been wraped in thier blankets to keep warm—as for myself you know I always prospered and fattened on cold weather and I do so now as I weighed 145½ pounds to-day and eat like a hog[.]

Inclosed is a Photo of the adjutant, a very good likeness—I would like a list of all that you have at home as I may have an opportunity this winter to compleat it—at least of those who are still living—alas! how few.

Lees left here yesterday for Baltimore to telegraph for a Sutler's tent—the idea of sleeping in these quarters or his wagon in such weather compleatly frightens him; he was to have returned to-day but did not, it may be that he is waiting for his goods or that he prefers the comfortable living of a city to that of Bolivar Hights; I think that he was rather astonished at *our* mode of living; it being a "leetle" more rough than he anticipated[.]

I received a note from the Paymaster yesterday stating that he would not be here until after the first of the month, and then he would pay us for 4 months if we had our Rolls ready—well, we *will* be ready for *him* before he is for us.

I am living on "tick" but that is of no account, I only feel solicitous about you, known that you had nothing when I left, *how* are you getting on? When the *pay does* arrive it will be several hundred dollars, but that is like "waite horse until grass grows"—I can only say to you and end my letter as I began—patience—patience[.]

Give my kisses to Clara (bless her) and my love to the boys—how I long to hear from you and them[.]

Your
Charley

P.S. I have been reading this letter over—the chyrography is bad, but my fingers are so infurnaly cold and cramped that I can not feel the pen—when I get my comfortable quarters I will make amends[.]

53

Warrington
Fauquier County
Va.
Nov. 10/62

Dear Mary,

This day and this place has witnessed one of the most imposing sights that mortal man ever beheld—George B. McClellan has left us—the mighty has departed—the hero is gone—*our* leader has been taken from us—our heart strings are snap[p]ed—our vitality—our life—our existance is paralized—we stand this day a huge mass of mourning mortality. Oh! what a sight! as we stood this day deployed in masses, thousands upon thousands of veterans—men whose sinues were hardened by toil—whose skins were bronzed by exposure, whose finer sensibilities were blunted by sights of carnage—there they stood (stretching as far as the eye could reach) waiting to take a last sad look upon him who had led them through victory, through defeat; through plenty and through privations—there they stood surrounded with all the "glitter and pomp of circumstantial war"—with gaudy uniforms and mournful thoughts—with "bristling bayonets" and breaking hearts—with sparkling eyes at the sight of one they loved and compressed lips and suppressed breathings of revenge for his enemies—as he rode through the lines not a word, not a murmer; sad and solemn were the beating hearts, moist were the eye and wet was many a sunburnt cheek—a funeral obsequies—until the over wrought heart could stand it no longer—military discipline *must* be broken, and as though each man had given away at the same instant, they sent up a shout—those thousands of hoarse voices—that reached the very dome of heaven and echoed back to earth again—woods and plains, valleys and mountains took up that shout and like the roar of an avalanch it went from craig to craig—then *all* was still, still as death, naught was heard but the suppressed commands of the colonels as they slowly marched their battalions to their respective quarters and quitely "broke ranks." The men then rushed—it would have been useless to have attempted to stop them, if desired—rushed to the spot where he was—they clung to his hands, they clasped his legs, they stop[p]ed his horse and in the frenzy of the moment they hurled their caps in the air and surrounded him in their bare heads—God! it was a sight witnessed but once in an age—but once in a centuary—I have seen many that are stamped indellabely upon my mind, but this day will out live them all.

Who our leader is to be the wise, the profound, the segacious, the *learned* "powers that be" have not yet condescended to inform us, we only know that the army of the Potomac is divided in three great corps, the 1st under Hooker, the 2nd (ours and Franklin's) under Sumner, the 3rd under Burnsides,[14] with (I believe) the latter as temporary commander of the whole—alas! my countrymen what a fall was there!"[15]—deep and loud are the curses that have ascended from this place to-day—our pride, our spirit is broken, our ambition dampened, glory vanished—God! I can not write—I must join the group of officers around the Camp fire and help them to curse the Catalines whose political intrigues has produced this result—oh! there *will* be a day of reckoning and then by heavens *our* time will come—delay but sweetens revenge.[16]

Oct. 11/62[17]

Dear Mary,

Well, the "jig is up" and Gen.l Burnsides is our commander (of the Army of the Potomac) a good soldier but not *our* General—he may be the equal, but has not *now* the confidence of the soldiers that McClellan had—threatened resignations are the order of the day, although the government will not accept them for such causes, yet they show the feeling of the army[.]

Lees talks of leaving here to-morrow (having sold out in two days) and will probabily reach Camden—I shall send this by him either to deliver in person or mail according to circumstances[.]

George appears considerably down on account (I think) of not hearing anything of his discharge, he goes moping around as though he had lost every friend in the world—do not tell Harriet as it would not help matters any here and only make it worse at home[.]

Give my kisses to Clara—bless her—and love to the boys[.]

Your
Charley

P.S. the *indications* are that we will leave here to-morrow morning, although we ("small fry") have not received any orders yet. I wrote to you on the 9th inst.—have not received any since yours of the 31st ult. except that of the 4th inst. from Lees[.]

54

Bivouac Near
Falmouth,
Va.
Nov. 17/62

Dear Mary,

Here we are within a mile or two of the Rappahannock River and about three miles from Fredericksburg, we have done some tall marching since Lees left us.

We left Warrenton on the 15th inst. and reached here to-day at 12½ o'clock P.M.—the rebs had a battery on the other side of the river (at the ford) and opened upon us, but were soon silenced by Pettits Guns[18] who opened upon them and made it so hot that they left their stand [of guns] and skedadled, but I suppose will steel them off to-night or reinforce them—we were ordered into action just now, but before we started the order was countermanded and I suppose that to-morrow will see a battle—in fact the men were too tired to fight with spirit as we marched 13 miles to-day and 17 miles yesterday and have had but one meal to-day, that was [?] [?] ½ o'clock this morning—'tis now [?] P.M.—we are having Virginia living again—I have not had meat for two days and the hard crackers are those which were originaly ship[p]ed to the Peninsular and back and are actualy full of Bugs and white worms simlar to maggots, except that they have black heads—it is horrable to contemplate, but hunger and costume can make one use[d] to almost any thing and we actualy eat them with a full knowledge that they are there; but it can only be done by biting into them and chewing away without looking at them—I am getting tired of this life and begin to feel as if I would like to *live* and *be* a *white man* once more—

I wrote to you on the night of the 14th inst. but when the men packed our things the next day at day-light they put my letter in one of the books—it is yet in the wagon, if I get at it before I have an opportunity to mail this I will send the two togeather.

I have not received any letter from you since yours of the 31st of October (except that brought by Lees) and feel exceedingly like looking in the face of one again.

Our cook (who is a contraband that Dutton got at Mannassas last March and been with us ever since) found himself last night on the farm of his wife's master and got a pass from me to visit her—alas! for human expectations—he found that she also had run away, taken her two children with her—the poor fellow was quite chop[?] fallen when he came back, but to-day while on the march he assertained from some slaves (who appeared to be posted) that they were safe in Alexandria—*that* consoled him for he now feels that they are *free* and he lives in the hopes that we may reach that place again.

Camp at Falmouth
Nov. 19/62

Dear Mary,

We moved to this place yesterday at day-light amidst a pelting rain which is continuing to-day—a regular north-eastern.

We now are opposite to the rebels, each in sight of the other, the Rappahannock River dividing the two armies. The prospect is that we will remain here for a day or two as we *must* build a bridge (pontoon or otherwise) before we can advance any farther, in the mean time we are being reinforced and they are being reinforced also, judging from the frequent arrival of cars at Fredericksburg, at least we suppose so by the whistling of the locomotives.

"New masters make new laws" and we have divisions and Grand divisions of the old Army of the Potomac—for instance we are the 1st Brigade (Gen.l Caldwell) 1st division (Gen.l Hancock) 2nd Corps de Armee (Gen.l Couch) 1st Grand Division, Army of the Potomac (Gen.l Sumner) with Gen.l Burnsides Commander in Chief.

Your letters, however, may be directed as usual, except, Hancocks division, instead of Richardson's.

There is not any mails to or from this place for the present, so I do not know when this will reach you, but I shall continue writing as usual and when they are opened (the mail routes) you will have something to read, even if it *is* stale.

Give my kisses to Clara and love to the boys—God bless you all! how I long to hear from you.

Your
Charley

P.S. Flour here is $20.00 per barrel, chickens $1.50 per pair, Butter $1.50[?] per pound and everything in proportion, Potatoes [?] per bushel[.]

55

[undated]

Mary,

Not having any thing to do, it raining too hard to go out and sit by the fire and too early to go to bed—i.e. to roll up in my blanket—I tak[e] up my pen to while away a few moments although I have not any thing to write about.

I had just written the above paragraph when I was asked if I "would like to see a paper three days old"—it is needless to say that down went the pen—it was the only paper (with *one* exception) that I have seen since I left Bolivar Hights—the 29th of last month.

George appears considerably down in spirits he says that he does "not care which comes first, the papers or the pay master" for he will leave with the arrival of either one; if the papers comes he will not wait for the Pay Master, and if the Pay Master comes first he will not wait for the papers—I hope that he will not take the latter course for it will be a clear case of *desertion* and he will be liable to be arrested for the same at any time no matter how *remote.*

Speaking of the Paymasters remindes me of a fact which came to light today—the General (Caldwell) had mislaid our Pay Rolls at the time he sent the others of the Brigade to Washington and to-day we found it out—although he said yesterday in my quarters that he "sent them off some time since"—Falstaff says "I love a liar" and this cowardly wretch, that holds a command, would have suited him (Falstaff) exactly—he is such a contemptable, mean, low, sneaking liar that not a man under him has a particle of confidence in the most unimportant word that he utters. We are endevouring now to get them off before the Pay Master starts, for fear that he (the Pay Master) may be on his road here while the Rolls are on their road there and then we would be compelled to wait another pay day for our funds—damn him (excuse me Mary but my indignation is great—both on account of myself and the injustice to the men) if I had my way I would whip him through the Camp. Now he is endevouring, with the dastardly spirit that is predominant in his character, to put the blame upon some of his subordinates but I hold him to his remarks in my quarters yesterday, which fortunatly was made in the presence of two witnesses—I have threatened to make complaint to Gen.l Hancock, if the regiment suffers by his neglect, and the craven is fightened out of his wits, for like all liars, all cowards, he stands in holy dread of his superiors, and he knows (as we *all* do) that Hancock has a contemptable opinion of his General-ship.

As my candle (the last that we have with us) is getting short, I will close for to-night.

Nov. 21/62

Rain—rain, more rain—this is the fourth day that it has rained incessantly—last night it poured—actualy came in torrents—the water came through our old tent as if we had not any thing between us and the heavens and yet *we* were better off than the men—God help them! To add to the misery of the present occasion we have not had a cracker since yesterday afternoon—it shows the differences between Generals—McClellan would *not* move faster than his supplies—some others move away *from theirs*—we marched 40 miles in three days and *now* have been five days waiting (like Micabaw) for "some thing to turn up" with nearly 25 miles of wagon route to bring our supplies—oh! "most wise, grave and potent seniors" at the White House, who would not be satisfied with any thing less than an "onward movement[.]"

Nov. 22/62

I have just been informed that a mail will leave immediately—we have not received any yet since we have been here[.]

Give my kisses to Clara and love to the boys[.]

Yrs[,]
Charley

Colonel Charles F. Johnson with his sword. The sword was paid for and presented to him by "the Officers and Privates of the 81st Reg." Courtesy of Mrs. Grace Johnson Lynch.

Mary Johnson and daughter Clara. Courtesy of Lucille and Richard Sicard.

The Johnson twins, Joseph and William. Charles Johnson may well have carried a copy of this tintype, along with the one above of Mary and daughter Clara, during his military service. Courtesy Lucille and Richard Sicard.

Clara Johnson, at age five in 1863. Courtesy of Mrs. Grace Johnson Lynch.

Bridge over the Chicahominy River on Mechanicsville Road, taken sometime in the spring or summer of 1862. One of the primary tasks of the Eighty-first Pennsylvania was the construction of such bridges, providing a link between the two halves of McClellan's army separated by the rain-swollen river. Library of Congress, Photographs and Prints Division, LC-B811-0913.

Battery B of the First New York Light Artillery, under the command of Captain Rufus D. Pettit, at Fort Richardson in the vicinity of Fair Oaks, Virginia, June 1862. "Pettit's guns" are mentioned in Johnson's description of a skirmish in November 1862. Library of Congress, Photographs and Prints Division, LC-B815-0476.

Union field hospital at Savage Station, Virginia, during the Seven Days' Battles in June 1862. This photograph is listed as having been "created/published" on June 30, 1862, the day Johnson was wounded. He was very likely initially treated at this field hospital or one similar to it. Such hospitals were generally improvised in farmhouses, barns, or even open fields. Casualties here appear to be waiting in the dirt of a farmer's backyard to be treated in one of the nearby tents. Library of Congress, Photographs and Prints Division, LC-B811-0491.

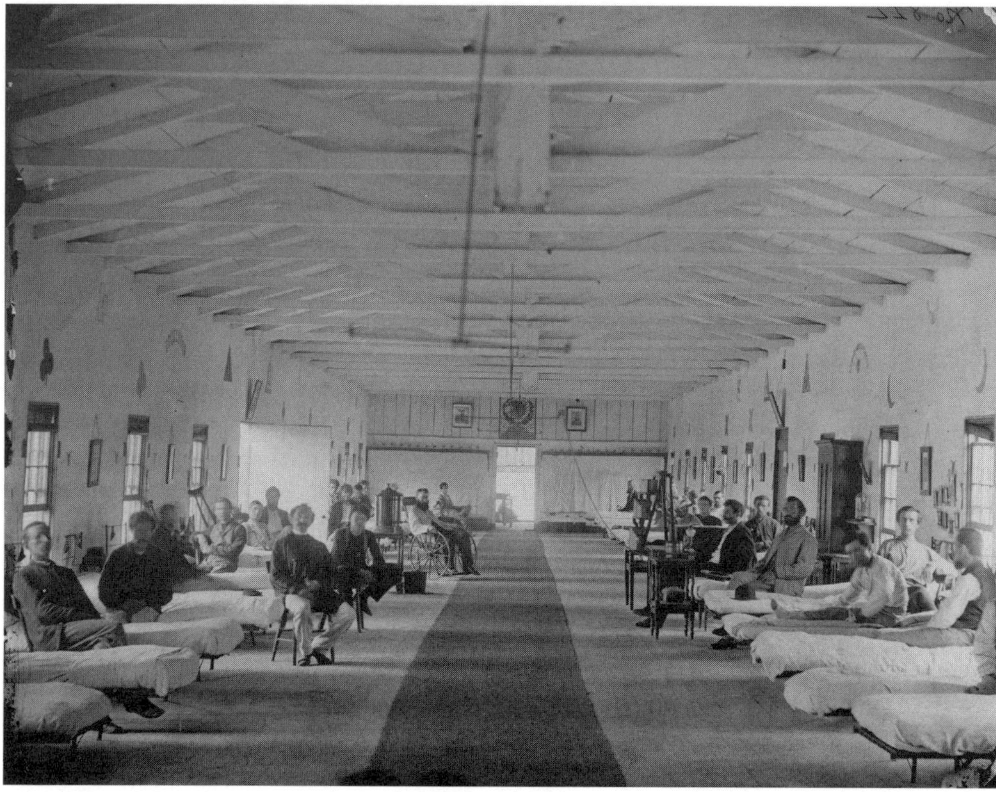

Patients in Ward K of the Armory Square Hospital, in Washington D.C. Civil War hospitals were noted for their overcrowding and lack of sanitation, but this one seems to have been cleaned up for the camera. Library of Congress, Photographs and Prints Division, LC-B817-7822.

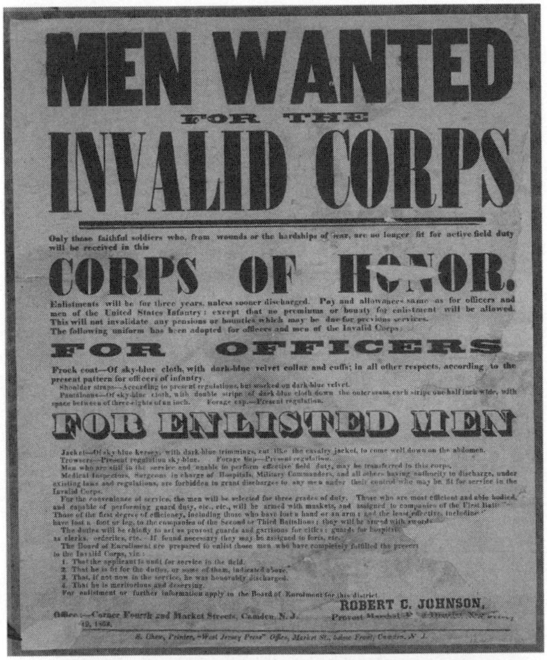

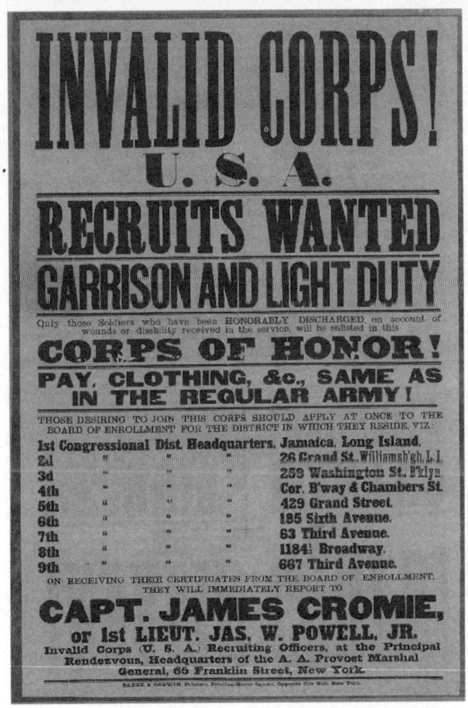

Early recruiting posters for the Invalid Corps. The army may have been sincere in its promise of "garrison and light duty," but the "clothing" of the newly created Corps was initially not the "same as in the regular army." The poster titled "Men Wanted for the Invalid Corps" was published in Camden, New Jersey, in the spring of 1863, and was likely seen by Colonel Johnson. Collection of the New-York Historical Society.

A rebel propaganda etching titled "Jamison's jayhawkers," purporting to show atrocities being committed by the Union's Seventh Kansas Regiment. Johnson described similar atrocities committed by rebel guerrillas in Kansas and Missouri, in a bitter internecine war where "extermination is the cry." Collection of the New-York Historical Society.

Company B of the Tenth Regiment of the Veteran Reserve Corps (formerly the Invalid Corps), April 1865, Washington, D.C. By this time the War Department had relented in its campaign to make members of the VRC wear special uniforms, and these men appear in standard Union army gear. Library of Congress, Photographs and Prints Division, LC-B817-7677.

The Union depot at White House Landing during the Peninsula Campaign of 1862. Two years later Johnson would command a mixed brigade at this post and repulse an attack by rebel raiders. It was during this engagement that Johnson urged a courier to "Tell the General my men are cripples, and they can't run." Library of Congress, Photographs and Prints Division, LC-B811-2485.

Drum Corps of the Tenth Veteran Reserve Corps "at leisure" in Washington. Library of Congress, Photographs and Prints Division, LC-B817-7688.

The Old Capitol Prison, at the corner of 1st and A Streets, NE, in Washington D.C., used to house Confederate POWs, political prisoners, and suspected spies. Members of Johnson's 18th Veteran Reserve Corps regiment were also assigned as guards to the prison, where, in 1865, the members of the Lincoln assassination conspiracy were held. Library of Congress, Photographs and Prints Division, LC-B815-1019.

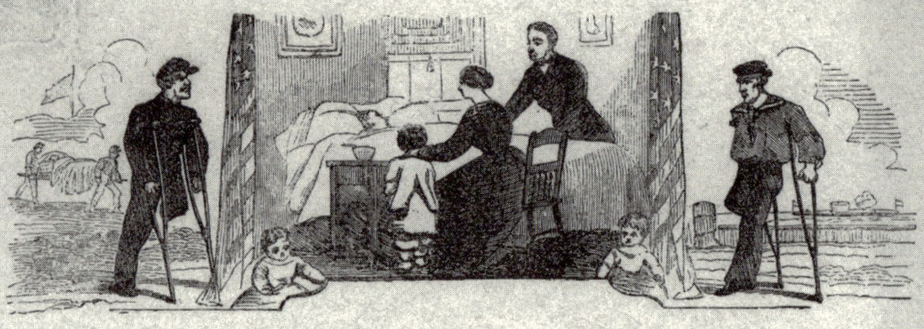

SOLDIERS HOME,

Race and Crown Streets, Philadelphia.

The Lady Managers of the Soldiers Home intend holding a Fair for the benefit of the Institution, and appeal to their fellow citizens for aid. They have secured the Academy of Music for the last week in October, and the first week in November next, and will have the entire house properly fitted up to accommodate all who are willing to aid them in their efforts to secure a permanent Home for the disabled Union Soldier.

The war is over. Peace once more blesses our beloved land. Can we, as Americans, forget the vast debt we owe to the brave spirits who periled life and limb, and have fought so bravely for our country, many of whom have lost health and limbs in the service, and are thereby prevented from earning for themselves an honest livelihood? Is it right that such men should be compelled to beg, or seek an asylum in our Almshouses, as paupers?

The Managers of the Soldiers Home determined, long since, to do what they could to render aid and comfort to this deserving class, and their modest Home has been the means of cheering the heart, and adding to the comfort of hundreds of our suffering defenders.

Finding their "Home" entirely too small to accommodate the many applicants now seeking admission, they make this appeal, in entire confidence, to those who have responded so promptly and cheerfully to all appeals made on behalf of our Soldiers since the war began.

The liberality of our PHILADELPHIA FIREMEN is proverbial, and the Committee take this method of presenting the claims of the Home to the various Companies, being fully satisfied that it is only necessary to let them know their aid is needed, to ensure its being liberally rendered.

Will you please take measures to interest your friends in behalf of this worthy Institution? The Fire Department was very successful at the Sanitary Fair, and it is desirable it should be so at this.

The "SOLDIERS HOME" has been in successful operation for about two years, and can be visited daily, Sundays excepted, between 9 A M. and 6 P. M., Corner of Race and Crown streets, Philadelphia. CALL AND SEE IT.

Donations of money, or of goods, suitable for the Fair, may be sent to the "Chairman of Fire Department of Fair."

MRS. R. P. KING, No. 522 Spruce Street.

Philadelphia, September, 1865.

A poster for the Soldiers Home in Philadelphia, published in September 1865. Library of Congress, Printed Ephemera Collection, Portfolio 159, Folder 5.

The Soldiers Home in Washington, D.C., sometime between 1880 and 1897. Institutions such as this would house tens of thousands of veterans disabled during the Civil War. Library of Congress, Photographs and Prints Division, LC-D4-4420.

Dining hall in the Soldiers Home in Hampton, Virginia, sometime between 1900 and 1906. Library of Congress, Photographs and Prints Division, LC-D428-823.

"Give my love to the boys and kisses to Clara, they all [the men at the post] have fell in love with her likeness." Clara Johnson, perhaps one of the likenesses carried by Charles Johnson during the war. Courtesy of Mrs. Grace Johnson Lynch.

4

"In the office we term them the '*Infidel* Corps' and me the 'Infidel Major'"

June 14, 1863–August 4, 1863

JOHNSON, still suffering from his wounds, resigned his commission at the end of November and retired to his home in Camden. Not content to sit out the rest of the war, Johnson chaired a meeting of the Philadelphia Committee of Retired Officers. This group, together with the Union League of Philadelphia, called for the creation of "another Arm of the Service known at first as the Invalid Corps."[1] The unit came into being in late spring 1863, and Johnson immediately requested another commission.

On June 10, 1863, the *Philadelphia Daily Evening Bulletin* reported that "Colonel Charles F. Johnson, late of the gallant eighty-first P.V. has been appointed a Major in the Invalid Corps. Colonel Johnson served in the Eighty-first through the campaigns in front of Washington and on the Peninsula, and was wounded while bravely fighting during the seven day's battles between the Chicahominy and James Rivers. He is as brave as a lion and a thoroughly competent leader, and we know that while his severe injuries prevent his going into the field actively, that he will be glad to serve his country in the Invalid Corps. No better appointment could be made."[2]

56

Neil House
Columbus
Ohio
June 14/63

Dear Mary,

Here I am safe (if not sound) without known what in the name of common sence to do with myself today. I suppose that I may as well give you my route. I left Phila. at 10½ P.M. the 11 inst. stop[p]ed at Altoona the next morning at 8 o'clock for 15 minutes for breakfast, and arrived at Pittsburg at 1 o'clock (356 miles) stop[p]ed 30 minutes, took dinner and took passage on the Pittsburg, Fort Wayne & Chicago R.R. to Crestline (189 miles) Ohio, stopping at Alliance for 15 minutes at 5 o'clock, for supper and arrived at Crestline at 8 o'clock, stopped 15 minutes and took passage on the Cleveland, Columbus & Cincinnatti R.R. for this place (59 miles) and arrived at 11½ o'clock last night, having travelled 604 miles. I was as comfortable as could be under the circumstances as I managed to keep my feet in an extra seet most of the time—this new ointment effectualy stops the itching whenever applied, and I shall remain in my room most of the day to give them as much rest as possable. I should here mention that there is a shorter route (but consumes more time) by the way of the Pittsburg, Columbus & Cincinnatti R.R. saving some 90 miles, but there is no connection and passangers must lay over in Pittsburg 12 hours, not reaching here until the following night—so I think the long route the best as it saves *nearly a day*.

I jumped into an omnibus last night and told the driver to take me to a hotel, not caring which, he brought me here, which is all correct as Col. Parrot is stopping here also.[3] I meet him this morning at breakfast and reported myself—he has not received anything from Washington concerning me, and did not know anything outside of my order which I presented to him, but says that he is glad that I am here as there is plenty to do—I am to call at his office in the State House (opposite the hotel) to-morrow morning—I saw him but a few moments—he is a light complected man, about Joe. Hufty's height, not quite so stoute, and about my age I should suppose—our interview was so brief and conversation so general that I am not able to form any idea of the man, either his intelectual or business capacity—however to-morrow will settle me—I have an invitation to call on him at his rooms any time to-day, which I may or may not accept. I intend to converse with several of the guests of the house in reference to him to-day, and find out if possable his general reputation—if I fail to pump them it will be the first time in my life.

Of course until my instructions arrive I can not tell anything about my life here—I have fully made up my mind to get a private boarding house if I am to be located at this place—where they do not have nigger *servants* for they are insorrably impudent.[4]

Give my love to the boys and many kisses to our darling[.]

Your
Charley

P.S. I forgot to say that the Col. does not ware a uniform—not the least insigna to indicate a military man.

I will write again to-morrow night so do not answer this[.]

57

Neil House
Columbus
Ohio
Sunday afternoon

Dear Mary,

I start this second letter to-day although I shall not end it until to-morrow, but the fact is, I have not "any thing else to do" and I truely feel like "a stranger amidst a throng"—I could quote poetry but I will not—

I have had another interview with my "Superior Officer" and have formed "an opinion as is an opinion," but I do not intend to state it just yet, for fear that I shall be compelled to alter it immediately—I shall waite until I get to *work* under him.

This morning I kept away from him and as I did not go to him, *he* came to *me* and we had a talk of three hours—"my goodness what were you talking about all that time," say you—well, I will tell you[.]

First on business—which ended thus—after getting my ideas on the various points, he remarked that to-morrow morning he would transfer *all* orders &c. in reference to the Invalid Corps in his possession over to me and give me the charge of the entire state, unless the government should designate something [page torn] in my instructions to alter the same—office hours from 9 o'clock A.M. until that days business is finished, be it 12 o'clock at noon or 12 at night, each day must be finished—to use his words "have the table cleared"—*mine* will not be much after the first week or so.

Then, I invited him to take a drink, he refused—"good," say you but it was not good, he refused to drink at the *bar,* but insisted upon goin up stairs to his room for something superior—we took a drink—we took a smoke—I offered some of my tobacco which is so superior to anything that is to be had in this town (excuse me—*city*) that he fell in love with it and I of course divided my stock.

Then we had a talk on Masonry—he is high, a "Knight Templer"—and he offered to introduce me to some promenent masons here, this conversation brought out several points to my advantage, among them an offer to introduce me to the Quartermaster Gen.l here and get me an allowance for rent of quarters (I am entitled to 4 rooms as a Major) also for wood to be consumed in said quarters—also to the Paymaster to get me commutation for horse feed &c. &c.

Then we had a talk on Odd Fellowship (he is a Past Grand) [.]

Then we had a talk on the Sons of Malta—he is one—which brought out the fact that he had passed several weeks at Beasley's Point, Cape May Co. and there became well acquainted with Dr. Cullen, Fitzgerald, and Geo. House of Camden[5]—which brought on a very general conversation as to where each of us served, who under, who we knew in the county, &c. &c. &c. &c. &c. He was the Speaker of the House of Representatives of Ohio at the time the rebellion broke out, and served in the "Army of the Cumberland," is an old acquaintance of Gen.l Howards &c. &c. and is down on the Regular Officers like thunder, was afraid first that I was one, was glad I was not—and that brought us to dinner time, when we parted—

June 15th

Well, I have been up to my eyes in business—have my pockets full of "orders," circulars, applications &c. &c. have rented a room, will furnish it to morrow and open office in due form—how long I may remain there it is impossable to tell, for if there is not other officers ordered here, I will be compelled to leave and take charge of the camp of rendezvous as we just now received orders to that effect—the Col. thinks of renting a Seminary that [is] vacant about 8 miles from here—I hope that they will send more officers here as I would much prefer office work to a command and the Col. appears disposed to retain me here if possable—however we must waite.

My feet is improving rapidly as I have not walked a mile for four days now—I cannot get my shoe on yet but it is on the back track.

I have purchased a few paper collars which I like exceedingly well; I gave 4 cents each for them—I think that they could be purchased in Philad. cheaper and I will send one on by mail before it is time to send my trunk so that you can send a 100 on which will last me nearly six months.

I will send you (at the proper time) a list of things to send in my trunk, and I will also write to day to Kelley to send my uniform to the house.

Give my love to the boys and many very many, kisses to Clara—how I miss you all.

As there is no deliveries from the Post Office here, direct your letters to

Maj. Chas. F. Johnson
Columbus,
Ohio

[tear in paper—PS Send] me the Inquirer, also a Sunday Paper—there is not a Philad. paper [in] the place, and they charge 5 cents for their little insignificant issues about the size of the Camden Journal, and *no news,* until they copy them from other papers.

58

Columbus, Ohio
June 16/63

D[ear] Mary,

I see that there is "high life below stares[?]" in Penn. again—well it was to be expected for the Rebs almost advertized it two weeks ago, and yet every thing is up side down when the time does come—how I wish we had Little Mac there to receive them again—the rumor here is that they have reached Harrisburg—query—I wonder if the State Treasuror has run to New York with the funds again.

If "the powers that be" would only take advantage of this move now and order Hooker to advance on Richmond at forced marches the rebs would get their bellies full of northern raids—but I suppose that the other course will be taken, to order him to *Washington* for *its* defence.

This state is promptly moving in the matter and collecting its forces—but I should not be surprised if the rebs were on the back track already—having done their damage leave before the back door is closed.

There is one thing that I will mention, and I only do so from well known your excitable nature—that is *keep cool—keep cool—keep cool* above all things *keep cool*!!!! from what you have told me in reference to your feelings on such a previous occasion, I would seriously, earnestly, and emphaticaly advise you to *keep cool*—do not think because they may reach Harrisburg that they are already in Camden—nor do not think even if they should reach *Lancaster* that they are at your door—rest assured that they will not get too far east to safely return, besides they could not afford to remain so high up any great length of time—it is a bold scheme and to be successful it must be *rapid*—off and on—so *keep cool*—no matter *what* reports may be rife in Philad—just quietly make up your mind *to remain at home* and abide the issue and having fully fixed your mind upon that *point* you will be astonished to find how little cause there is for any nervousness on your part.[6]

I write in this style not that *I* apprehend any danger in the least to you or your locality, but that you may not give yourself many hours of anxiety as would be the case if you paid attention to every "fart that sails upon the wind."

They can not, they *dare* not remain long or travell too far east, to expose their flank and rear to the forces in the state of New York and the North West, which would be the case if they left the mountainous regions of Pennsylvania to march on Phila—so *keep cool.*

I have not received any instructions from Washington yet and until I do, I shall not have much to attend too—for the appropreations for our Corps is so mixed up and orders so conflicting that no one appears disposed to assume any responsibility and until there is instructions more in detail, I shall not have much to do.

I walk across the street to the Capitol ask if "any orders have been received"—answered, "no," get a bach of fresh applications, look at them, put them in my pocket and walk out—after dinner go through the same performance with like result; until I have quite a formidable pile of papers waiting for action—phew! how I will sweat when the machine does start working; however, not to be caught napping I quietly arrange every document so as to go straight at it when the time does come—perhaps it is all for the best as it gives my feet plenty of rest and *that* is some compensation for being idle, but, my heavens! how the time does hang upon ones hand—days are almost weeks—it appears to me that I have been here a month.

The City is all excitement to-day as there is a State Convention to nominate a Governor for the Republican Ticket and politics with raids is all the go—I set and listen but do not participate.

Give my love to the boys and kisses to Clara—I begin to long for a letter[.]

Your
Charley

59

Columbus, Ohio
June 21/63

Dear Mary,

Yours of the 17th inst. came to hand yesterday afternoon and it looked like "an old familiar face" of by gone days.

Who is Edward C. Johnson, I can not recall him to mind. What is the object of Saml. C. Luchess visit is it to attend to the Temples?[7] I suppose that you are glad of the probable visit of Mrs. Shields. If Jim Parsons is likely to get out of employment *why* does he not "dip into" the "six months men," there must be plenty of chances for him—by-the-way, it is lucky that I secured my appointment when I did, for I know that I could not have withstood the "pressure."

And "little Clara often talks of her Papa," does she—God bless her! and her "Papa" often *thinks* of her—if you do not have her likeness taken by the time you send the trunk, be sure and send all the ambrotypes that I had with me when I was away before—oh! how I miss the "sweet communion" that I often had with them—I will *never* leave home again without all your pictures—

there is a consolation "devoutedly to be wished" in gazing upon the images of those we love.

I am sorry, very sorry that the boys are derilect in their studies; they should be ashamed of themselves—I hope that they will do better.

I will send William an answer in accordance with the tone of his.

Well, Mary, I am in my new quarters, I came here on Friday night, and thereby reduced my expenses considerably, for the hotel fare was $2.50 per day, or $17.50 per week—this is $6.00 per week and *more* accomidations. I have the front room and it is about the size that ours would be if the closet and third story stairs was included in it—the furniture consists of a cottage bedstead, beauro, washstand, a small and large table, towel rack, three cain-seat chairs and a stuffed seat rocking—nothing extravagent but comfortable.

The family of Mrs. Prester consists of a married daughter and husband and their other daughters, ages between about 6 and 14 years. They all appear like very nice folks, but as "a new broom always sweeps clean," I do not intend to form any definite opinion in regard to them. I have been informed by Lieut. Parrott that they were wealthy during the life of Mr. Preston, in fact every thing indicates that, for there is a general appearance of "decayed respectability," a kind of "light of other days is faded" about the place, as well as considerable refinement in their manners. The girls are quite musicians and are thumping the piano and singing. I made a bargin that they was all to consider me a "quite, domesticated, settled, old gentleman" and to "let me go and come as one of the family" "no fuss, no cerimony, then I would remain, if they did not I would have to go" that "my object in getting into a private family was to get as much like *home* as possable." They consented and said that was just what they wanted—we will see.

Mary, oh! Mary, (by-the-way they use that infurnal oh! here like the Marylanders)—Mary, I have made a discovery—ha! ha! ha! ah!!—he! he! he! e!!—hi! hi! hi! i!! oh! my—yes I have made a discovery—I have penetrated into the profound depths of the unknown—I have come like the sparkling bubbles to the surface with a mind filled to overflowing with a knowledge of the essence of polished society—I have discovered—hold! prepare thy self—let it not steel upon you unperceptably and

"o'come you, without your knowledge,
Like a summer cloud to the up turned gaize of mortals
Without their special wounder"[8]

Nerve thy self for the shock—prepare thy self for the fearful revalations—I have discovered—ho! ho! ho! oh!!!!—we—i.e. us—I mean the family—

ourselves—we use—"ye Gods! that controll the universe" how shall I speak it; we use (oh! out with it Charly) well, we use napkin *rings* [underlined twice]!!!!!! ergo, I have discovered their use—well, what is it? why bless you it saves *washing*—ah! ha!!—ah! ha!! ah! ha!! yes that is it—saves washing, for each one know his napkin by the ring and when he is done eating he rolls it up and shoves it in his ring—I tried the plan of putting mine into *my* ring in a pecularly way and behold! at the next meal, there it was just as I left it—I tried another kind of fold and there it was just as I left it again—grand, great magnificance, glorious—saves washing.

Mary a cockney who arrives in this country commences to write a history of "Columbia and the Columbians" before he is here 24 hours and I suppose that *I* might be excused for doing the same after having been in the place one week.

The City is on the eastern bank of a (canal I call it) they call it the Sciota *River*—the streets run at right angles like Philad. north and south, east and west, the principle streets are all about as wide as arch street, the square about the size of those at Philad. and are intersected by streets about as wide as Hamilton—the houses on all the streets, except High street (which is the business street and has a city Passenger Rail way) are built in cottage style and have yards front, back and both sides, in fact many squares contain but three or four dwellings which gives the place quite a country appearance especialy as *none* of the streets are paved—all MacAdamized—dust is plenty and I suppose mud also—there is many cottages—you might call them Mansions that occupy a whole square. The houses are all bricks, the Stores, Churches Colleges &c. being ornamented with bases, door and window sills and caps, and cornices of gray granit—there is no exceptions to this—I have not seen a public building that is not ornamented with gray granit—like the stone in Dr. Jayne's building 3rd & Chestnut. The Churches are quite numerous and *all* large, in fact there is not any in Philad. that excells them and very few that equals them in size or variety of archetecture—the Medical College is a pure gothic (brick and gray granit) all wings and recesses, towers and pinicles, turretts and gables, while the gothic is carried out the full extent, there is not a single front (or wing even) that resembles the other—we read of a building being started by the father, an addition built by the son, another by the grandson and so on through several generations, each building according to his own ideas, until it becomes a castle, well this has precisely that appearance.

The Capitol is a fine marble building rather larger than Girard College, surrmounted by a tremendious dome, and is situated in the centre of the City, on a lot about a square and a half each way; the floors, steps and railings are all of different coloured marbles, on some of the railings each seperate piece being of different kinds.

The Male gender of inhabitants has the usual appearance of Western men—solid, substantial farmer-like men, plain and somewhat uncouth—I have not seen an *exquisite* since I have been here.

The Women have a fashion, which they adhear to most religiously, of wharing these little jaunty hats, white and black, young and old, all have them—I have seen woman as old and as stout as Mother Johnson with them on—in fact in the week that I have been here, I have not seen over 50 bonnets and nearly all of them were travellers—Spanish bodices and nothing on the shoulders is the walking or out-doors costume—by having those hats, they have their hair in but two styles, viz. in nets or cut short, those that can curl them do so, those that can not has it straight and about as long as Clara's. As a general rule they dress expensive.

The Col. kindly went to Cincinnatti in my place yesterday—I was glad of it, although I would have liked to see as much as I can while out here, but just now there is two draw-backs, first my feet, next the pocket, for although my transportation would be furnished, I of course must pay my hotel bills, however, when I do get a little ahead, I shall endevour to travell a little at Uncle Sam's expence.

I sent you a letter on Friday that I wish I had not sent, as there is no use of my troubling you with my troubles; if you will only put it in the fire and imagine that I did not send it, I will be satisfied.

Another Philadelphian reported here yesterday a 1st Lieut Alex. Black[9] I do not know him.

In the top left-hand draw in the secretary is an iron *punch* send it in trunk by George, if I keep on I will get a trunk *full*—however, I either do now or *will* want them all.

I did not get the papers until I had your letter, although I inquired every day for them. I then told him that they must be there and after a hunt he found them—then he caught it in true Johnson style. They were the Inquirer of the 15th-16-17-18, the Mercury, Transcript, and Dispatch of the 14th and Democrat of the 13th eight papers in all and plenty of reading matter for to-day (Sunday)—if it had not been for them the day would have been long indeed, I feel very thankful for your kind considerations.

Well, I gess that I might as well stop.

Give my love to the boys—if they do not do better I will stop sending it to them—and Many kisses to Clara[.]

yr[.]
Charley

P.S. direct to me in care of Col. E. A. Parrott

A.A. Prov. Mar. Genl.
Columbus
Ohio

then it will be put in his box and I will be more certain of getting it[.]

60

Columbus
Ohio
June 29/63

Dear Mary,

I this day received a letter from you without date, but as there was one from Joe on the back dated 26 inst. I suppose that yours was the same.

> Hail! Thrice hail! the happy inclosure,
> "The sweet intelligence of those dear eyes,
> (Blest be the art that can immortalize;
> The Art that baffles Time's Tyrannic Claim
> To quench it,) here shines on me still the same."[10]

I have gazed, and gazed, and still gazed, and will continue to do so "from dewy morn until solemn eve" upon that picture of innocence—God bless her!

I have unwrapped it to take another look and can only say, in the fullness of my heart—God bless her!

It wants something else—it wants *all* your pictures, to compleat *my* picture gallery.

I wrote you on the 27th to call on Cassaday for my Masonic Certificate,[11] but it arrived by the next mail—I owe him $2.12 which I will forward to you soon to pay him.

I get my washing done by the Month by the woman that washes for Mrs. Preston and it is a decided improvement on the cloths.

I find that my position here is likely to be very elaborate in its details as I am the Senior Officer and hence "Commander of the Post" and as such must draw *all* the requisitions for Commissary and Quartermaster Stores, Muster all troops (i.e. Invalid Corps) for pay &c. the same as a Brig. Genl. there is a darn sight more responsibility here as Major than in the field as Colonel. Tomorrow I muster all my forces for pay—in the office we term them the "*Infidel* Corps" and me the "Infidel Major" to designate me from Major Bierce the A.A. Genl.[12]

I received a bill from Kelly to-day and he informs me that the uniform was sent home, so I shall expect the trunk soon.

You wish to know something about the threatened invasion of Ohio, well, we are getting ready—slow—slower—slowest—to-day and every day this week all places of business closes at 3 o'clock P.M. and the town (city) assembles at the Capitol to get recruits and to be recruited. I do not think that they come very fast, although nearer the Ohio river they are up and doing, but this place is eminently secessh, and nothing but the "iron hoof of war" would wake them up.

In the multiplicity of my business I have many quear (and some funny) sceans; I enclose you one sample of many espistols that I have to over haul—it was handed to me by Gov. Todd to answer.[13]

Tell Jose to continue in his determination to raise in his class and if he does not succeed this time to "never give up," but go at it with a stronger determination to succeed the next—I like the tone of his letter.

I hope that Willies sickness is only temporary.

When you send the trunk send the *key* in a letter—hereafter I shall have a duplicate, if I had have had one when I left I could have brought it with me—it is a wonder I did not think of it.

The Inquirer of the 24th and 27th came to-day.

As the Mail will close in a few minutes I must close,

Yr[.]
Charly

P.S. Do not forget my love to the Boys and many, very many kisses to Clara—*I* nearly forgot it[.]

June 30

By the time I arrived at the Post Office, the Mail had closed, so all my haste was thrown away.

Inclosed is a likeness of Maj. Bierce—the asst. adj. Genl. of the Provost Marshals—the office is getting all theirs taken—I shall do so some time hence with my uniform on.

61

[letterhead: Office A.A. Provost Marshal General of Ohio]

Columbus, Ohio, July 8 = 1863

Dear Mary,

Yours of the 5th came to hand yesterday, when I wrote to the Boys.

You think that the Coat "must be high," well it is—$40.00 for Coat, $4.50

sholder straps, total coat $44.50, pants 12.00 so I suppose they must be "fine[.]"

In reference to Clara's likeness, I think that I wrote you that I was highly pleased with it; also that the Preston's were in extacies over it, especially the children who have borrowed it time and again to show to their companions—don't you think that she looks about 8 years old? I think so—have you a *full length* of her with curles? if so send me one also.

You are right in supposing that I thought of "when we meet" on the night of the 5th in fact I thought of nothing else at that time and rehearsed my adventures to the family that night.

I have not washed my belts yet, but intend doing so next Sunday, when I can dry them while I am in my room.

The "bullet mould and other fixings" that you speak of, I do not want; as the cartradges are of the patent kind they save all that trouble, however they will do no hurt[?] here.

Your[s] of the 6th came to-day—I cannot tell yet weather I will be compelled to take command of the barracks or not, and will not be able to answer that question until every thing is settled in regard to them[.]

You acknowledge the receipt of all my letters except that of the *2nd inst*—did you get it?

My eruption appears to be leaving me rapidly—I use the Syrup (Weaver's) with religious punctuality and will continue to do so as long as it acts so favourably[.]

I am glad that Willie is improving, and hope that his appetite will return—for Heavens sake Mary don't *you* loose flesh—I would not have you thin again for a brick house.

Tell Clara that I will not forget to send her a kiss again, I do not know how I happen to do so, for I am very particular to end my letters with "love to boys" and "kiss to Clara"—tell her I will keep her "branch of Posie" on my table so that I can see it all the time.

I should say that the Key came all right. You think that I should "laugh when I see the Magnesia," well bless your soul! I expect that I will laugh at more things than *that* when I open the trunk, or else you have changed some if not considerable.

Yesterday and last night was quite a gala day here, over the fall of Vicksburg.[14]—as soon as it was confirmed all the bells in town were rung including, church bells, fire bells, hall bells, dinner bells, tea bells, cow bells, gongs &c. &c. from every house that had a bell—towards dark Cannons, guns, pistols and crackers, were fired and at night bonfires were lit at every corner, some so large (2 and 3 stories high) that the fire engines were out near them to prevent the surrounding houses burning—in fact two of them were so large that the Provost Marshal of the City ordered the steam engines to play upon them to prevent the heat from igniting the wood work of the buildings near by—every one appeared crazy—the display of Roman Candles, sky-rockets, and all kinds of fireworks exceeded that of the 4th as day does night—the air was literly filled with them flying in all directions.

The last two days has been very heavy in my department, and I can not get any assistance until the various districts are filled with Recruiting Officers as all who are ordered to report here are sent out immediately—for the Prov. Mar. Genl. of the U.S. is constantly urging us for recruits of the first class saying that they want them immediately[.]

Give my love to the boys and many kisses to Clara[.]

Hastly[,]
Charley

P.S. have you noticed that [m]y letters appear to reach their destination much sooner than th[e]y first did[?]

The Capitol is alive with the constant arrival of Volunteers under the last call—they are coming in by hundreds from all parts of the state.

62

[letterhead: Office of A.A.P.M. General for Ohio, Columbus]

July 18 = 1863

Dear Mary,

Yours of the 15th came to hand to-day signed—Polly—Polly; that is not half as sweet as Mary—

I put my slippers on and if I did not mention them, it was unintentional for I assure you that I feel proud of them as well as all other things that you do.

You "had a good look and a good talk with them"—the reb prisoners—I hope to heavens! Mary, that you too are not becoming secesh—as for me, my love for the Union is fast becoming lost in my *hate* for the south; the longer this war last[s] the more deadly do I feel towards the arch-fiends who are creating all this disaster to our country—I don't know but what, if I was able, I would go into the field again.

You "should like to whisper in that gentleman's ear that men are *all heartless*"—what is the matter, has something new turned up or is that a fling at me? if so, I do not divine the cause[.]

I do not think that you need have any fear of a riot, in resisting the draft, near you—[in] that as New York has put the authorities on their guard and any similar attempt would be likely to be crushed in the bed—here we have had three or four counties resisting the enrollment but, thank God! Col. Parrott is a man that does not stand any nonsence—when he is ordered to do a thing, he does it, wille, nille, and "though the heavens should fall" it is done, and done effectualy—every thing is fixed here and when the draft *is* ordered you may rest assured that it will be carried through if half the population of Ohio go to their graves.[15]

But we fear no trouble—if you could have seen the turn out on the Call of the Governor, who issued a call for the Militia-men to meet the supposed invasion—over 50,000 men marched into the various camps, each bringing their own blankets and cups—they came so thick and fast that the Gov. was forced to tellegraph all over the state to stop them, and was forced to send half of each company on the grounds home—this is the midst of harvest too, when hands were being paid $2.00 per day—there is no doubting of the loyalty of the "hardy yeomanry" of Ohio. There were no distinction of party—Democrats as well as Republicans—the Gov. was like the man that "drew the Elephant," he did not know what to do with it.

I have taken the half bottle of Magnesia and if it does not purify the blood, it will certainly clean the stomach for the dose to-day has given me four stools and a half—the half stool was an insain attempt to break wind without letting my breetches down—it was a "breach of confidence—however I shall continue to follow the perscription "come weal, come wo."

I received a letter to-day from Geo. Chambers who is teribaly exercised about the draft—as his brother Jim is drafte[d] in [the] 14th ward, he feels that his turn will come next and writes to me to "make my calculations" so as to remit the amount due him as early as I can—if he is not drafted, then he will not want it and I can retain it as long as I desire—I wrote to him that if he is drafted, to borrow the money and I will certainly pay it at next pay day—also if he must pay for the use of it, that I will settle for the discount—for I could not concientiously use his money for nothing while he was paying to some for his own use[.] But, as I do not fear but what his chance is as good as the many thousands who will not be called for, I do not feel uneasy about it.[16]

Give my love to the boys and kisses to Clara—you did not say in your last, how your health is[.]

Your
Charley

P.S. This Salve of Weaver's is splendid, it drys the eruption in twenty-four hours, *after* it comes to a head, and feels like ice upon a fevered brain, so cool and plesent is the sensation—I yet have the carpet slipper on[.]

On reading this over I find it full of errors—but let it go—I could not better it to-day for some how or another all day (in fact for the last two or three days) I have a kind of dread hanging over me, that I can not shake off although I try—a feeling as if something dreadful was about hapening—it is a new sensation to *me*[.]

63

[letterhead: Office of A.A.P.M. General for Ohio]

Columbus, July 23 = 1863

Dear Mary,

Yours of the 20th and the boys (with your endorsement & Florence's note) and the Inquirer of the 14th all came to hand to-day. The Inquirer of the 13th & 16th and Despatch of the 12th came yesterday—you will perceive how late they are and the irregular times that they arrive—do not send the *Inquirer* any more unless there should be something particular in it, then mark that point.

I am glad that the 10th N.J. is near home again, on John's account; but I do not think that it will be for any great length of time; I take it to be mear precautionary measure on the part of the government, and as soon as the apparent necessity has disappeared—off they go again—this is my idea—at a distance.

I am glad that you have formed some agreeable aquaintances whereby time—grim and rugged as he is—may pass more smoothly—*who* are the Process'? I remember the name but cannot *locate* them—however, it is im material, if they are agreeable to *you* I am satisified no matter *who* they are, and can thank God! that you have at least *some* enjoyment—there is nothing, Mary, like a hearty laugh now and then to break the cobwebs that dull cares constantly weaves around our hearts.

You ask about your Store bill—*do not pay it—keep the little money you have*—I can not be paid until the 1st of September and you had better hold on to *what you have.*

I received a letter to-day from George Chamber and *that* debt is all right, as he escaped the draft—he says that he is sorry that he wrote now for fear that I might suppose that he was impatient for the money.

If you get into so tight a box again as you was for heavens sake, Mary, tell me, and I will endevour to raise the wind here in some manner or another—it is true that I am in the midst of strangers but a fertile brain, indominable perserversence, and plenty of brass, can accomplish great feats, and as I possess all these to *some* extent, I know of no one who has a better right to demand thier use than my family: and even if it would be disagreeable to use said recourses under ordinary circumstances; I would rather practice them than have you want, or even feel mean before your acquaintances.

I am sorry for George Deal—did he give up the Police—and if so can he get on again? what is he doing?[17]

I have not played Chess with Mrs. Preston, because I have found a *gentleman* to play with, which is more agreeable than a lady—more so as he is deaf, which is a good quality for a chessplayer—we do not waste any time in *talking*—besides, although my boarding house is as comfortable in *every* respect as I could expect any place to be while absent from that only spot on earth—*home*! yet I do not exactly like Mrs. P.—in fact, I never *dis*-like many women, as you know—but the longer and more often that I leave home—the more faults I see in them—I know not how it is, but, I some times think that there is but *one* woman—as she *should* be—and *that* woman, is one that I call *mine*!—if the folks at the house believe *all* that I tell them they will think my wife the most perfect woman created.

I wrote you on the 18th inst. which I suppose you have received—the irregularity of our letters is my fault, which I will remidy—but, I have been endevouring to get our correspondence in some shape—so as to make each letter an answer to the last—the inquiries made and the subjects discused would be more fresh—but—as it can not be, without making a great gap in our correspondence, I give it up—for I would not be compelled to waite another five days for a letter again for a mint. Hereafter I shall write twice a week letter or no letter.

You will please give Charley Welsh[18] my respects for his kindness and when you see him again tell him that request of Florence is all "*bosh*"—"*bosh*"—for he has the very information that he asks (except the price paid and from whom purchased) and *that* the government has *never* [underlined twice] asked for before—as for the other part of his note; he has the certificates of my superior officers (as well as my own) on file, making the statements that he now requires—however I shall write to him although (I now feel that he is only playing with me) and comply with his demands—if that *was* the cause of the delay he would have notified me long since—gammon Mary—gammon—damn gammon all of it. I will write to him and if something is not done soon, I will give a power of attorny to some one else and take the case out of his hands.

Jose tells me that the streets of Camden has become infested with a set of desperados—that Mother was stoped &c. &c. for God sake, Mary, dont you go out after dark with out company—in times like these, unprincipled men take advantage of every excitement to practice their evil deeds—and the authorities (it appears to me) hesitate so long for fear of blood-shed—by God! if I had the power—the law to the fullest extent should be enforced—enforced in the most minute perticulars if it required additional grave-yards to bury the dead—yes if the road to justice had to be paved with human skulls—once *convince* unprincipled men that retribution—swift and shure—will follow the least infringement of law—that the sharp sword of Justice is out of the scabbord, cutting right and left as she hews her way along—once convince them of *this* and the cause for such severity will be removed—because sound[r]els are cowards, either physicaly or mentaly.[19]

I still have my carpet slipper on, but expect to be able to use my shoes in a few days—the idea that you sugest of "driving the humour out" and not "dry it up" will answer very well in cases where the patient can endure it—but in my case I would be compelled to tare the flesh to pieces to ease the itching and stop the swelling—as it is I generaly draw the point of a needle across the sores so deep that I frequently bring blood—if it was any where else except the feet I could get along better—except one spot—the Penis—where thank God! it did not come *this* time—hevens Mary! you have no idea of the agony that I endured when it was there—I shudder to think of it.

You do not say how *your* health is in your last—give my love to the boys and kisses to Clara—I have written this in a fine hand (for me to write) as I felt like giving you a *long* letter with out increasing the pages—I guess that I have succeeded[.]

Your
Charley

P.S. *who* did you purchase that smoking tobacco from—*what* did you pay—it is not like that which I have had—it is *not* Lynchburg by a long shot—I wish that I could sell it or give it away for it is not worth smoking—who ever you procured it from stuck you Mary[.]

64

[letterhead: Office of A.A.P.M. General for Ohio]

Columbus, Aug. 2 = 1863

Your letter of the 29th inst. came to hand to-day (Sunday) and it is scarcely necessary for me to say that I came to the office this morning to get it—the fact is that so little have I to amuse me—so little have I to interest me here, that if it was not for your letters I would feel like "bidding adue to the world"—I have formed no association since I arrived, in fact do not know a dozen persons out side of the office and the boarding house, and have no inclination to do so. I have received many invitations to visit, but have declined *all* for two reasons—first, from inclination; second, as they have come through Mrs. Preston, they naturaly come from the lady portion of the families, and as I do not think that it is proper for a married person to form associations with the opposite sex in the absence of ones partner; more especialy with those who are *entire* strangers to that partner—hence I have preemptory refused.

You speak of our living togeather—God knows that life, to me, is but one continual round of the horse in the Mill without you and the family; but as I hold my position here subject to so many probabilities, and possibilities of a *change* that I do not think that it would be advisable or wise to incur the expenses necessary to alter our present mode of life—however of that we can *talk* more fully when we meet again, for I fully expect to see you as soon as we have funds sufficient to incur the expense—of *that* time I intend to leave you the sole judge.

George Deal need not "think it strange" that I do not write, for if he did not think it worth wile to call on me when I left—and he known that I *could not* walk much and hence could not call on him—he certainly could not have cared much about it—and if he waits for me to commence the correspondence, he will waite a long time I assure you—I seldom *commence* a correspondence with any one, unless my interest (called business) prompt it, but invariably *answer all* letters.

Clara still harpes on that baby—Mary I believe that I wrote a paragraph in my last in reference to my feelings on that subject, I wish that it was erased—for I believe that it is the first time in my life that I ever alluded to *that* subject in writing—it shall be the last—for when I think of it I (you need not laugh) actualy feel small for expressing such desires—it kind of looks like a "viciated taste"[20]

I wrote you a short time since that I played chess with a gentleman hard of hearing—his name is Whitmore and is a Batchlor and has rooms in one of the numerous buildings rented for that purpose here, and eates at Mrs. Prestons—he is "one of the family," that is, has been eating there for over twenty years. Well to get at the subject, night before last while riding out with a lady friend (they do not walk here, it is buggy-buggy) he was stop[p]ed by having a pistol pointed at his head and some demand made of him—he could not hear and the lady was too frightened to know—but the *action* was sufficient—with considerable presence of mind he pretended not to understand and telling the man that he could not hear, handed him his ear-trumpet and requesting him to speak through it—while the ruffian was doing so he siezed a hold of the wrist of the hand that held the pistol and jumped out of the buggy—then commenced a struggle for supremacy which lasted until each were considerably bruised and tired out, he then offered a compromise—viz. that each should go their way without hindrance from the other, the offer was accepted and they let go thier holds and parted. I mention this to show you that we too are in the *fashion* as well the larger cities of north and east.

I expect my likeness to be done by Tuesday and I will forward them by adams express with some funds—say $40.00 or $45.00 which I will have for you—if they are not done I will forward the money without them, for I expect that you want it—I will send them (likeness) by mail—I will write you the day that I ship the funds[.]

Give my love to the Boys and many kisses to Clara[.]

Yr[.]
Charley

P.S I wrote you on the 29th & 30th ult.

65

[letterhead: Office of A.A.P.M. General for Ohio]

Columbus, Aug. 3rd 1863

Yours of the 1st inst. came to hand to day, it is considerably ahead of the time I expected.

You neglected to tell me of the trick that Cunningham intended to play upon me—let it come! I think that I can reciprocate without any loss to myself.

I am glad—extreamly glad, to hear of your determination "not to give people cause to talk about you"—not that they could have any effect upon me, but I would have my wife like that of Caesar's, "not only pure, but *above* suspicion"—you do not know Mary, what a consolation it is to me to feel the sweet consolation of the *utmost* confidence in the woman I love, and to *know* that her sence of propriety is such that coupled with her virtuous mind, she "could do no wrong"—oh! it is a consumation that many would prize as thier life.

I am astonished to hear of the opperation of Franks, not astonished to hear of any ones dishonesty, but I did not think that he had brains enough to conceive an idea much less to execute one.

I have six pictures of myself to-day, there was a "misunderstanding" on the part of the opporator and he only printed that number and did not color any, but will have the other ready by "to-morrow if the sun shines" and it is *not* shining.

Now Mary—for the pith of my letter—I have some money to send you and I am afraid to send it for fear I will want it—why—why—"oh there is the rub"—well read for your self and then you will know as much as I do—the following "order" came to-day[.]

"The Provost Marshal General directs me to say that the services of Maj. C. F. Johnson and 1st Lieut. J. M. Cress are imperatively wanted elsewhere and to warn them to be ready to move, and obey with great promptitude orders which are now being made out and will be sent them" signed &c.&c.

There you have it—*when? where?* for *what?* you know as much as I do—but go it is I suppose, there is one thing the "order" has brought out, and that is a strong, emphatic and universal regret in the entire office—the Col. is as "mad as a march hare," and cursed *some*—the first I have heard him use.

Now if the "order"—damn these "orders" does not come to-morrow I shall have the ballance of my pictures, if it does I will be able to send you but 3 or 4—in fact it required some determination to hold any, when *that* order came, for a dead set was made of one for "just one major."

Aug = 4 = 1863

The "order" has not yet arrived, but I have succeeded in getting *one months* pay (July) out of the Paymaster here on account of my leaving—which is quite an unusual favour I assure you—so I will send you by Adams express to-day the sum of $175.00[.] I would have sent a few more dollars but I do not know where in the thunder they will send me and I would rather have a few dollars in my pocket—however this will answer your present wants—pay Lees $35.00 Bill Hufty (if you should see him) $16.00 and then do just as you please with the remainder—I would advise you to *hold on to it* [underlined four times]—for you would not have enough to pay any one else in full and the money will be just as good in your hands until next pay day as in any one elses—besides I may get at a post where there is no Paymaster and then I would be like it is in the service uncertain; *very* uncertain, or, if I take a command, I can not get paid except when they are *regulary mustered* as in the field—so you had better look out for *Number one—number one* [underlined twice].

Upon reading this over I think that I had better express myself a *little* stronger, and say that it is my *earnest wish* that you retain the funds (after paying the two little accounts mentioned) to meet such contingencies as might arise—of course I mean you to pay such accounts as *you* have incured for living &c.

I have inclosed in the package by Express four of my pictures—I will send the ballance by mail if they are ready before I leave—if not I will make arrangements to have them forwarded to you by one of the clerks in the office.

I will write you the instant I get my "orders" and advise you of thier purport[.]

Give my love to the boys and kisses to Clara[.]

Yr[.]
Charly

P.S. I *have paid* the freight—upon the package[.]

5

"Extermination is the cry"

August 8, 1863–December 7, 1863

"THE ORDER," when it finally arrived, sent Johnson to St. Louis, where he became the provost marshal's inspector general for the state of Missouri. The position involved traveling to the various Union outposts and garrisons throughout the state and filing reports on their condition. It also meant supervising the formation of companies and then regiments of the Invalid Corps and getting them ready for duty. During this period Johnson was exposed to the brutal realities of guerrilla warfare in the border states and wrote of the plight of the thousands of refugees fleeing the war zone.

In October, Johnson was appointed acting superintendent of recruiting for Missouri, serving in this capacity until January 1864.

66

Hansen's House
St. Louis, Mo.
Aug. 8th, 1863

Dear Mary,

Here I am "on the banks of the Mississippi"—the last place in the world that I would have thought of—for my mind was fully made up that they would send me still farther north-west. I left Columbus at 11:35 O'clock Friday night and did not reach this place until 12½ O'clock this morning, a long and tedious travell; if the Ohio & Mississippi Rail Road is "one of *the* roads" of the South-West then they are "slow coaches" for it took nearly twice the time to travell from Cincinnati to St. Louis as it does from Philadelphia to Pittsburg, about the same distance, and "nary" a sleeping car at that.—Moreover, nevertheless, we had but two meals during the day—viz; breakfast at Seymour, Indiana at 10½ o'clock a.m., and (I do not know weather it was dinner or supper) at Olney, Illinois, at 5½ o'clock P.M.

I have not yet seen Col. Alexander nor does any one know where he resides—but I have found his office and will call there this morning, and if he is not *very* religious, will report to him to-day—[1]

This "House" is $2.50 per day and of course I shall leave it as soon as I find *what kind* of duties the Col. will require of me—*he is a regular*—I do not anticipate much from him—however "we will see" as the blind man said. By-the-way, Mary, if you know any old woman that is an oricle on "good and bad days" you may consult her when I recall to your mind the fact that my appointment was made on *Friday*—I left home on *Friday*—my order to report here, is dated on *Friday*—and I left Columbus on *Friday*—ha! ha!! well, *if* that is an unlucky day—it is compensated for by the fact that I reported at Columbus on *Sunday* ("the better the day, the better the deed") and will report at St. Louis on *Sunday*—so one will balance the other.

I looked at the Directory this morning to endevour to find where Alva Stites is, but I can not, perhaps I have the wrong name, is it Livingston?—that is my impression—if I am correct the name is not down in the Directory—tell me the name and location and I will call on him if possable.[2]

As the mail will close soon, I will stop and write more fully in my next—I was anxious to let you know that I arrived safe, so penned these few lines—give many; very many kisses to Clara, and when you write to the boys give my love—did they get a letter from me last week?[3]

Yr[.]
Charly

67

St. Louis, Mo.
Aug. 10 = 1863

Dear Mary,

I wrote to you yesterday of my arrival and now sit down to write more fully—sit down with the persperation oozing out of every pour—by-the-way, I prespire more in one day now than I ever did before in a week—month, yes, a whole summer—I actualy *wet* two hankerchiefs a day and a paper collar last[s] about three *minutes*—I seldom put one on, for before I can get down stairs it will "caflumix." Is this a signe of returning health or is it weakness? I think the former, as I weigh *four pounds* heavier than when I left home and I think that I am increasing.

Yesterday after I had written to you, I remembered the street that Alva Stites is in and I started to find it—I had scarce left the steps when I heard "hello! Colonel, my God! what are you doing here?"—who should it be but

Ex-Col. Fredricks of the 27th Ill. (an old friend of Dutten's) who I knew in Philad. and is now in business here through him I found the store of Mr. Livingston and I called upon Alva this morning—he fairly yelled and jumped, or rather he fairly jumped and *did* yell when he saw me—we had a long talk of about almost every thing—except Mary Davis and neither of us "ever mentioned her"[.][4]

I reported to Col. Alexander to-day—he is a tall, thin, gray haired, billious old Man—crooked, positive, precise and *very* gentlemanly—now you may think that very paridoxal, but it is true nevertheless: he is a stern disciplinarian, has quear ideas and insists upon their being carried out, but does it in so smooth, quiet and genteal a style that it does not grate upon the feelings.

They have eight full Companies of the Invalid Corps here, with about 75 unassined men, (making over 400 men) in Camped about 2½ miles below St. Louis on a high hill on the banks of the Mississippi river, and I was immediately ordered to the Command of the same—well thinks I, here is Camp life again—now I have enjoyed the luxery of a bed inside of a *house* so long that I did not relish it, but I "jumped at conclusions" too quick—however, I went down, looked at it, and assumed *command* by comming back to the Col. and requesting his opinion, if I could not be sufficiently in *command* by boarding elsewhere and attending to the duties through the day—thinks I, I may as well knock the old fellow in the head a good lick at once, when to my surprise he said, "Major of course, suite your self and what ever you do or want let me know and I will see that it is carried out"—so I shall board in some private house near the camp—I have engaged one, but can not be accomidated before a couple of weeks, at $4.00 per week—

I found an old acquaintance in the camp, a Cap.t Hicks formaly of the 88th "Penn." Vols. who I knew very well in Philad.—he was one of the Committee with me that was appointed by the Meeting of Resigned Officers at Philad.[5]—there was also two other officers, captains Rice and Russell[6] who served in Sumner's old Corps and knew me very well but I did not remember them, they were so pleased at my being in command that they offered to go on a spree if I would consent.

Mary, some how or another I think that I am pretty devilish lucky getting along with people, for Col. Alexander has a fearful reputation here among military men—yet while I was eating my dinner he sent for me and after a long talk adopted nearly all my sugestions; many of them were on the Provost business of which I had nothing to do with and [he] showed me some of his private correspondence with the government, and finaly requested that I would delay the command of the camp for a few days, saying that he long had wanted a man upon whose discretion and judgement he could rely and he thought that I was that man, and asked if I would undertake a "Secreat Mission" for him in the lower part of the state—I of course accepted the offer and will leave here to-morrow morning at day-light and proceed to Potosi and from hence to Ironton and then return to St. Louis—I go in Citizens Dress and as a citizen—it showes a great deal of confidence in the "damn stern old regular" as they call him here—I hope to the Lord that I will not disappoint him.

Of St. Louis, I of course can not speak yet, but of a Sunday night in St. Louis, I *can,* for I have passed one here=we had a thunder storm all the afternoon and part of the evening and when it slacked up, I took a walk to ease my bones, and "nosey-like," I walked into all kinds of places: 1st I saw a signe, "Trevoli" and I walked in; there sat about 300 people drinking Lager Beer and a full Brass Band playing and *not* "sacred music" either—the next place "Arcadia" where 5 or 6 Billiards Tables were occupied—the next place "——Bower" (forgot what *kind* of "bower" it was) but the first room I entered there was 5 men *shooting* at a mark, the room behind, some 6 or 7 tables engaged with Domonoes, on the side a large garden where they were drinking under trees, grape vines, awnings &c. with huge fans turning by machenery to enable them to "keep cool"—the next place a "Restaurant" where they were playing euchre—well I came to the conclusion that if Rail Roads *are* slow—the people as individuals are *fast* enough, and I retired to my bed highly impressed with the morality of St. Louis.

One constantly learns something by knocking about from "Post to Pillor"—now I never fully understood (not "to put so fine a point upon it") the luxury of shitting (bah! you dirty fellow! never mind Mary, "a dirty subject requires dirty words") I never fully understood it until I arrived here—I thought that the water closets in Washington were "swel[l]" but they are surpassed here—you enjoy the opperation in little lattice worked boxes (to let the air in) and have a stream of water constantly run[n]ing under you (to carry off the affluvia that might effect your delicate nasal nerves) and a *fan* to cool oneself as he strains (thereby equilizing the heat) piles of news papers to read (there by uniting "profit and pleasure") while piles of "soft and strong" paper surround you (thereby preventing the Piles)—now if "that ain't enjoying the thing hugely" I do not know anything about it—why I shall be apt to take double doses of Magnesia while I stay in the house, if "only for the fun of the thing"—but then I guess the *water* will answer, for if that at Columbus was hard, this is harder, for it is so full of limestone that it is the color of milk.

Give my love to the boys and kisses to Clara—

Charly

P.S. I shall expect your letter via Columbus, to-morrow, but blast it I shall be off and will not get it for 3 or 4 days—I wish we had a private tellegraph of our own, whew! wouldn’t the “merchene” work and the “lightning fly?”
I should have mentioned that I will leave my trunk &c. in the Hotel and travell with my valice when I leave to-morrow, also that I drew my milage from Columbus to St. Louis—it cost me $15.00 to come and I received $25.70—making $10.70 clean, I go to morrow with transportation tickets, the Col. wanted me to try the milage but I was afraid that *his* orders would not be as omnipotant as those of the Sec. of War and told him so, and he procured me transportation and yet Mary, do you think it, I had to tell him *how* to do it—for he actualy did not know the process—bah! talk of your *regulars*!

68

St. Louis, Mo.
Aug. 13 = 1863

Dear Mary,

Here I am back again, sound and alive.—I would not have returned so soon but I felt anxious to get your letter, which I expected, via Columbus, yesterday and I hurried up my work with astonishing dispatch—and did not get paid for it, for no letter came; although there was one from Harry as well as some from Columbus, but *the letter* was not there—however, I expect it in “due course of mail[.]”

I have been in the “rural districts” since I wrote my last—I have been in the land of corn-cakes and log-houses, in a section of the country where there was no roads—or rather where the roads were so indifferent that a waggon could not be used, except from some few points to others at short distances, where every man, woman & child went on horse-back. In a section of the country where men thought nothing of gone to *church* with Bowie-knife and Pistol in their belts—in fact, I have been in the “bushwacking” country.[7]

I left here on the 11th inst. and went by rail to Potosi, finished my business there by dark or a little after, and passed a very plesant evening with the family of a Mr. Sam.l Singer, an old resident of Harrisburg, Penn., who has been living there (Potosi) for some 15 years and made his “pile,” having two lead mines, three or four saw mills, besides considerable other property—finding that we were both Pennsylvanians, we began to talk—it is astonishing that *men* should do such things, is it not?—and discovered that we both knew a number of persons, and that brought an invitation to visit his house; as I was stopping at a log-house *hotel*, I of course accepted and remained there all night and had my breakfast and left with the offer that, when ever I come that way again if I did not call directly *there* and make that my stopping place it would give offence—a safe offer for it is not very likely that I shall ever see them again although I shall long remember his hospitable *palace* (for such it was) and equaly hospitable family—there appear to be but two classes in the interior, southern and western part of this state, the rich and poor—the rich being very rich—the poor, very poor.

I had one of my joking spells on while there and kept the family in a roar the whole time—the "old codger"—for he is a gray headed old man—offered me, that if I would only settle down, fetch my "family out," that he would build me a house and he "be damned if I should not go to Congress"—what do you think of *that?* I guess I will *not* accept.

I left Potosi on the morning of the 12th, and arrived at Iron City by noon—took a stage, with out springs, and drawn by four mules and passed over the "Pilot-Knob Mountain" to Ironton—this Mountain, in fact several around it, is almost one solid mass of iron, hence every thing is iron of some kind—Ironvill, Iron Gap, Iron Tunnel, Iron City, Ironton, Iron Mountain Rail Road &c. &c. I finished my business and left in the night and arrived at St. Louis this morning—took a short nap and wrote out my report, which pleased the Col. so much that he insisted that I should read it over again,—he said that he would have thought it impossable to have collected such a mass of evidence (under so unfavourable circumstances) under a week—*he* did not know that it was the desire to hear from Mary, that done the work—he advised me to go and lay down and take a nap, so I took his advise and *went,* but wrote this instead of sleeping. I think that I mentioned in a previous letter, that some how I appeared to have the facalty of getting along with people—well I still think so—for the Col. (after hearing my report) gave me my choice to go to camp or take an office in the building with him—it is scarcely necesary to say that I jumped at the offer and choosed the latter—so tomorrow I shall be installed—to day I have nothing to do, for he told me not to *dare* come back again to-day.

I find some dificulty of getting board here, as the usual stile is to rent furnished rooms and eat at the hotels, renting the rooms and engaging the board by the month—I do not like it, for I have a great dislike to putting myself out of reach in case of sickness in the night—however I shall adopt some plan soon—the manner I mentioned cost from $30 to $35 per month "rather steep," but as I will commute my quarters by being in the office it will pay the board and that is better than being in camp and paying $4.00 per week and *no* commutation of quarters[.]

Aug. 14 = 1863

I had got thus far in writing when Alva Stites knocked at the door and after a talk he engaged to call in the evening which he did—now Mary, I will tell you some thing which I want you to keep to yourself by all means, I would not have the Stites to know it for any thing—especialy as coming from me—do not breath a word to any one—St. Louis has "brought him out"—he says that he has been to Church but *once* since he came here—has visited all the Theatres and is posted on all the Lager Beer Gardens, in fact I meet him (at his sugestion) at the "Trevoli" where we drank three or four glasses of Lager and sat until 11½ o'clock and when I said "let us go to bed," he looked rather surprised and asked if I "always went to bed so *early*"—I mention this, not to his disparagement, for I do not think that he is ruined by any means—but I mention it mearly to show the decided change that this fast town has made in his quiet life—I would not have one of the boys to "get his growth" here for half it is worth—another thing he told me that I promised not to say any thing about—that is that Livingston is not the man for a deceant young man to live with—I will give you one among the many instances that he cited—at the supper table one evening he (Livingston) asked the hired-girl "Jane here, I want you" she came to him, "well what is it"—"oh" said he, "I only want to know, how is your ass to-night" when *Mrs.* Livington remarked "how is *your* ass"—now I think when people are so low, vulgar, and dirty onary as this it is what one might term "damn common"—this I give you as a sample of the usual conversation at the table—he is Irish and she is English and God help any refined American in that case—now put this to the discription that I gave you in my last of the character of the place as displayed on Sunday evenings and you will not wonder that he is no longer a *boy,* but promises to be a fast man—I do not think, however, that it has altered his principles yet—what it may do in course of time I do not know—keep this to *your self* for God sake!

To day I received my order placing me on duty at the office and at my suggestion the Colonel dated it back to the day when I first reported so that I could commute my quarters from that time—he has ordered a desk &c. for me and introduces me to all that come as the person to whom they shall look for information or orders in his absence—what he intends to make of me he does not say, but has written on to Washington asking that I be permantly detailed in the office as long as I remain—this one of the Clerks tell me. To-day he told me to "go and come just to suit myself"—not to "consider myself a clerk by any means"; as he does not believe in an *officer* working much when he can find others to do it, I suppose he wants to impress me with the same idea—well, I generaly am an apt scholar and I think that I can manage by *hard* exertion to learn "how not to do," although I told him to-day that I did not believe that the government would permit me to remain in the office when there was so many men in camp. [H]e thinks that they will especialy as another major has reported (major Steavens of Wisconsin) and *he* is ordered to Camp.[8]

On Monday I leave here again for a couple of days on another trip for the Col. down in the southern part of the state—he is so pleased with the result of the last that he has forwarded a copy of my report to Washington to-day—I think that I can get along with the Old Codger if nothing serious happens[.]

I wrote yesterday to Harry and would have mailed the first part of this to you but held on expecting your letter to-day, but it did not come—I shall mail this to-morrow weather I hear from you or not—I feel very anxious to hear if you received the $175.00 that I sent you the 4th inst. by gracious! that is *ten* days ago, and Harrys letter reached Columbus in two day[s] and reached here in two day[s]—being written on the 9th (Sunday) and reached me on the 13th (Thursday). I wonder where in the devil your letter has gone to—for I *know* that it *must* be on the way at the proper time—however patience old boy, to-morrow will fetch it "right side up with care"—I have got a batch of letters coming as I wrote to you on the 4th, 6th, 7th, 9th & 10th. I suppose that the answers will come all in a heap.

As it is now striking 11 o'clock and the mosquetoes have discovered my light I will close—we are compelled to sleep under mosqueto nets here for they are thick enough to darken the street lamps[.]

August 15 = 1863

Hot-hot-hot—then stop for breath and say—Hot-Hot-Hot and if the persperation does not wet your shirt through, you have no idea of what is *Hot.* [T]he sweat is actualy running down my fingers on the pen-holder.

Yours of the 8th inst. (via Columbus) and of the 11th inst., direct, came to hand to-day, and now, I see the cause of the delay, viz: the funds not coming to hand as early as it should—I never thought of that or I would have supposed the case at once—however I *have* heard, and you *have* the funds so it is all right.

I am pleased to learn that the boys are enjoying themselves so much and hope that it may improve them physicaly, as also that you are ocasionaly bidding "dull care begone."

As for my "repremanding" you for short letters, why God bless you! I never thought of such a thing—although I believe I once did make a play upon some quotations (that were applicable to the case) on account of one of your short letters, but Mary, I never intended it for a repremand or in a spirit of fault-finding, at least I did not *feel* so at the time.

I hope that you may succeed in obtaining that "change" without any serious difficulty and that your health may be the better for it—for I realy do believe that you will *never* be a well woman until that "change" does take place.

So the pictures disapointed you did they, well so they did me—I did not suppose that I was so stern in my expression although they told me at the office (at Columbus) that it was my natural expression "when buisly engaged" but "not when talking"—I endevoured to look pleased by thinking of you and how in the devil it was not so I can not conceive—but, I suppose I must be getting that way—the darkness of the picture I suppose is accounted for by the lightness of the clothing.

Is Cunningham on duty in *Philad.*—can you tell me exactly *what* the regiment is doing?

I said in the previous part of this letter that I did not know exactly what the Col. intended to do with me—well! to-day I got *another* "order" and I am the "Inspector for the State of Missouri" that is that part that lies under the jurisdiction of the Prov. Mar. General and my duties will be to visit and examine the books, papers, work, vouchers, accounts &c. of all the Prov. Mar. of the various districts in the entire state and if wrong to set them right and "instruct them"—"ah! there is the rub," that word "instruct["] a [good] deal of "trouble may come"—for I have got to "learn by heart" (as the children say) all the laws relative to the Draft, a book of some 57 Pages and about 150 orders & circulars—jewilikers! but here is head-work before me.

If I make a few more changes I shall be a walking encyclopedia, for when I entered the army I had to learn "tactics"—the[n] the laws relative to the Invalid Corps, which embraced Subsistance and Quartermasters department, now the Draft—what next? *I* do not know, unless they put me in a Fort. This birth will give me an opportunity of visiting *every* part of Missouri and be very easy in between times; as the Col. remarked today, after you get back and *take a few days to rest* I will send you off in another direction"—the idea of "taking a few days to *rest*" over a hundred or so miles of travell in rail road cars is decidedly *rich.*

To day I engaged a room at $8.00 per month, and will move in it perhaps to-night and eat at the Everett House at $20.00 per month, they want $45.00 per month in the same house for boarding and lodging—I endevoured to obtain my meals at a private boarding house (they do not lodge their boarders here) and they wanted $25.00 a month for them—"salty" is it not? By this arrangement I will live for about $6.53⅓ cts. per week, but then my board goes on there or not, if I am away say two days a week it will cost about $9.00 per week to live—so we go one day up the other down, but even *that* is at about half that it would cost if I was detailed in Washington City—perhaps the next place that I may get into may be better, for I realy do not expect to stay here *very* long—you would be surprised at the way that the Invalid officers have been sent to all parts of the United States.

I guess that I had better stop this letter or you will get tired of reading it.

Give many kisses to Clara and my love to the boys when you write to them—as for yourself I can only say that last night I did kiss you, for I passed nearly the whole night along side of that window at Olive Street with my head on your breast as "of old"—we were single again—by George I felt mad when I awoke in the morning.

Your
Charley

69

St. Louis, Mo.
Aug. 19 = 1863

Dear Mary,

I have just returned to this place after a hot ride—hot! no!! that is a faint word to express the state of the weather—first *boiling* and then after there is no more greace to come out then commenced the scorching and roasting—I am now expearencing the pleasing sensation of having the sweat running down my fingers on to the pen holder—hot travelling, yes, fat woman felt fussy and fumed furiously, lean woman leaned languidly back (like withered lilies on a lake), shabby slipshod servants sat silently and sadly on the shady side of the cars, yea! babies bawled bravely, fretfully and furiously, cinders crept into your clothes and dust stuck stubbornly to the skin, yea, varily it *was* hot!

I have been to Arcadia Valley in the south of Missouri, and it is one beautifull spot, surrounded by the Ozark Mountains (in fact compleatly hemmed in) and is about 10 miles across either way and the ground, at the interval of about every 400 achres is raised in little knobs about thirty feet high on the top of which they have built their houses—originaly farm houses but now (that is before the war) fast being altered in mansions for summer residence.

There is no "public houses" there and Brig. Gen.l McCormick[9] (who I met there and has command of the forces there) invited me to remain all night when he was stopping at a Dr. Barrar; of course I accepted and slept within about two squares of our picket line—Marmaduke & Prices' forces (7000 strong) were just on the other side of the hills; as they call the mountains here; it felt something like old times to hear the "orders" for pickets, reserves &c.[10] But the best of the joke was that this Dr. Barrar is a very religious man and the agent of the Bible Society happened to be there and of course there was "family worship"—jewilikins! I was in a box—but, thank the Lord! I survived and am "here to tell the tale," the agent and I was roomed together (separate beds) and do you not think that *he* had the assurance to ask me if I would "unite with *him* in prayer" (mind you *after* I had suffered one attack down stairs) I quietly told him to "pray away old boy I guess you need it"—"I came here to *sleep* and not waste my time," well, he first looked astonished, then rolled up his eyes, then groaned and then doubled up like a jack-knife—what he did *after* that I do not know for I was asleep.

When I arrived here (to-day) I found a letter from the Boys—no it was not either, it was from Jose, of the 10th inst. and came via Columbus. Also yours of the 12th & 14th inst. You wish that "they would make up their minds" that my services would be required on East—I have wished *that* thousands, yes tens of thousands of times—first I detest the place and next I would rather be living in mud knee deep nearer *home*, where there would be a prospect of seeing you all once in a while, than in a palace here without that prospect.

Why did not George shoot that infernal nigger—by heavens, *that* is one of the blessings out here—a nigger is a nigger and if he presumes to be any thing else "down goes his house" and "no questions asked" if he is a *free* nigger; a slave would not *dare* to be any thing else but a nigger.[11]

Alva Stites and I had a conversation last Sunday evening about Mary and (he requested me not to mention the subject so keep mum) I can tell you pretty emphatically, if not classicly, that so far as he is concerned "she is gone up a spout"—he keeps her letters for two or three weeks and then writes about a half a page of note paper, he says that he thinks that is the best way of stopping the correspondence, that is gradualy—her letters contain nothing but abuse of you and the family and that convinces him that she has no principles—he thinks that your quarrel with her has brought out her true character and that he "made a lucky escape"—do not mention this, for our conversation was confidential—in fact I "drew him on" and he could not help it.

Your idea of William in reference to the Mare and mine are similar—I do not expect to ever receive another cent from him, if I was near enough to get at him I would put some hot coals under his feet that would make him dance more lively than he has for some time—by the way a good joke was perpertrated by Mary Davis, she told Alva that her parents did not intend that thier folks should ever associate with the Johnson family again, ha! ha!![12]

How much farther am I from home than I was in Columbus? Just double the distance, about 1200 miles, and I think—and it is with great reluctance that I am forced to think so—that it is intirely to far for you to travell, especialy without your husband—beside it would involve an expenditure of

$35.00 each way—if you remained two or three weeks, and you should not go home on less, it would cost about $100.00—so we will have to trust to fate or our good luck to get nearer togeather shortly. I do not think that I will be here long, I have a kind of abiding faith in my good luck.

Give my love to the boys and many kisses to Clara[.]

Yr[.]
Charly

P.S. Before closing I would like to mention one point—I did not intend to do so, but think that it is my *duty*—I did not intend mentioning the subject for fear that you would not appreciate *exactly* my reasons and motives, but prefered rather to let the matter remain entirely on your judgement, discrimination and sence of propriety—but after thinking over the matter for several days I have come to the conclusion of mentioning the subject to you. It is this, do you not think that you and the Process[13] are becoming a *little* too intimate—with her I have nothing to say, but it is of *him* I speak—now you are to judge how often it would be right, be proper or prudent for a married woman to accompany a gentleman during her husbands absence, especialy when that gentleman is an *entire stranger* to that husband—now do not jump at conclusions until I get through—I know that his wife accompanies you, and on that account did not at first think much of the subject, in fact when you wrote that you had taken evening walks, gone to Ice Cream Saloons, visited the Public Park &c., I thought nothing of the affair—it was right—as every thing is that my wife does, but when you talk of gone to watering places, it began to look as if you in your *thoughtlessness* was liable to place yourself in a position that the world would be apt to take advantage of and slander your fair fame—now I do not intend objecting to your making that visit but I want you to look well over, *all over* the matter before you do go—I know that I at a distance am not able to judge fully upon the subject, I know that you frequently move in matters that suite your fancy with out full deliberation, I know that you do not stop to weigh every feather in the cap of those who please, I know that you are as free from guile as the child at the breast, hence I came to the conclusion that you did not look at the subject in all its bearings—if you stop[p]ed to consider at all and I thought that I would mention the subject to you—think it well over Mary, then do just as you please, just as you think right, proper and prudent—I *know* that I can leave any subject in your hands if your attention is once called to it.
P.P.S. I shall leave here again the day after to-morrow for the northern part of the state, but will return by Saturday night.

I changed my boarding house and moved into my room this morning and moved out again this afternoon—when I went there I examined the bed clothing (as usual) and the sheets were stained as though the parties there had the bad disorder, I asked for clean bed clothing, and was told that it was all in the wash and would not be ready for use for two or three days so I just moved again, I am now at the Barnum House and pay $1.50 ($1.00 less than the other house) per day by taking board by the month—it is $5.00 more a month than I would pay if I rented a room and eat elsewhere—I would rather pay it than run the risk—by heaven it makes my flesh crawl to think what would have been the consequence if I had not looked at the sheets.

70

St. Louis, Mo.
Aug. 23rd 1863

Dear Mary,

I have just returned from the prairie lands of Missouri (they are about 400 miles in extent) and would have written to you last night upon my arrival, so that it could go by the mid-night mail, but I did not reach here until 11 o'clock P.M. and compleatly "used up"—so much so that I went to bed without any supper, having ate but one meal (breakfast) that day and travelled between 2 & 300 miles—I find that this "Inspection" is likely to make irrigular correspondence by my being so frequently absent and that at irregular intirvels and uncertain lengths of time, but rest assured Mary, that the letters shall go from here as frequently as possable, for the only consolation, the only pleasure, in fact the only companionship that I have is writing to you and reading your letters.

I am heartly tired of this infurnal place and will get out of it as soon as I possably can with safety, that is, as soon as I can with a certainty of getting *east*—I would start (or endevour to do so) a ball in motion to have me taken from here, but I am afraid that I might be sent farther off, and then I would wish I had let it alone—however, there is a prospect of a batallion of the Corps being ordered from here and the Colonel has been directed that he shall send a Field Officer with them when the order reaches him, and I have asked *him* as a special favour, that if they are ordered east that I may be sent with them, he would not promise posatively but, I think that it is all right if they do go east, for he said that I "deserved some favours on account of the prompt manner in which I executed my orders," would not promise, but "would take it into serious consideration"—I think *if* they go "eastward ho!" that I will be there. God grant that such may be the order and then farewell—thrice happy farewell to St. Louis—the spot where you dare not *look* at a man with out paying a "picune"[14] and if you *speak* a "bit, sir!" is the cost—a "bit" here is twelve and a half cents.

To-morrow (Monday) I inspect the offices of two districts in St. Louis and on Tuesday I leave here for one of three places, either Hannibel (on the Mississippi—near Iowa) or Jefferson City (on the Missouri River) or St. Joseph (on the boarders of Kansas) one of the three which I can not tell until to-morrow, such is the uncertainty of military life.

I have been quite under the weather the last few days, but feel considerably better to-day, a general prostration of the whole physical system, attributed to the excessive heat, mainly—perhaps the constant travelling about has a little to do with it as the water constantly changes, with change of locality and meals very irregular, some times one on top of another, some times none at all, as per yesterday.

While I was absent on this last trip the officers at the Camp waited upon the Colonel and solicited that he would "send Maj. Johnson to the command of the camp"—the Col. told them that he did not doubt but that they would like me there, but "gentlemen, he is of too much assistance—too valuable here to detail him there"—Maj. Steven[15] (the commander of the Camp) was among the number—I have promised this morning to go down and visit them once a day, every day that I am in St. Louis—they are stuck on their Rolls, accounts &c.—the dunces, I have not had any more experiences in those affairs than most of them, but if they *must* have advice, why, it don't cost anything to give it, so I will "elucidate."

As I desire to send this by the 11 o'clock a.m. mail, I will make it some what shorter than my last two letters.

Give my love to the Boys (I suppose that they are home by this time) and many kisses to Clara—I hope that your next, which I expect to-morrow, will convey the intelligence that you are improving in health.

your
Charly

71

St. Louis, Mo.
August 29/63

Dear Mary,

I am here again at last and as my last trip contained considerable variety and some adventure, I will endevour to give it to you in diary form; and as Marcutio would do "begin at the beginning," even if the whole story should be like Hamlet told Polonius his reading was, "words, words, words."

My usual proceeding upon receiving an order to inspect a Head Quarters is to proceed to the Quarter Master's Department and get transportation by "the most direct, and usual travelled rout," upon gone there this time they informed me that the "direct rout" was closed by Guerillas, that the "usual travelled rout"; viz; by steam-boat up the Missouri, was dangerous, *very* dangerous, and cited as an instance that a few days before or rather nights before, that while a steam boat was "wooding up" at a landing but five miles from Lexington, a band of about 60 Guerillas seized her and took *all* the Negroes that were aboard (30 in number) ashore and while one man held a pine[?] torch up to their faces another shot them, killing the whole 30 darkies; in the mean time another party had drag[g]ed the passangers out of their births and shot them *all*—eight citizens and three soldiers—and did not leave a soul aboard (out-side of the *crew* of the boat) except *two woman*—the Captain and Chambermaid have been arrested as accomplices, as they voluntery told the Guerillas where the passangers were and the Chamber Maid wanted them to kill the woman—the pair of them *will* hang—this is one of the incidents that is almost daily occuring on the Missouri River, but was told me as being applicable to my case as it occured near Lexington—I did *not* take the "usual travelled rout," but procurred transportation from St. Louis to Macon City (via the North Missouri R.R.) thence to Hamilton (via the Hannibel & St. Joseph R.R.) thence (by Stage of 55 miles) to Lexington—by refering to the Map you will see that my course was something like this [drawing of his roundabout route] while the dotted line is the "most direct" route—thus giving me a travell of over 300 miles more than necessary and nearly half of that by stage.

I left St. Louis at 4 o'clock A.M. on the 25th and a cold, biting, *frosty* morning it was—[in] fact—the frost was so heavy that you could have written your name on the boards, well, as the change was sudden and one left without breakfast, I felt it—at sunrise we crossed the "Mighty Missouri" and there I succeeded in getting a cup of (hem! ah! hem!!!!!!) coffee and amused myself while crossing in blowing first my fingers, second the (ah-ha!) coffee, thirdly creation generaly, we stop[p]ed for breakfast at 9½ (ye Gods!) o'clock at Warrenton and reached Macon City at 1½ o'clock—left immediately, stop[p]ing at Brookfield at 4½ for dinner, and reached Hamilton at 7 o'clock P.M. and remained over night.

Hamilton is built as if each man had "squatted" down without know[ing] that he had a neighbor or that it was intended to make a *place* of it—no streets, no enclosures to the house (they do not know what a *garden* is "out west") no nothing but the shanties, and they are located like the men in a game of Checkers when it is about half finished. However as it is situated in the midst of the Prairie I thought that I would enjoy two boasted sights, viz; sun set and sun rise on the Prairie—well I seen the sun set and it was a humbug and I went to bed in "the best room in the house[.]"

Let me describe it—first there was *no* post bedstead—if it had a post I could not see it, no carpet on the floor, one chair and a small pine table on which was a cracked bowel and a no handle pitcher—no water though there *was* a towel spread over it—a rough board partition and no plaster on the celean—well I turned in by the light of the "pale moon's misty beams" and looked up at the lathes as they grinned down at me and fell asleep only to awaken with an old feeling "still so gently o'er me stealing" and slip[p]ed out of bed—struck a match—and great Heavens! the bugs—no, not *bugs,* but all one bug, they were so thick—why Mary there was not holes and cracks enough to hold them all and they just run "around loose"—well I put on my drawers and stockings and turned in, thinks I, it will take you some time to discover that passage and by that time I will be asleep and then it will not matter.

I arose at the break of day to see the "sun rise on the Prairie"—humbug! again—took my breakfast and went to the *Stage Office* i.e. an old shed—and found that the Stage would carry nine persons, but there was six men, two women and four children there already and pretty soon there came another woman (weighing 360 or 630 pounds, it don't matter which) with five children, a trunk, a band-box, a clothes basket full and a willow couch[?]—here was a mess, nine grown persons and nine children—the agent finaly offered if some of the gentleman would let the ladies ride in the coach that he would send them down in a hack—well your humble servant step[p]ed out immediately (glad of the opportunity) and so did two others, the rest refused and consequently the whole party of them were packed in togeather and sent off—the men growling, the women quarrelling and the children squalling—joy be with them.

About an hour after we were started off with a pair of horses and a little light waggon—the *we* consisted of a young man (about 22 years of age) named McPherson—a tall, long, gaunt, thin necked specimen of the production of Kentucky, who could drink (as young as he was) as much bad whisky as Bill Moore and could *eat* as much tobacco as John Cunningham, he had just returned from the north, where he had been educated, but his Father ("the Govourner") thinking that it was a little too hot at home sent him into Missouri to look up a farm of a friend of the family who had been compelled to leave on account of his Union sentiments—and this was his errand.

The other passanger was a quiet, sober, steady, farmerlike man of about 55 or 58 years of age and named Hedgges—*he* was drove from his farm (about 15 miles below Lexington) about 2 years since and was just on his road to endevour to see or at least hear of his family—he was armed with authority to accompany any scouting parties that might go into his neighbourhood—These points I learned through our conversation, which of course touched upon all topics, from the price of corn to "how to save the country" if we *only* had the power. We journe[ye]d this way over the Prairies to Knoxville where we stop[p]ed to feed and be feed—and here we came near being left behind as the driver told us that his instructions was to take us to Knoxville and if we wanted to go any further we must pay $6.00—well, as we *had* paid our fare, we came to the conclusion 1st that we would not pay $6.00, 2nd that we would not stay in Knoxville, 3rd that we would *go* to Lexington, and 4th that his team and none other should take us—that if he did not drive we would do so ourselves and hire a guide—a careless display of the butts of our pistols made him suddenly change his mind and "*he drove.*"

Upon leaving Knoxville you leave the Prairie Lands and enter the hilly country that bounds both sides of the Missouri—for we were coming back to that stream again—here the country is pretty and wild flowers in profusion, I saw some splendid specimens of Mountain Phlox, and caught a young Dove, but let it go again—but then to enhance the beauty of the scene, we were getting into the Guerrilla district where every bush might contain a Joe—as we crossed the "Crooked Hills["] (on the margin of Crooked River) we met an ox cart containing an old woman, a girl about 17 years old, two boys about 14 & 12 and two girls about 10 & 7 years—she was moving "north," the Guerrillas had murdered her husband and drove her out, burning down the place, she left; but the night before we meet her they visited her cart and took her older son (about 19 years old) out and shot him before her eyes, and then actualy *ravished* her daughter—the girl's disordered dress, swollen eyes and downcast looks, almost told the tale without the use of words—we gave them a little to purchase some necessities at the next town and bid them God speed—Mary this is war in Missouri, (I passed *seven* such parties) my God! if I was only able to stand the constant use of the saddle and had a few good men, how I would cut down the sons of bitches—the cry has gone forth through all Missouri—"ask no quarters—give no quarters" and it will be lived up to and extermination is the cry—the Militia is now ordered (after the 9th of Sept.) to hang *every man* who does not enroll himself at that date to hunt Guerillas—to remove his family south and destroy his houses and crops—that will make them show their hands—no "neither side" men—and I assure you Mary that the Militia will execute *that* order, for nearly all have felt the effects of the "Secreat Joe[.]"

But that is a digression and as I have not consumed half of my journey I will resume the subject and endevour to not get astray again—but I tell you that I am getting rabid—well, there let that go—when we reached Richmond our Kentuck friend left us to wend his way eastward, here they informed us that as we would not reach Lexington until after night it would not be safe travelling especially in the "Bottoms"—let me stop a moment to explain—the Missouri River has a bluff either upon one side or the other, if it stops on one side (and it generaly does after a strech of 8 or 10 miles) it will appear upon the other, on the side that has no bluff, the land is low, flat and filled with a dense growth of large trees and thick brush and this is called the "bottoms"; these bottoms are from 3 to 8 miles wide and then comes the Hills (simlar to the bluffs) which gives the place the appearance as if the Missouri River had at one time been a broad shallow stream from 3 to 8 miles wide, but at the present time it is what I would call a *long*—very *long creek* [*creek* underlined twice]—it is not as wide as the Schylekill at Fairmount (except when flooded and then the bottoms being covered it has the appearance of a mighty stream) I speak of the natural bed of the river as found at all times except during a "rise."

Well, they advised us to remain at Richmond, Hedgges got frightened and agnised, I insisted upon gone though and Kentuck offered to go along, but we dispensed with his services and started on after I had Pooh! Poohed! the Landlord and called his arguments a "weak devise of a hotel-keeper" (I wonder where the devil I ever got that expression) however I succeeded in getting Hedgges up to the "sticking point" after haranging him on his family, his wife, the prattling little ones &c. by George when I think of it, I believe I got eloquent on the subject, but I felt that *I* would have went through a whole host of Guerrilaas to see *my* wife and children after a two years seperation.

Well we started and sure enough night did come before we reached the bottoms so we cocked our pistols and kept watch, one out each side of the waggon and the driver ahead, when we were with in about four miles of the river—"halt" thundered through the bush—"halt" it was—"who comes there"—a pause, the question repeated "who comes there?" "Friends" said I, "if you are friends, foes if you are foes"—"hump! that is no answer" said the voice, "well damn you, step out into the Moonlight and I will answer the question," I whispered to Hodgges to be sure of his aim and to the driver to be ready for a dash—there was a pause—when three men step[p]ed into the road in *blue* uniforms—"who are you?" said I—"the 1st Missouri Militia" was the answer. "Why in the devil did you not just say so before?" said I—"who are you?" was the answer to my question "Union men" I answered, "is Major Johnson in that waggon"—"yes"—"then it is all right" one of them step[p]ed up and said that the "way bill" called for three more passangers than the stage tonight—who the driver informed them was coming in a private hack and that the steam boat was sent across for us under charge of a party of soldiers to prevent her capture, that we being so long they had fears that we were stop[p]ed on the "bottoms" and they had come out to meet us—I will here mention than when I first started out to inspect, the Military Authorities was constantly tellegraphing to Col. Alexander to know if I was the party that I represented myself to be—you see the whole state (out side of St. Louis) is under Martial Law—the Col. to prevent any errors sends word that I am coming and to "give him all the assistance he requires"—they having received that word and seeing my name upon the "way bill" (for it is rigidly inspected) sent these parties to "see me through" for the Guerillas do not give an officer time to say his prayers—they told us to move on but to make "assuance double sure" I told them that the driver did not know the road and for them to pilot us, which they did, I prefering to have their backs to us rather than our backs to them as we had only their word for it—we however reached the boat and crossed the Missouri in safety and landed in Lexington.

Lexington is a flourishing little place of about 6000 inhabitants and supports three hotels about like Englishes in size where the boys play billiards and the men drink corn whiskey. After supper I found that Capt. Cormengo (the Provost Marshal) was in St. Louis, but that his chief clerk lived in "old town" and Capt. Ophol[16] of the 2nd Regular Cavalry, who was the Officer of the Day kindly offered to pilot me out there, I accepted his offer and mounted the saddle and reached there at about 11½ o'clock P.M. found him in bed, woke him up stated my business and made arraigement with him to inspect the office at day-light the next day so that I could leave at 9 o'clock A.M. in the stage, and thus save 24 hours. Having attended to my business I had to go the rounds with the Captain as I did not know the road back and might be arrested in the bargain—Mary, it felt like old time to visit the posts at midnight—upon our return the Captain bet that his horse could beat mine, I accepted the offer and we had a mile race at 1 o'clock in the morning by the light of the Moon it reminded me of the times when Conner[17] and myself did the same thing in Virginia.

The next morning (27th inst.) I was up at day break and made my inspection and when I went out to the coach (after breakfast) I found Capt Ophal, Chief Clerk Fanley and a Major, endevouring to bribe the driver and go and leave me so that I would be compelled to remain until next morning, but he would not move unless *I* took my name off the "way bill." I asked them no, and left—I was the *only* passenger in the coach and you may rest assured that it was a lonely 55 miles ride—at Knoxville we changed horses and driver, this driver was sick and did not want to go, but as there was no other he could not help it, well after we had left Knoxville for about 12 or 13 miles he fell from his seat and I was in a pickle, I tell you, however thinks I this won't do, so I got him in side, fixed the cussions so that he could lay down and I mounted the box—whop! thinks I, here is a go—suppose I cannot handle four horses—I tried it *very* delicately at first, then got bolder and finaly used the whip—hurrah! here is Charly Johnson the Engraver, the Chesnut Street clerk, *Colonel* Johnson driving a four horse coach across the Prairies of Missouri—was my first thought, my next was *which* was the right road or rather *path* for they cross each other like the bars on a prison window—ugh! that is a horrid similie—however I trusted to the horses and reached Kingston, where the driver got some medicine and offered to procure a man to drive, but no—I intended to take *that* stage into Hamilton, and I *did* take it into Hamilton flying, for the horses "smelt the stable" and I am blast if I could hold them—phew! how we went the last few miles—I believe that they'd run away with me, but I did not let on; and do you believe it the Agent of the Stage Company (the skin-flint) refused to *pay* me a half days wages for driving his infurnal old coach—he offered to treat me to some tangled foot, corn whiskey, but as I had a glass of *that* two days before—I respectfully positively and emphaticaly declined—heavens! I can taste and *smell* it yet.

I retired to bed with a great deal of the feeling senominous to that which I suppose the Martyrs of old experianced when they were led to the stake—they know that they would be burnt but could not help it; I knew that I would be bit, but I could not help it—if you ever *should* travell that way, which God forbid! put up at the Hamilton House, kept by Jacob Brosins, and ask for Room No. 3, the "best room in the house" at least so they assured me.

The next morning (28th) I left in the cars and arrived in St. Louis at mid-night.

Mary the South West—the *great* South West is a humbug, a myth—a nothing—all the houses (a very few excepted) are one story frames or log—no gardens, no enclosures even—no comforts—no conveniences—plenty to eat and no one knows how to cook it—since I left Columbus, Ohio, I have not ate a single deceant meal out side of St. Louis—the rail roads make only 14 and 15 miles per hour and give you but two meals a day so miserably are they arranged—I will give you an instance,—on our way down we stoped at Brookfield at 4 o'clock P.M. for *dinner* on our way up stoped at the same place at 10 o'clock A.M. for dinner so it is all through—I think that I can speak with some experience as I have travelled over 1700 miles since I arrived here on the 9th inst.

As I have not been to the office yet to report I should lay this aside, especialy as I expect a letter there from you—I did not intend to make this so long and if you get tired of reading it you must excuse me by saying, "he could not help it—he is just as fond of writing as he is of talking and he *must* do it even if he does not say any thing[.]"

Afternoon—yours of the 22nd & 24th and Harry's of the 23rd inst. was at the office waiting for me—Harry tells me that Willie is something like Joe was last summer, I hope that he is mistaken, is it so? poor fellow, Mary, get him all the ice that he requires (if possable) at *any* cost for I know what it is to want that article during a fever—beside money is of but little value if we do not use it for our absolute necessities—get him ice at all cost—I would rather do without any every comfort that I have than that he should be deprived of it—bless his good natured soul.

Alva does know all about your skert his mother told him, but he asked me all about it—and I "laid her out straight" don't mention any thing of our conversation about Mary to his folks—she has lost a Beaux certain.

Poor Jenny! she has had her first affliction—how are her prospects? is Lizzie with them yet?

I am glad that your judgement has led you to take the course that you did with the trip to Atlantic City—I *knew* that if you only stop[p]ed to think that such would be your decision—you have been too correct all your life for me not to have supposed so.

I shall wait quite anxiously for your next to hear from Willie again[.]

Give my love to him (tell him I am thinking of him) and to Joe and kisses to Clara.

Your
Charly

P.S. Monday or Tuesday I expect to get a Months pay and I will forward you some funds immediately—how is your bank? dry, I expect.

72

St. Louis, Mo.
August 31 = 1863

Dear Mary,

I have just received a letter from you without date, conveying the dreadfull intelligence of the actions of that damn scound[r]el Reed.[18] You ask for sympathy—I know that you need it and wish that I was near you to assure you that this is not the result of any want of care or foresight upon your part; nor the want of any proper training on the part of the children by you—no! no!!

it could have happened at any time by the contact of a damn scound[r]el—a hyprocritical son-of-a-bitch as that, with innocent children, and I glory Mary, in your strength of mind in advising me of the case, notwithstanding the advice of "all hands" to the contrary, and I fully appreciate your feelings and motives; you did right Mary by apprising me of it so early and I feel that so far as *you* have the power, that the honour of the family will not suffer in my absence—but Mary you have not power enough for revenge, not power enough to satisfy that insatible thirst for blood, that desire to tare his cursed carcase to peices, that longing to grind his mangled corpse beneath my feet—oh God! that I could only annialate time and distance!—but thank God *my* disposition is such that I can nurse my wrath, I can keep my resentment warm for months, yea! years if necessary, and when the time *does* come—for come it will as sure as there is a God in heaven—when it does come that I can reach for him, he shall know—he shall feel what a Father's revenge for a son's wrongs is like.[19]

In the mean time, Mary, I shall rely upon Harry to take care that the honour, the pride, the outraged feelings of myself and family are avenged—as I would do him and his if he was in my situation—I know that he is volent and impetious but *all* the violence and impetuosity that he possesses will not *more* than satisfy my cravens—let him pitch in rough-shod and I will stand all the expenses that he may be put out, yes even to the last farthing.

You ask me not to interfear—can the caged Lion do any thing but roar?—I can not do any thing but write—by the God of Heaven if something is not done with him, I shall be tempted to break all bond here and appear upon the scean myself—*that* I can not do without some loss of my own honour, but I would rather sacrifice *that* yes everything than not have revenge.

You tell me that you will take the case in hands—what is your plans? I know that you will do *all* that a *woman* can do—but Great God! a woman can not do enough in this case with out appearing before the public and my love for you, my great respect for your finer feelings would not desire *that*—no! let the matter [rest] with Harry and if he does not act—then let it rest with *me* and I will abide my time—the difficulty in my reaching him will only add strength to my feelings when I *do* reach him.

I would like to know exactly the extent of his nefarious practices, *I must know,* so that I can act understandingly.

In the mean time you can console yourself that no blame can rest with you, for no human foresight could have devined such an act—and endevour to impress upon the boys the enormity of the crime—be careful of that, Mary, for these practices once instilled into children seldom ceases until they grow to man hood—watch them carefully without their knowing it.

I am glad to hear that Willie is improving and hope that the next will bring news of his continuing so—Give my love to him and Joe and kisses to Clara.

I must close this with four pages as I have been ordered to Inspect the Camp and Officers and Men at Camp Alexander this morning as they will be mustered for duty to-day—such is the exingencies of the service, move when you are ordered, ah! little do they know the state of my feelings!

Charly

73

St. Louis, Mo.
September 2 = 1863

Dear Mary,

Your tellegraph of 5:40 P.M. of August 28th came to hand at 11:30 this morning it was left with Maj. Johnson at the Pay Department and when I called to day for my pay I received it—he said that he did not know where to send it although it was directed to "Office A.A.P.M. Genl." damn him if it had not been for Lieut. Cress (45th Co. I.C.) I would have floored him immediately, for the sucker had been to our office to get the Colonel to let him keep a man of the Invalid Corps in his office, but the Col. refused—I think that was the "cause of the Milk in the Coca Nut."

I showed the tellegraph to the Colonel and he advised me to tellegraph back to you and if you said "come or that it was necessary to come" that he "would assume the responsibility and give me leave"—I told him that I thought that it was on account of the illness of Willie—I did not want to tell him the facts.

We this day received orders from Washington to send 8 companies of the 1st Batallion of I.C. to Indianapolis and the Colonel gave me the choice of command or not—I refused.[20] 1st because I wanted to hear from you in answer to my tellegraph today, 2nd if you said "Come" I could through him, if I took command I could not, but must get ready to move and then make application from the A.A.P.M. Genl. of Indiana—he might be a gentleman or not—but he would certanly not give it immediately upon my arrival—could not in fact—3rd it would put me in the field only 4 or 5 hours nearer home and that post might be more definite than this—here I can trust to chances and beside am not permanently in command of a batallion and hence am more movable[.] on the whole I thought as the Colonel did, viz; that my chances of getting east were better by waiting—it may be so or not, but the "die is cast"—I *know* that I can get any thing out of Col. Alexander that is reasonable if *within his power to give it* and that he is disposed to help me along—

in fact he said that he would rather lose any two men under him, than lose me, but that he would not let his interest stand in my way if I said I could better myself by gone, I thanked him and candidly told him that I would rather remain with him unless I could get near my family and *that* would break *all* other ties of course—I think from what he told Capt. Bush,[21] that I will be recommended by him for promotion if the government forms regiments of the Invalid Corps—he has big influence at Washington with the "regulars."

This Captain Bush is a "regular" and was for a long time Adjutant of the Col.'s Regiment and is now on duty here as assistant Inspector—he is the exact image of Harry and has his ways in every respect except being so very hasty in temper—he has passed nearly all his time in the service on the frontier among the Indians—we are together nearly all the time. I write this letter and will mail it—simply because I can not help writing, although I expect to hear from my tellegraph before this is half way home. Another reason is, that if your tellegraph will not require me to come home immediately, you will know much sooner *why* the answer to yours was delayed.

The non deliverance of your tellegraph fully accounts for my not getting any letters as I suppose that *you* was waiting for *my* message.

I shall close without touching the subject most in my mind until I hear from you.

Give my love to the boys and kisses to Clara and may God bless you and keep you firm in this your day of trial[.]

Charley

74

St. Louis, Mo.
September 3 = 1863

Dear Mary,

Yours of the 30th ult. and also answer to my tellegraph of yesterday ("It is not") came to hand this morning. I am glad that you can get along without me, although I could have left here if necessary, yet I did not like to impose upon the good nature of Col. Alexander unless it was actualy requisite; because, by taking a "leave of absence" *now,* it might prevent my getting one at some future time when it might possably be more needed.

Before answering your letter, I wish to say that I recall all that part of my last that desires Harry to go at Reed "rough=shod." I do so for two reasons; 1st that I do not want to get Harry in a scrape, 2nd that I have a plan of my own that I will put into opperation when ever I get near Reed—be it a month, a year or an age hence—one, and the only one that will satisfy *me,* no matter what legal course you may take; with that I do not want to interfear by any means, my arrangements can come in afterwards.

The cause of the delay in answering your tellegraph was explained in my letter of yesterday, had it ever reached *this* office it would have been attended to correctly.

So Dr. Cullin recommends that they be taken from school and put to *work*—well, Mary, the idea of taken them from school may as well be dismissed at once—unless it may be for a sufficient length of time for them to recover their health—if that should require their absence from school I of course am satisfied; but as to putting them to *work*, that can not, must not and shall *not* [underlined twice] be considered for a moment. Why what is to be gained by it?

I suppose that the object is to have them *employed* so as to prevent their having opportunities and also to tire them out so that they will not have desires to practice that vile habit—if that is the case, working will not remedy the matter; for there is no place, no circumstances, no surroundings that will prevent that—no! it *must* be done by moral culture, by impressing upon their minds the bad results and the crime of that nefarious practice—besides are we to destroy their opportunities for intellectual improvement? *That* would be only making matters worse to my mind—Dr. Carles has not recommended it and I have *more* confidence in him than any other Doctor in Camden or perhaps elsewere, especialy an alopathy.[22]

I know, Mary, that you are in a dilemma and scarce know what to do, and beside have, I have no doubt, a score of advisers each sugesting different courses to pursue, now, Mary, I want you to stop and think, quietly and calmly (if you can) as to the best course to adopt—think it over by *your self* for I have an abiding faith in your good common sence and having thought of and adopted a course of treatment to pursue towards them (the boys) then consult *Dr. Carles* as to its effects upon their *health* (nothing else) and then "go a head" and let *all*, the whole class of advisers (meddlers I may call them) go to the devil.

I never knew a theory as a *preventative* for the practice of these cases but that it has failed—no! no! the remidy is the advice of parents, the prevention of opportunities as much as possable, the obedience of the child and his strong *mind*—a mind strong enough to overcome his desires. Now I speak advisably on this subject, for I have seen in my time case after case, and *know* as much as any practitioner of medicine as to the difficulties of *conquering the practice*—*they* of course know better than I do, as to the remedies to *restore the physical condition of the constitution* and in that I submit to them—work! pshaw! *that* will not stop it, but, it *will* put them in the world as "hewers of wood and drawers of water"—what! send them upon the world with out *all* the education that we can give them and then not gain the object for which we strive?—why it is adding one evil to another—you consult Carles and never mind Cullen or any other doctor or their friends either and I warrent that you will be as near right as you can get—the more you listen to what "every body" says the more difficult the case will appear to you and the less you will know how to manage it—I mean so far as preventations of future practice is conserned; the course that you have adopted towards Reed I have nothing to say about, in *that* you can consult Cassaday for he will give *you* justice if any one can, for he is good in bringing criminals to the bar—as for *my justice,* that I reserve for myself at the first opportunity that I get, even if it is years hence and even if the *law* does feel satisfied with Reed's punishment.

You desire me to write to the boys, Mary, that is a difficult task, to *write* to children so young as they, I could *talk* much better; you can say any thing that you think proper and tell them that I wrote it—do you not think that the better course to persue? if not I will write. You can get some ideas of the *effects* of these habits from a little book that is on either the top or next to the top shelf in the secretary—it has the name on the side the "Decline of Manhood," (in fact I think that there is two books there of the same nature) from it you can talk advisedly to them about the subject.[23]

Let me know if you still think it best for me to write[.]

Has Bill Hufty been mustered out? is he doing any thing now?

I would have written to Harry but I have forgot his address will you send it to me?

Give my love to the poor boys and tell them that upon their future conduct will depend my love—poor fellows I suppose that they feel bad enough it must crush their spirit—damn that scound[r]el's soul. but waite oh! waite until *my* turn comes.

Give many kisses to Clara[.]

Charley

P.S. I will forward you either to-day or tomorrow the sum of $100.00 either by Adam's Express or by Draft (which ever is the best and cheapest) and will notify you of it. I could send you more, but I have retained my month's board (on the 19th inst) and also enough money to pay my way home—*that* I will keep about me *always* in future so as to be ready for any emergency that may arise.

How will your funds be with this $100.00 in your possession?

P.P.S. I have ship[p]ed the money this afternoon by Adams Express and paid the expressage (75 cents) one thing I forgot to mention in reference to the boys viz; encourage them to go out and play with such boys as you consider proper—don't let them set and mope about the house—give them the bat and ball and any athletic exercise that you can induce them to take—keep both their mind and body employed[.]

I write this against the wall of the Post Office[.]

75

St. Louis, Mo.
September 9/1863

Dear Mary,

I feel kind of despondant to-day, a feeling of lonelyness and so resort to my usual solice of writing a letter.

It is the usual opporations of the army. A man is ordered to a new locality—unknown and amidst strangers—he meets others in like situation—each feels that they are thrown togeather with the possability if not probility of their being togeather for month[s], perhaps years and being strangers in a strange place each has to depend upon the other to smooth off the rough edges of life, hence it is encumbent upon him to add his mite to the general store of pleasure, by that means a strong feeling of association (in some cases of friendship) arises. Then on comes an "order" and they are seperated—those that go, do so with mingled feelings of regret at the seperation and wonderment as to whether those whom they are to meet will be as plesant and friendly as those they leave—those who remain do so with the same feelings of regret at the seperation and a knowledge that *they* have new men to meet and new associations to form, which may perhaps last for years or be sundered as the former ones were as soon as a friendly feeling has been formed.

Six Companies of the Invalid Corps (the 33rd, 35th, 36th, 40th, 44th & 45th) left here yesterday for Indianapolis and I accompanied them to Illinois Town (across the Mississippi) and many was the hearty grasp of the hand that showed that the heart was with it—was exchanged between myself and the Officers—two of which were Philadelphians whom I knew at home, and several who served in the army of the Potomac, some in our old Corps—we parted with the *hope* that we might meet again but *felt* that we never would, at least not as officers; especially those who reside in remote quarters of the Country.

I thought that perhaps this feeling was peculiar to those who are but recently in the service, but old Army Officers say the same thing and say that they "never *liked* a man" but either he or they were "ordered off."

We have two more Companies ready to ship as soon as they receive their regular designation (numbers) from Washington.

I have enduced the Colonel to ship the companies as soon as organized—not keeping them until a Batallion is formed—my object is two fold—1st that the organization would not get so large as to require me to go to Camp to take command. 2nd that if the authorities found that to be the case they would ultimately come to the conclusion that it is not requisite for me to remain here hence *I* would be "ordered off"—at least such is my impressions and trusting to that "fickle jade, fortune"—who has seldom deserted me for any length of time—I will run the risk of being sent *east,* I may miss it, but I am disposed to "trust to luck."

The Colonel is authorized to dispose of the 2nd Batallion as he may deem proper, and he will this week send the four companies of that class to the various Hospitals in the state as guards for the same, and by that means virtualy break up the Camp. *He* thinks by that means that he can keep me in the office, *I* think different although I would not for the world that he should suppose the true cause of my advice for he is extreamly clever to me, but there is one star (brighter than *all* others) that bids me follow—that is *home;* I may perhaps in my endevours to get there be sent farther off, but will risk it.

September 10 = 63

While waiting for an answer to my letters of the 2nd & 3rd I will give you a feint description of St. Louis. It is elevated about 20 feet above the Mississippi River by the levee—the levee is an incline plane running into the river and paved with sand stone, to which flat bottom boats are attached to act as wharfs for they do not know what such an article is here, and when they land goods they have to put the heavy articles at the bottom to prevent the whole from sliding into the river. The streets are (with but 3 or 4 exceptions) narrow and crooked, even the main streets, the thoroughfares, the promenades are so crooked that they have an elbow at every half mile, in fact it looks as if every ward had laid out the streets to suit itself without any regard as to where they would connect with the streets of the adjoining wards, and if *that was* [*was* underlined twice] the case they have succeeded admirably, for every half mile or so they are just like Hamilton & Berkly streets are at West street—this is all through the city. They are paved with large pieces of Limestone, which being soft is readly ground into powder by the vehicles to the depth of two or three inches, said powder pervades every particle of the dress and hide of pedestrians, yes it actualy settles on the lungs and being of a gluetinous nature it farely macadamizes them. When it rains this powder or dust becomes like a thin paste or glue which can not be brushed off the boots but is *scraped* off with a knife, and as they *never* clean the streets—at least not since I have been here (a month to-day) and I have been told by persons who have resided here for several years that *they* do not remember such an occurance—then I may say, as they never clean the streets, we are blessed with the dust or mud at all times—a half hours rain this morning made them over shoe top.

The houses are built without any regard to order, regularity, or style of archetect and you frequently see buildings that cost 20–30 yes $50,000 on little narrow alleys scarce wide enough for a waggon to pass through, while shabby, half finished buildings will be put up on the main streets.

The Business portion of the city has an active pushing, restless kind of an air, a great deal like New York on a small scale, but then they have no "private residence section" like all other places that I have been in—that is to say no section where the "business men" reside, where every thing is clean, neat and orderly—no! it is the same confounded irregularity everywhere.*

Every third or fourth shanty is a "Beer Saloon" which are patronized extensively as four fifths of the population are Dutch—although they can speak English they will persist in gabbling German, of the other fifth of the inhabitants one half are Irish, the remainder are of all nations—the old French stock of the original settlers appear to have merged into the Dutch.[24]

There is one thing that I can honestly say—that is, that I have not seen a pretty woman since I came here—that is a symetrically formed and classicaly featured woman, one who has an *intellectual* expression and by-the-way the same may be said of the men—it is Dutch—Dutch—all over Dutch.

Speaking of the Dutch reminds me, that there is a Saloon opposite to the Hotel, kept by a Dutch-Frenchman, named Louis P. Ebert who formaly attended in the Bolivar House for old man Carles and knows the whole family—he speaks very highly of the Doctor and wanted me to send his respects to him—so you can tell the Doctor when you see him—he is making money rapidly having the best "Weiss Beer" and "Oyster Saloon" in the city—he tells me that the Doctor was out of his head at one time on account of the death of his first wife, also that one of the girls was turned out of the house by the old man on account of prostitution—did you ever hear of these cases?

This "Weiss Beer" i.e. White beer is made from the fermintation of wheat and contains a carbonic gas, some what like Mineral water—I never seen it until I arrived here and as it is said to be the most *healthy* drink in existence I am endevouring to cultivate a taste for it—do you think that I will succeed?

*[footnote written along the side margin of the page:] There is over a dozen City Passenger Rail ways in the city, here and there the houses (by some volcanic explosion or *accident*) are forced back a few feet, thus widening the street, but then they stick a shed in the centre and call it a Market House[.]

September 11, 1863

Yours of the 6th just at hand where in you charge yourself with neglecting the requisite precautions for the security of the Children. Mary, you should not feel so, for this thing could have happened under *any* circumstances and all the precaution that you or any one else could have exercised would not have prevented it—why bless your soul, *who* would have thought of inquiring about any man (especially one of his age) in regard to *that* particular crime? No one! And beside, Mary, it comes with a bad grace (I think) for any one to inform you *now* that they knew all about this thing before—they either lie or have acted with very little respect to you by conceiling it until *you* made the discovery—oh! I have seen so many people like that in my time why I would wager my existence against an apple that if you had asked these very people (in a general way) "What kind of man is Mr. Reed?" that they would have given him a good reputation—No! No! Mary, do not blame yourself, for all the inquiries that you could have made would not have revieled the true state of affairs—*people are afraid*—but having once made the discovery without them, then they are profuse in their advice—it is the way of the world—want help and all stand back, but convince the world that you do not need assistance and they come in multitudes to offer it.

You say that you are to go to the Spring Garden Hall and do not know what for—now Mary, I want to recall to your mind my sentiments as expressed in a former letter in regard to your judgement—do not let *any one* lead you around without your knowing *what* it is for—you should have made Harry tell you what he intended so that you could have had time to think over it, before you acted—if he refused why then let it go bye and do not act, if he could not rely upon your judgement, and secrecy, you should not upon his, *I* would not act thus with you and I have no more confidence in following (or letting you follow) any one *blind* than I have in myself goin it blind.

We can *talk* of your "starting business" when we are clear of the world, but as yet we have some $300.00 to pay, *after* that we will discuss that affair.

My breaking out is as usual one week in every three—that is one week sick with it and two weeks well—it however is not so severe as formaly; the neck and feet (anckles particularly) are only effected and they not so bad as while in Columbus, occasionaly the eyelids katch it a little.

I shall be glad to see that picture of our little darling and shall count the days until it comes.

Your ideas and mine are running on the same time—Christmas—for I shall shurely get home at that time *if possable,* if I should not before.

I received the Despatch yesterday with the description of that Scound[r]el on the wrapper—*what is the color of his eyes?*—I am afraid that I would not know him if I meet him—I should curse my very existence if I should pass him by unknowingly.

Give my love to the boys—tell them that I live in the hopes of seeing them grow to be such just, upright and honorable men as to be a credit to their parents and an ornament to society—give many kisses to Clara, and my wishes (I nearly said prayers) that God may continue to lead you through your troubles to a happy termination.

Charly

76

St. Louis Mo.
September 19 = 1863

Dear Mary,

I have just returned from a trip of 659 miles, having left here last Monday (14th inst.) on one of those floating palaces—a Mississippi River steamer—the Die Vernon, to Hannibal (150 miles). These steamers, Mary, are great institutions—you could place two such boats as the Stockson or Steavens inside of them with ease—this one (the Die Vernon) is a three deck boat, the Cabin or Saloon being quite as long as from the house to West Street; you can judge of its length when I state that it contained 9 chandeliers each at full distance from the other and had state rooms on each side of the saloon capable of accomidating between two and three hundred people, two to a room, why the Barber shop alone is as large as our two parlors combined. As we did not reach Hannibal until the next day, we had all sorts of amusements to while away the time, a half a dozen tables at one end of the saloon being occupied by gentlemen drinking, smoking and playing Euchre, whist &c. (no gambling allowed) while the Ladies at the other end amused themselves with playing the Piano and singing; later in the evening the Music struck up (they have several good Musicians on the boat) and they danced until after mid-night. I fell in with some officers on their way to Fort Leavenworth, Fort Scott &c. and we had a quiet game of Euchre until bed-time.

Hannibal is like most country towns situated on a couple of streets and has at present 8000 inhabitants, whos principle occupation is the manufacture of Tobacco.

Having finished my business at 12 o'clock PM. I left in the day train, for St. Joseph, but it was a *way* train, and appeared as if it intended to remain on the *way* until eternity—I got tired and step[p]ed off in Macon City and put up at a Hotel for the night, and left the following day (16th inst.) at noon.

Macon Cit—oh! ah!—ah hem! *City* is a true western town—does not boast of a single street, the houses having been squatted down without any regard to order or regularity—well they look as if they had come down in a thundering shower and had been left standing just as they fell. It has about 1000 inhabitants and 20 groggeries (called *Hotels*) making about one tavern to every 50 men, women and children.

I left there at noon (as I before stated) at as about 5 o'clock, when a few miles below Utica we felt a thumpity, bumpity—umpity, dumpity—a jumpity, jumpity—a whibley, whobly and a chur bumpt—a halt and an inquiry of "what is the matter"—well the wheels of one of the cars had broke and we had been gone (for about three times the length of the train) over the sleepers and there we were high and dry, with one end of the car stuck in the clay bank—it was lucky that it did not occur a few moments sooner or we would have had a somersault down a steep gully, well, Mary, we were five hours getting it on the track and then they locked the wheels and draged it seven miles to a sideling, then went back for the rear cars—the consquence was that instead of reaching St. Joseph by 10 o'clock P.M. of that day we did not get there until 6 o'clock the next morning with the passangers of three cars crammed into two, for such is the extensive and thorough arrangements of this road (the through line to the "*Great* West") that they make no provisions for accidents, but if one *does* occur the train must do the best that they can with out expecting help for if they do, they wont get it. However we managed very well, for several Ladies and Gentlemen got on at Utica to attend a meeting of Union Ladies at Kingston, dressed for the occasion with Flags &c. and as it was clearly demonstrated they *they* would not reach there they came to the conclusion to sing the patriotic songs in the cars, that was prepared for the folks at Kingston, and we had quite a lively time of it, with songs resitations, comical speeches &c.—one man constituted himself manager of the performance and required every one to add his mite to the evenings entertainment and by the time morning did arrive we would have been just as well satisified as not to have gone another 100 miles as not.

St. Joseph or St. Jo. (as they call it out here) is one of the greatest business little places that I have visited, with a population about the same as Camden (about 15000) it has street after street of stores with a stock of goods if not quite as extensive, certainly equal in variety both in kind and quality to either Philad. or New York, in fact they bost that they have every thing that is in the eastern markets and I think that they do. The City is built considerably like some men's whiskers "extensively laid out but thinly settled"—it covers more ground than Camden without any large lots in it as we have. It was originaly built upon the face of several hills and when they started to grade the streets they took the base of the hills as the guide and consequently they left the houses on the top considerably elevated in the air; to remedy that defect they walled up the face of the banks with gray stone and built steps up to the houses, so that although the streets are *level* the houses are *hilly*, and all over the town you find residences that require you to ascend three flights of steps to get to the front door, some of them as high as a three story house.

They have quite a number of Hotels, two of which equals Girard House in Philad. in extent and finish—which is a "big thing" for a little place the size of Camden, but it is the outlet for all travell to the "far west[.]"

I became acquainted with—of course you did, did you ever go any where without getting acquaintance—well I meet a little Dutch man, D. W. Bertran, Surgeon of the Post—who is the very facsimile of Charly Meeves, hight, size, hair[,] eyes, manners &c. as near a like as two peas; we drank a bottle of wine togeather and then I visited his house and passed a very plesant evening with his family, consisting of wife and one child, a little girl about six years old, who sung and played upon the Piano for me. After I had left he sent to the Hotel a bottle of Brandy and wild cherries with his compliments, which came very handy—I mean the Brandy not the compliments—as it was cold and frosty and I had not my over coat with me.

I left St. Jo. at 5 o'clock A.M. yesterday and reached here last night at midnight and put up at the Planter's House, as I had a quarrel with Barnum just before I left on Monday—the circumstances are these—on Monday morning I put on my uniform to have my likeness taken and I left my pistol (Sharp's) in my other coat pocket, hanging in my room, when I returned to dinner I went up for the Pistol but it was gone—I informed Barnum of it and required him to inquire into the matter, but he endevoured to browbeat me out of it and I pitched in roughshod and we had a lively time of it for a while but as I had but a few minutes to spare to reach the boat, I had to talk fast to say all that I wished—and you know that I *can* talk sometimes—well, the up shot of it was that I demanded my bill and left; I had so little time to spare that I had to leave my trunk and valice there, but took my sword and left it in charge of Alva as I passed to the boat—I will call on him to-day and if it [the pistol] is not recovered or paid for I shall either prosecute him or advertize him in the papers—I would not have lost it for something as it is like an old friend, besides the revolver is too large to carry and I must have some arms with me as I travell about and I am not able to purchase another for I feel as if I would rather run the risks than spend that amount for a pistol.

Upon arriving at the office I found your letters of the 11th & 15th inst. and the Dispatch of the 13th inst.

You wish to know what I think of the manner that you acted when you discovered Reed's viliany—you did right Mary, in not arresting him on Willie's evidence while he was sick—no Mary, "first besure you are right, *then* go a head[.]"

You think that Mrs. Livingston has the "appearance and manners of a highly educated Lady"—well shey may have *that appearance*—but she is *not*—I have never seen her, mind you! but I *know* her and him too, if Alva is to be believed and I know that I can put confidence in his veracity—as for the "boarding school" education, I can only say that it *may* be so—but I know that *all* foreigners have been *great* people at home—beside Alva describes her family (at Pittsburg I think) as being very common people although making money—again "Mrs. S. told you" how does she know except for what *they* told her—bah! do you remember Mrs. Shields "maid in the kitchen and lady in the parlor" affair—You want me to "call on them"—"I respectfully decline"—the day that I first called at his place of business, he was ungentlemanly enough to holla from the back of the store "Alva oh Alva" and ordered him off on some business and cut our conversation short and I had to leave—he did not know who I was, but that makes no difference—it was the set and manner that stamped him in my mind as "no gentleman"—I never have insinuated to Alva that I noticed it, but quietly drawed him out in regard to them and my first impressions are confirmed—well, let them go!

So you are making great preparations for Christmas are you—well now, I am gone to disappoint you for I do not intend to say one word to "check" your anticipations.

I regret very much to hear of Will Hufty's proceedings, I was in hopes that he would get at something as soon as he came home—how does Uncle George get on?[25]

I inclose a likeness of Cap. Spencer of the Invalid Corps,[26] he left here on Monday with his Company for Columbus Ohio. I also have one of Col. Alexander but will keep it until he returns (he is in Minnesota now) for his signature and will then forward it home, also some copies of my own which will be done by Monday—I think that they are superior to those that I had taken at Columbus.

Give my love to the boys and encourage them to write to me also kisses to Clara and tell her if she spells for me when I get home I will give her just what ever she asks for[.]

mmm
Charly

77

St. Louis, Mo.
September 21 = 1863

Dear Mary,

Yours of the 17th came to hand to-day and I am astonished at Middleton—no! I am not either (when I think of it) for it is all that you could expect of a *church-man*—damn them! if ever the Almighty forgives me for having visited such places in years gone bye, I will promise him *never* to do so again.[27]

I have every confidence in Cassaday although he too is a churchman, but, Mary there is a *stronger* tie between us than that of hollow religion—a tie whose fraternal strength is so great that Church-ties are but "ropes of sand" beside it.

If Middleton becomes implicated in any, yes the least particle, with that scound[r]el, *he* will find that his official position has but little weight to save him—he will awake up to the fact that the Mayorality of a one horse town like Camden is but an insignificant position in this world, however great *he* may suppose it to be—do not let that have any effect upon you Mary, for neither he, nor his *office,* is any bar to the course of law, justice or *revenge* of outraged parents.

The course that you have taken in reference to the boys is very commendable and you should persist in not allowing any one to speak of the affair to them or in their presence—it only wounds their *pride,* which if persisted in would have the effect of hardening their feelings and ultimitly make them perfectly callous to their future life, and I have great faith in the effects of an honorable pride upon the actions of any one, even in a child—once destroy *that* and we become mear brutes.

I have not received any letter from Cunningham since I have been here, but I have had several from Geo. Chambers, in fact we have kept up (that does not sound grammatical) a continual correspondence.

Alva and I took our usual Sunday afternoon walk yesterday and he handed me Mary Davis' last letter to him to read, (do not mention that fact) she is retrograding very much in her writing which he observed and could not account for—he little knew that *you* was the author or rathe[r] the reviewer of her former letters—I did not intimate the cause to him—I mention this to show you the great confidence that he is getting to have in me—in fact he generaly consults me on every move that he makes and stands in daily dread that I may be "ordered off," I think that if I was to leave here that this place would be a desert to him—poor fellow—he has strong principles of honor in him and I encourage them as much as possable.

He does not look for any letters from you while I am here, as he thinks that he is to hear from my family through me.

You are right "St. Louis and I are not friends"—I should have mentioned in my description of this place one of the causes of the expence of living here, viz; rents, would you believe it, that a small house of five rooms, say parlor, dining-room, kitchen and two bed-rooms, rents for from $600.00 to a $1000.00 per year—Col. Alexander lives nearly two miles from the business part of the city in a house (which he describes) about the size of ours, but a *little* more stilish, and pays $2000.00 per year rent—you could not rent a deceant residence of *any kind* for less than $800.00 per year. How the duce people live I can not conceive, nor can the people here explain.

Give my love to the boys and kisses to Clara[.]

Yr[.]
Charley

P.S. I am very busy as the Col. is still absent and will be so for several days and most of *his* work has fallen on me, he having left orders that I should be consulted by all the clerks in reference to their work while he was absent—I feel honoured by his confidence, but it keeps me in constant dread that I may not be able to satisfy him.

78

St. Louis, Mo.
September 28 = 1863

Dear Mary,

Yours of the 23rd inst. arrived to-day and it *was* a surprise—for I was expecting Claras likeness and when I opened the paper the back of the card was towards me, and I turned it fully expecting to see her when lo! the face of all the faces in this world look right at me—the very eyes appeared to twinkle and lips to smile at my surprise—God how I could have hug[g]ed you just then! It is good Mary.

Sam.l K. Brown was Captain of Co. D of the 81st and lost the *use* of his leg at Antietam—I signed some papers for pension &c. for him while at Columbus, and I suppose he wants some more—well, let him come for he is a good fellow and a *perfect* gentleman if there ever was one.[28]

That must have been a "high time" between Harry and Maria—did Harry strike her, or was she hurt while he was endevouring to prevent her attacking him? Is the Children there yet? What has become of Bill Moore, does he do any thing for his family &c. &c.?[29]

I can see you, you little goose you, with your trembling and your needle bobbing up and down on account of other peoples quarrells—I wish that I had been home! I would have walked her out of the house on a "double quick"—darn her eyes! I would have taught her the necessity of keeping her "shin-digs" at home and not endevour to bring you into it too.

So you have turned Mrs. Toodles[30] have you and attend auctions—well, I am pleased to hear that "My (your) Machine works beautifully"—that is, I suppose you mean the Washing Machine.

I am afraid, Mary, that you are making such extensive preparations for me, for Christmas, that I will be compelled to "bust" to do justice to your kindness and labor.

I have not written to Jones yet, in fact to no one else for two or three weeks past, except to you—some how I have not felt like it, but will do so soon, but *not for publication.*

I begin to feel a little more like the thing since I have secured private boarding—I have not been there long enough to tell how I will like the inmates of the house—the living appears to be good and plain, which will answer as I expect to dispence with the "side dishes"—the "Macaroni and Cheese a la Italiani," the "Calf's Brains and Maderia sauce," the "Apple fritters and Brandy dip," the "Fresh Trout and Butter Sauce" &c. &c. &c.! also the after Claps—the choice "between eight or ten varieties of Pastery—the "Blanc Manges," the "Chansilled a la Francise," the Puddings with "cold sauces" and "Rum dips," the almonds, Pecans, Rasins, Grapes &c. &c. &c. and lastly the Cup of strong Coffee and Cake to wash down and to *hold* down the huge conglomerated mass that one swollows during the hour or hour and a half that it takes to Masticate the dinner, but then thank God! we eat now with the full conviction (even if it is not so) that it is *clean* and beside one does not have his appitite tempted to gussle down a mass of very palitable food which is likely to produce Dyspepsia even if it is "good feeding"—no ringing the bell and ordering "ice water" at any hour of the night, now—no setting the boots out of the door to be blacking during the night—have to do that myself now—fact is, Mary, if I had continued Hotel life much longer I would not be "worth a Continental Cuss" for a *poor man*—I am glad that I am out of it for my own good independent of the *cost.*

One meets with some queer people in this world as they "knock around"—for instance a Deputy Provost that I stuck for $180.00 by reporting in such a manner that the government "disallowed" that amount on his bills—instead of kicking up a row as some others attempted, he quietly said that he "be damned if he did not admire my independence" and saying that I had "done all the mischief to him that I could" he sent me (as one of the Commission) a special invitation to attend the State Fair at Heminia, Mo.;[31] accompaning the invitation was a notice that rooms were engaged for me for the three days of the Fair at the Hotel, all free "including wine for dinner" and also inclosing a Rail Road ticket there and back—well it was such a "huge affair" that I could not stand it—my modesty revolted and I declined with "many considerations of my highest esteem &c. &c."

I called on Alva one day last week to tell him that I had moved so that he would know where to call on Sunday afternoon as usual, and I met and was introduced to Livingston. Mary, I am astonished, surprised, yes astounded that neither you or the Stites or any one else could not read that man—why every trait of his character is stamped on his countinance, his actions, his conversation *all over him.* Mary, he is a liar, a hypocrite and a——well I would not trust *my* pocket-book in his keeping—now this is a bold asertion against a man—that man a stranger—but I will risk my reputation for veracity—for judgement of mankind that *my* estimate of that man will turn out true—jot this down in your memory—for I *feel, know* that I am correct—Great God! *he* never could have taken one of *my* boys from home—he invited me to call on him, but—I have seen enough in only one interview to satisfy me.

The Col. has at length come to the conclusion that the War Department intends to let me remain here in the Office and he has created a seperate department in the office and placed me in charge with instruction to so arrange it that it will not interfear with my duties as Inspector—and what do you think is that department—nothing more or less than a "Detective Department for the Arrest of Deserters, Disloyal persons, &c. &c."[32] And I have a room full of Clerks writing out lists &c. with a whole Corps of Detectives, spies, special agents &c. "waiting orders" every morning—I have the lists laid on my Desk by noon each day, fix them up by night and issue the orders, assigne the parties to carry them out &c. the next morning early, so that with all the huge work of that Department added to me, I scarce feel the difference—I have the power to call for as many clerks as I need and all the Military force that I may require or think necessary to carry out any of my orders. I systemized this department for the Col. (he used to attend to it himself) some three weeks ago and it worked so smooth while I was at it that he stuck me there for good—I tell you Mary, it is dangerous to make ones self useful in this world.

Tell the Boys that I want a letter from them—I do not care on what subject they write so that they do write, give my love to them and kisses to Clara and tell her I am expecting that likeness with the baby[.]

your
Charly

P.S. I inclose Col. Alexader's carte de visite it is a splended likeness of the old man—he is sixty odd years old[.]

I would like you to acknowledge the receipt of these "physiogs" as I send them[.][33]

79

St. Louis, Mo.
October 2 = 1863

Dear Mary,

Yours of the 27th—8th inst arrived this morning and I feel very sorry that you should get the "blues" over "unpleasant dreams" about me; there is enough of the realities of this life, Mary, that has a tendency to make one wish that they had never entered the world, realities that we bare up against nobly and deturmandly and why should we then, let a few "fantasies of the brain" have even a passing thought? Dreams! Dreams!—I wish I could remember Mercutio's description of dreams, I would give it to you; but as I never like to quote incorrectly I will pass it bye.[34]

Joe Smith's sacrifice of his claim against the State of Pennsylvania was "heavy" that is true—one fifth of the claim—but I suppose that he thought that it was clear gain as none of it was expected when we entered the service; he is generaly pretty sharp on money matters, but you go and see Ford and tell him what you have heard and that I requested you to call and get his advice as what you should do in the matter—he will give you the exact state of the affair—then advise me—if we *must* sell, 80 cents on the dollar is better than none—I have forgotten if you ever received my commission of Lieut. Col. from him or not; if not inquire for it while you are there—it strickes me that he gave me a receipt for it, look among the papers in the pigeon hole of the desk and in the cash box, if I have it, it will be in one or the other places.[35]

Do you think that the boys indifference (Joe's especial) at school is the result of a broken spirit? Endevour, Mary, to find the *cause*—for it is impossable to remidy a defect without removing the primary cause of that defect; if we would kill the tree we must strike at the root.

Capt. Bush is a single man and I think is looking rather cross-eyed at the Colonel's daughter—however, *that* is a mere suggestion of mine without any thing definite to lay a foundation upon. He does not room with me, as he came to the conclusion of renting a furnished room and eat[ing] at a hotel as he did not like to be confined to the exact minute for his meals—I have retained the room to myself and pay $30.00 per month—it is about as well that it should be so for I prefer being by myself so far as rooming is concerned. There are four of us at the boarding house (or rather five) a Mr. Huntington and wife (he is the Superintendent of the 5th Street Passenger

Rail Road) an Englishman named Daily—he is a Teacher and a Mr. Hahn, a commission Merchant who is "gone in strong" after Mrs. Silver's daughter. [*H*]*e* is "one of the family" I suppose.

My health is very good, except that day before yesterday I had one of those old fashioned billious heachaches and vomited nearly all the morning—about a quart of perfectly green matter—and did not get out of bed until afternoon, when I went to the office and "got jessig" from the Colonel for "daring to come out when I (he) had ordered you to remain in bed," "now go back at once," but I did not—to-day I am "first rate," the cleaning out I got has done me good.

That agency for Lillies safes is too much in "embrio" to talk about *now*—as I know nothing about either them, the proffits, or Process—it would take something *definite* to make me change at present—I had enough once before of giving up a *paying* position for a doubtfull one—no, Mary, when I make a change again it must be for something *at least* as sure as the one that I now hold—the prospect of living at home once more is a big inducement though—as you say "if we have luck" I can talk over the matter in person.[36]

Yesterday afternoon (after the Colonel had raked me over the coals for disobeying his order to remain home) he forwarded the following to Col. Fry, Prov. Mar. Genl.[37]

"In compliance with your letter to me that any particular case of a very deserving officer should be brought to your official notice, I would recommend Major Johnson as such an officer. Since he has been on duty with me he has won my entire confidence and has performed his duties in a perfectly satisfactory manner.

I should regret to loose him but under the circumstances would be much gratified to see his advancement as a just reward for his services and merit."

What effect it will have remains to be seen—they are organizing Regiments and appointing Colonels for them and he (the Col.) says that I *must* have one of the posts if he can get it for me, even if I do not come in my regular turn—the above was showen to me by a clerk who said that the colonel added something personal that he would not let me see—the Colonel does not know that I am aware of the above.

I will forward to you by Adam's Express (this afternoon) $100.00 and pay the expressage upon it.

I enclose you a likeness of "our Dutch Captain," who is on duty here awaiting his transfer to the Invalid Corps—he has an invoice of Swiss Cottages &c.[38] coming "from home" and has informed me that I shall have "something goot to send to your frow, masure."

Give my love to the boys and many kisses to Clare—I shall await her likeness with anxiety—bye-the-way I introduced the folks at the house to "my family" and they "thought I ought to be proud of them" so I *am*[.]

Your
Charley

80

[letterhead: State of Missouri Office of the Act'y Ass't Provost Marshal General U.S.A. St, Louis]

October 5 = 1863

Dear Mary,

I write in great haste and as I leave here in a few minutes to investigate another case I must be brief.

I this day received my appointment as *Lieut. Colonel* in the Invalid Corps to rank as such from the 29th of September.

They Charge $9.50 here for sholder straps and I think that they could be bought for about $5.00 in Philad. so I want you to send me a pair embroidered on *dark blue* [*blue* underlined twice] *velvet*—that is the regulation for the Invalid Corps—send them as soon as possable as I may be ordered off at any moment to the regiment that I suppose I am to be assigned to—I pray to God that it may be "due east," one thing certain is that it can not be *farther* off as there is no Invalid Soldier in any other direction from here than east—or north east—however trust to luck.[39]

I expected a note from you to-day but suppose that I will get it to-morrow when I will write more fully.

Give my love to the Boys and Kisses to Clara[.]

Yr[.]
Charly

81

St. Louis, Mo.
October 7 = 1863

Dear Mary,

Yours of the 1st inst. was received this day—and I was rather startled to find that you thought "that St. Louis had turned up some attraction very agreeable to you or I would certainly received one sooner"—startled first, that such an idea should for an instant enter your precious head even in the faintest manner—why bless your soul! the dark paul of absence that surrounds me here only serves to make the halo that surrounds *home* the more attractive by its contrast—no! No! Mary, I *might* possably forget you (for a few moments) while near you, but absent—*never!* it is impossable.

Again if you refer to the *dates* of my letters you will find that I wrote to you on the 24th ult.—four days previous to the letter that you complain of as being so long—*your* letter to me you will perceive has been *six* days on the way here—I have been absent from home since the night of the 12th of June, 116 days in which time I have written 45 letters (including this) making one letter every 2½ days, some of them covering three and four days—it is true that since I have been "Inspecter" my letters have occassionaly been irregular on account of my absence from St. Louis, but as for attractions, pshaw! do not *think* of it again Mary for it makes me feel uneasy to feel or know that you would harbor such thoughts especialy when every days absence strengthens the bonds of affection for you and our little ones.

You think Capt. Bush a rake, do you, well Mary you have *never* been *more* mistaken in your life—why! the Lord help you! he is a very St. Augustine in that respect, a very Priest of Chastity—bless my soul! *I* never knew a man that was as indifferent to woman of *any* kind as he is—a "rake"—well that is good—why let me tell you that he is an old man—yea varly a settled, staid, staunch old man—why Mary he keeps up his field hours in setting and rising—keeps time with the chickens—and does not vary one half minute in any of his meals—he neither drinks, chews, smokes nor swares—ha! ha!! a rake—rich—good—no! no!! Mary take another look and guess again—imagine him without *whiskers* and then perhaps you can hit nearer the mark—now if you had accused Parrott of *that* you perhaps could have claimed some credit for reading men from their photographs.

You think that with Col. Alexander flattery "would perhaps tickle his fancy a little"—wrong again—for the least attempt at such stuff would damn the individual for ever; he would think that you had some designe on him—I have seen *that* tried and heard him say (after the parties left) "that man is a damn sneak"—"an infurnal raskell[.]"

I heard of Mother Davis' sickness through Joe but more definitly from Alva's letter from his Mother—you must have had your hands full—my God! how I wish that I could take some of the trouble and anxiety off of you.

As for Joe, I will cut his hide for him, I tell you, and you can tell *him* that I shall not forget *all* and *every* act of misconduct of his when I come home, I will bring him a Christmas present that *he* will not forget in a hurry—why! the infernal young scamp—and I wrote him such a kind letter on last Saturday. Mary, you must use harsh measures with him—that is *knock him down*—flat, straighten him right out—use a club, a *club*, you must *whip* him with *that* cowhide (or one like it) if you get some one to tie him first—he *must* have *that* whipping by *you* [underlined twice] or he will think that you are not able to master him—or you can not do it again if you want to—give him *that* whipping for heavens sake or he will be your master, oh! God! but *I* will settle him when I get home, if it is a years hence.

We are having great weather here now, on Sunday it *snowed,* Monday warm, Tuesday cold—over-coats and gloves and at night by way of variety it rained, cold rain with tremendous peals of thunder and vivid lightning—thunder, lightning, raining and freezing at the same time—all the fires are going on at a great rate.

Speaking of fires reminds me that some one has adopted a new plan of stop[p]ing the navigation of the Mississippi by burning the Steam boats, we avarrage about 1½ boat every 24 hours for the last week or ten days, to such an extent is it carried on that nearly *all* the first class boats of St. Louis are destroyed.

I informed you in my last (very hastly) of my promotion to the Lieut. Colonelcy. You perceive from the date that it took place before Col. Alexander's recommendation reached Washington—he now says it must be a full Colonel, but I think that I must waite my turn, unless I could bring *political* influence into play and *that* I can not—well, I would rather get my advancement upon *merit* alone than any other manner—if I *do* reach that point it will be by the recommendations of my *military* commanders and that speaks for a man in stronger terms than all the Politicians in the world—especialy when those superior Officers are *regulars* recommending *volunteers* to positions in the *regular army,* for such they consider the Invalid Corps will be as soon as Congress meets.[40]

The Colonel when congratulating me remarked that he was "glad and sorry," "glad of my promotion and sorry that it would call me away"—the old man spoke as if he ment it for he displayed considerable feeling on the subject which is a very unusual thing for him; that is to *show* his feelings one way or the other.

Since my appoint[ment] has been received, I have been very busy in the Office fixing up things generaly—the Colonel is so firmly fixed in the idea that I *must* and *will* be "ordered off" that he is getting me to "arrange that Colonel so that it will work smooth when you leave"—"arrange this colonel for me"—arrange the other colonel &c. &c."

I forwarded to you on the 2nd inst. $100.00 by Adam's Express—I always mention this in two successive letters for fear that one may misscarry.

I have just had a good laugh at Capt. Bush, having told him your opinion of him—it nearly knocked him on his hinder, he throwed up his hands, opened his eyes and began to "protest," amidst a universal roar of laughter from all hands, for it was so opposite to his true character that they roared at the joke—the more *he* "protested" the more they all offered their affidavits that it was so—he "protested" that he would never have another likeness struck off and instantly an offer was made to raise a purse for "the gratuous distribution of the likeness of the rakish officer" ha! ha!! ha!!!—I know that you will not thank me for it but Mary, the joke was too good to be lost—but I promise you to "never do so again"—ha! ha!! I can not write an account of the "flashes of wit and flow of humor" that is flying around me at his expense while he "protests" so I will close.

Give my love to Willie and tell him I will answer his letter to-morrow and many kisses to Clara[.]

Your
Charly

82

St. Louis, Mo.
November 4 = 1863

Dear Mary,

I wrote to you this morning and as I like to give you all the information that I possess, especialy when that information has a good prospective, I will squeese in a little time to write again to-day.

I this moment received an order assigning me to the 16th Regiment Invalid Corps, Col. Chas. M. Prevost, Commanding, the Headquarters is at *Harrisburg Penn.*

I also received an order that I am to "remain" on duty at St. Louis, Mo. "until further orders."

The following is the location of the various companies, by which you will see that they are *all* of Pennsylvania *organization,* although of course the *men* are from different states.

Co. A at Williamsport, Pa.
" B " Troy
Co. C at Harrisburg, Pa.
" D " Chambersberg "
" E " Huntingdon "
" F " Meadville & Waterford "
" G " McClellan Hospital, Nicetown, Phila.
" H " Broad & Cherry St. "
" I " Chester, Pa.
" K " in Summit House Hospital near Phila.

Now what I mean by "a good prospective" is that the Regiment is not likely to be ordered out of the State—as would be the case if one part was in one State and another in some other State, then they would be moved to be united in the same state or an officer would be ordered to each state, hence I think that if, or when I am "ordered off" it will be to good Old Pennsylvania.

The second order "to remain on duty here["]—rather implies that while the Companies are so scattered they will not want any Lieut. Col. there; but after Christmas I can make a push to be ordered to my command with perfect confidence, *knowing* that it is *all* in Penn.

Col. Alexander claped his spectacles on in "double quick time" when I told him and sat down to read and digest the orders—"why Colonel," said he, "how you frightened me—I thought you was off." Thinks I, yes and after I get my leave of absence out of you old Boy I will be "off" or break a neck in "the endevour," if I can not do it in any other manner I will work upon his sympathies and get him to ask for the removal—however we will discuss *that* "when I get home."

Yr[.]
Charly

83

St. Louis, Mo.
November 17 = 1863

Dear Mary,

Yours of the 13th inst arrived this day and I really can not tell you why or how it is that *my letters* "are so far apart," as I am sure that I have answered yours *immediately* upon their arrival. I have been thinking the same thing in reference to your letters—well—well—I wrote three last week without regard to the receipt of any from you and *now* I hope that they will work all right again.

You must be in a high state of excitement in regard to the robberies in Camden, but Mary, do controll yourself as much as possable and not participate in the "huge surmises"—the "wonderful suposes" of the garrilous old woman of the neighborhood. Robbery has *always* been the result of winter and has ever been more frequent during "hard times" than at other periods and I do not suppose that it is any worse *now* than usual, except that more notice is taken of it.

I am glad that you have resolved not to go out at night for fear of insult—damn that fellow if I had been there *he* would not have troubled any more woman—"cuss" him—insult *you*—I do not think any thing of *some women* being spoken to; for women frequently bring this on themselves—but *you*—I know that you are so far the opposite, that his offers *must* have been so [?]iously as to have been a direct and premeditated insult that required some good kicking. Our Company sometimes bring us into trouble—is Mrs. Process as careful of her conduct in the street as you are?[41]

There is one thing that I like about this western country, viz: that few men insult each other, because each man is prepared for such an encounter, and each know it, hence *all* are guarded in their intercourse—few men have recourse to the "*laws* delay." There is another thing about St. Louis, that is, that *no* respectable woman *ever* goes into the street alone after dark, in fact under *no circumstances* will she enter the street at night unless accompanied by a gentleman, and *he* is always ready for any emergency, unless he is too cowardly to resent an insult—in that case he is "nobody."

I have seen three stabing and shooting cases here in one week, in all of which the parties showed that the opposite were the aggressors and that was the last of it—it is a quick way for any *gentleman* of any courage to get his redress.

I think that I have mentioned a Mr. Daley who boarded at the house—well, he has left us for New York and the morning (yesterday) that he left, he came to my bedside before day light to formaly present me with a rough, black, stone jug—around which we have passed many a plesant evening, while smoking our pipes in our rooms, and I have placed the inclosed inscription upon its sides.[42] Mrs. Silvers, says, that the latter clause will never be carried out for if I leave, *that* jug shall be kept in the family as a momento of the "lively spirits that she had to controll"—she (by-the-way) is an old acquaintance of Mrs. Preston, with whom I boarded in Columbus, and Dr. Silvers is a native of Philad—so you see that I have come, as the boy said of his Father to "know them just as *easy*"—for the Doctor is acquainted with quite a number of Philadephians and Jerseymen that I know and we have some old fashioned talks together, as I have to post him, for it is a number of years since he was there.

Give my love to the boys and many kisses to our darling, who I hope is fully recovered from her cold by this time,

Your
Charly

P.S. Mrs. Alexander has a letter from the Colonel and I think from the delay that he has experienced at Wilmington that you will not see him.

84

St. Louis, Mo.
November 21 = 1863

Dear Mary,

Yours of the 18th inst came to hand to-day[.]

You say that Willie acknowledged mine of the 11th & 12th inst.—I have not received it yet—did he direct it right?

Mary, our little darling must be very sick, *very* sick when you are compelled to get the boys to answer my letters—my God! I hope that it will not result seriously—My Heaven! how little does those who are absent a few miles know what is transpiring at home!—here I have been happy—*very happy* in anticipation of my coming visit while you have been miserable, fatigued, worn-out with sickness at the very spot upon which *my* happiness was centered.

It is needless to tell you Mary not to spare any expense for her benefit—let money go—let it "flow like water" if it is requisite—and at the same time save your self as much as possable—hire a nurse and then you can save considerable loss of sleep which is *one* of the cause being worn-out while attending sickness—for God sake! dont you break your self down too.

Oh! how I wish that I was home to relieve you as in times past.

If any thing should happen that would absolutly require my presence at home tellegraph me and direct your tellegraph as you do your letters in *care of Col. Alexander A.A.P.M.G.* so that it will not get astray as the former did—be sure to name *Col. Alexander* as there are several Prov. Mar. here in the various Military offices—in fact you might add (to make it doubly sure) 5th & Pine Street.

You have not informed me of the disease that she has.

Col. Alexander has not yet returned and is waiting at Wilmington, Del. for the members of the Board who are absent from that place—and Capt. Bush has taken up the Superintendancy of Recruiting for him, which requires his (Bush's) absence from the office nearly all day, and as the Ordinance and Recruiting Officer of the Invalid Corps is yet on "leave"—and I having *all* his duties to attend to for them in connection with my own, I am so busy that I scarce have time to eat—hence this letter must be short.

Give my love to the Boys and many kisses to Clara—God bless her!

Yr[.]
Charly

P.S. Write soon and let me know how she is—for I will be all anxiety until I hear from you[.]

85

[letterhead: State of Missouri
Office of Act'g Ass't Provost Marshal General U.S.A.]

St. Louis, November 23 = 1863

Dear Mary,

I received Willie's letter of the 17th inst. this morning and find that Clara's sickness is the Thyphoid Fever—and very fearfull that it may either prove lingering or leave her with some bodley disease—the other alternative I will not—dare not—think of. I can not tell how uneasy, how upset I have been since I received your letter—if it was not that I have been so *very* busy since, I do not know what I would have done—even in the midst of all my writing of "Special Orders," "General Orders" &c. I see her before me; and you with your worried countinance sticks like wax to me—God! I hope that your next (which I expect to-morrow) will bring some glad tidings.

Col. Alexander has not returned and we started the State Recruiting or rather the "General Depot, Recruiting Service Missouri Volunteers" to-day and it has been a perfect *rush* for all hands—I have laid my work aside to write these hasty lines today and will write more at length when I get your next—due to-morrow.

I understand to-day that *all* the officers of the Invalid Corps are to be examined before an "Examining Board" between now and the 1st of January next—I suppose they intend to "weed out" this arm of the service before it is made a perminant thing.[43]

Give my love to the Boys and many kisses to our little Pet[.]

Yr[.]
Charly

86

[letterhead: Head Quarters, Recruiting Service, Missouri Vols.
Office of Act'g Ass't Provost Marshal General for Missouri]

St. Louis, November 26, 1863

Dear Mary,

This being Thanksgiving Day and the office being closed since 11 o'clock A.M. I thought that I could not better enjoy myself than write a few lines to you—

Well! the "jig is up"—the "cat's back is "broke"—and I am "in for it" as the heading of this letter shows—to-day the Colonel informed me that he would place the above in my charge—"darn his buttons" say I—for I actualy do not understand *all* the duties of the "Superintendent of Recruiting for the State" which is his title and *my* work, and per consequence I have got to "fall too" and "read up" the Recruiting Regulations"—I tell you what it is Mary, when I saw (yesterday) three furniture cars filled with books, blanks, vouchers, accounts, desks &c. &c., I thought that *somebody* would sweat unless they were posted and I little dreamed that *I* was that some body. To show you the extent of that Department I will mention that I have one Captain (Acting Asst. Quarter Master) one Lieutenant and five clerks and am compelled to appoint two more tomorrow. Blast the thing! if I do not get somebody in a scrape before I get through, I will be a "lucky Dog" that is all—this is all in connection with my former duties, the Colonel say that I have *that* so systemized that, *that* part of the affair can not bother me much,—hump! I guess that I had better not *systemize this* or another Department will be added—when I mentioned this to him he said "Oh! never mind Colonel, you may purchase all the Desks that you want and detail the whole Company for Clerks if you desire it, but I would rather that you take charge of it for the present."

Capt. Bush leaves here to-morrow morning at day-light for 15 days, he is gone nearly 700 miles *west*, on a hunting excursion on the Prairies—Buffalo, Elk, Dear &c.—near Fort Larimah, his old quarters. When he return[s] then—then—then—oh my![44]

Col. Alexander requested me to state to you that he was detained so long at Wilmington that he was compelled to go through Philad. without missing a connection, being but 30 minutes there—in fact he was not able to go to Washington even, hence the impossability of calling on you—I am sorry for I *did* want you to see the "old codger." When I *showed* a regret (for I did not express it) he remarked "never mind Colonel, if we have luck you will soon *see* them yourself and that is better than having some one see them for you"—I guess that he was right *there* although I wanted *both.*

Night before last I was very much astonished to meet Mr. Markely of Camden, in the street here as we both were with Company, we had but a few moments togeather. I went to the "Lindell" twice yesterday but could not see him, he said that he would leave today and offered to carry any thing that I desired, if I see him (I shall make another attempt) I will send this by him if not, then by mail.

I am waiting anxiously for your next (due Saturday) to hear of our little Darling's improvement—I say improvement for I have settled my mind that such is to be the intelligence. They say that "absence conquers Love" but *I* can give the lie to that old proverb, for the longer I am from home—"sweet home," the greater are the longings to see, hear and feel the "loved ones" that make that spot so bright, and

"Time moves on with laggard steps"

as the day[s] decrease their number that holds me here—if I could only move them with Rail Road speed, and then the cars with lightening speed how quickly it would be done.

Give my love to the Boys and many kisses to Clara[.]

Yr[.]
Charly

87

[letterhead: Head Quarters, Recruiting Service, Missouri Vols.
Office of Act'g Ass't Provost Marshal General for Missouri]

Saint Louis, December 7, 1863

Dear Mary,

It is now 9 o'clock P.M. and I am just through my days work and I hasten to write to you (before I go to get some supper) so that it will leave by this night's Mail.

I received your tellegram this morning (directed to Lieut. Col. *Smith*) and I answered it immediately, and I regret that it was impossable for me to leave to-day for my desk was literaly piled up with papers (although I worked from 9½ o'clock A.M. until 5 o'clock P.M. on yesterday—Sunday to keep the work down so that I could get off for home soon) and as the accounts embraced several thousand dollars the Colonel was not willing to entrust it in other hands (damn his confidence) for fear that they might stick him for some hundreds of dollars, hence he would not say go—well! I do not say that I can blame *him* although I felt very sorry for I *knew* that you wanted me by your side in your affliction and I longed to be there, because I felt that you was wishing for me.

Had I have got permission to leave I could not have done so until to-morrow evening (to-day it was impossable) and that would not bring me in Camden until Friday afternoon late; which would be too late even for the funeral much less to assist you in your affliction and difficulty incidental to the funeral; and as it (even being too late) would necessarly *shorten* my stay with you, when I did get there, I submited with the best grace that I could.

The death of Mother Davis was of course expected and did not surprise me—well—well! poor Old Soul she has had a long life and passed a good one and has passed from a world of trouble to a better home—if there is such.[45]

I received your letter of the 3rd inst. this afternoon in which you appear to forshadow Mother's death, so I suppose that you also was not surprised although these things, even if we *do* expect them, startle us when they come—I can not or rather *will not* write what I could say, but I feel that I could soften your grief considerably if I was there—however I soon will be and then my dear you can pour out your trouble, for I come prepared to listen and console. I feel that you have had enough to try any woman, and more than your share of trouble since I left home this time—God bless you! how my heart yearns for an opportunity to share your burdens with you; as "Misery loves Company" so does affliction love some one to lean upon and sympathize with them even if they can not remove the burden or restore the bright page of life—I know all this—I feel all this, and am more than ever eager for the time of my departure from this accursed hole.

I could go on and write pages but as it amounts to only words on paper and I know that thousands are not worth one where the sound of the voice is heard—I shall stop—while I could *talk* for hours I feel that I can not *write*—at least write any thing that will answer the purpose.

As it takes from eight to nine or ten days for me to get an answer to my letters, you may answer this if you can do so immediately, but I hope to be on my road home before I could get an answer to my next letter to you.

Give my love to the Boys and many kisses to Clara[.]

Yr[.]
Charly

P.S. I feel a kind of gloom because I *know* that you will be disappointed at my not getting home—God bless you!

6

"The same old thing, except being *shot at*"

January 6, 1864–May 5, 1864

JOHNSON was able to spend Christmas 1863 with his family. Sometime during this period he also traveled to Washington on business that apparently had to do with the Invalid Corps. While there, he no doubt continued his efforts to procure an assignment to a post closer to home but had to return to St. Louis in January 1864.

88

St. Louis, Mo.
December [January] 6, 1864[1]

Dear Mary,

Here I am at last, writing by the dim flickering of a half frozen gas metre, here after a long and tedious ride which can be best illustrated by a detailed account of my journey—I left Philad. at 10½ o'clock and went all night until we were about 12 or 14 miles from Pittsburg, when the truck of the tender broke and we were detained nearly *three* hours and arrived at Pittsburg in the afternoon of Sunday just as it commenced snowing like "all blazes" and continued to do so until I left at 2¼ o'clock Monday morning.

While prowling (for I can call it by no other name) I stumbled across Dr. G. A. Palmer the Brigade Surgeon of Gen.l Howard, afterwards the Medical Director of Richardson's Division, he was ordered from Carlisle Barracks, Pa to report at St. Louis—of course we "Coaliced" immediately.

Dec. [Jan.] 7 = I had just written the above when the gas "froze up" so I continue this morning.

While waiting for the cars to start (2¼ o'clock Monday Morning) I was surprised by being spoken to by a number of the 8th Illinois cavalry who were on their road home as veterans—they frequently served under me during reconizance—I did not know them but they did me.

We left Pittsburg with some 4 inches of snow and were stoped twice before we arrived at Cristaline[2] to remove the wrecks of two trains that broke down and finaly reached Indianapolis at 10 o'clock at night and found that no trains had arrived from St. Louis for two days, so we were compelled to "lay over," and had to sleep in beds with two and three in it, as every place was full, in fact I did not get a place to sleep until after Midnight, having ran all over the city in 10 inches of snow and the thermomiter at 12 degrees below zero.

We left on Tuesday (I am so cold I can scarce write) at 9 o'clock and when 94 miles from St. Louis we found another train off the track, the snow having packed so high and hard on the track that the cars could not remain on it for any length of time with any certainty hence we ran very slow—well, we had either to "clear the track" or stay all night, so we went to work, having built large fires with fence rails, and finaly succeeded—in short we arrived at East St. Louis at 5 o'clock on Wednesday morning—instead of Monday evening as I expected when I left home, and there we had to foot it across the Mississippi on the ice with lanterns and the thermomiter at 10 degrees below Zero, by George it *was* cold.

The weather has been 24 degress below Zero here for some day[s] but it has "let up" to-day and looks like more snow—whole trains of Hogs have frozen while on the different roads.

I have not had time to get my pay yet but will do so to-day or to-morrow and forward to you immediately and write at the same time—I am ashamed of this scrawl but can not help it[.]

Give my love to the Boys and kisses to Clare[.]

Yr[.]
Charley

89

[letterhead: Head Quarters, Recruiting Service, Missouri Vols.
Office of Act'g Ass't Provost Marshal General for Missouri]

St. Louis January 15, 1864

Dear Mary,

This is the day that I should have received an answer to my letter of the 7th inst.—I suppose that it will come however either by this afternoon or tomorrow morning's mail.

Lt. Col. Frederick is here on a few days leave of absence—he was ordered to Indianapolis as one of the members of the "Examining Board" to examine the Line Officers of the Corps at that place—I am free to admit that I do not understand it—for if the Field Officers *are* to be examined why are they not examined *before they* sit in judgement upon their inferiors. Varily! Varily! we can exclaim with Hamlet:

> "There is more betwix Heaven and Earth
> Than is drempt of in your phylosophy."[3]

The Inspector General U.S. (Col. Marcy)[4] was here this morning and intruded his official nose into all manner of corners and nooks and propounded all sorts of inquiries as to the "whys and wherefores" of this, that, and the other—blast these Washington officials they do stir us poor devils up once in a while—if he was satisfied with the office or not I do not know and as Col. Alexander says *he* does not "care a damn" why of course I do not care either so we let it go for what it is worth.

I have just received an "order" from Washington—not to leave here, no! but an order assigning me to my Regiment—it is the 18th (81st reversed) and the Headquarters are at *Indianapolis, Ind.a*—it is mearly a notice of my assignment nothing more—no orders to leave here or any thing else, those I suppose will come hereafter—the organization is as follows, viz.;

Col. Chas. F. Johnson
Lt. Col. N. T. Colby
Maj. Martin Flood   do not know where in the devil they are[5]
4 companies at Indianapolis, Ind.
1 " " Jeffersonville, "
4 " " Louisville, Kentucky
and 1 " " Camp Joe Holt, Indiana

Where in the thunder the last place is I do not know and more than that, do not care, for although it is one days less travell between home and here, yet it is a Western Regiment, or rather a regiment located "out west," and that is enough for me blast! it I say—I have "cussed" some this day, I regret to say, but—I could not help it, for I some how have fed myself with the hope that I might get into Penn. or the New England states, although the latter would not be any nearer to my home than here, and not as near as Indianapolis, yet it would get me from this confounded *"west"*—blast it, I have it worse than ever, since I have returned from home—oh! there is no spot so sweet as that little one called Camden.

However "grin and bear it" is the Motto—I will acknowledge the receipt of the "order" blast the "orders"! this afternoon and awaite the future ones—I of course do not know until I get at my regiment, if it is likely to be located any length of time at that place (or places I should say more properly) in fact do not know yet if I will be ordered to it at all and until that is definitely known we might as well let the thing pass as a matter of general information.

Send me the number 18 in your next letter—you have both in the cash box—by-the-way Mary, that jumps me over seven Lieut. Cols. as I should have ranked as 25th on the list if promoted by regular rotations.

As I expect a letter from you to-morrow I will close.

Give my love to the Boys and kisses to Clara[.]

Your
Charley

It is hardly worth while to speculate upon military orders or movements but the fact of my regiment being so scatered it looks as if I would not be ordered to it in a hurry, unless it should be ordered to be collected togeather or sent to some other post—

but what *is* the use of surmising "sufficient for the day is the evil thereof[.]"

90

[letterhead: Head Quarters, Recruiting Service, Missouri Vols.
Office of Act'g Ass't Provost Marshal General for Missouri]

St. Louis, January 19, 1864

Dear Mary,

At last! A[t] long, *long*, at last it has come. Heavens how anxiously have I looked for it—yours of the 14th inst. came today, the fact is, I had made up my mind to tellegraph to you if I had not secured a letter within 24 hours—although my judgement told me that there was not anything wrong with you, yet my heart—that cowardly member of the body *feared* that there was—and it said "use the wires Charley—while common sence said "waite"—it has been seventeen days (oh what an age!) since I have seen or *heared* from you all.

I here inclose Clara's (God bless her!) weekly installment—the truth is that I had forgot all about it—you need not tell her or the Boys that such was the case—but my mind was on the rack about other things.

Well, Mary, my orders are here at last—to-day (within an hour) I received them—here they are.

"Col. Chas. F. Johnson is relieved from his present duties and will report to Col. Conrad Baker, 1st Indiana Cavalry, A.A.P.M. Gen.l at Indianapolis, Ind to *assume command of the 18th Regiment Invalid Corps.*"

I suppose, from my previous orders that my Headquarters will be at Indianapolis unless Col. Baker has the power to change them, that he can do only by express order from Washington.

Here goes for a Barrack's life—farewell to all Citizens dress—henceforth it is uniform—uniform—Reville—Tattoo—drill &c. the same old thing, except being *shot at.*

Col. Alexander will not relieve me for a couple of days, yet—in fact is so upset by this order that he can not think of *who* is to take charge of my Department.

I have a plan in my head whereby we can get togeather again, but as it will depend upon the state of affairs there (Indianapolis) and the probable permnancy of the affair, that I will waite until I get there and then we will discuss it in full.

This is a very disconnected letter, but I wish to say so much and have such little time to say it in that I scarce know how to write, for with instructions to all my force, collating documents, assorting and collecting papers I am "over head and ears" with business, for now that I am leaving I wish to leave as "clean" an office as possable, so as to retain my hitherto good reputation with the Colonel, so that if I ever (which God forbid) should be required to refer to *him* I can do so with perfect safety.

As I will have left here by the time you receive this, you had best direct your answer to

Col. C. F. Johnson
18th Reg. Inv. Corp
Care of Col. C. Baker
A.A.P.M. Gen.l
Indianapolis, Ind.

I do not know where my Camp or Barracks are, but will make such arrangements with him as to get it—if an other address is required of course I will advise you immediately—I will write just before leaving here[.]

Give my love to the Boys and kisses to Clara—I suppose she will receive these[.]

Yr[.]
Charly

P.S. the inclosed installments are up to next Saturday being three weeks pay—seventy-five cents—thirty each for the Boys and fifteen for that little prattler[.]

91

[letterhead: Head Quarters, Recruiting Service, Missouri Vols.
Office of Act'g Ass't Provost Marshal General for Missouri]

St. Louis, January 26 1864

Dear Mary,

I have just time to inform you (according to promise) that I leave here this day at 3 o'clock—provided the ice will permit us to walk over—passangers cross, their baggage follow when convenient.

I will write you immediately upon my arrival at Indianapolis, that is, as soon as I am *located.*

I have been feated for the last few days to the extent of my capacity—a Party at Silver's—a Supper by the Provost Marshal's and their Deputies and to-day a Dinner by the Officers connected with our office.

I inclose twenty-five (25) cents my weekly installment to the children up to Saturday next, 30th inst.

No answer to my letter of the 15th inst. or any subsequent one[.] Give my love to the Boys and kisses to Clara[.]

Yrs hastly[,]
Charly

P.S. I inclose likness of Lt. Mann[ar]ing.

92

[letterhead: Head Quarters Military Prison
Camp Morton
Indianapolis, Ind.]—

January 27, 1864[6]

Dear Mary,

I arrived at Indianapolis this morning at 4 o'clock and immediately proceed to this place Burnside Barracks—I use the above heading because my trunk has not arrived and they have no other paper present—this camp Morton is attached to Burnside Barracks and under the commander of the Barracks (Col. Stevens).[7] We have here one full Regiment of the I.C.—the 5th and parts of three other, viz. 17th, 18th and 23rd.—[8] I have five companies here and a Major—and at Camp Morton (which we guard) we have over 3500 Rebel Prisoners.

Lt. Col. Fredericks is attached to the 5th Reg. permanently.

I reported to Col. Baker this morning and after being ordered to take command of my Regiment, we had a talk and the result is that I will leave here to-morrow morning and proceed to Jeffersonville, New Albany, and one or two other places to inspect all the troops in the Invalid Corps in the various places in the Southern part of the State. The fact is that there is a conflict of authority between the A.A.P.M.G. for Kentucky and Indiana in reference to the Invalid Corps—they never could get it straight, so Col. Baker (saying that he had "heard of my executive abilities") thought that I had better go down with full power and make such a report that he could forward it to Washington with his approval and bring the thing to a focus. He also insinuated that he *might* create a Department (similar to this, but extending over several Counties) down there and asked, if he did do so, how I would like to take the command[.] *that* question I could not answer until I had seen it and fully understood what was wanted of me—that I had rather take a rest from *organizing* Deparments &c. &c. he laughed and said that I had been suggested to him sometime since—that he had been told that "Col. Johnson was just the man for such work" and that "since talking with you Colonel I believe it to be so"—so it rather looks as if I was intended to have a "big thing" under me.

They are in daily expectation of the Examining Board's arrival, as they are nearly through [with] their work at Washington and this is the next post to be visited—phew! may-be they will want some other commander for the "Southern Indiana Department."

I have not received any letter from you since your answer to mine of the 13th inst. I certainly expected some letters at this post—more as I received one from Harry, directed to me here, and saying that you informed him of my change, hence as you knew of it, I expected one.

I have just received my orders from Col. Baker—I am also to proceed to Louisville, Kentucky for the same object.

As the waggon leaves here for the afternoon's mail I must close—I will give you a full description of the Barracks &c. in some future letter—I must now go over and take command and overhaul my Major's actions.

Yr[.]
Charly

P.S. I wrote to you on the 15th, 17th, 19th, 21st, 24th, 26th, and this, answers are due for the first four—gads! I hope that they will hurry along[.]

I open this to say that yours of the 23rd inst (in answer to mine of the 19th inst) just arrived—in reference to our getting togeather we will discuss as soon as I can see how and where my Regiment is to be situated and you can rest assured that I will do so as soon as possable.

Direct to me (naming Regiment) Burnside Barracks, Indianapolis, Ind.

93

Washington D.C.
February 10 = 1864

Dear Mary,

I have *seen* (not received) my written orders—I am ordered before the board for examination and from the cold and extreamly *Military* manner in which I have been received I do not expect any mercy.

I am to be examined to-morrow at 12 O'Clock—Col. Rush[9] asked me when I would be ready, I answered "just when you choose"—I thought if I was to "go up a spout" I might as well go at once and not be at any extra expence here, for "go" I *will* to all intense and purposes—damn them.

I will either write or Paddy like[10] bring my next letter as soon as I am through with the Board, I guess it will be Paddy like for I fully expect to get permission to "leave" instanter.

This letter is short but it contains enough for twenty[.]

Yr[.]
Charley

94

[letterhead: Head Quarters Military Prison
Camp Morton
Indianapolis, Ind.]

Feb. 17th = 1864

Dear Mary,

I have only time to write a few lines to inform you of my arrival here last night—instead of the night before last as anticipated.

The Government informed Col. Baker (who was *very* glad to see me) that his request could not be granted, as "Col. Johnson would in all probability be absolutely required for other duties" this communication was however written upon the day of my *arrival* at Washington—I would rather it were written upon the day of my *departure* from the same place.[11]

Col. Stevens has asked as a favor (he has no right to *order,* so mixed up are our orders) that I take command of the entire Burnside Barracks and (to use his own words) "run the machine" leaving him to attend to Camp Morton alone, as he has always been very clever I consented and am up to my eyes in business, as I have the executive affairs of the 18th Reg. to attend to in connection therewith.

I will write to you more fully at some future day but this is written while the Mail Carrier is waiting at the desk.

Give my love to the Boys and Kisses to Clara,

Yr[.]
Charley

95

Headquarters 18th Reg. I.C.
Indianapolis, Ind.
February 20 = 1864

Dear Mary,

I avail myself of a few moments leisure to write to you to-day. I have [been], and am, up to my eyes in business in endevouring to bring the 18th Regiment "up to the mark" and make it compete with the 5th regiment and some older ones here. I have a fine Major (a perfect soldier) who was a Lieut. Col. in a Wisconsin Regiment and who has taken a great interest in our regimental organization, otherwise my task would have been more difficult—he is a *perfect gentleman* in every respects—and I do not often say as much of any man, but in this case I can not say otherwise.[12]

We have a number of cases of Small Pox here, particulary in the Rebel Prisoners, and as a precaution I have been vaccinated and think that it will "take" as there is a constant irritation of my arm.

We are enjoying winter to perfection, and I sleep on a straw bed with *seven* blankets over me, kindly loaned by the Quartermaster of the Post—we have not been without snow since the 1st of December and water freezes in every vessil in the quarters to such an extent that it requires a hatchet to cut it in the mornings. Nevertheless I feel "first rate" my "back-door-trots" having entirely stop[p]ed, except that my cough has returned again, and I wish that you would get that recipe from Mother as I am out of Medicine.

Col. Baker has forwarded an other request for me to be detailed in his office "if only temporary"—he told me that if I had only requested two days sooner that I should have had command of the City of Indianapolis which he gave to Col. Warner[13] of the Invalid Corps and offered to "get clean of him" if I sayed so, but of course I refused to be cognizant of any such transactions as Col. Warner is proving himself a good officer.

This afternoon we are to have a "Brigade Review"—that is a Review of the three and a half regiments of the Corps and I am to be the Reviewing officer—the A.A.P.M. Gen.l for Ind. the Govaner of the State[14] &c. &c. are to be present—Col. Steven[s] backed out as (he said) he had all that he could attend to at Camp Morton, and Col. Warner did the same thing having (as he said) "so much to do in town," so I quietly remarked "Damn it gentlemen, I will take charge of the affair and will not disgrace the Corps"—weither that promise was rash or not I do not know, but I shall do my best I assure you.

Col. Stevens (who is a member of the Examining Board) appears to think that I am to be placed in some good position from the statements that I made to him (candidly) of my examination. however *that* is all in the "womb of time."

Give my love to the Boys and many kisses to Clara.

Yr.
Charley

I inclose two weeks instalment which I believe is correct[.]

96

Burnside Barracks
Indianapolis, Ind.
February 24 = 1864

Dear Mary,

I avail myself of a few moments leisure this morning to "drop" a few lines to you. I have been and am *very* busy this few days past as I have been put in Command of Burnside Barracks with its eighteen companies (a larger Command than I ever had before) and am engaged in changing the entire aspect of affairs and am endevouring (and by George *will*) make things look different by dividing and sub-dividing the responsibility of all parties; for instant, I have divided the forces into three regiments (of six companies each) under the command of Lt. Col. Frederick, Majors Gardiner & Flood and set them to work as a miniture Brigade, with myself at the head—the command is fully as large as our Brigade was in the field when I left—and with taring down and moving Guard House, building Barracks, grading the ground, and white washing *every thing* (over a hundred and fifty men at *that* alone) it keeps me busy—I expect that with my usual luck that as soon as I get *this* place in a shape to suit me (and there is immence work to do to accomplish that) that I will be ordered elsewhere or be permited to "leave" the service.

The Board is here, or rather have been ordered here to meet on the 23rd inst. (yesterday) but have not yet made their august apperance, although all the Field Officers have been notified to meet them and some of the Line Officers consequently there is considerable "nervous debility" apparent throughout the command with said parties—thank God! I can laugh at them now even if I do "go by the board" and I must say that I do not like the looks of things just now as this Board is a new one and I am not on it—it "kinder" looks as if I was not intended to live longer than the Gods intended[.][15]

"Those whom the Gods love! die *early*."

My Lieut. Colonel has been ordered to report to me and also to report to the Board, so I will see him in a "few days"—I hope that he will be as good an officer as my staid, steady, sober sided, gray haired Major, whose sole ambition appears to be to do just as I desire.

I will forward to day two or three papers containing a description of our celebration on the "glorious 22nd" one of them, the "Sentinal" is copperhead but you will perceive that even *that* does not speak disparagingly of the Corps.[16] I must say that I felt proud of them as every officer and *man* did his best and we took "In-*gee*-ana" entirely in the back—I am working like the devil to bring the 18th Regiment up to the mark, even if I am forced to leave it, they shall give me the credit of leaving a good regiment and shall not be able to point to it and say "his command showes that he is not qualified" but rather that I may say "My regiment speaks for me gentlemen[.]"

Give my love to the Boys and Kisses to Clare—I begin to feel anxious to hear from you[.]

Your
Charley

97

Burnside Barracks
Indianapolis, Ind
February 28 – 1864

Dear Mary,

Yours of the 23rd and 24th inst. came to hand last night and I hasten today to answer having just finished a thorough inspection (monthly) of the entire Barracks, Hospital, Prison, Books &c. &c. as I am to Muster the force here for pay tomorrow—and am forced to divide my labor into two days, as it is more than I can get through with in one—it is not exactly according to Hoyle (nor Regulations either) but I will make it answer.

You say that you are using a powerful Tonic (given to you by Chambers) why what is the matter with you, and what kind of Medicine is it?

I am indeed sorry that you have the Salt Rheum and can and do sympathize with you, for a more troublesome disease could not be imagined, especially as it is not a fatle one—but Mary, you know the remidy—one dozen of "Citrate of Magnesia," one half bottle every three days—try it.

You had best send that Draft to me—that was what I informed you to do at the time that I told you of it—you can send it inclosed per. mail, it will be perfectly safe, I guess, and quite as convenient as "cussing" to a Power of Atterny.

My Lieut. Colonel has turned up and Lo! and behold! he is the very officer that the Board (damn them) offered to set while I was being examined and to whom they gave the headings of his examination, he was examined three days after I was and has had his report of his case three or four day[s]—no partiality in *that* case—well, Mary, he is not worth a "Continental damn" (excuse the language) although he has passed "the Board" and I regret it—not that he passed, but that he does not know any thing, however I have set him to work and by George he either *shall* do his duty (despite of the parciality of the Board) or get relieved from duty here—it makes me furious.[17]

I have come to the conclusion not to die yet awhile, and have come to that conclusion from the fact that I have gained some eight pounds of flesh—yesterday I weighed 142 pounds. There goes the call for Dress Parade and I must close.

Col. Baker intends to renew his application for me at his office and Stevens does not want me to leave here, as I have (so he says) "worked such wonders in the Barracks since I have had command, that he would like me to finish a job so well begun."

Give my love to the Boys and many kisses to Clare[.]

Yr[.]
Charley

98

Burnside Barracks
March 3 = 1864

Dear Mary,

Yours of the 27th came to hand yesterday and I would have answered it at the time as is my usual practace, but I have been so "run down" with my duties that I scarce have time to "answer the call of Nature" as this infurnal Mustering has kept me busy; when I inform you that I have "the Muster for Pay" rolls of nineteen Companies to examine and verify, each giving the full Military history of each man and every roll quadruplicated and that in connection with my duties as "Commandant of Burnside Barracks," you can see that I have not had many idle moments, especialy as the Rolls *must* be forwarded in "three day[s] from muster"—thank God I have done it up in the given time and will have my returns in all "O.K." This being Commander of the 18th Regiment, Commander of the Barracks and Mustering Officer and President of an Investigating Board (which meets nightly) is not what it is "cracked up" to be, but as Col. Stevens says "no matter what the Examining Board may say of you theoreticaly, I can sware to your services practicaly" and as he is a member of the board it amounts to some thing as "part payment."

While writing the above another company has reported to me for duty, from Cincinatti—so we go.

The Paymaster has "no funds" but "expects in a day or so" and hence I can not ship as promptly as usual—this "In-gee-ana" is a great place for I have not yet been able to get lumber for my quarters and in fact have not been able to get my milage from Washington to this place but will "in a day or so"—the old song.

I regret exceedingly Mary that as your letter indicates, you are in an exceedingly nervous state and I hope and pray that I may soon be able to fix things so that we may be togeather again—I should know by this time, so the Members of the Board—two of whom are here—inform me, of the result of my examination so I may expect it shortly, in fact daily, and be it either way we will be togeather shortly, so Mary keep your spirits up and do your best to fight against that feeling that I know and feel is undermining your constitution—I know that when we get togeather again that I can knock it as "dead as a door nail" or I will "bust" in the attempt.

I gave yesterday a letter of introduction to a Capt. Rice of the 5th who I expect will call on you, also my address (verbaly) to Mrs. Gardiner wife of Major Gardener of the 5th who promised to call on you, but I do not expect it, as she did not get it in writing, and "out of sight, out of mind" you know is an old and true adage.[18]

I received a letter from Alva Stites which was forwarded to Washington to me and sent back by the Prov. Mar. Gen.l here—so it has travelled "some."

Pshaw! there goes the call for Dress Parade and I must close [.] Well "there is no rest for the wicked" and I suppose I am classed under that head—It will not do for *me* to miss *that* as *I* have just issued an order threatening to Court-Marshal any officer who does not appear upon the Parade.

By-the-way—the Government dismissed one of My Captains at my request, for "intoxication and conduct unbecoming an officer and a Gentleman" and it has made all the post as strict as possable, they have got it into their heads that I have only to ask the "powers that be" and "off goes their heads" poor devils! they little know that I stand in the like fear.[19]

Give my love to the Boys and many kisses to Clara.

Your
Charley

99

Burnside Barracks
March 9 = 1864

Dear Mary,

I yesterday forwarded per Adams Express the sum of $150.00 also the Draft which I might as well have not forwarded at all for I realy believe that I did not endorse it—to tell you the truth I have not thought of *self* scarcly one moment this last two weeks, and I did not endorse it at the time that I received it for fear that it might be lost and my impression is that in my haste (at the time of shipment) that I forgot to do so.

I will send you a Power of Attorny for you to do so—I[t] cost more than postage but I will pay it for my damn infurnal negligence but the fact is that I had so much to attend to at the time that I scarce know if I was on my head or heels and did not get any thing to eat until night. I am writing this while a horse is being saddled and if I can get to the express office before it leaves it will be all right—if not why—damn it! I scarce know what to say—I feel so infurnally out-done at my cursed negligence—it is true you do not want to use the money, but if you did the error would still be there and that is what makes me so mad[.]

I have just returned from town and (although I rode at a full run on the saddle) I was just 30 minutes too late to stop the Draft—so keep it and I will send a Power of Attorny as soon as I can get to town to have one executed.

Upon my return I received your letter of the 1st [or 7th] inst. and I regret to say that I have not answered Alva's letter, but will do so as soon as possable.

As for the list of questions and answers before the Board; you can tell Harry that it will not avail anything for the whole thing is put[?] in a *political* shape—officers are passing and not passing in accordance with the pressure that they bear upon the Sec. of War and if he can do any thing in that line, he had best do it—Andy Curtin[20] is all powerfull in that direction in regard to the Invalid Corps—if any member of Congress from Penn. could be influenced it would help me to a certainty you can tell him in *Confidence*—he is not to let it be known—that the Sec. of War (who is not my friend) has my papers under consideration—I expect nothing and hence will not be disappointed—however he can work from that—Col. Stevens has offered me (as Commander of the Post) a leave of absence for seven days if I desire it—and *he* to take the responsibility—I have not accepted it as I do not know that I could effect any thing by my personal importunities and I may want it for other purposes, beside it would opperate against me as one evidence of my neglect of duty—at least it could be so construed. So I will waite until it is absolutly necessary.

Two Field Officers (whom *I* instructed and prepared for examination) have passed and I am assisting the third who I *believe* will pass—*I* certainly should do so and will if *Politics* does not interfear—however we will waite—in the mean time if Harry can get an imperative demand that I pass it would help me—but let him act cautiously and [not] "pitch in" too roughly—I have not spoken of this matter before, but I have not been idle.

Give my love to the Boys and kisses to Clara.

Yr[.]
Charley

100

Burnside Barracks
March 13 = 1864

Dear Mary,

It is now 5 o'clock in the morning—hence I write this by the light of the lamp—but as yesterday was the proper time for me to write and I was so "run in the ground" that I could not have tried I thought that I would get up before Reveille this morning and make sure of it.

I should have received your letter in answer to mine of the 6th to-day but as the mails are "uncartain—sure" and we have only one on Sundays—I do not expect it until tomorrow.

I [and] All hands (of the Field Officers) have been before the Board of Examination and as our fate is fixed—even if we do not know it—and as Congress is likely to pass the bill making us—no I will write more definitly, for it may not be *us*—well as Congress is likely to pass the bill making the Invalid Corps a fixture in this great, glorious, free and independent country, in such a form as to create Brigades—*we*—the immaculate *we*—us—ourselves are now busly engaged in endevouring to make certain parties Brigadiers—and have sent Col. Frederick to St. Louis for letters, signatures &c. for the benefit of Col. Stevens.

I would not rush into the work but as all of the examining Board are fighting for it and as I thin[k] that many of them do not stand well with me, why—I would "pitch in" for the Devil to defeat them if possable.

I expect that we will be "sucked in" all around for as soon as the Corps is a "fixed fact" that every petty Politician will endevour to obtain a position for himself or some "friend" and "poor we's" will be as Shuttlecocks between the Battledoms—knocked from one side to the other, some times underneath some times sent up flying, but at last suffered to "fall to the ground."

The Corps appears to me to be fated to constant Legislation—that is to say, that Politicians will be constantly endevouring to mend or alter it, some from pure motives, others from interested ones, as it will always have the *appearance* of being a "fat place" hence the outs will always be pulling at the ins. As for myself, I have quietly determined to meet any fate like a man—I have been informed that the cause of my not receiving any notice of the report of my case is due to the Sec.y of War who is on the stand with me—how true *that* is I do not know—but I suppose that there is something in it as the Board *must* have made *some kind* of report long before this—however I am not loosing friends I assure you—I will cite one instance—I called upon the A.A.P.M.G. for Ind. yesterday for an expression of opinion in regard to Col. Stevens for Brig. Genl. and urged him to see Gov. Morton, when he (Col. Baker) gave me a letter of introduction wherein he used the terms (speaking of the bearer, myself) that he was "one of the most accomplished gentlemen, efficient soldiers, and honest men that I (Col. Baker) have met with during my official careare[.]" So you see that if Old Stanton holds on much longer I will add a little more salt to my rod that is in pickle.[21]

Give my love to the Boys and many Kisses to Clare—you have not mentioned her in any of your letters recently[.]

Your
Charly

101

Burnside Barracks
March 15 = 1864

Dear Mary,

Yours of the 12th inst. has just arrived, amidst a most violent snow storm—in fact it has snowed for the last three concecitive days and while writing this it is falling so fast and thick that I can not see across the Barracks[.]

You need not be anyways alarmed (that "anyways" is not *very* gramatical, but let it go) at my over-taxing my health, for I actualy "wax fat" upon my work—the constant excitement, the out-doors work and the regular activity rather helps me than otherwise; as my increase of weight attests.

The only detriment is my frequent riding in the saddle which sometimes hurts my testicles—if I was sure of my position I would secure a horse and Buggey and by that means obviate *that* diffculty.

As for my "working for other people" you are mistaken, Mary, for I am working for myself for I will either maintain my reputation (if I remain) or I will *leave* a reputation that the Board or Secretary of War can not "gainsay"—hence it is for myself.

As for my giving it up just *now*—*that* is out of the question, for if I should resigne and leave I would create an impression with my friends that I was *forced* to do so, and that impression would be so firm and appear so plausable that I could not remove it—hence I would have the "name[??] without the game"—No! No!! if I *must* leave, I will leave a favourable record and perhaps *take* with me a favourable record that will give the lie to all asertions to the contrary.

Joes determination to succeed pleases me very much—and why should it not? for it is "daddy all over"—as "determaned as the devil" when his mind is once made up—even *I* can see Charley Johnson in him.

Apropos of my hard work I can say that I have passed *two* evenings with *Ladies* (now do not get frightened, I "haint goin" to run away with them) in the City of Indianapolis or rather I passed two evenings with the family of an acquaintance that I have cultivated here; which was quite a relief, as it has been the first time since I left St. Louis that I have even *talked* to a female or visited a private residence, (except while at home that short time) and I cite this to show that I have time even for recreation, so you see that I am not killing myself with work when I can spare *two* nights for pleasure.

I have standing invitations with other *friends* (as the world goes) for Dinners, suppers, and Evenings and in fact quite a number of invitations to "make my [self] at home"—none of which I expect to acept, for I could not be happy or even *pleased* with any one while I knew or felt that my wife was miserable at home, even if I had the inclination to go—

The Corps here stands very high and the light blue coat is the pass-port into society, especialy if it has a double row of buttons down the front—I can cite one instance of that fact—at the Theatre they have Opera Glasses to hire by leaving the price with the man—that security has *never* been asked of an Officer of the Invalid Corps while it is demanded of every officer of every other arm of the service.[22]

Give my love to the Boys and Kisses to Clara[.]

Yr[.]
Charley

102

[letterhead: Head Quarters Post Commandant, Madison Ind.]

March 24 1864

Dear Mary,

I write a few hasty lines from this point while waiting for the boat to take me down the Ohio to Louisville, Ky. I am on another tour of inspection to ascertain if there are any and if so how many men there are in the 2nd Battalion of the Invalid Corps fit for transfer into the 1st Bat.[23]—I found over

120 in the four companies at this post—the Commandant of which is my old friend J. W. Cress who reported to me at Columbus Ohio, and is now a captain and perfectly crazy to get into my regiment with or without his Company, and wants to give up this command (a fine post) for that purpose.

Madison is a fine little city of about 1200 inhabitants, and is on the banks of the river, built into a bowl (If I may so term it) for it is completely surrounded by mountains—I took a ride on the surrounding hills and it was truly a very pretty sight, the road winding around the side of the soring mountains (over 500 feet high) and encompassing the whole city, with the swift running Ohio flowing directly through the centre of the valley—it reminded me very much of Easton, Pa.

I am very glad that I did *not* endorse that Draft or I would have been Compelled to have borrowed money, as it was I retained $70.00 and left the $100.00 with the Brother-in-Law of Col. Stevens to ship by Adam's Express, you can get it by calling at the office—directed as coming from me—I would have shiped it myself but it was after Bank hours and he cashed the Draft for me and I did not want to carry it all with me so I left him to ship it.

There goes the whistle of the steam boat and I must close.

Give my love to the boys and kisses to Clara—direct, as usual, I expect to get to Indianapolis in three days if possable—I visit Louisville, Ky, Jeffersonville & New Albany Indiana and perhaps—if things work right—also Lexington, Ky.

Yr[.]
Charly

103

Burnside Barracks
March 30 = 1864

Dear Mary,

I avail myself of a few leisure moments (while the horse is being saddled) to scrawl a few lines, so that the great laps of time that has frequently ocurred between our letters laterly may be avoided—although I have not anything important or I believe interesting to communicate.

Between the excessively bad weather and the want of Carpenters tools I have not commenced my quarters yet, but expect to do so in a day or two—we have had terrable weather here this Month—rain, snow, freezing, snow, sun-shine, snow, rain, clear cold and icey, then rain again &c. &c. to the end of this month occasionaly enlivened by winds that fairly take the hair off the head; and would do so if it was not cut so *short*, "according to regulations."

I have been (and will be) especialy busy for some time, as I am the only Field Officer on duty in the Barracks—my Lieut. Col. (Colby) detailed at Indianapolis, Major Flood on detached service—Col. Steaven at Camp Morton, Lieut. Col. Fredericks in Court Martial, and Maj. Gardiner on detached service—I have been to Indianapolis but once since my return (Saturday) and then only to hand in my report and come immediately back again—The Court Martial has taken five Line officer[s] from me for members of its Board and the Board of Examination (now in session) has from four to six of the others before them each day—hence I may say that I am "driving the machine" alone with two more companies added to the command yesterday.

There was an attempt to remove us to Johnson's Island (in Lake Erie)[24] but the authorities here decided that they could not spare us, so I suppose that it has failed, although I understand that it will be renewed—I wish that it would succeed, for it is one of the "garden spots of the Country"—so said—I have never been there, but I *do know* that they have splendid quarters for the officer[s]—two story brick buildings and fine barracks for the men—beside one view I take of it is—and perhaps that is the most weighty one with me—that if once there we will remain "during the war."

To day I received my order that the "Veteran Reserve Corps" sceases to "belong exclusively" to the Provost Marshal Gen.l Department, we now (or will hereafter) report to the Commandant of the Department (Gen.l Hinslerman) so you see that we are again "in the Army"—being as our name implies Veteran *Reserves*.[25] Understand me I do not suppose for a moment that it will alter our duties in the least, but that things will "jog along" as usual—although I regret that the change has taken place (personaly) for two reasons—first I do not like Hinslerman and second (and most important) I have won the good opinion of Col. Baker, and could (as they all say) get "just what ever he askes for"—I have now got to win the favourable opinion of "Old Col. Persimson" the Commander of the District of Indiana—Col. Baker tells me that I stand "A No. 1" there, although I have seen him but once and that for but about twenty minutes, when he invited me (just as I was leaving him) to call at the house and see him and his family—a pretty good "omen."

There—I guess I have "spun out" and will close, as the orderly say[s] "horse ready, Col."

Last Sunday I had a billious attack but took some "Compound Cathartic Pills[“] and now feel rejuvenated again.

Give my love to the Boys and kisses to Clare and tell her to think of her "Papa" (I believe that is the term) when she puts on that "nosed" Hat.[26]

Yr[.]
Charley

I enclose fifty cents for the children, will you tell me how I stand as I have lost all run of the account[.]

104

H.Qrs. Burnside Barracks
April 7 = 1864

Dear Mary,

Yours of the 1st and 2nd inst. both came to hand last evening and I hasten to answer for fear of another "rap over the knuckles" as we term a "reminder" from Headquarters.

So Mrs. Leed has a Son, has she? And you wished it was yours—I thought that you did not wish any more boys, or is the prospect so gloomy that you have at last come to the conclusion that you would take either sex so as to get a baby? "A dear darling duck of a baby" ah! Mary that thing is "played out"—or more properly or correctly or definitly speaking "*I* am played out"—I am sorry (for your sake) that I can not accomidate *you,* as for my self I rather like it, for I am clear of, as the old woman would say, "a world of trouble."[27]

I shall have my likeness taken the first clear day that I can take time enough to go to town. We intend to have all the officers taken at these Barracks and exchange with each other.

I regret very Much to hear that you have the neuralgia—for Heaven's sake Mary try the battery before it gets too much head way—do not forget or neglect the battery.[28]

You ask if you shall proceed with house cleaning—well Mary, I think that you might as well, for I really do not know what to say *just at present*—this call for all the Malitia-men indicates a change—the Commandant of the Department also desires to send some of us to Johnson's Island, again there is an attempt to consolidate all the Veteran Reserves at Washington, all of which movements are possable but none of them probable, yet it indicates that a change may and in fact is likely to occur and that in a short time—the government is determined to take *all* in the Field that are available and that must necessarly make some changes in the location of the Corps—the only question so far as *this* post is concerned is, can they get along with less than they have here at present? if so some *must* go to other stations and I feel satisfied if that does take place that I will be of the party—if the Prisoners at Camp Morton are not removed, because Col. Stevens having charge of them will be the one likely to remain with them. These are only surmises of mine and it will take a little time to decide—Many of the officers who have brought their families here recently are regretting it now as they say that they have destroyed their homes and will be compelled to leave their families for a short time in a strange place—however a Month will decide it and in that time I will have my quarters up and then I will expect a visit (at least) from you, but in the mean time you had best act just as if you did not expect to leave for six months at least.

What the duce possessed Maxwell to make the request to be buried in Canada? was he a native of the place? A Mighty poor Compliment to his wife to have his remains removed so far from her, my request always has been to have my carcass taken near my home, then if any one desired to respect it they could—and if they did not God knowes strangers would not[.]

Give my love to the Boys and many kisses to Clare who has frightened me very much with her wants[.]

yr[.]
Charly

105

Burnside Barracks
Indianapolis, Ind.
April 26 = 1864

Dear Mary,

Yours of the 22nd inst. arrived this morning and I am very much pleased to find that the Boys are to accompany you on your visit to this "Windy City of the Plains" (as Whitney of St. Louis calls it) for I think that the Change and novelty would do them good—both amuse and instruct them very much—it will give them an insite to life in some of its phases, that they could not otherwise aquire, independent of the pleasure that it would give me.

I can scarcely say that I like your plan of locking up the house for so long a time without any one being in it, but I suppose that you have arranged "all for the best."

The knives, forks, spoons &c. that you speak of bringing will be very acceptable and save me, for I had them down on my list of "articles to be purchased."

News paper rumors, Camp Rumors and other rumors are so rife here as to what they intend to do with the Corps, that some of the officers are getting frightened out of their faculties but I tell them to push a head for I am and will if the whole thing is busted up the next day.

We are informed (unofficially) by the Prov. Mar. Gen.l that our uniform coat will be a *dark blue* and advise all of us who require new uniforms to purchase the dark blue—now I made a lucky hit for I was on the point of ordering a new suit (had selected the cloth) but thought that I had better waite and take that money for making my nest a little more comfortable for the birds that would soon be flying in this direction[29]—by-the-way could not Harry get you a ticket to Pittsburg and back it would save half of the fare, if not for all of you why for one or two—try it Mary.

Dr. Newcomer and myself constitute a Board to examine all the attendants, nurses &c. at the Hospitals of this city (Indianapolis) to either discharge, send to the field or Vet. Res. Corps, as we may deem proper.

The following is a list of such articles as you may bring with you if you will

4 or 5 pillow cases—enough for the family
sheets for three beds
Table Cloths
Towels

these articles can be folded up in the trunks and will not make much bulk—I would also like 2 or 3 doz. of Parlor Matches and 5 lbs of smoking tobacco of the same kind as the inclosed lables—I purchased it at Front & Market St. if I should think of any thing else I will write you in time.

I inclose two likenesses—both spendid of Howard & Sumner.[30]

Give my love to the Boys and kisses to Clare,

Charley

106

Metropolitan Hotel
Washington DC
May 5 = 1864

Dear Mary,

I have just received my orders, this 3 o'clock P.M.—I am ordered to report to Brig. Gen.l Briggs at Draft Rendezvous at that infernal *hole* Alexandria, V*a* where six companies await me.[31]

Lt. Col. Colby is *accidently* transferred to the 19th Reg. and I have been promised that Maj. Flood would be promoted to the Lieut. Colancy of the 18th. and that my regiment (18th) would be filled with 10 of the 1st Batl. Companies immediately.

I leave tomorrow morning you need not answer this but waite until my next when I will be able to inform you how to direct yours.

Yours Hastly
Charly

7

"Tell the general my men are cripples, and they can't run"

May 7, 1864–June 22, 1864

SPRING 1864 marked the start of what was to be a nearly year-long campaign to wear down the Confederacy until it could no longer resist. Human beings by the tens of thousands were fed into the machinary of war, and ambulance trains stretched for miles to hospitals north and south. In this struggle the Veteran Reserve Corps would play its part, filling garrison and provost posts, guarding prisoners, and escorting draftees so that more-able-bodied men could go to the front. Johnson's regiment would be called on to perform duties that only six months earlier would have been thought far beyond the capabilities of an Invalid Corps.

107

City Hotel
Alexandria, Va.
May 7/64

Dear Mary,

Here I am in Dixie once more—I visited "Camp Briggs" yesterday—pshaw!—What a contrast to the one I left. It is new, *all* new, but three barracks built and only two Line Officers quarters up[,] the mess looks like a lumber yard with its piles of boards—grounds not graded—not drained or in fact not anything as the six companies have been here but two weeks—Oh! Work! Work!! Work!!!

I have not yet taken command but will do so to day as the Major who has had command was absent yesterday—I shall start my quarters immediately, but until they are finished I will be compelled to "board out"—it will take at least a month for me to fix up for you I think—but it *shall* be done as soon as possable—of course I can not describe any thing of the mode of living &c. yet—except to state that the Camp—that is the Camp in prospective is about a mile above Alexandria and is very nicely located upon a hill at the margin of the Potomac and I think as pleasant and healthy a location as there is about this "cussed" shore.

I contemplate finishing a cottage-shape quarters for myself that is in the midst of a clump of trees—if lumber and workmen (among the men) can be found, it will go up as if the devil was under it poking it with his pitchfork.

I understand that the Regiment is Assigned to furnish the escorts for all the Drafted men that are forwarded to this Department—hence it will spoil all drills as one half of the men are absent nearly all the time upon that Duty—in fact one squad just returned from New Orleans where the[y] had conducted some Drafted Men, being absent four weeks—so that my regiment is likely to be "scattered over all creation."

There goes the Breakfast gong so I will close and then proceed hem! hem! And "Take Command"—by-the-way Bald. Hufty and I are occupying the same room at this house, *he* is likely to remain here for a week or two before he can get orders, and a chance to proceed to his Company.

Give my love to the boys and kisses to Clara,

Charly

P.S. You may direct your answer to me

Camp Briggs
Alexandria, Va.

as I will establish a Post Courier and make arrangements with the Post Office before your answer can reach me[.]

108

May 11 = 1864
Camp Briggs
Alexandria, Va

Dear Mary,

Yours of the 9th (Mailed yesterday) arrived here this morning.

You are right in supposing that I would rather be here than in Washington, although I do not like this section of the Country nor the unfinished state of the barracks[.] Most especialy as the government has decided to not build any more but require the men to live in tents during the hot weather—had I have been here a week sooner I would have had the lumber for the whole ten barracks and then I could have had a Camp to suite myself—but "so must it be"—I shall jog on however and gradualy work the thing through and have it to my liking by the time (I suppose) that they move me to some other spot as is my luck, at least ever since I have been in this Corps no matter at what station or on what duty—I am falling into my usual luck, viz; getting the good opinion of the Commander Brig. Gen. Briggs,[1] who to-day is endeavoring to get the government to make Camp Briggs an exception to the general order although I scarce think that he will succeed.

This is a queer (to me) command—except some twenty carpenters at work on the quarters, I have not thirty men in camp the whole of them being detailed to various points, in fact I received an order last night between 12 & 1 o'clock for 200 men and three officers when by George I had but 150 men and *not one* officer on the grounds—why my command is so much "under my nose" that I am compelled to keep a book to know where in the devil they are, or I would loose them half the time—if this thing continues, this will be one lazy life for me and any thing but that of a soldier—no drills, no dress parades &c. &c.

Your suggestion in regard to bringing things is good and while I think of it I will name some, say sheets & pillow cases for three beds, towels, one half dozen each knives, forks, plates, cups & saucers, glasses, spoons &c. I would not have you bring many things or prepare for a *permanant* residence for I realy and candidly do believe that we will be moved from here before the summer is over, especialy if Grant is successful for the base of supplies is now being moved to Aquire Creek[2] and we *may* (some of the Corps certainly) be shoved down and as it is my fate to be "moved on" why I expect (as usual) to be among the first—so do not expect a *permanant* residence with me; at present at least. If we do leave this and go farther to the front it will be to live in tents and of course I could not could not think of subjecting you and the little ones to such an undignified mode of life—Mind I am not talking against your coming, for I have decided on *that* but guarding you against preparing and expecting a *perminant* residence—it may last until fall, may last longer and may not last a month—I have sceased to feel decided on that point.

I am shoving my building along and feel confident that (if they do not say "move") I will send for you as soon as I receive my next pay[.]

Give my love to the Boys and many kisses to the Girl that "only hints for bread[.]"

Yr[.]
Charley

P.S. As I "lie upon my pallet of straw"—and *that* is no poetical "flight of fancy" I assure you—this afternoon, I found the following in a paper which I send, not that it is applicable to you by any means, but, that there is a veine of humor running through it, hence I "forward" it as we say "a la" Militara

[printed poem:]

Summary of Wedded Bliss.
God bless the wives,
They fill our lives
With little bees and honey!
They ease life's shocks,
They mend our socks,
But—don't they spend the money!

When we are sick,
They heal us quick
That is if they love us;
If not, we die,
And yet they cry,
And raise tombstones above us.

P.P.S.—There you once objected to this P.P.S. but it *must* come *now*—I write at 1 o'clock in the morning—I have just received "orders"—damn there orders—to move my regiment (entire) to-morrow—or I should say to-day—to Belle Plains with 3 days rations and 200 rounds of ammunition per man so alas! farewell to all our plans and projects for the present—the next dodge will be (I expect) to be ordered to Fredericksburg—damn them—well, well, "there is no rest for the wicked" in this Mundane sphere—Mary, I regret it exceedingly, but you may as well prepare yourself for a prolonged residence without your "liege lord"—Curse their ugley pictures—I must close this hastly as I have but a few hours sleep before I "move" for after that I get none more for some time as I take some thousand Drafted Men & Volunteers under my charge—I report to Gen.l J. J. Abercrombie[3] for duty—who in the devil *he* is I know not—so good night or rather good morning[.]

You need not answer this until I write again which I shall as soon as possable and inform you how to direct[.]

109

[letterhead: U.S. Sanitary Commission]

Belle Plains, Va
May 14, 1864

Dear Mary,

I hastly write to you from the Sany. Com.[4] boat.—I was ordered yesterday to the Command of the Hospital at Fredericksburg, but the order was countermanded at night and one hundred of my men sent to Fort Delaware in charge of 380 Officers, Prisoners among whom was Genls Stewart & Johnson[5]—I am now awaiting further orders—if waggons can be procured to carry the knapsacks &c. of the men & myself to Fredericksburg—there is over 7000 Prisoners here and Col. Hoffman[6] (who has charge of the prisoners of the U.S.) is desirous that I should have controll of all prisoners but Gen.l Abercrombie wants me at Fredericksburg—I do not know which will win.

Address me in care of Gen.l Abercrombie, Belle Plains, Va.

Give love &c. and kisses &c.

Hastly[,]
Charly

P.S. living in Huts[?] and everything is to perfection.

110

Belle Plains, Va.
May 15 = 1864[7]

Dear Mary,

While waiting

Belle Plains Va.
May 17[?] = 1864

I had just written the above commencement of a letter to you when I was ordered off with 1300 Prisoners to Point Lookout, Md. I went down with two steamers (600 in one and 700 in the other) with 250 Vet. Res. as Guards—a small guard but as we had a Gun Boat to accompany us it was sufficient—we reached Point Lookout at 11 O'clock P.M. and had to work until eight o'clock the next morning to get through with counting, searching, examining &c. &c. so I was considerably "used up"—I returned here to-night and found four more companies of the Corps here—they are unassigned—the Gen.l (Abercrombie) has informed me that *all* the Corps that will be sent here shall be under my charge and to hold myself prepared to "manage a Brigade"—to use his own words—

Now *that* is all very pretty but unfortunately it is "played out" and I can only say "damn the Brigade" (excuse the profanity, but it is the result of the "*Field*") for I would much rather have a regiment in barracks than a division in the field—some of the Corps are very sour at my having (as they term it) the "Pioneer force"—well they could have the *honor* (hem!) if[?] they desire[?] it and I could say "God speed" them with all my heart although my post as Commander of the escort of Rebel Prisoners *is* of "some P[?]kious" to all the officers here—but "Blast their eyes" it has killed all my "cherished hopes" that is of once more living with those that I love so dearly and *that* is of more importance to *me* than "empty honor" especialy when that honor is accompanied with considerable work, and to add to all the rest, I have ascertained since my return that a horse kicked my acting Quartermaster and broke his leg and that he has been sent to Washington by the Surgeons, and not having a single officer that I can spare or have confidence in (for that post) I must play the Quartermaster myself.

By-the-way tell George Deal that the said acting Quartermaster is Captain Thibaut (pronounced Tea-bold) of the 4th New York reg.[8]

I shall write to George in the morning in reference to the Sutlership.[9]

Yours of the 12th reached me to-night via Alexandria and the "fond hopes" in reference to the Companionship of Nancy[10] is all knocked in the head—not any more to your regret than to mine—damn the luck—excuse me Mary for I would not hurt your feelings by such "forcable" language but I have felt (and fear have *used* some) like "definite expressions" these few days past—some officers are now envying my post—well they would be whelcome to it—

Give my love to the Boys and kisses to Clara—if I have a lot of Prisoners to send east again I shall endevour to command the escort[.]

Yours in tribulation[,]
Charley

P.S. May 18 (4 o'clock a.m.) I open this (for the lack of something else to do) to inform you that we are laying under arms, waiting for Mosby[11] and his party to attempt to cut off our base of supplies, he is around our flanks in force and evidiently intending either to stop the suplies to those in front or rescue the Prisoners of whom we have seven thousand yet here, in fact they come faster than we can ship them—Should he be foolish enough to attempt to ride through us you will hear of some "stiff work" being done by the Vet. Res. Corps—we can not *march* nor endure the fatigues of field service, but by the eternal Moses, we will show the country how we can *fight*, should the enemy attack us.

111

H.Qrs Vet. Res. Corps
Belle Plains, VA
May 22 1864

Dear Mary,

I sit down on this calm, clear, warm Sunday morning to pay my devotions at *my* shrine, while you I suppose are at the "House of God" paying your devotions at *your* shrine.

The prospects are that we will leave this spot shortly as the base of supplies will be changed—if we go to Aquire Creek landing[12] there is a prospect that the Vet. Res. Corp will be detailed as Provost Guard and your humble servant as Provost Marshall, at least so I have been informed (verbaly) from the "top of the hill" i.e. General's Headquarters.

I am getting along as comfortably as a man can under the circumstances—I have a tick filled with hay and laid upon three boards, with cedar brush about a foot deep scattered all over the tent (which by-the-way is an old Hospital tent that my acting Quartermaster "froze upon" at Alexandria[)]—the most that troubles me is the eating, it is true that we get "fresh shad" caught at the very foot of our camp but "*nary* conscience" they only charge just one dollar per foot for them, that is, a shad 12 inches long is $1.00, larger ones in proportion.

I have not received a letter from you since I left Alexandria (10 days) except one addressed to me at that place although I know that they are about some where—I am inclined to think that they must have passed this point and went down to the front. I wrote to you on the 11th, 14th & 17th which I suppose you received by this time be sure and direct to me in care of Brig.l Gen. J. J. Abercrombie, Belle Plains Va.[13]

I had one of my old fashioned attacks of billious headache yesterday and laid all night last night with iced cloths on my head that is when my vomiting did not jerk it off—the Sanitary Commission here furnished me the ice and the Medical Director the Doctor so between the two I was very nearly "cured to death"—to-day I am the better for my cleaning out but feel week and sore in the stomach however a little Cornstarch for dinner and I will be Marked "Right Side up" again—oh! how I missed your finger[s] about my head last night. My Adjutant, two or three orderlies and a little Counterband[14] (who we have picked up) were my nurses and they went at it with such a will that if I had not "cleared the shanty" and locked the door, i.e. tied the flap of the tent, they would have had every known and unknown remedy that could be found crammed down me before morning.

I have received notice that my regiment is attached to the 2nd Brigade of the Vet. Res. Corps, Brigade Headquarters at Alexandria, Va., Commander not yet selected. Some "thumb-sucking" sucker I suppose.

My sick are increasing rapidly and to-day I have sent them to the field hospital at the landing with word that they may expect to put up a "few more" sent from the accomidation of this Corps alone.

Give my love to the Boys and Mary very many kisses to our darling (God! how I would like to feel her curles about my face).

Your
Charley

P.S. I believe that I did not tell you that I have met some of the wounded of the 81st P. V[?]. enroute for Washington—oh! how they prayed that I would be in command again, they say that "it is not the same regiment as when you [were] with us Colonel"—poor fellows it did me good to hear them talk—I secured them an extra attention and some extra nourishment and left them with their blessings.

112

Port Clinton, Va
opposite Port Royal
on the Rappahonock
May 26 = 1864

Dear Mary,

Here we are ("invalids") in the rain without any tents &c.—we left Belle Plains on the afternoon of the 24 and arrived here last night, I had but 336 men when I started as there were over 180 who could not march two miles and were sent in boats, but the General had forwarded nearly all his force to Grant and was compelled (he said) to take as many of us as possable—to say that we are a "used up party" is but a slight expression of the condition of all of us. I have 300 men out somewhere, and God knows when they will get here—it is to use the lightest word—a damn outrage and in direct opposition to *all* the pledges of the Government in reference to the Corps[15]—but however "a change will come o'er the spirit of our dreams" pretty soon if not I shall throw up and leave the service.

We expect to cross the river to-day and then I am to have the choice of encamping ground out of compliment to the conduct of the men while on the march—I had the march to myself by orders and did not reach here for some 7 or 8 hours after the other force, but I *did* come[.] I came without a straggler, for I put over 45 in the waggon train that failed after the first two miles, the rest came in solid with a regular funeral step—snails! What nonsence it is to put such men out here. They are now clustered togeather to endeavour to keep each other dry, for it has rained all day (in fact all night) and not one yard of canvass do we own while able bodied men here are provided with tents—well so must it be.[16]

Grant has thrown his left wing around to Hanover Courthouse and the prospect is that (so far as I can judge that he will in a very short time occupy the very ground that the politicians hounded at McClellan about—*this* I suppose will be all right for Grant bah!

I have not heard from you since I left Alexandria 12th inst. just two weeks and by George I begin to feel like seeing the light of one of those little black bordered envelopes. I suppose that this change of location destroys the chances of seeing a Mail for some days again, and by that time I expect that we will be off again—if Grant continues to throw his left around—*our* next front will in all probibility be at the White House or West Point on the Penninsula once more.[17]

Give my love to the boys and m[an?]y kisses to Clara[.]

Yr.
Charley

113

Port Royal, Va
May 28, 1864

Dear Mary,

I seize the opportunity of sending a few lines to you by Jonathan Kirkbride, who is just leaving here. I have written to you on the 11th, 14th, 17th, 23rd, 26th—which I suppose (or *hope*) you have received. I have not received any answer to either of them—It is now nearly three weeks since I received any word from you—I[f] any thing should go wrong at home *tellegraph* to me at this place or perhaps it would be best if you should be *compelled* to tellegraph to do so to me "In Genl. Abercrombie's Command" that will be most likely to reach me, for I expect that we will leave here in a few days for either the White House or West Point on the York River.

I have a nice position at present, so far as work or exposure is concerned—as my force is *all* detailed at Hospital and on Contrabrand duty. Here *I* have "nothing to do" comparatively—the General said that hence forth while in his department "Colonel you *shall* be entirely ornamental, we do not want you to be useful, as you have worked enough to entitle you to rest." So to use the army phrase—I "have a soft thing"—

Kirkbride can *tell* you more than I can *write.*

Give my love to the boys and many kisses to Clara[.]

Yours[,]
Charley

114

Board Steamer Lizzie Baker
Chesepeake Bay
June 1, 1864

Dear Mary,

Here we are on the "briney deep" steaming away for the White House on the Pamunkey River—how things change in a short time—this day and this *hour,* two years ago I was just resting from the heat and bristle of the Fair Oaks fight, now I am gone to within 15 or 18 Miles of the same spot—I can say that I do not like the change as I did not enjoy very good health on the Peninsula before (confound this boat! how it shakes I can scarcely write) but to return—perhaps my post here *this* time may not cause the exposure that my post then did, *that* may make a difference, if it does not and I can not get a change I shall leave the service and not waite until I get compleatly broken down as I did before—I feel very indignant as this Corps "organized for Provost Guards and Guards in Cities" of "men not fit for the field" but "fit only for such service" (I quote the order organizing the Corps) should be sent to this infernal spot—and kept knocking around half the United States—I would not feel so did I not know that *all the other* regiments are yet in and around Washington City—it is true that *my* (individual) duties *may* be lighter here than there, but I am tired of this eternal moving about and at remote points from home—as for the other officers and *men* their duties are more severe than they can stand and more than the government promised that they should be; it is telling upon them—four officers has been sent to the Washington Hospital sick up to the present time, being one-fifth of the number—the "Pioneer Regiment" and all that sort of thing is all very pretty on *paper* but it "don't pay" either us or the government as it cost Uncle Sam the expense of one steamer (at $195.00 per day) and three Barges at I do not know what cost per day, to convey us to our present destination to get one man's work out of three men, for *that* is the ratio of our detail for the present duty, for instance if they want the labor of fifty men, they are compelled to detail one hundred and fifty to get it done—I can not see that the government saves anything by keeping us at this post where we are constantly being changed from locality to locality.

I have not received any word from you yet but suppose that you have received my letters and also that you have (confound this shaking) forwarded yours; I suppose that they will all come in a heap as they are following us about the country.

I do not know exactly *when* or *where* I can mail this but will endevour to get it off at Yorktown if possable—I started a Post Office (on my own hook) at Port Royal and forwarded over 3000 letters from that point and have nearly one bushel aboard that came in after the last boat had left for Washington—I[t] was a great accomidation for the forces passing through and gave employment to some of the men who could not handle a musket and I have a number of such with me.

Give my love to the Boys and many kisses to Clara[.]

Yr[.]
Charley

P.S. That Sutlership for George must remain in "status quo" for the present as sutlers are not allowed so near the front[.]

115

White House, Va
June 4 = 1864

Dear Mary,

I wrote to you yesterday morning and I believe that I some what ridiculed your idea of my having the command of a Brigade or rather being a Brigadeer General—well the letter was scarce mailed before *my* idea of matters was changed by *facts* for before the day was ended I took command of the 4th Provisional Brigade at this Post and I now have the following command, viz;

18th Reg. Vet. Res. Corps
3 Companies 11 " " " "
1 " 10 " " "
38 Wisconsin Vol. Infantry
37 " " "
1 Battalion 1 Minnesota
179 New York " "
132 in Ohio " "
1 Bat 39 New York
1 Provisional *regiment* composed of nearly 1500 men of all regiments; among whom are some of the officers and men of the old 81st who were glad to see me once more, I assume, particularly as Commanding a Brigade of such size—this Provisional *Regiment* is compossed of all the officers and men who are returning to their old regiments and

is likely to swell to some 2000 strong, they are on duty here until further orders.

I have command of all the infantry for the defense of this Post, having the business Right and Centre (including three Redoubts and four rifle pits) while the Cavalry has the Left wing—My Command extends over nearly two miles and all orders for details of every kind are issued by me, that is so far as the Infantry are concerned.

Some of the Colonels &c. did not like the idea at first of "coming into the field to be Commanded by an Invalid," they did not like the *light blue*—but a "change has come over the spirit of their dreams" within the last 36 hours: for my waggons not having arrived, and I not having my "chicken fixens" they nearly *all* have been to my quarters to either offer me some little article of Camp furniture as a *gift* or loan or to request that I would get them detailed permanently under me (numbers of such request have been made) the former I invariably refuse, being determined to show them that if I *must* be in the field, that I am a Soldier yet, the latter of course I can not grant, but of one thing you can rest assured that is that as the *old soldiers* pass to the field they begin to entertain more respect for the *light blues.*

While on this subject of Brigade (for I do not know that I shall ever devote a *whole* letter to it again) I will mention that of the vast number that I command to-night—I may not have a single one to-morrow but all be filled by new regiments and yet *all* may remain a week and a half a dozen more added—the General told me to-day to prepare myself for enough men to make a division for he "intended" that I should be *useful* "now" as he had made me "*ornamental* at Port Royal"—it produces *work* but it also gives me *position* and no thanks to Washington or any one else but my own exertions "tarn-ation sink seize them."

As it is now 12 o'clock and I must be up at 4 in the morning to send off 800 Rebs to Point Lookout[18] and some 2000 men as waggon Guards to the front (some to return and others to report to their Corps Commanders) I will close, but not by signing myself "as usual" "Commanding 4th Prov. Brig."

Give my love to the Boys (I have not had time to write that letter to them yet) and many kisses to Clara.

Yrs[,]
Charly

P.S. Direct to me as usual in Care of Gen.l Abercrombie, White House, Va, be sure to write Col. 18 V.R.C. for I would not have any one to think I care a damn about the present title[.]

116

H.Qrs. 4th Prov. Brig.
White House, Va.
June 6 = 1864

Dear Mary,

Having a "breathing spell" this evening and it being too infurnely hot to sleep I thought that I would sweat awhile over this sheet of paper and give you some few disjointed ideas and rambling intelligence.

We have a rumor here that Harry McKeen[19] is killed, if it is so I suppose that you have received the information before this, I hope that the rumor may prove incorrect as the *gentleman* who is home on a "flesh wound" (as one of the officers of the old 81st remarked to me yesterday) will get entirely "too big for his boots" and the little town of Camden will not be sufficiently extensive for him to "spread out"—I expect that he will emigrate to New York City or perhaps go "booted and spured" to visit Europe to "astonish the natives" of that classic portion of this Mundane sphere.[20]

Last night we were up in "arms and eager for the fray," for we could hear the rattle of musketry for nearly two hours—Lee attempted to break through our lines and failed; but if he had this post would have been the place he would have drove for to cut off Grant's supplies—now while I am writing they are at it again to night—I expect before I finish to receive "orders" to get my men in readyness—I have 53 companies all told under my command, being 13 more than is requisite for a *Major General's* command and I feel (while this infernal rattle of musketry is gone on) that I have more responsibility than I should have; but if the Rebs *does* succeed in getting here there is one thing certain—I will fight—how *scientifically* it may be done would be demonstrated at or after the time of the fight—of one thing I am certain that is that the General after having rode along my line (after I had it formed) told me that I could not have disposed of my forces to a better advantage—and he is an old "regular." Some of the commanders of regiments here who did not like to be required to report to "an Invalid" (as they termed it) have since said to me that they felt more security since I took command of the Brigade than they did before, they now are perfectly pleased and "didn't want to change" but change they do for I have sent off to the front three full and parts of two more regiments and received nearly five others in their place—it is constantly go and come—those that arrive require to be located, rationed, &c. &c. immediately, details for waggon trains (as escorts) for Pickets, for guards, for Rebel prisoners, for guards when they are shipped to various points, for Provost guards, in fact for every thing that must come through me and I assure you that the *work* fully makes me pay for the *honor*—the one advantage is that I invariably detail the Vet. Res. for the best and easyest posts and they deserve it for they have no business here at all.[21]

There they go at it again in the front—I wonder what in the devil they are at now!—blast it how I hate to hear that firing and not have a "finger in the pie" it makes my blood warm to fever heat—if we could *march* I suppose that they would have us out there before this, but we *can't* and that settles the hash.

I wrote you on the 4th and forwarded it to Washington by a Sergeant and I suppose that you have received it before this. I have not received but *two* letters from you since I left Alexandra (the 12th of May) viz: yours of the 24th and 28th inst. our mail is regular now every day and letters passed through my office today postmarked at Philad- the 3rd and 4th inst. I wonder where in the devil *mine* (or rather yours) has gone to, for I know that you have answered mine, blast it, I do want to hear from home once more—give my love to the boys and kisses to Clara.

P.S. do you direct your letters in care of J. J. Abercrombe at White House, Va?

Charley

117

HQs 4th Prov. Brig.
June 8 = 1864

Dear Mary,

To-day we are enjoying the favour of a "Southern Sun"—in fact, "basking 'neath the refulgent rays" of "firey Sol"—if this heat is the cause of that "firing of the Southern hart" that we read so much of, it is all right, but it "don't fire the Northern hart" by "a darned sight," but one thing it does and that is, it opens the Northern "hide" and produces an effect somewhat like a shower bath on a small—no by George! a *large* scale—paper collars are recumbent "down in the market"—if not the market, they are down the neck—starch stands about as much show as a man would passing through Pluto's dominion with a pound of powder in each pocket—provided they have pockets "away down there"—but to return to the subject of heat

11 o'clock, P.M.

The subject of my previous page was cut short this afternoon by the arrival of a regiment that I must place in line, just as I finished another reported, and while at supper (Pamunky River Cat-fish) a third reported which kept me flying—heat or no heat—and I have just got through after making my details for the waggon train that starts at 4.30 tomorrow morning—and as there is a "hole in the ballad" of heat I rather guess that I will not resume the subject.

I now have under my command the following

2 Batt. Vet. Res. Corps
39th Wisconsin
38th "
1st Minnesota
132nd Ohio
138th "
142nd "
155th Ohio[22]

1 regiment just reported on the boat to land in the morning, if it had landed it would have made *ten* regiments—the magnitude of the force fairly frightens me when I think of it.

I draw one consolation (however) for all the work that it brings, and that is, that if the "suckers" or "any other man" at Washington sent me down here to prevent my occupying a prominent position, they have missed it most damnably.

I shall reduce my force to-morrow by sending off three regiments, leaving seven regiments yet on hand "to be accounted for" as we say in Military reports.—I guess that I will close to-night and retire to my "virtuous couch"—hurmp! "needs must when the devil drives[.]"

June 9th

Having been recuperated, refreshed, renovated, resusicated and invigorated by a four hours sleep, I am enabled to finish this letter—by George I might as well when I am on the last page.

The day after tomorrow will make *one month* in which I have received but *two* letters (and they both within the same mail)—by Heavens it is too bad—*two* letters a month—I do wonder where in the devil they have got to—if *no* letters from the vicinity of home passed through the office, I would not think so much of it—for I could then suppose that the mail miscarried or was stop[p]ed, but *every day* the men receive letters post marked Philad- at about three to five days old[.]

'Tis true 'tis strange,
Tis strange 'tis true.

Give my love to the Boys and many kisses to Clara[.]

Yr[.]
Charly

118

Hd.Qrs. 4th Prov. Brig.
White House, Va.
June 11 = 1864

Dear Mary,

Yours of the 8th inst. arrived this morning by the hands of Mr. Robert Patton—to say that it gave me pleasure is but a feeble word to express my emotions on receiving this communication fresh from your hands—rather call it joy or anything short of frenzy.

He offered to carry a letter to you, but as it was 11 o'clock a.m. when I rode up to the tent and he left at 12 o'clock and I being busy engaged in embarking and forwarding some 5000 troops to Bermuda Hundred to Genl. Butler,[23] which weakened my line of defense and required that I should bring up my reserves and in fact change my lines more or less, I actually have not had time to write—he caught me at a very busy and unpropitious moment for a letter for you—*now* I am through for a while and seize this opportunity.

I have discovered the cause of my not receiving the letters regular, viz. all letters arriving in Washington for the Vet. Res. Corps are sent to the office of the Prov. Mar. Genl. to be forwarded by him—we have nearly two bushels there which they have neglected to forward to us—I wrote a stinging *"personal"* letter to Wisewell[24] today which I think will produce the mail.

I wrote you a letter a day or two ago in reference to the death of Harry McKeen and *Col.* Wilson[25] in which you will see that you and I appear to have had the same thoughts at about the same time—I regret the death of Harry exceedingly, for let the world say what they may he was always the square thing to *me* in all our transactions with each other—he had queer ways (so we all have)—that made him many enemies, but as some of them were towards me it did not alter my feeling formed from old association—as for the slacker, now at the "head of affairs of state," I have waisted ink enough on him already.

You appear to be laboring under an error in reference to my present position[.] I am *not* a *Brigadier* yet, but a Colonel commanding a Brigade, which makes a vast difference in more than one point, first it adds more labor but it does *not* (darn the flies) add more *pay*, but it does add honor, power and position which compensates for the work—another difference between the Colonel commanding and a Brigadier, is that when the Brigade sceases to exist—the "Col. Comd.g" sceases to exist—so you need not build or buy *that* "big brick house" yet a while.

You will be compelled, Mary, to borrow some funds until I can get the opportunity to send my pay account to Washington for *here* we are actualy in the field and may not see a Paymaster for months—as soon as I get an opportunity I will do so and get the person to Express some of the funds to you from that front.

You say that a "notice of my good luck appeared in this Morning's North American," what was the purport of it? I would like to know, as I did not suppose that *any one* knew of my being here.[26]

I wrote you on the 26th & 28th of last month the 1st, (3rd & 4th you answer[ed]), 6th & 9th of this month did you receive *all* of them, I would like to know as I keep a record of all sent—When you next write direct to Col. Chas. F. Johnson, Care of Brig. Genl. J. J. Abercrombie and do *not* put the Vet. Res. Corps then it will not get into the Prov. Mar. Genl. office.

Give my love to the Boys and kisses to Clara,

Charly

I would send you some funds out of my pocket, but one *slight* impediment interveans—I have but $1.50 hence it is "on possable"—so borrow Mary, borrow and do not let yourself want—

119

H.Qrs. 4th Provisional Brig.
White House, Va
June 15, 1864

Dear Mary,

Yours of the 31st ult arrived this day with over a bushel and a half of mail matter from the office of the Prov. Mar. Genl.—I had twenty-seven letters some of them nearly a month old.

We are still at this Post—as the heading of the letter indicates—all the forces have left but my Brigade and one regiment of niggers—hem! I mean one regiment of troops of "African Decent."[27] in fact every thing is cleared out, Quartermasters, Commissary and all and we are only holding the place until Hunter arrives[28] as there is a waggon train here for him with over 80,000 rations which we have parked inside of our works—

Grant has moved and left our front uncovered so that we are practicing that price of Liberty—"eternal vigilence" and it behoves us to do so for the Reb. Cavalry and Guerrilers are constantly appearing within a short distance of us, they however are not in sufficient force to show their noses to any extent and disappear whenever I send out any Cavalry—we sleep under Arms (the old tune that I practiced before so often) and keep every man within near or in the rifle pits at all times.

We should have left here yesterday and would have done so immediately upon the embarcation of the 18th Corps if it had not been for protecting Hunter's stores—now God knows when *he* will arrive, if he does not hurry up the Rebs will discover our small command and make *us* hurry up, probably a little faster than is comfortable—I remember one "skedaddle" from this place before and would not be surprised at a second—they can send their Cavalry and be darned to H——for I have *my* front completly fortified and two batteries mounted in their redoubts, with six guns each—the left is in nearly the same fix and two gunboats in the Parmunkey, which are so situated as to cover us if we are drove into our interier lines,—for I have a rifle pit near the river bank as a last resort—so you see that all *we* can do, has been done.

Three days since the General appointed a Medical Board to examine every man in the Vet. Res. Corps with the view of our being sent out of the "field," the Board consisted of former Army Surgeons (the Medical Director one of them) and they reported that *four-fifths* of the entire command as "wholy unfit for marching" and but *five* men fit for "the exposure incident to the field" and recommended that we be "sent to some post where the men can have good quarters and the proper diet" also that if we are retained here we will only "fill Hospitals and over-burden the Ambulances"—this report has been forwarded to Genl. Grant—so the prospect is that we will be sent to Washington again—Damn them! I hope that they will be satisfied *now* that the Vet. Res. Corps are an "Invalid Corps" in fact and that the mear altering of the *name* does not alter the *men*.[29]

When we leave here we go to Yorktown! rather ominous that, for the base of supplies to be shifted so far from Richmond—oh! I could *talk* my ideas but I will *write* them—I can only say "don't believe things because they are in the papers."

Give my love to the boys and many kisses to Clare.

Your
Charly

P.S. I do not know *when* this will leave as all communication with Washington (or any place else) is cut off from this point at present[.]

120

Hd.Qrs. 4th Provisional Brig.
White House, Va.
June 18 = 1864

Dear Mary,

Here we are yet, cut off from the world and all its contaminating vices, free from the vanities of a worldly life, removed beyond the snaires that constantly environ the inexperienced, out of the reach of those strifes that ambition beget—, far away from the pomp and show of a gaudy world.—hem! hem!! ah! hem!!! *that* is *one* side of the picture, perhaps the most phylosolical one that could be taken; by George! if there is not phylosophy in that view, there is nothing in any view; for the other side of the picture is as follows—between 3000 and 4000 men squat[t]ed behind rifle pits at a point on the Pamunky river called the White House, afraid to go a mile out side of said works for fear of being "gobbled up," afraid to go to sleep for fear of being "gobbled up," afraid to go to the sink (no matter how much you have the "back-door trots") for fear of an attack and "all be gobbled up"—yes here we are on the Historical and Classical grounds of by-gone days—, it is plesant to sit on the porch of the house overlooking the serpantine Pamunky (it is very crooked) and think that it was *here* that the "Father of his Country"—Washington first met his wife, *here* he sat many evenings and poured forth that "tale of love" that melted her heart and made her "all his own"—it is pleasant to sit beside the chimney stacks (all that is left of the White House) and permit the mind to go wandering back to the night that *here* he *married* her who he won on the porch of yonder house—omiting any thoughts as to *what* took place on the same night *after* the above ceremony—all this may be very plesant if one could thus ruminate without the ear being streched to catch the sound of the rifle on "the Picket line" or constantly keep his mind on the rack to devise modes of attack or defence (especially the latter) to prevent being "gobbled up" should said attack occur.

I believe I said—(hem! I *know* I wrote) that we were cut off from the world, well, Mary, we *are*, as effectualy as if we were not in it—the fact is that this post is no post, in other words the base of supplies is on the James river, of which I suppose you are aware before this, and we would have been off from here one week ago, but—ah! Many men, and women too have been lost with their buts!—well, but there were 150,000 rations in waggons that with the ambulances would strech out five miles, that were parked inside of the rifle pits here that are designed to feed Hunter's and Sheridan's forces,[30] who are *supposed* to be making their way down here from the Valley, and the powers that be *supposed* that they would be here several days since, so they removed all the forces that they thought could be spared, stop[p]ed the mail at this front, removed the tellegraph, ordered off all the transports &c. except just enough to carry us off "*after* Hunter arrived"—but as Hunter has not arrived, we are still here until he does, entirely cut off from all communication with the "outside barbarians," i.e. the world, and will so remain until Hunter *does* come, unless the Rebs come in such a force as to make us do as we did in '62, "git up and git" from this "classic region" located upon this particular spot of the Sacred Soil—[31]

Genl. Abercrombe has been relieved from the Dept. of Suplies and been ordered to an other "historical spot," ycleped Yorktown—we accompany him there.[32] It is *supposed* (for we realy do not know anything, and have not for a week) that he is to command the garrison at that place, if that is so, he will endevour to retain us with him, provided the order from Grant is not all ready at that place for us to proceed to Washington—at least such he told me, he would like to do—I said "nothing but kept up a devil of a thinking."

The Prov. Marshal sent me word that he intended to send a messenger through in the morning and offered to convey a letter for me—hence this rambling scrawl, for I really have not anothing to write about, but I could not resist the opportunity—we are all packed up for a start at any time—my trunk and *every thing* except that on my back has gone a week since, for we *may* leave in a hurry.

Charley

P.S. (on the *first* page)[33] Give my love to the boys and many, very many kisses to Clara—all our provisions has "run out" and the sutlers run off, so we are on Salt-Pork and Hard-tack once more—"oh! it is sweet to *live* for ones country"—I believe the text is to "*die* for ones country" but I prefer the other version.

121

On Board Steamer Webster
York Bay VA
June 22 = 1864

Dear Mary,

After having taken a good wash and changed my clothes (the first time for three weeks) I feel like—I was about to say an officer and Soldier, but I *will* say—like a white man once more, and avail myself of the few hours that I have at my leisure to give you a few lines since my last.

Well, Mary, I have "smelt the smoke of battle" once more—not "from afar" but in the midst—on last Monday (20th) the Rebel Gen.l Hampton[34] with about 4000 men (some estimate it as 6 and 8,000) attacked our lines at the White House at 5 o'clock in the morning under cover of a thick fog—the first indication that I had was a volley from the Pickets for the videttes fell back to the left of the works leaving my entire front uncovered, and the Pickets immediately followed suit by falling—damn it to speak [it] plain—by running back on my line—I immediately mounted my horse and lead (for they would not go at first) them back to their post—again the Rebs drove us back and again I lead them on—the same thing occurred a third time—it was so foggy that you could not see fifty feet from you and we met[?] almost face to face each time before we were aware of the location of each other—at about 6½ o'clock the mist cleared up and then I found that they had possession of our Picket line and I ordered the artillery to open when they fell back under cover of the woods—while this skirmishing was gone on I had called for 25 volunteers and one officer to rush out in advance and take a small rifle pit which commanded a portion[??] of their lines—the 25th N.Y. Cav. (dismounted) step[p]ed out—the fire of the Rebs was so hot for them and their Lieutenant (a brave fellow) fell[35]—they hesitated when (I do not know what seized *me*) but I stuck spurs into my horse leaped the pits and cried follow me and with a yell they did come—I on a full loape, they at a full run—we took it, poured a volley into them from our Sharpes Carbines and drove them back and held the place the whole day—As I rode back the "Johnneys" took special pride in scattering the dust about my horse—that act of mine fixed my reputation with the whole Brigade and they received me with a shout as I reached the pits again—now for an unpleasant fact—Genl. Abercrombie (who I understand is receiving great credit for the "defense of the White House) started[?] for his boat the instant the Rebs opened their artillery and did not once leave it during the whole fight nor did he send me a single order or word of advice—as the attack was made upon *my* portion of the line and mine *only*, I had all the work to do—three of his aids came out and informed me that the Gen.l had retired (they did *not say* under shelter of the Gun Boats) and offered their services to me—it was a ticklish position for if successful *he* would receive all the credit; if a failure *I* would be censored for assuming responsibilities not authorized—I hesitated one moment—got mad—mad as the devil—and 'pitched in'—changed the artillery, shifted some of the forces, and fixed up to suit my own ideas—sent his Aids with order[s] to parties saying "the Genl. (meaning Abercrombie) orders you thus and so—in my issuing orders in that manner I actualy commanded two Colonels who ranked me—but *they* never stop[p]ed to ask any questions—they looked and acted as though they were darn glad to have some one either take the responsibility, or *show* them what to do—Well, the up shot of the whole affair was that after trying for *seven hours* (from 5 am to 12 pm) the Rebs came to the conclusion that there was "no use knocking, for they could not come in" and retired—our loss was small the men all being under cover—only one man wounded in the Vet. Res.[36] I did not receive a report of the other before I left—I have received hearty shakes of the hands and very flattering complements from nearly every officer at the Post for my actions except Gen.l Abercrombie who I think rather felt his position when the danger was passed—*he* congratulated the Gun Boats for their share of the victory and *no one else,* when it is a notorious fact to all in the front that they fired but *two* shots that reached the enemy all others falling short, either in our picket line or inside of the rifle pits—I sent to them twice to either increase their range at least a half mile or stop firing, the second time I sent word that it was "all darn nonsense"—but the Gen.l says they "rendered efficient service" so we must let it go.[37]

Directly after the fight was over Genl. Getty (his successor) arrived and relieved him—in the afternoon Genl. Sheridan arrived with his cavalry, but did not cross the bridge until next morning (we remaining under arms all night in the pits) and he started out for Hampton but was checked about three miles out and was compelled to call on all the Infantry to advance to his support—as they will be compelled to march entirely across the Peninsula to City Point, he tellegraphed to Grant to know what to do with us and Grant ordered us to embark immediately for Washington City[38]—so we are now on our way and I hope to Heavens that the Government is satisfied with sending Sick men to the front—although, now that it is all over, I am not sorry that I went, because the Vet. Res. Corps under my command were the *first* if not the only ones that have been under fire as Vet. Res., because, I had an opportunity to show my self to my new command, and I did! as well as sticking another "feather in my Cap"—every Regular present has either offered me letters of introduction to their friends or invitations to visit their families—another reason is, that I have for some time had a hankering to hear the shots and shells once more and I *have*—two shells bursted directly under my horse and did not "turn a hair"—I have quite a large piece of one of them that grazed my head—I could not resist the temptation of stop[p]ing to pick it up while the enemies sharpshooters were pelting us—the Aids and myself were out side, on the Picket line watching some change of the Rebel column at the time and they seeing several horsemen togeather let drive—we scattered when the second shell came (the one of which I have the piece) the Adj. Gen.l who was dashing apast me for the pits cried out as I was stooping to pick up the piece "Damn it Colonel get under cover—I really believe that you would stop here to eat your Breakfast if you took the notion"—

I shall mail this as soon as I get to Washington and write you as soon as I get my order locating me again—I will draw my pay as soon as I get there and express you some funds of which I know you stand in need.

Give my love to the Boys, and kisses to Clara,

ever,
Charly

P.S. 23rd—Arrived at Washington this P.M. at 3 o'clock leave immediately for Alexandria Va[.]

8

"All the rich are sechesh and *all* the poor are staunch union"

June 26, 1864–October 7, 1864

THE Eighteenth went north to Washington to rest and refit, after which Johnson and his men were sent into Maryland to resume their usual duties as provost marshals, depot guards, and escorts for prisoners and draftees. Various of Johnson's companies were also detailed to protect the vital Baltimore & Ohio Railroad, as the war drew to its final, bloody climax.

122

Cliffburne Barracks
June 26 = 1864

Dear Mary,

I hastily mailed a letter to you on the 23rd as I was leaving Washington for Alexandria, Va.

Yesterday we left the latter place and arrived at this, which is the Depot Camp for the organization of the Corps for the East—it is very plesantly situated about two miles above Washington (out 17th Street). We were ordered to this place to "recuperate"—the fact is that the Men are so extremaly and infurnaly used up that they are not "worth a Continental Cuss" and I will loose about 200 men who will be compelled to be transfered to the 2nd Batl—on my road here (four miles marching) seven fell in the streets and I had to send ambulances after my arrival to gather up the sick (not "wounded").

The Government ordered a sufficient number of Barracks to be vacated for our accommodation [of] the men—and issued wall tents for the Field and staff in which we are now living as the Mansion (Headquarters) is full, with officers permanently located at this place—for Myself it just answers, as I prefer a tent to a house in this hot weather—the only draw back is that there is no accommodation for you for a visit—however we will remain here only long enough to get the men "set up" and then be off again—I have claimed a right to be located at some good spot, either north or west (I want to get out of the Department of Washington) of this place and hope to succeed—to Morrow (Monday) I shall go to the City and work up all the influence that I can for that object—I shall strike for the New England states if possable.

They have here a Field and Staff Officers Mess, what it cost I do not know but judging from the "set of the table" it is "some," for they "live like fighting Cocks"—Breakfast from 7 to 9 o'clock A.M. Lunch at 1 o'clock and Dinner at 5 o'clock and the latter from "Soup to Raisins" in a word it is "playing soldiers" in comparison to that which I have heretofor experienced.

Col. Woodward[1] is in command of the Post and appears to be a perfect "white man" although he is the son of that sechess Judge Woodward of Pennsylvania[2]—you perceive that my Brigadeship is "numbered among the things that were," and I am under a Colonel of our Corps—*that* is one of the great incentives for my removal as soon as I get the regiment in shape again.

I shall draw my pay to-morrow and also endevour to get a few days leave of absence to slip home for the 4th of July if possable—I do not know how I will succeed but "nothing ventured—nothing gained."

Yours of the 9th & 11th just reached me—I can not say that I admire your plan of letting the Boys have their own way in leaving school it is giving them their own way too much—in fact it is insubordination in the extreme for so such children to dictate their course of action—keep them at school—even if they do *not* learn anything—give them this and they will demand something more before a Month has elapsed—by heavens I will settle with them when I next see them—if they "bully rag" you they *shall not* me.

Direct to me (18th Reg. V.R.C.) at Cliffburne Barracks, Washington, D.C.—our mails will be regular now—at least for the present.

Give many kisses to Clara for me[.]

y[long squiggle]
Charly

P.S. Did you receive my letters of May 26th, June 1st, 8 & 9th, 11th, 15th, 18th, & 22 & 23nd [?]

123

Cliffburne Barracks
Washington, D.C.
June 27 = 1864

Dear Mary,

I this day forwarded to you (per Adam's Express) the sum of $100.00, having received my pay for the Month of May—I will send you the like sum in four or five days—say 1st or 2nd of July—that is provided I am not ordered off to Kamkatcha—Madigasca, Timboocoo or some other infurnaly outlandish locality—the fact is, I would not be surprised at being ordered anywhere, except Phila- and *that* would surprise me.

To-Morrow Col. Woodward leaves here temporarly and I assume command of this Post—well I came here to rest—"recuperate" (so said the order) and *guess* that I will recuperate—"over the left." We have exceedingly hot weather here—thermomoeter (yesterday) at 105 degrees in the shade at 10 o'clock A.M.

My action at the fight at the White House is beginning to attract some attention at Washington as some several persons (unknown to me) has been to the various departments and speaking in rather glowing terms of my conduct—Col. Wisewell informed me—he rode out to see me for that purpose—that he had "made a special report in regard to me and took it in person to the Secretary of War and waited until it was read" and followed it with the remark "you have pleased the old man to death"[3]—we (the 18th) are termed among the Corps here "the war torn veterans" and I have been introduced to scores of officers as the "Hero of the White House"—"the Man that saved Sheridan" &c. &c. until damn it I begin to think that I did *some thing* somewhere or somehow—although I have not opened my lips to a soul except you, in regard to the fight at all—not thinking that it was a matter worth mentioning—it was a fight and nothing more—but they appear to be tickled at the idea that 2000 men *under an "Invalid"* should repulse between 5 and 6000 picked troops under such leaders as Hampton and Fitz Hugh Lee.[4]

There are great "tribulation[s]" here among the Corps Officers in regard to the Senate confirming our appointments and if no action is taken as to *who* Lincoln will reappoint, as the appointments fall to the ground you know if they (the Senate) do not take some action and we must be all reappointed to await the action of the next Senate[5]—beside it is brooked around that quite a number of officers have been omited on the list sent in for confermation—several Colonels "left out in the cold," which puts them "up the spout" for if their Names are not there the Senate can not confirm and if Lincoln will not send their names in of course he will not reappoint—I have (*between our selves*) been informed semi-officially that "you are all right Colonel"—"just keep quiet and move along as usual"—so I do, and would under *any case,* but at the same time I "keep an eye to the lee-ward"—blast their pictures! *if* they sent *me* to the front because I was of "no account," they just missed the mark—for to give you some idea of how the matter stands *now,* there has been four applications by commanders of regiments to be ordered to the front—seaking for "either a grave or fame" especially the *latter,* but it is "no go" for the state of my men has demonstrated that the Corps can not stand the exposure incidental to the field.

Give my love to the boys and kisses to Clara[.]

Your
Charly

P.S. the expressage is paid on the $100.00[.]

124

Cliffburne Barracks
July 10 = 1864

Dear Mary,

I did not succeed in leaving Phila. at 8 o'clock A.M. yesterday as contemplated, as that train did not connect with Washington and as it would have cost $2.00 for "Cab hire" at Baltimore, I laid over at Phila. until 12 o'clock PM. but preferred not returning home as I could have remained but one and a half hour, so I went to the store to remain; when there I received a tellegraph dispatch that the Headquarters of the regiment was removed to Laurel Station (the place that you went to go to William's) on the Washington Branch of the Baltimore and Ohio Rail Road—I however was compelled to go to Washington to report.

I arrived later in the afternoon and at this place at 9 o'clock last evening.

I was first ordered to join my regiment, but afterwards ordered to these Barracks for the present as they expect to organize a Brigade and place me in Command—I will endevour to find out the full particulars to-day from a private conversation that I am to have with Wisewell—there were too many present yesterday—

I am now occupying the "bed and board" of Col. Woodward (who will return on Friday next), as all my traps, Horse &c. &c. are at Laurel Station—I have not even succeeded in a clean shirt—as my trunk is still at the Depot "awaiting approaching events."

From the News in the paper to-day, I should not be surprised if I took a Brigade to meet these "ruthless invaders" up towards the Monocacy somewhere—if I do get one, by heavens! I will have the "star" or nothing[6]

Give my love to the boys—I am glad that I did not bring them with me—and many kisses to Clare, and take to yourself the fervent prayers of one who seldom suplicates for favors[.]

your
Charly

Answer by directing to these Barracks[.]

Afternoon
Metropolitan Hotel

I leave this 3 P.M. for Laurel Station—(between us there is a great scare here and all the Malitia are called out to fill the place of the Vet. Res. Corp. who will follow me towards the "front" i.e. Baltimore (some what changed is that "*front*")[7] I am afraid that this move of the Rebs will kill my commanding a Brigade, blast their buttons!—shoot that is moderate language anyhow[.]

Direct to me at Laurel Station Md.

125

Laurel Station
July 14 = 1864[8]

Dear Mary,

Here I am "alive and kicking" but would not have sworn to it the last three days or nights as it was quite old fashioned sleeping out on the Rail Road without removing even spurs and having the horse saddled all night—but as they made up their Minds to not visit me at the post—I had all my labor for nothing, although I have no doubt but that the entire party would have been captured as my forces are not strong enough at any one point to make any show if numbers should come, as my six companies are spread from one mile this side of Anapolis Junction from here to Washington—I believe that I lost several men at Beltsville and the post above me (the Junction) was deserted and I left without any support north—the fact is they got very much frightened at Anapolis and removed all their men from the Rail Road, absolutely deserted it and attempted to remove some of my men but I soon put a stop to that and sent word to Baltimore that as long as I had a man that this culvert here and that at Savage's Switch would be preserved[.] some of the beauties (100 day men) actually got a locomotive and sent an order for my men to get on and leave—a written order from a 100 day Colonel to my men—hang him if I had not been very busy at the time I would have arrested him, but I guess that he will not attempt to interfear again with *my* command.

I shipped my trunk &c. on Monday night to Washington so I must write this with a lead pencil.

Direct at Laurel Station, Md—I can not find you the county as I believe that three—Prince George, Annarundel & Howard all meet at this place but I think that it is Prince George.

Give my love to the boys and many kisses to Clare—I have been thrice glad that I did not bring the boys with me, but will send for them when this all blows over[.]

Charly

126

Laurel Station
Prince George Co.
Md.
July 16 = 1864

Dear Mary,

Yours of the 11th inst. came to hand yesterday—the del[a]y being I suppose attributed to the suspension of the Mails between here and the North.

You ask me to call on Mr. Spencer at Spencerville, should I ever get that way—well I was at Spencerville the night previous to the receipt of your letter, but as the Rebs were picketing just then above and I had but two men (mounted) with me, I of course "didn't stay long just thar," but last night I started again with six mounted men and went through to Mechanicsville and back by midnight, taking a bye-road to return, making the ride 30 miles, between a little before dark and mid-night and I can assure you that [I] slept "some" afterwards. I called upon Mr. Spencer on my way out and acknowledged the obligation—he was both surprised and pleased that such trouble should be taken to do so.

I visited Bill Davis[9] about five minutes; not that I felt any interest in *him* or his family, but that I could *use him* for the interest of the government, by being able to rely upon any information that he could, and I felt would give me in reference to the loyalty of the inhabitants of this section, for Laurel is so violently Sechesh that I can not place *any* dependence upon their statements and I have written for orders to arrest certain families in this County, also Montgomery and Howard; and if I get the authority I will astonish some of the "upper crust" of this section of the state, and I suppose that I will get a "splendid reputation" from them, but blast their ugly hides! they attempted to get my command cut off and I will pay them back with interest.[10]

I also received your letter of the 13th; two of the 14th, and one of the 31st of *June*—they just reached me—I do not know if there are any more (like unborn babes) "on their way" or not, but if so, I suppose (like the said babes) [they] will "be delivered" in "due corse of time."

I can not say that I admire the likeness much, the shade of the right side is too dark and I think that the cheeks are colored too much—however as all the officers say that it is good, I suppose it must be so—I will want *one dozen* [?] to go around. You do not express any opinion upon the subject.

You speak of coming here on a visit—all very good, but—waite until I write in reference to the subject as I am in doubts as to my remaining at this post—as I have not a Colonels command here, only three companies and a Major with me—I shall go to Washington early next week and then will know something more definite on that point—that is if a Soldier can know any thing about his future actions, I prefer remaining here and if I can I will secure boarding for you in some private house.

Give my love to the boys—Bill's folks wanted me to promise to send them there but I would not—and give many kisses to Clara[.]

Charley

P.S. I did not see your beautiful neice.[11]

127

HdQrs 18th Reg. V.R.C.
Laurel
Prince George Coy.
Md.
July 19 = 1864

Dear Mary,

By George! that is a military heading (except the "dear Mary") but never mind it may not be a military ending—I am actually in that condition that I *must* write for I have "nothing else to do" to while away the time.

The Poet Young says,

"Oh! for a lodge in some vast wilderness,
Amidst a contiguity of shade."[12]

which has been paraphrased to read (excuse the lewdness of the joke) "oh! for a lodge in some vast widow's nest, amidst a contiguity of hair."

The quotation was recalled to my mind as I like him, wanted some change and did not get it and like the jester who distorted his lines—*didn't get it*—so the two slipped into my idle brain together: I might however, in the absence of both, console myself with Hollands extract of "Bitter Sweet"

"The fountain of joy is fed by tears,
And love is let by the breath of sighs;
The deepest griefs and the wildest fears
Have holiest ministries."[13]

but then *that* is "*Cold* Comfort." as the poor Man, (who was up to his knees in snow) said as he looked into the "Restaurant" window.

Strange "freiks of fancy" some times seize me, while laying in this little log hut—isolated from the world, although the world is all around me; and in its busiest form, i.e. the constant whirl of the locomotive as it hastens on—it reminds me of Tom Moore's

> "Oh! well may we hope, when this short life is gone,
> To meet in some world of more permanent bliss;
> For a smile, or a grasp of the hand hast'ning on,
> Is all that we enjoy of each other in this."[14]

There! I am not agoin to become religious—not by a "long shot," although I did come *very* near gone to church last Sunday for want of "something else to do" by George! I came very near it; heavens! help the poor church if I *had,* how the plaster would have rattled down upon the head[s] of the audience—no! I mean congregation—I believe *that* is the proper term to use.

It is a singular thing, that while engaged in the midst of the turmoil of battle or the hurry incident thereto, at the times when we should think most of those we love, that love scarce effects us (so busy is the mind) yet as soon as *that* is over, it redounds with tenfold force and make us as Baily writes

> "Who sayes he loves and is not wretched, lies;
> x x x x x
> 'Tis the most reasonable thing in Nature"[15]

Now while in the field all I asked for was to be "near home" since I have been in the Corps all I have asked is, for "home to be near me," *that* is the only draw-back that I feel (the chance shots are of no account) I have only asked like Carleton,[16]

> "Oh! smiles of love shine on me
> In rays of light devine,
> To chase the hideous spectres
> From off this path of mine."

July 20, 1864

I had just finished the above when I received information that I could capture a desperate character some eight miles from here; so I mounted immediately and with two men set out after having procured a guide—upon arriving at his house, the "bird had flown," but ascertaining that he was at the

"Furnace" (Inn) some 10 miles across from his residence, I determined not to be baulked, I procured another guide (to cut across the Country) and started and reached the spot at mid-night. The proprietor of the residence was very much frightened to find me standing in the centre of his room at—

"———the hour when Night had driven
Her car half round the sable heaven;
While Mortals lost in gentle sleep,
Forgot to smile, or ceased to weep."[17]

for I did not deem it proper to pass through the cerimony of knocking on the door when I found it unfastened: he denied that the man was *in the house* but upon my threatening to arrest *him* and then walk all over his property, he informed me that the long-looked for was on the hay mow in the barn and there sure enough I found him with three other ruffians sound asleep; here I was stuck to tell which was the man, for I had no description of him, so I resorted to the dodge of calling his name in a very earnest and friendly tone to which he readily answered—"Come out side quick Luke," said I, "what's in the wind," said he, "Come" I replied in a very cautious and serious tone, and but he came into the full glare of the Moon, I took a good look at him instantly as he turned to retreat into the barn; "it is of no use Luke," said I, "for I know you now, and would much rather take you alive than dead; but take you I will"—he caught a glimps of the two men that I had with me, with their revolver[s] in their hands and (I suppose) thought with Falstaff

"Discretion *is* the better part of valor"[18]

and succumbed—well to make the story short I marched him to camp and this morning forwarded him to Washington.

I know that with my rank I should not go upon such expiditions, but the fact is that I have such an infurnal, eturnal and inveterated hatred to the trators (which is increasing every day) that I can not help "dipping in" on every occasion, especialy when I think how the "Sympathizers" (oh! what a mild term) of this locality endevoured to get this little band of *"Invalids"* "gobbled up" by the enemy on this last raid—by-the-way, quite a complement was paid me by themselves, for I discovered through one of the *few* union men of this section that the reason that the rebs did not attempt to destroy the bridge at the Laurel was that they (the "sympathizers") informed the rebs that it "would require at least 5 or 600 men to dislodge me as I had a good position and evidently intended to fight it out at that point"—they could not spare that number and it would take *too long a time* to "whipe us out" for them to stop, and so did not come, although urged to do so by several of the prominant residence of this place—as soon as I get all the "dots" so as not [to] involve some poor people here, I shall make a "clean sweep" of them—there is one thing that you can rely upon, viz; all the rich are sechesh and *all* the poor are staunch union, at heart at least although quite a number are afraid to "come out of the wilderness."

By-the-way I forgot to mention in my last that Bill Davis was *drafted* in the last draft and had to sell his horse to raise his little $300—had to "raise the wind" to get out of the wind, i.e. draft.

Yesterday I received my Parchment (called Commission) from the President as Colonel so now I am fixed—at least as long as the war last[s].[19]

I expect a letter from you this afternoon—should I not get it I will mail this to night so that it will leave in the morning as we have but one mail north per day 7:30 a.m.

I have just received some information in reference to the "sharp practice" of some more of these infurnal scoundrels about here—it makes me repeat the lines of Tom Moore

> "Oh for a scurge to curse the slave,
> whose reason, like a deadly blight,
> Carries o'er the councils of the brave,
> And blasts them in their hour of Might!
> May Life's unblessed cup for him
> Be drugg'd with treacheries to the brim,—
> With hopes, that but allure to fly,
> With joys, that vanish while he sips,
> Like Dead Sea fruits, that tempt the eye,
> But turn to ashes on the lips!
> His Country's Curse, his children's shame,
> Out Cast of virtue, peace and fame,
> May he at last, with lips of flame
> On the parch'd desert thirsting die,—
> While lakes, that shone in mockery nigh,
> Are fading off, untouch'd, untasted,
> Like the once glorious hopes he blasted!
> And, when from earth his spirit flies,
> Just Prophet, let the damn'd one dwell
> Full in sight of Paradise,
> Beholding heav'n and feeling hell!"[20]

I find that my "poetical fancy" is both becoming strong in language and lengthy so for fear of wearing you I guess that I had better close.

Give my love to the boys and kisses to Clara[.]

Yr.
Charly

P.S. I will go to Washington tomorrow and endevour to ascertain how long I am likely to remain here and inform you of the prospects.

128

Laurel Md
Aug 26 = 1864

Dear Mary,

Yours of the 24th inst. arrived this evening, and as the Boys leave tomorrow morning I forward this by them. They both have made strong promises to do their utmost towards their advancement at School when they return—Willie threatens to advance one class immediately and Joe to pass for the High School examination—I hope that they will both fullfill their promises.

They have been a luxery to me—an expensive one it is true—but a luxery nevertheless and one that I regret to part with, but I think as you say, they are more needfull to you, than to me, beside I could not make it as fine fun for them were they with me regularly, for this time I gave them one continual round of pleasure, which has cost me nearly $90.00—an avarage of $10.00 each per week (counting board) but it was money well invested—it paid me and I think that (the sight of life considering) it paid them.

Your statement of the condition in which Mary presented herself does not surprise me in the least—the only surprise is that she had funds enough to get home at all—I suppose that there is enough of you all to make her look respectable at least.

You say that she may visit me after she gets fixed up a little—I would like very much to see her, but there is two difficulties in the way, first, I would not know where to put her if she did come, for she could not come and go in a day—next is that I will not be likely to be here as I shall visit Washington the first of the week to make a change if possable; so if she desires any thing of or with me she had better write—is she stopping with you?

"Mary says that Charly was never in the Confederate employ"—before making any remarks upon that point I will mearly drop a hint that the words *Rebel* employ would sound better Mary, than that word Confederate, which is used only by either the Rebels themselves or their sympathizers—however Charly may possably never have been in their employ, but if my memory serves me right *she* stated in one of her letters that he had joined the City

Guards at Savananah at the commencement of the rebellion—and that before they thought of conscripting, and *that* Company was at the taking of Fort Paulaski[21]—again I have the impression that he either was working at a "Government Foundry" (as they term it) or working at a Foundry that was supplying them with the means of murdering the loyal Citizens—I mean munitions of war.[22]

Now, I have always entertained the affections of a brother for Mary, but that never extended to Charly, and even if it did, it would soon be lost for a brother who was a traitor to his Country—I went into this war from Principle, but that is fast becoming Hatred, which is increasing as their treason and barbarity to those who fall into their hands continue—look at the actions of Moseby's men within a week, but a few miles from here—men shot, some their brains knocked out, two with their throats cut, *all after they had surrendered,* yes! some who were laying upon the ground wounded were deliberately murdered—may the curses of God! follow them through this life and the life to come.

Give my kisses to Clara[.]
Yr[.]
Charly

129

Laurel, Md
Sept. 5, 1864

Dear Mary,

I this day forwarded per Adams Express the sum of $100.00 the expressage *not* paid—I was not able to get to Washington (being busy) and had the Adjutant to express it and forgot to tell him to pay the expressage, hence it is not paid.

To-night I ship part of my regiment to Washington for duty and have but two Companies with me—the prospect is that the whole regiment will be ordered there this winter, in fact—I was informed that Gen.l Auger[23] had decided to give me command of one of the Forts at that place, and as they are making changes daily I may get my orders at any moment.

Excuse brevity on account of business as I must go to Savage[24] to see that the men there are ready.

Your
Charly

I enclose a likness of one of the Lieuts put it with the others[.]

130

Laurel, Md
Sept. 9th 1864

Dear Mary,

Yours of the 7th inst. came to hand this day.

I have entirely recovered from the effects of my grand summersault, except an occasional twitch in the right sholder—of no account.[25]

You think that I must be "much pleased at the prospect of moving." I am, but not for the cause that you suppose—that, "there is more excitement in Washington than in the little village of Laurel" for that is what does not "suit me exactly" at the present—, for I would rather be alone in the dreary waste of some desolate desert, than again mingle in society, with its brilliant surface that is polished over only to conceil the rotteness that is festering beneath—

"I would rather be a toad
and feed upon the vapor of a dungeon"[26]

than be compelled (because it is exigent) to listen to the gibbering of these chattering apes, misnamed humanity.

But, I am glad of the change in that direction (the only time in my military life that I do not feel dissatisfied with the prospect of being on duty in Washington) because I then can have opportunities of having my regiment filled and cared for by the "powers that be," which I have not now, and also, because there may be a prospect of my regiment *all* being on duty at one place, so that I can bring it up to that standard that I desire, beside giving employment to my mind.

If you would send me a box of collars, when you send the Coat—I would like it, provided you can purchase them for less than $5.00 per hundred; that is the price here—14½ inch, "English style D" is what this box is marked.

Give my love to the Boys and many, very many kisses to our pet,

Your,
Charly

131

Laurel, MD
Oct. 5, 1864

Dear Mary,

I left Philad- at 10.30 P.M. yesterday as expected, but upon arriving at Baltimore I found that the train did not stop at either Laurel or the Junction, so

I was forced to remain in Balt. from 3.30 until 7 o'clock and arrived here at 8 o'clock, "just in the nick of time," for my orders to move entered one end of camp as I entered the other.

I am ordered to Washington with the two companies for duty—the other two will remain, one at Laurel, the other at Hyattsville—but there is an ambiguity about the order that leaves me in the dark in reference to my Staff, however I will know by night as I have sent to Washington for that purpose—perhaps before the mail closes for this[.]

I write in haste but I will enclose the "flights of fancy" that I promised to forward and as they are voluminous, it will serve to amuse, perhaps, but to occupy, certainly, your spare time until my next.

I have not read the enclosed but mearly looked at the dates so as to *page* them for your convenience.[27]

Give love to [the] Boys and kisses to Clare[.]

Hastily[,]
Charly

P.S. I open this to say that the entire headquarters "move" tomorrow at daylight—do not answer this but waite until I write from Washington with directions, which I shall do to-morrow night[.]

132

East Capitol Hill Barracks
Washington, D.C.
Oct. 7 – 1864

Dear Mary,

I have only time to inform you of my whereabouts as the "penny-post" will leave in three minutes—I will write more fully tomorrow—Direct your answer to my last (from Laurel) to me as follows

East Capitol Hill Barracks
East Capitol & 3rd St.
Washington, D.C.

Give my love to Boys and kisses to Clara and excuse brevity *this time*[.]

Charly

9

"They do not permit the Vet. Res. Corps to remain idle"

October 13, 1864–December 11, 1864

JOHNSON would spend the rest of the war in Washington, commanding his regiment and superintending the transportation of troops through the city, among other duties. During this time Lincoln was reelected, Atlanta was taken, Sherman marched to the sea, and Lee surrendered his Army of Northern Virginia. Then came shattering news: the assassination of Abraham Lincoln. Colonel Johnson personally signed the order assigning three men of his command to the honor guard that escorted "the remains of the late President of the United States" to his home in Springfield.[1] The letters we have to Mary end well before this, in December 1864, when Johnson was finally able to bring Mary and the children to live with him.

133

East Capitol Hill Barracks
Washington, D.C.
Oct. 13 = 1864

Dear Mary,

I take my pen in hand without the least idea of what to write, as things remain here just as at my last, hence I have nothing to record.

I have not received any word from you since I left home, although I suppose that there are answers to my three that I wrote, some where on the road. It is one of the bores of changing headquarters, that the mail *will* get missed in spite of all precautions to the contrary and I suppose that this is the case in this instance—the fact is, that the entire regiment has not received a single letter since our arrival here, except those which were sent to us from the Laurel Post Office—I have made every attempt at the Post Office at the Bureau and elsewhere to get a Mail, but each place insist that there is not any for us although I know that there *must* be plenty somewhere. I begin to feel very anxious to hear from you in regard to your health and also if you received the package (it almost amounted to a package) that I forwarded to you from Laurel in accordance with promise.

I have not got my order through for my Cottage yet, it has passed through nearly all the "approved," but has stuck in the Quartermaster General's Office, on account I believe of some difficulty about some Cottages previously built for officers of the Corps, they having exceeded the estimated cost—some them costing the Government nearly $2800.00 each, so the Department are rather doubtful of ordering any more, but as I have some very good parties following mine up I do not despair yet, for I have good backing and strong workers.

I have received word (verbaly) that two new and full companies have been added to the regiment, and also have succeeded in getting one of my detached companies ordered to these barracks—I think that by hard work and constant driving that I will get things in some thing like a shape.

The duties here are very heavy for the men of our Corps, as the details are constant—for instance now while writing I have but *two men* in Camp not on duty; to-morrow I will not have a Camp guard of any kind—this morning I had to discharge all the Prisoners in the Guard House to fill an order for a guard at the Old Capitol Prison[2]—so you see that they do not permit the Vet. Res. Corps to remain idle, at least in Washington: the Corps should have at least 3000 more men here for the duties that they now are doing.

Of course it increeses my idle moments by taking all the men for details outside of the barracks—a Colonel here in command of troops has but little to do, for the simple reason that he has no troops to command, personaly.

I received a long letter from Alva Stites yesterday, via Laurel, which I shall answer tonight, he is well.

I wrote to George Deal in reference to the Sutlership and sent it to you as I do not know his address—I suppose that it arrived, and also suppose that he has or had come to the conclusion that the Sutlership was all "bosh"—well, I do not think that half of the people will know me until after I am snugly laid under the sod, and then it will not make much difference to *me,* in fact do not much now.

Give my love to the Boys and kisses to Clara[.]

Charly

134

East Capitol Hill Barracks
Washington, D.C.
Oct. 20 = 1864

Dear Mary,

Yours of the 19th inst. arrived this day—none other however, that you mailed from Camden has yet arrived.

You think that you could find plenty to write if we did not differ in regard to the Presidency—why bless your soul! Mary, "spit it out" to the full extent of your desires if it will either relieve you or furnish food for a letter, for like you the letter is to me a "well spring of pleasure" and the longer the sweeter.[3]

Letters! they are the blessed messengers that make the heart's blood forward fly through every artery, coursing the whole system until it rebounds again at the starting point—letters! they weave the golden flowers of rememberance of the past, like well remembered echos thrilling upon the ear; they bring forth the hidden treasures that are conceiled in the recesses of Memory's Cave and send the bright thoughts forth from their dungeon to the glorious shrine of the present, brightning all with a halo so pure that naught can dim its etherial lustre while they come upon us in the shape of glorious visions lighting up the whole of our existance.

"Though in Time's record nearly naught,
They are Eternity to Thought,"[4]

and wipe all darkness from the refulgent brow of the future and drive the dead leaves from our past as———there the adjutant, blast him! has stuck a dozen papers under my nose and broke the thought—well! let it go, perhaps it is best for I might have went so far that I could not have got back to-night.

I have a dead woman in my quarters to-night, she was a Laundress of the 6th regiment that was too sick to be removed when I ordered the others to uncase the premises so I (of course) let her remain and now she has "step[p]ed out" for good, well poor soul! perhaps she is better off—who knows? I am sure I do not—only she might as well have died upon the hands of her (or her husbands) regiment.

I have no news yet about my quarters, but am promised a positive answer tomorrow morning by 12 o'clock.

I have ordered the sutler here to "vamouse" by Saturday night so that the way may be clear for George[.][5]

Give love to the Boys and kisses to Clare[.]

Charley

135

East Capitol Hill Barracks
Washington, D.C.
Oct. 31 = 1864

Dear Mary,

I wrote to you on the 25th and 28th inst. to which I have not received any answer—the latter, however, I suppose you did not receive until yesterday morning as Sunday intervened; I expect that I will get an answer to that tomorrow, the answer to the former, I have no doubt has gone on a "fall excurtion."

The Adjutant will leave here tomorrow for home (Michigan) on a twenty days leave of absence, the first since he entered the service—two years and four months—and that will make me very busy for a few days, for I regret to say that I have not a Lieutenant in the command with brains enough to fill his place, without consuming more time to teach him than it would take me to do the work myself: that with the revising of the Muster and Pay Rolls of my regiment and the detachments of the 6th and 19th regiments (which I had to muster to-day) will make me "hurry up the cakes" for the next three days.

To-day I was informed at Headquarters (blast their ugley pictures) that it was contemplated to put me in Command of Sherbourn Barracks in addition to mine, as "it wanted some energetic officer to take a hold of it"—a good inducement for a fellow to work like the devil, truly—but I backed down for the present, although I expect that it will come before the winter is out—the fact is they want to get something more for me to do and they scarcly know what, at least so it appears, for a few days since, they asked me if I did not think that a Cavalry regiment of the Corps would not suit me, for they wanted to organize one and thought that I had "just about *dash* enough to make it sell"; but I soon asked them out of that as I could fall back upon the Surgeon with my testicles, that "settled that hash"—a number of Field Officers here are crazy for the chance—they are welcome to it, for I have no desire to be riding through the mud of Virginia every two or three days to hunt Mosby's Guerillas or any one elses.[6] They remind me of the story of the Sailor who attended an exhibition of a Juggler, who was performing over a Magazine, and while Jack was gazing with open-mouth wonder at the tricks, the Magazine by some accident exploded, throwing the Tar into a neighbouring yard upon his back, and when he saw the severed bodies of the audience, heads, arms, legs &c. flying through the air, he "wondered what in the devil the fellow would get at next."

I have secured the lumber for your tables and tomorrow I will set a Carpenter to work at them—I am gradualy sneaking, for that is the honest word, sneaking one thing after another out of the government by sugesting this advantage, that improvement &c. &c.—gads! if they do not get the building finished soon, I will have "all the modern improvements" upon it before they know exactly what they are about.

I purchased a little single bed-stead (cottage) to-day for Clara, it is second hand, having been used by an Officer and will be equal to new after it gets a coat of varnish, I paid only $2.50 for it.

I have not succeeded in a school for the Boys yet, but think that there must be some in the other end of the city, I will take a scoute in that direction as soon as I get time.[7]

I will be at home on election day for certain, having received permission today to go and the offer to give me a *pass* instead of a leave of absence, so that it will not count against me in case I should want a leave at some future time—this being near headquarters and getting intimate with them posts a man in all the "ins and outs" of the government—military I mean.

Give my love to the boys and kisses to Clara[.]

Yr[.]
Charley

136

East Capitol Hill Barracks
Washington, D.C.
Nov. 17 = 1864

Dear Mary,

Yours of the 15th arrived this evening, inclosing a letter from Clara, which will serve me for a Month, for it will take all of that to decipher it—she is death on periods I percieve, however you need not tell her (bless her little soul!) that it is all Greek to me.

The Lord's Prayer &c. is in a little frame, I would like you to bring it with you, for it is a curiousity and will not require any space to carry.

I will not have but one Chest made as I perceive that you are partial to your old one and the three (if I had another) with my trunk would be to much to lug around.

George arrived here this morning and has not see[n] the former Sutler yet and I think, myself, that when he does, it will not amount to much, for the fellow has a Washington idea of the value of his old shanty.

The Plasterers are at work upon the quarters but I really do not think that they will be ready for occupasion before the 1st of the month, although they say otherwise—every thing is progressing and I see no draw-backs on the time I fixed—the *first.*

I received verbal information yesterday that I am to have additional duties to perform, that an order was being prepared for me to take (in addition to these barracks) command of the Soldiers Rest, the Baltimore Depot and to have command of the troops on the rail road as far as Annapolis Junction—it does not involve my changing quarters but will use up all my spare time, of which I have plenty just now.

There is as high as 2 and 3000 troops passing through the "Rest" in a day, many of them commanded by Colonels who leave their men to go strol[l]ing around the City, and the Government wants some Colonel there who will not be out ranked and also to "have snap enough to *compell* them to remain with their troops" (I use their words) "hence we want you"—I would have been there today but Giles thought that the order did not give me power enough and it is being re-modeled so as to make me the "I am" along that road and at its terminous—it will require my officers (those on duty) to examine all officers passes and give me the power to decide where there is any doubt, if he shall proceed or return, so that it will require considerable of my time until I get the Machine in good running order; about that time I suppose I will be detailed for some other duty—well "so must it be."

You had best bring some of that washing soap with you as it is, as I informed you 25 cts. per. cake here.

Give my love to the Boys and kisses to my little correspondent[.]

Charly

137

East Capitol Hill Barracks
Washington, D.C.
Nov. 21 = 1864

Dear Mary,

Yours of the 20th (mailed on the *19th*) arrived this evening.

You wish to know what I would do in reference to borrowing Mary's trunk, I think, if it would hold all that; the Chest would that you could easly send it back by express, or on the other hand you could bring the Chest and if we can dispence with it we could easly convert it into kindling wood—the question is simply one of economy, is the chest worth more in Camden to you here than the cost of expressage in the Trunk? if it is leave it, if not bring it—that is my point of view, the *value* you can settle to suit yourself.

Y[ou] desire me to send for the things as soon as possable, well Mary, I really can not before the first of the Month for I have not the funds, as I possess but 5 cents and am now letting my board run on, if they were sent they would of course lie at the Office until that time, however, I will send you word, so that you can ship them by the 1st or so that they may arrive here about the 1st.

We have had five day[s] of constant rain which has retarded the plastering for they can not mend the roof unless it clears off (one day would answer) and then they will "pile in" I have arranged so that my quarters should be done the first thing with the same idea that you possessed, viz; to make fires so as to heat the rooms and dry the plaster.

You perceive by this time that my estimate of character and judgement of human nature has not fallen off any—I always[s] said and thought that Charly Redding was an infurnal mean cuss, to use the mildest terms possable, and it is one of the inegmas of life how a woman can be hoodwinked time and again by such scoundrels and still place any confidence in them.

I have got out of the Post Commandership of the Soldiers Rest and Depot and now only command the troops there, which of course is only a nominal thing, so far as the labor is concerned, as I attend to it at the Barracks and only visit them officialy every second day, although the responsibility still rests with me, but as I have selected the best Officers and very best men (let none others go) I feel perfectly easy upon that score and decidely easy at the loss of the mental labor—I do not know what in the thunder they will try next with me.

I had another application to day for a servant (in fact two) but as they had a harlot appearance I sent them flying—if you could get a decent darky you had best for these who go out here are (it appears to me) tickled with the notice from white—men I was about to say, but will not—scamps and they the filthy sons of suckers appear bent upon tickling them—so low does a bad Soldier sink himself—I intend, the first one that I catch to trot them out before the Command at Dress Parade and make an example of him—these Washington Niggers have become so accostamed to Soldiers and Washington Soldiers so accostamed to them they actualy fratranize—although the Nigger that I have engaged is so old and infurnal ugly that I do not think there will be any back door business, yet I would prefer a northern dark if you can suite yourself, if not we will hold on to this.[8]

Give my love to the Boys and kisses to Clara[.]

Charly

138

H.Qrs. 18th Reg. Vet. Res. Corps
Washington, D.C.
Nov. 25 = 1864

Dear Mary,

Yours of the 23rd inst. arrived today.

I have but a brief time to reply, for I am up to my eyes endevouring to ferret out a most outrageous case of rape committed last evening upon a little girl, about 6 or 7 years old, in this vacinity, by a soldier of the Vet. Res. Corps. The little thing is expected to die before morning from the loss of blood, and I am examining *every man* from first to last, in camp and out, in Depot, Soldiers Rest and every where else to either catch the scoundle or vindicate my regiment—the latter I hope and pray for it was a most foul crime and unless we either clear our command or bring the villian to justice the whole Corps will suffer—I have informed the Headquarters of the affair and recommended that the same thing may be done through out the entire city at the same time—talk about the "*poor* soldier" bah!—I think that the estimate that the Regulars use to put upon the mass of men under them, is nearer correct than the morbid sympathy exercised at the present day.

I am glad that you have secured a black girl at home; for you can best please yourself and beside bring one into a strange place so that you can break her in before she can make any acquaintance.—I have informed the other that she is not wanted.

They are pushing up my portion of the building—but the weather is against me and it is slow work, though I am in hopes of its being ready for your things by the 1st but do not expect it to be ready for you for a few days after, as I shall make shure of its not making you sick—I do not forget Col. Colby's case and have no desire to bring you and the children yet a while, certain.[9]

Give love to the Boys and kisses to Clara—I realy can not make out her letter, but will write (or rather print) one for the little thing as soon as I get time.

Charly

139

East Capitol Hill Barracks
Washington, D.C.
Dec. 1 = 1864

Dear Mary,

Yours of the 25th ult. arrived two days since and strange as it may appear I have not had time to answer it until this moment, and that, I fear but briefly—I have had a new kink added to my duties, as receiving and forwarding officer for the 1st Corps of Veterans under Genl. Hancock[10] and yesterday a new duty was added that required me to be up all night and I expect all of to-night—in fact, it will require at least two days and nights, perhaps three, and no sleep except "cat-naps"—so you see that I am driving *five* horses at present, viz; the Barracks, the Depot, the Soldiers Rest, the 1st Corps Recruiting Office, and the last named duty which (*confidentially*) is no more or less than the shipment of two Army Corps through Washington and being responsable that no straggling takes place—it is true that the last duty will end in two days, and well it may, for between transports, Rail Road Trains, Tellegraffs, posting Guards, Closing Drinking Saloons (on the Rout &c). I am compleatly be addled—you need not mention any thing of this last duty—at least until after the papers notice the movement and I suppose that they will get it about the time that it is done, for we are moving quietly and all my orders are *confidential.*

Yours of the 29th arrived this evening inclosing Bill of Lading of goods shiped per Phil. Wil. & Balt. R.R. you do not say if the freight is paid or not—however it matters little for I will discover that when I send for the goods.

The Plasters will not get the White Coat upon the quarters before Monday so that it will be several days yet before we can venture in there, but it is just as well for the Pay Department is out of Funds and will be for some ten days or two weeks—blast it! it could not happen at a worse time than this—if the goods are not paid for, I will borrow and get them at the barracks—damn the Pay Department.

I am sorry that you can not get your Girl, for I have discharged the one I engaged and can not get her now—you had best employ one at home and bring her along—that is the advise of *all* the Ladies that I have asked in reference to the girls—none would recommend a Washington Nigger.

I have not had time to see about the Boys schooling yet—I do nothing but ride from point to point—horse sweating—and as soon as I land at any of the offices (I have three) there is any quantity of paper to be answered that consumes all the time. This afternoon I laid down to get some sleep for to-nights work when I had to get up to see Genl. Hancock and the Military Governor—so it goes—there is "no rest for the wicked in this world"—talk of the work of the field, by George! I have done more in one week in this Corps than I did in a Month in the Field.

Give my love to the Boys and Kisses to Clara[.]

yr[.]
Charly

140

Washington, DC
Dec. 3 = 1864

Dear Mary,

Yours of the 2nd inst. arrived this evening and I assure you that there is not any thing the matter with me either mentaly or physicaly, except that for the last three days I have been worked to death and absolutely have no time to eat or sleep.

On the evening of the 30th ult. I was ordered to attend to the troops passing through Washington to prevent straggling, as they were expected that night I of course had no sleep—they did not arrive until the next morning and it took nearly all day—at the same time I was ordered to attend to the recruits of the "1st Corps" and had that office to organize *at once*—lodge & feed them, register them &c. which took me until near bed time, when the tellegraph announced "more trains on the road," as they were not expected for three hours I fixed all up and had *two* hours sleep that night and then was busy until noon of the next day (2nd) then had the "1st Corps" office to visit and was there until 11 o'clock at night, when I went to bed and was routed out this morning at day-light, making only seven hours sleep in three nights and working like the mischief each day—to-morrow morning I turn out at 3 o'clock to go at it again—I intended to go to bed at supper time to night, but your anxiety to know if any thing was the matter stop[p]ed me to answer—if this thing was to continue for a week it would lay me up—but I expect that it will end in two more nights. I have received the credit of having pass more troops through the city in the same time and less straggling for the number, than has taken place since the war—in fact but fifteen men slip[p]ed through my hands and they were nearly all captured by the Mounted Men that I had posted about the town, and I did the whole of it with only 60 Cavalry and 70 Infantry men, when the Military Governor offered me 300 men and thought that it would take nearer 500 than that number.

The goods reached here and are now in store under lock and key—I have not had time to look at them—the trunk and carpets are in my bed room all O.K. they were cheep in transportation as they cost only $5.20 for the lot—borrowed money, for I am in the same fix as you are as the Paymaster is out of funds—I shall go in person on Monday and if I can not raise it from him I think that I will get my pay account cashed by an outsider if it does not cost too much.

The building is nearly finished, the rough coat of plaster is quite dry (I have a stove in each room) and the white coat will be put on Monday. I think that by constant fires—day and night that it will be safe by the last of the week for sleeping purposes; by that time, or before, the carpenter will be done, so I may expect to have you about that time.

I will forward funds as soon as I can get a hold of them, which of course I shall do in some manner.

Give my love to the Boys and Kisses to Clara[.]

Charly

Do not mention any thing about the *great number* of troops passing, as the government keeps it quiet and no one here (not even my own officers) dream of the extent of the Movement, as they see only those who pass during the day.

I wrote to you on the 1st inst. and directed as this is.

George has closed out and I moved his shanty for him to-day, he goes into opperation on Monday.

I enclose $2.00, all I have[.]

141

East Capitol Hill Barracks
Washington, D.C.
Dec. 6 = 1864

Dear Mary,

Yours of the 5th inst. arrived this day, and I am truely sorry that you was so uneasy in regard to me—why, it appears that I was regular in my answers except *one* that I laid over for two days, and I assure you, that, as strange as it may appear, I really could not find time to answer that before I did except on one occasion when I did attempt it and fell asleep with the pen in my hand and slept my time out (two hours) at the desk until aroused by the guard at the quarters in accordance with my orders—but, Mary, I will endevour to avoid it in future no matter what may occour, for I really would prefer any amount of pain and exertion upon my part than one moments anxiety should be experienced by you.

I suppose that I must look out for a Nigger at last—well, alack a day! I will have a happy time of it—but you bring one if *possable* for I do not think that I can get any to suit, although I will try, and not get "weary" in the cause.

Pay Master has no funds yet and to-day thought that it would come in a few days, some three or four—I will have a proposition to advance when it does come, about your debts—it will be tight squeezing for the first month or so—in fact now that we are behind hand, it does not appear that we will *ever* get up square again.

You say that Adaline Hufty[11] is the only one of my relations who has visited you—well, Mary, there will be some trouble saved in the way of letter writing—and that is some consolation.

I met Mr. Process[12] in the street to day and like a damn fool did not know him—he stop[p]ed me with "ain't this Col. Johnson" and stuck out his hand—I took it and said "yes it is"—trying to recall the man, "when do you expect your wife" said he; "not for some time" I replyed, still holding his hand "you have the advantage of me, your face is familiar but I can not recall your name"—"my name is Process" said he, and I slung his hand off, step[p]ed up and looked in his eye; he step[p]ed off to the car and got in—I let it go at that as it was in broad day-light, I was in uniform and in the presence of some of my men, for it was just at the Depot—Damn his impudence I will get a chance at him when we will not be so conspicious, as I would not bring *your name* in public. The building is progressing at about the usual rate—I gave both the Carpenters and Plasters a severe rub to-day and think that it will be gone on a little more lively after this—I know that it will be ready by the time that we are, but I want all the advantage of time, so as to dry the wall thoroughly.

Give my love to the Boys and kisses to Clara[.]

Yr[.]
Charley

142

[Lynch transcription]

December 11, 1864
East Capitol Hill Barracks
Washington, D.C.[13]

Dear Mary,

Yours of the 8th inst. arrived this day.

You say that you are surprised at my actions with [Process] at your letter—why! My God! did you expect me to extend the hand of welcome and friendship to him?—to the man who has dared to pollute the chaste person of *my* wife? by a lecherous kiss?—I say lecherous on your own representations as I know not the man—or thing—but—you yourself say that it is the "promptings of his love of woman[.]" And pray could a man love (honestly) more women than his wife—we all know where that "love of woman" would lead the man who does not confine himself to the most strict rules of propriety—what would you think of my actions if you heard that "my love of woman" had induced me to do such things in your absence? What but that I had some base designs upon them, and justly would you come to that conclusion—

It is all very well to talk of his "friendship" bah! if that "friendship" ends in insult what it is worth? or if that "friendship["] is only for the ultimate object of insult, what is it worth? Nearly a year and a half ago I cautioned you (while I was at Columbus, Ohio) with that man's actions—do you remember a certain Post Script? I while a stranger to him foresaw exactly where his "friendship" would end—and thought then that there was a great deal of *disinterested* "friendship" on his part—men are not apt to be so damn clever to other men's wives (strangers especially) for "friendship[.]"

Again, you say that "he is a gentleman"—God help me! if I have lived a life so virtuous as not to be able to appreciate the fact, that a "gentleman" is one who takes advantage of a husbands absence to insult his wife—I aspire to be a gentleman, nor must I show attention to every lady I meet and then kiss her at the first opportunity to stamp me as such! If so then let me be no "gentleman" for I doubt the position and equaly doubt that every wife would defend me (as you have him) when that husband undertook to resent the insult offered to him—I wish to God! now, I had shot him on the spot.

Again you express a regret that you ever mentioned the subject to me and berate your "unruly member"—Mary, Mary, that is the last wish that I ever expected to hear you express—a wish that you had kept me in ignorance of an indignity offered to you that I might live in good fellowship with the offender. Great God! A desire to conceil an action which if breathed by other lips than yours would have made it horrible indeed, especialy if the information had come to me after I had extended the hospitality of a friend to him and you had joined me in that hospitality—oh! look at it—at the result.

Again, you say that you regret having mentioned it "unless I want every one to know that my husband has lost confidence in me"—now, Mary, you do me great injustice by that remark, for I do not publish my actions to the world, or I would not have avoided a scean that day, and again I have *not* lost confidence in you in the least particular nor have I insinuated such at any time but can I not have confidence in you and at the same time can you not be insulted, many a virtuous woman has been so offended—as God is my Judje! I entertain for you the most true, pure, holy and undying love and faith—if I did not, I would not care a "cuss" for any ones actions towards you, but, as I do, I feel disposed to resent it, and in so doing I certainly did not expect you (of all others) to be the defender of those actions and stamp *me* (your defender) as a ruffian and him, the offender, as a "gentleman"—God! God! either I have lived far too fast for this world or the world has progressed too fast for me[.]

Your
Charley

I shall write again about Monday or Tuesday and set the time for you to come on[.]

10

"Kisses to Clara"

October 9, 1866

JOHNSON'S war-time letters to Mary end here, on a discordant note, seemingly rare in their relationship. The rift was apparently not serious, and Mary and the children moved south to share Johnson's life in Washington.

Johnson moved to Bowling Green, Kentucky, in June 1866, and served as the chief superintendent of the Freedmen's Bureau for the Southern Subdistrict of Kentucky until July 1867. Among other duties, he monitored the progress of schools for newly emancipated slaves, mediated disputes between freedmen and their employers, and arrested suspected terrorists and "regulators," precursors of the Ku Klux Klan. The Lynch family had only one letter from this period, in which Johnson refers to others to and from Mary, but none of these appears to have survived.

Debilitated by chronic diarrhea and still suffering from his wounds, Charles F. Johnson died on July 28, 1867.

143

Bowling Green, KY
Oct. 9, 1866

Dear Mary,

Yours of the 3rd inst. (dated *Sept*) is at hand, acknowledging the receipt of mine of the 29th ult. On the 27th ult. I forwarded $150.00 to you (through Lockwood, per Adam's Express) and also forwarded a letter the same day; the receipt of the letter you acknowledged in your last, but there is no mention in either letter of your having received the funds. I begin to feel anxious—not for its safety (for I have the receipt) but that you may be in straightened circumstances by its non-arrival—if you have not received it by this time send me word *at once,* that I may hunt it up.

I have thus far paid all of Joe's bills out of my scanty funds and started him fresh from the 8th inst. free of board &c. He will have $26.66 as his pay for last month—he being carried on the rolls from the date of his acceptance of appointment, which will give him a chance to pay some of his borrowed money; and if I can settle a part of his board bill for this month, and I will try to my utmost to do so, it will enable him to get ahead of this world in his pecuniary affairs. I sometimes feel a regret that the Almighty has set his Countinance against self Destruction—if it was not so how easily could we "shuffle off this mortal coil" and escape the trials, tribulations and vexations of this Mundane Sphere—I feel that the dreaded uncertainty of the future is more preferable to the *certainty* of the present—and am fast becoming disgusted with my self, the world and its concomitants—there is one tie—my wife and children! *they* fill my soul to the very depth, breath and highth of its ideal Grace—oh! with what strength do they fill my whole being, to the very level of every day's life, by sunshine and Candle light—as freely, as forcably, as strongly as man strives for Right—with all the purity of Childhood's faith—and if God chooses, I will love them better after death.

This, this only can reconcile one to the contemptable nothingness of this life—the Wife!—the Children! how they rise before me at every step I take—ever accompanying me on the journey through the labyrinth of life, clinging (through memory) with such tenacity—that we are *never alone*—the woods, the streams, the clouds—not a leaf but speaks in eloquent silance of the absent loved ones—not a flower—the wild violet, the cultivated verbena but recalls the past with its thousands of fond remem[b]erances and forces us to cling tenaciously to life; and so we trudge along, (thankfully for the few gleams of peace that are seen through the clouds of trouble) with the happy knowledge that a few fleet-swerving years will end the pilgrimage, no matter what the Shrine that we halt at.

Give kisses to Clara and believe me as ever your

Charley

Notes

Introduction

1. Gessbury to Johnson, November 15, 1855, Johnson Papers. Any item noted as being from the "Johnson Papers" derives from the collection of letters and documents preserved by the Lynch and Sicard families, and made available for use in this book. Letters from Johnson himself, either to his wife Mary or to his children, are referred to as "Letter."

2. There is a second note from Gessbury, almost identical to the first but written at "Red Bank," and inscribed on June 23, 1859, for Johnson's daughter Clara. This seems to indicate both that Gessbury was a fixture on the waterfront at Camden and that he was accustomed to turning out such notes, perhaps for a gratuity.

3. Douglas C. Baynton, "Disability and the Justification of Inequality in American History," in *The New Disability History: American Perspectives,* ed. Paul K. Longmore and Lauri Umansky (New York: New York University Press, 2001), 52.

4. Anna L. Boyden, *Echoes from Hospital and White House: A Record of Mrs. Rebecca R. Pomeroy's Experience in War-Times* (Boston: D. Lothrop, 1884), 189.

5. Stewart Brooks, *Civil War Medicine* (Springfield, Ill.: Charles C. Thomas, 1966), 39.

6. Bruce Catton, *Glory Road* (Garden City, N.Y.: Doubleday, 1952), 322.

7. Gerard A. Patterson gives the following figures for the Gettysburg wounded: Confederate wounded taken back with the army: 8,000; Confederate wounded left on the battlefield: 5,500; Confederate wounded captured during the battle: 1,800; total Confederate wounded: 15,300; total Federal wounded: 14,500. Gerard A. Patterson, *Debris of Battle: The Wounded of Gettysburg* (Mechanicsburg, Pa.: Stackpole Books, 1997), 3, 48, 57.

8. James M. McPherson, *Battle Cry of Freedom: The Civil War Era* (New York: Ballantine Books, 1989), 487. The commonly accepted treatments for wounds and disease were sometimes lethal. The most basic forms of sanitation were neglected, with doctors who knew nothing of aseptic technique moving from patient to patient while wiping their hands on the same bloody towel. Men who complained of diarrhea were given laxatives "to purge" their bowels, and the appearance of infection was praised as "lauditory pus." The inadequate organization of hospitals and frontline aid stations and the failure to provide men going into combat with bandages in anticipation of injury turned serious wounds into lethal ones and relatively minor infections into debilitating disease. See Bell Irvin Wiley, *The Life of Billy Yank: The Common Soldier of the Union* (Indianapolis: Bobbs-Merill, 1952), 124–51; also George Worthington Adams, *Doctors in Blue: The Medical History of the Union Army in the Civil War* (New York: Henry Shulman, 1952); Brooks, *Civil War Medicine.*

9. For a discussion of illness in the army during the Civil War, see "The Depths of Suffering" in Wiley, *Life of Billy Yank,* 124–51.

10. Civil War combat veterans, who coined the term *soldier's heart,* obviously had far more understanding and empathy for those who suffered from post-traumatic stress disorder than did either the civilians or the medical professionals of the time. Indeed, it was not until World War I that shell shock became recognized by the medical establishment as a disability in its own right. Two particularly poignant, if fictional, accounts of soldier's heart or shell shock are Gary Paulsen, *Soldier's Heart: Being the Story of the Enlistment and Due Service of the Boy Charley Goddard in the First Minnesota Volunteers* (New York: Delacorte, 1998), and "Soldier's Home" by Ernest Hemingway, in *In Our Time* (1925; reprint, New York: Charles Scribner's Sons, 1958), 89–101. For an excellent overview of the struggle to win acceptance for post-traumatic stress disorder as a medical diagnosis, see Judith Lewis Herman, *Trauma and Recovery* (New York: Basic Books, 1992).

11. Theda Skocpol, *Protecting Soldiers and Mothers: The Political Origins of Social Policy in the United States* (Cambridge: Harvard University Press, 1992), 109. This represented 16.85 percent of the total number of Union veterans still living. A much higher figure is given by William H. Glasson, who cites a figure of 467,927 disability pensions granted by 1888. Glasson, *Federal Military Pensions in the United States* (New York: Oxford University Press, 1918), 138.

12. McPherson, *Battle Cry of Freedom,* ix. Two notable exceptions are *Gone for a Soldier: The Civil War Memoirs of Private Alfred Bellard,* ed. David Herbert Donald (Boston: Little, Brown, 1975), and the privately published *Portrait of Elnathan Keeler: A Union Soldier,* ed. Helen Klass (Wappinger Falls, N.Y.: Goldleif Reproductions, 1977).

13. Oliver Otis Howard, *The Autobiography of Oliver Otis Howard, Major General United States Army* (New York: Baker & Taylor, 1908); Joseph E. Crowell, *The Young Volunteer: The Everyday Experiences of a Soldier Boy in the Civil War* (New York: G. W. Dillingham, 1906).

14. Lynn Manning, "The Magic Wand," in *Staring Back: The Disability Experience from the Inside Out,* ed. Kenny Fries, (New York: Plume, 1997), 165.

15. Paul K. Longmore and Lauri Umansky, "Disability History: From the Margins to the Mainstream," in *The New Disability History* (New York: New York University Press, 2001), 6.

16. Rosemarie Garland Thomson, *Extraordinary Bodies: Figuring Physical Disability in American Culture and Literature* (New York: Columbia University Press, 1997), 6.

17. Henri-Jacques Stiker, *A History of Disability* (Ann Arbor: University of Michigan Press, 1997). See in particular "The Bible and Disability: The Cult of God," 23–37. Stiker notes how "Legal uncleanness was attached to the disabled" in the Book of Leviticus and how "The community of Qumram [practitioners of Essene Judaism] excluded the disabled of all kinds. This was a ritual exclusion, since it was in the name of the sanctity of the congregation or community that the exclusion was proclaimed." For a discussion of disability in the classical world, see Robert Garland, *The Eye of the Beholder: Deformity and Disability in the Graeco-Roman World* (Ithaca, N.Y.: Cornell University Press, 1995).

Although Americans of the nineteenth century prided themselves on having made a clean break with the traditions and constraints of the Old World, their notions of disability were largely transplanted from European society. If anything, American frontier society, with its emphasis on rugged independence, might have been even more critical of those having perceptible disabilities. For a general discussion of the social roles imposed on people with disabilities, see Herbert C. Covey, *Social Perceptions of People with Disabilities in History* (Springfield, Ill.: Charles C. Thomas, 1998), 6–25.

18. "Invested with meanings that far outstrip their biological bases, figures such as the cripple, the quadroon, the queer, the outsider, the whore are taxonomical, ideological products marked by socially determined stigmata, defined through representation, and excluded from social power and status" (Thomson, *Extraordinary Bodies,* 5). For a discussion of how this has worked in one form of mass culture, see Martin F. Norden, *The Cinema of Isolation: A History of Physical Disability in the Movies* (New Brunswick, N.J.: Rutgers University Press, 1994).

19. Thomson, *Extraordinary Bodies,* 36. Discussion of the "just world" theory is presented in Melvin Lerner, *The Belief in a Just World: A Fundamental Delusion* (New York: Plenum, 1980). That this view was prevalent in nineteenth-century America is confirmed by K. Walter Hickel in "Medicine, Bureaucracy, and Social Welfare: The Politics of Disability Compensation for American Veterans of World War I." Hickel states that disability, along with its economic effects of "unemployment, poverty, and dependence," was most commonly seen as "a preordained fate, a divine stigma incurred at birth, or a result of individual moral flaws and self-destructive habits such as criminality, alcoholism, and sexual promiscuity" *New Disability History,* 241.

20. Bruce Catton, *A Stillness at Appomattox* (Garden City, N.Y.: Doubleday, 1953), 143.

21. Byron Stinson, "The Invalid Corps," *Civil War Times Illustrated* (May 1971), 23.

22. Longmore and Umansky, *New Disability History,* 19.

23. Much of the material on Johnson's family is taken from Grace Johnson Lynch, *From Whence We Came,* a genealogy of the extended Johnson family, self-published in 1985. The volume is an invaluable resource, including as it does not only information on Charles and Mary Johnson, their ancesters, and direct descendants, but also on their cousins and in-laws the Huftys, the Blackistons, and the Davises, some of whom are mentioned in the Johnson letters.

24. The committee made a series of recommendations, among them that every ferry boat on the river be provided with a life boat "made of metal, fire proof, capable of sustaining . . . fifty persons, with life-lines attached to the gunwale at suitable distance," that they also carry life preservers and that the ferry operators be required to observe other stipulations intended to minimize the danger of explosion and fire. *Cummings Evening Bulletin,* Philadelphia, March 28, 1856, quoted on p. 74 of Lynch.

25. Lynch, *From Whence We Came,* 11–12.

26. Ibid., 32, 43.

27. Ryan Lindbuchler, *History of the 81st P.V.I., "The Fighting Chippewas": The Story of the 81st Pennsylvania Volunteer Infantry Regiment in the American Civil War* (81st Pennsylvania Infantry Regiment, Company K Civil War Reenactment Unit, 1992), 2. Ryan Lindbuchler is the author of this history, which is based principally on the research of Robert Mischak.

28. Letter, September 19, 1861.

29. Letter, October 19, 1861.

30. The certificate was enclosed with Johnson's letter of November 17, 1863.

31. Blackiston stipulated in his 1821 will that his seven slaves "be free and fully discharged from slavery to me and to me heirs," from two to five years after his death. Lynch, *From Whence We Came,* 20–21.

32. Letter, June 19, 1863. The rest of the letter is not included here, as it deals mainly with items such as Johnson's ruined laundry, which was apparently the cause of this racist outburst.

33. Letter, January 10, 1862.

34. Letter, April 8, 1862. The details of the 81st Regiment's history are taken from Lindbuchler, *History of the 81st P.V.A.* For a detailed account of the campaign as a whole, see Stephen W. Sears, *To the Gates of Richmond: The Peninsula Campaign* (New York: Ticknor & Fields, 1992).

35. Letter, April 8, 1862.

36. Lindbuchler, *History of the 81st P.V.A.,* 5.

37. Ibid.

38. Ibid., 6.

39. Charles F. Johnson, Carded Medical Records of the Civil War, Volunteer Units, 81st Pennsylvania Volunteer Infantry, entry 534, RG 94, Records of the Adjutant General's Office, National Archives and Records Administration, Washington, D.C. (hereafter cited as National Archives).

40. Charles F. Johnson to Secretary of War Stanton, August 13, 1866, National Archives Microfilm Publication M 1064 (J 351 CB 1866), Records of the Appointment, Commission, and Personal Branch ca. 1775–1917, Letters Received 1863–94, National Archives.

41. J. H. Taylor, Special Orders No. 9, extract, Headquarters, Army of the Potomac, November 24, 1862, Johnson Papers.

42. *The Camden and Gloucester Directory of 1863–1864:* Containing the Names of the Inhabitants, Their Occupations, and Dwelling Houses: A List of the Streets, Lanes, and Alleys, the City Offices, Public Institutions &c (Camden, N.J.: O. Durang, W. Hindman, H. Curts, 1864), 70.

43. See note 41 above.

44. Charles F. Johnson to Secretary of War Stanton, May 26, 1863, Johnson Papers.

45. RHR to Charles F. Johnson, June 10, 1863, Letters Sent May 1863–Sept. 1866, vol. 1., entry 290, Records of the Provost Marshal General's Bureau, Veteran Reserve Corps Branch, RG 110, National Archives. Also *Camden Democrat,* June 13, 1863: "A meritorious appointment—We are pleased to learn that Col. Charles F. Johnson, late of the 81st Pennsylvania Volunteers, has received from the War Department his commission as Major in the Invalid Corps." In Lynch, *From Whence We Came,* 75.

46. U.S. War Department, *The War of the Rebellion: A Compilation of the Official Records of the Union and Confederate Armies,* 128 vol. (hereafter cited as *Official Records*), series 3, vol. 5, (Washington, D.C.: GPO, 1880–1901), 543.

47. McPherson, *Battle Cry of Freedom,* 427, 429–31.

48. *Official Records,* series 3, vol. 5, 543.

49. "The Invalids," *United States Service Magazine* (Sept. 1864): 236; John C. Fitzpatrick, "The Invalid Regiment and Its Colonel," *Daughters of the American Revolution Magazine* (Nov. 1919): 649–53.

50. Glasson, *Federal Military Pensions,* 55.

51. "The Naval Hospital Establishment," *United States Service Magazine* (Sept. 1864): 261–62.

52. "Homes for Discharged Invalid Soldiers," *United States Service Magazine* (Sept. 1864): 489, 490, 492. Among the charitable societies concerned with the plight of veterans who were disabled was the Sanitary Commission, a volunteer organization that dealt primarily with improving conditions in military camps and hospitals. To support its work the commission organized fundraisers in all the major northern cities, where disabled veterans were often in attendance, in some cases taking the opportunity to ask money from passers-by, either for themselves or for the commission. For example: "A crowd followed armless Berry who carried on his strong back legless Smith—who in turn dressed and fed Berry. These two had become great friends and, like Siamese twins, were inseparable. . . . I had obtained permission for the three men, Smith, Berry, and Mudge [another disabled veteran], to remain in the trophy department [at the Fair] where, each day, many greenbacks were crowded into their pockets." Adelaide W. Smith, "Mesdames Grant and McClellan Head Subscription Lists," in *Noble Women of the North,* ed. Sylvia G. L. Dannett (New York: Thomas Yoseloff, 1959), 275.

53. "Homes for Discharged Invalid Soldiers," *United States Service Magazine* (Sept. 1864): 492–93. There were concerns about disabled Invalid Corps officers as well. A memo from the Provost Marshal General's Office in Washington, which had charge of organizing the corps, noted that "Officers of the Invalid Corps, coming as they do from different arms of the Service, and from Regiments in which every variety of discipline has been practiced or omitted" would require especially close supervision by their superiors. Provost Marshal General's Office to Maj. W.H.A.A. Provost Marshal General, Louisville, Ky., August 18, 1863, Letters Sent May 1863–Sept. 1866, vol. 1, entry 290, Provost Marshal General's Bureau, RG 110, National Archives.

54. George Parsons Lathrop, *History of the Union League of Philadelphia.* (Philadelphia: J. B. Lippincott, 1884), 52.

55 *Official Records,* series 3, vol. 3, 193–194.

56. *Official Records,* series 3, vol. 5, 544. General Order 212, issued on July 9, 1863, elaborated on what did and did not constitute a disqualifying disability. Included in the list of eligible men were those with "epilepsy, if the seizures do not occur more frequently than once a month," "paralysis, if confined to one upper extremity," "impeded respiration following injuries of the chest, pneumonia, or pleurisy," "chronic disorders of the kidneys or bladder," "loss of sight of right eye, partial loss of sight of both eyes," "loss of an arm, forearm, hand, thigh, leg or foot," "extensive, deep, and adherent cicatrices of lower extremities," and a long list of other disabilities. In most instances, officers and enlisted men would no longer have the option of continuing in the army or accepting a medical discharge, as had been the case before, and all medical discharges for those with listed disabilities were ordered stopped (*Official Records,* series 3, vol. 5, 544). The only exceptions listed were those "who have lost an arm, forearm, hand, thigh, leg, or foot, [who] may be discharged . . . if they so elect" *Orders, Letters, Circulars Concerning the Invalid Corps, 1863,* G.O. 212, 3–5, Research Collection, Boston Public Library.

The list of conditions that *did* exclude a man from consideration began with "Manifest imbecility or insanity," and continued on through "[p]aralysis or chorea," "confirmed consumption, cancer, aneurism of important arteries," and "inveterate and extensive disease of the skin." Also included were deafness, "dumbness, permanent loss of voice," "incurable deformities of either jaw," "total loss of sight," as well as several conditions seemingly unrelated to a soldier's ability to guard prisoners or attend to hospital patients. Among these last were "[t]otal loss, or nearly total loss, of penis," and "[h]abitual or confirmed intemperance, or solitary vice, sufficient in degree to have materially enfeebled the constitution"—a common euphemism for masturbation. *Orders, Letters, Circulars,* 6.

57. *Official Records,* series 3, vol. 5, 544–45.

58. *Official Records,* series 3, vol. 3, 1001.

59. Ibid., 1000–1001.

60. "Proceedings of a Board of Officers to Examine Candidates for Inv. or V.R. Corps," Correspondence and Reports Relating to Persons in Veteran Reserve Corps Organizations 1863–65, box 3, entry 305, Provost Marshal General's Bureau, RG 110, National Archives. The accuracy of this sample was more or less confirmed by a more general survey, reproduced in a report of March 17, 1866, showing that "[o]f every 100 of its officers, 82 were disabled by gunshot wounds, 13 by disease, 5 by accidental injuries." *Official Records,* series 3, vol. 5, 682.

61. *Official Records,* series 3, vol. 5, 552.

62. Ibid.

63. Donald, *Gone for a Soldier,* 236.

64. John W. De Forest, *Miss Ravenel's Conversion from Secession to Loyalty* (New York: Harper & Brothers, 1939), 311.

65. "The Invalid Corps," by Frank Wilder, 1863, in Paul Glass, *Singing Soldiers* (New York: De Capo Press, 1968), 142.

66. Provost Marshal General's Office, May 28, 1863, Records of Office Subdivisions 1862–66, Veteran Reserve Corps Branch, General Records, Correspondence, Letters Sent May 1863–Sept. 1866, vol. 1, entry 290, Provost Marshal General's Bureau, RG 110, National Archives.

67. *Official Records,* series 3, vol. 5, 549.

68. Letter, June 4, 1864.

69. *Official Records,* series 3, vol. 3, 193–94.

70. Klein to Secretary of War Stanton, August 20, 1863, Letters Received 1862–64, Office of the Acting Assistant Provost Marshal General, State of Missouri, box 1, entry 4167, Provost Marshal General's Bureau, RG 110, National Archives. The writers of this petition, some eighty-one men, also protested that "our privileges were infringed on, both by depriving us of the pay for our Horses, and by placing us in an Invalid Corps on Infantry duty instead of Cavalry." The Provost Marshal General's Bureau replied on September 8, 1863, directing that "all turbulent cavalry" be returned to their original regiments. Colonel R. H. Rush, Assistant to the Provost Marshal General, to Col. E. B. Alexander, Sept. 8, 1863, Letters Received 1862–64, Office of the Acting Assistant Provost Marshal General, State of Missouri, box 1, entry 4167, Provost Marshal General's Bureau, RG 110, National Archives.

This confusion over the purpose and makeup of the Invalid Corps was not confined to prospective members. The congressional debate over a joint resolution to "suspend any order mustering out the officers of the Veteran Reserve corps" in part revolved around the issue of whether these officers were, because of their service-related disabilities, dependent on the government of the United States for their livelihood. *Congressional Globe,* 39th Cong., 1st sess., Dec. 4, 1865–Feb. 21, 1866, 36, pt. 1: 43–45.

71. R. H. Rush to Col. James B. Fry, May 25, 1863, Records of Office Subdivisions, 1862–66, Veteran Reserve Corps Branch, General Records, Correspondence, Letters Sent May 1863–Sept. 1866, vol. 1, entry 290, Provost Marshal General's Bureau, RG 110, National Archives.

72. Crowell, *Young Volunteer,* 457. Crowell enlisted in a New Jersey regiment in August 1862, fought at Antietam, and was wounded at Chancellorsville. He entered the Invalid Corps as a second lieutenant in January 1864. *Field Record of the Officers of the U.S. Army Veteran Reserve Corps, From the Commencement to the Close of the Rebellion* (Washington, D.C.: Scriver & Swing, 1865), 36.

73. Letter, June 29, 1863.

74. Letter, August 8, 1863.

75. F. B. Heitman, *Historical Register of the United States Army from Its Organization: September 29, 1789, to September 29, 1889* (Washington, D.C.: The National Tribune, 1890), 156.

76. McPherson, *Battle Cry of Freedom,* 784–88. See also Michael Fellman, *Inside War: The Guerilla Conflict in Missouri during the American Civil War* (New York: Oxford University Press, 1989).

77. Johnson to Alexander, August 13, 1863, Letters Received 1862–64, Office of the Acting Assistant Provost Marshal General, State of Missouri, box 1, entry 4167, Provost Marshal General's Bureau, RG 110, National Archives.

78. Johnson to Alexander, August 19, 1863, Letters Received 1862–64, Office of the Acting Assistant Provost Marshal General, State of Missouri, box 1, entry 4167, Provost Marshal General's Bureau, RG 110, National Archives.

79. Johnson to Alexander, August 29, 1863, Letters Received 1862–64, Office of the Acting Assistant Provost Marshal General, State of Missouri, box 1, entry 4167, Provost Marshal General's Bureau, RG 110, National Archives.

80. Letter, August 29, 1863.

81. Letter, August 15, 1863.

82. Letter, August 19, 1863.

83. Letter, August 13, 1863.

84. Letter, June 18, 1864.

85. Letter, June 16, 1863.

86. Letter, August 8, 1863.

87. Letter, September 21, 1863.

88. Letter, August 29, 1863.

89. Letter, August 31, 1863.

90. Letter, January 29, 1864; February 1, 1864; March 3, 1864.

91. Letter, December 11, 1864.

92. Letter, September 3, 1863; September 29, 1863 (letter not included here).

93. Letter, April 7, 1864.

94. Letter, January 19, 1864.

95. *Official Records,* series 3, vol. 5, 560–66.

96. Ibid., 560.

97. Ibid.

98. Harrison Gardner, *Diary of Harrison Gardner,* Civil War Miscellaneous Collection, United States Army Military History Institute Carlisle, Pa., 18 (hereafter cited as USAMHI).

99. Donald, *Gone for a Soldier,* 239.

100. For a description of wartime Washington, see Margaret Leech, *Reveille in Washington: 1860–1865* (New York: Harper & Brothers, 1941).

101. Donald, *Gone for a Soldier,* 264.

102. *Official Records,* series 3, vol. 5, 561.

103. Ibid., 563–64.

104. Ibid., 565.

105. Stinson, "Invalid Corps," 24; also McPherson, *Battle Cry of Freedom,* 609–11.

106. Gardner, *Diary of Harrison Gardner,* 30.

107. Frederick H. Dyer lists the 18th Regiment as being organized "at Washington, D.C. May 5, 1864, by consolidation of ten 1st battalion companies." Johnson's history submitted to Provost Marshal Fry on September 30, 1864, however, has the regiment forming on January 16 of that year at Indianapolis, and a letter from Johnson to Fry dated January 15 acknowledges "the receipt, this day, of the order organizing the Eighteenth Regiment, Invalid Corps." Dyer, *A Compendium of the War of the Rebellion* (Wilmington, N.C.: Broadfoot, 1994), 1742; Johnson to Fry, September 30, 1864, and Johnson to Fry, January 15, 1864, both in Veteran Reserve Corps, Letters Received 1864, entry 297, Provost Marshal General's Bureau, RG 110, National Archives.

During January and February of 1864, Johnson made trips to Louisville, Kentucky, and Washington D.C., apparently on regimental business. He was back with the regiment for good, however, by February 17.

108. Johnson to Fry, September 30, 1864, Veteran Reserve Corps, Letters Received 1864, entry 297, Provost Marshal General's Bureau, RG 110, National Archives.

109. Letter, January 27, 1864.

110. Letter, February 20, 1864.

111. Book Records of Volunteer Union Organizations, 18th Veteran Reserve Corps, Regimental Descriptive Book, vol. 1, 208–209, Adjutant General's Office, RG 94, National Archives. A look at a random page from the regimental descriptive list of the 81st Pennsylvania, by contrast, shows that of twenty-nine men in Company K, all of whom enlisted with Johnson in September 1861, seventeen were born in Pennsylvania, two in New Jersey, one in New York, one in Ohio, five in Ireland, two in Wales, and one in Germany. Twenty-three of the twenty-nine were listed as "laborers," along with one painter, shoemaker, blacksmith, carpenter, engineer, and moulder. Book Records of Volunteer Union Organizations, 81st Pennsylvania Volunteer Infantry, vol. 1, Adjutant General's Office, RG 94, National Archives.

112. Samuel A. Craig, *Memoirs of Civil War and Reconstruction.* Civil War Times Illustrated Collection, USAMHI, 40.

113. Ibid., 32–62.

114. Ibid., 63.

115. Ibid., 63.

116. Ibid., 64–65. A. J. Warner was commander of the 17th Regiment, and his "firible manner" extended to those outside the Corps attempting to infringe on his

authority. "I learn with surprise," he wrote to Captain Wilcox, the head of the soldiers' home in Indianapolis, "that details of my men for various duties have been made and Ordered away without the knowledge of myself or Company commanders. This is a strange proceeding and can not be permited. My Officers all are forbidden hereafter to respect any order for details not coming through these Head Quarters." Warner to Wilcox, February 9, 1864, Books Records of Volunteer Union Organizations, 17th Veteran Reserve Corps, Regimental Letter, Endorsements, Order and Discharge Book, vol. 5, Adjutant General's Office, RG 94, National Archives.

Disabled residents of the soldiers' homes might have had to endure the discipline and supervision of Captain Wilcox but not the men assigned to the Invalid Corps.

117. *Official Records,* series 3, vol. 4, 188.

118. *Official Records,* series 3, vol. 5, 552.

119. Gardner, *Diary of Harrison Gardner,* 24.

120. *Official Records,* series 3, vol. 5, 547.

121. Correspondence, Reports, and Other Records Relating to Officers and Enlisted Men in the Veteran Reserve Corps, 1863–65, entry 305, Provost Marshal General's Bureau, RG 110, National Archives.

122. Letter, March 9, 1864.

123. Gardner, *Diary of Harrison Gardner,* 12.

124. Letter, April 26, 1864. Less than a month earlier, "General Order No. 4" from headquarters in Indianapolis had insisted that "Every soldier arrested for disorderly dress will be immediately punished by confinement and hard labor or other severity and before he is Discharged from arrest will be got in good order." The order refers to the "slovenly condition" of noncommissioned officers and soldiers in general but also specifically insists that "all non-commissioned officers and soldiers . . . shall wear the uniform of their respective regiments or Corps." March 30, 1864, General Order No. 4, Book Records of Volunteer Union Organizations, 17th Veteran Reserve Corps Regimental Books, vol. 6, Adjutant General's Office, RG 94, National Archives.

125. Letter, May 5, 1864.

126. Letter, May 11, 1864.

127. McPherson, *Battle Cry of Freedom,* 722.

128. Gardner, *Diary of Harrison Gardner,* 37.

129. *Official Records,* series 3, vol. 5, 554.

130. Letter, May 26, 1864.

131. Letter, June 18, 1864.

132. Letter, June 6, 1864.

133. *Official Records,* series 3, vol. 5, 555.

134. Charles F. Johnson to Brig. General Fry, J 103, Veteran Reserve Corps, Letters Received 1864, entry 297, Provost Marshal General's Bureau, RG 110, National Archives.

135. *Official Records,* series 1, vol. 36, pt. 3, 781–82.

136. Letter, June 27, 1864.

137. Charles F. Johnson, Special Orders No. 12, July 1, 1864, Regimental Consolidated Report, Letter and Order Book, vol. 4, Book Records of the Adjutant General's Office, 18th Veteran Reserve Corps, Adjutant General's Office, RG 94, National Archives.

138. Consolidated Morning Report of July 1, 1864, Regimental Consolidated Morning Report, Letter and Order Book, vol. 4, Book Records of the Adjutant General's Office, 18th Veteran Reserve Corps, Adjutant General's Office, RG 94, National Archives.

139. R. E. Johnston, to M. N. Wisewell, October 1, 1864, Veteran Reserve Corps, Letters Received 1864, entry 297, Provost Marshal General's Bureau, RG 110, National Archives.

140. Ibid.

141. Letter, July 10, 1864.

142. Donald, *Gone for a Soldier,* 270–71.

143. R. E. Johnston, to M. N. Wisewell, October 1, 1864, Veteran Reserve Corps, Letters Received 1864, entry 297, Provost Marshal General's Bureau, RG 110, National Archives.

144. This same cavalry regiment had fought at White House Landing with the 18th VRC, as part of Johnson's "provisional brigade." For details of Early's assault on Washington, and Lincoln coming under fire, see Catton, *Stillness at Appomattox,* 258–66; Robert E. Denny, *The Civil War Years: A Day-by-Day Chronicle of the Life of a Nation* (New York: Sterling, 1992), 434–36; Leech, *Reveille in Washington,* 329–46.

145. R. E. Johnston, to M. N. Wisewell, October 1, 1864, Veteran Reserve Corps, Letters Received 1864, entry 297, Provost Marshal General's Bureau, RG 110, National Archives. Gardner's description of the battle is in his journal entry of July 12, 1864: "The men in the skirmish line made a charge on their line simultaneously with the firing of the guns from this fort [Stevens] and drove them back and kept it up until near 12 p.m." (Gardner, *Diary of Harrison Gardner,* 53).

146. See Martin D. Hardin, "The Defense of Washington against Early's Attack in July, 1864," in *Military Essays and Recollections: Papers Read before the Commandery of the State of Illinois, Military Order of the Loyal Legion of the United States,* vol. 2 (Wilmington, N.C.: Broadfoot, 1992), 121–44.

147. See, for example, the records of the courts-martial of Frank M. Buss (June 17, 1865), Patrick Cassady (May 27, 1865), and Peter H. Shultes (December 12, 1864). Private Shultes was arrested for calling Colonel Johnson "'you damned son of a bitch' or words to that effect" to his face. A number of men were also court-martialed on September 24, 1865, for signing a petition to the "Military State Agent of Pensylvania" complaining of "systematic bad treatment from our officers." Order Book, Companies A–I, Book Records of Volunteer Union Organizations, 18th Regiment Veteran Reserve Corps, vol. 5, Records of the Adjutant General's Office, RG 94, National Archives.

148. Charles F. Johnson, Special Order No. 40, April 20, 1865, Regimental Letter and Order Book, Book Records of Volunteer Union Organizations, 18th Regiment Veteran Reserve Corps, vol. 4, Records of the Adjutant General's Office, RG 94, National Archives.

149. Craig, *Memoirs of Civil War and Reconstruction,* 70–71.

150. Peter Gamache, "The Civil War Experiences of Sergeant Peter Gamache," (Carlisle, Pa.: USAMHI), 9. Gamache, from Northboro, Massachusetts, enlisted in the 34th Massachusetts Volunteer Infantry in July 1862. He was wounded at Fisher's Hill on September 22, 1864, promoted to sergeant, and transferred to the VRC in March 1865, where he was a member of Company F of Johnson's 18th Regiment.

151. *Official Records,* series 3, vol. 5, 682.

152. *Congressional Globe,* 39th Cong., 1st sess., Dec. 4, 1865–Feb. 21, 1866, 36, pt. 1: 38.

153. In August 1866, Johnson wrote to Secretary of War Stanton "to respectfully request that an assignment to duty (with my present rank) with one of the four regiments of the Veteran Reserve Corps authorized in the bill providing for the reorganizing of the Army of the United States." Charles F. Johnson to Secretary of War Stanton, August 13, 1866, National Archives Microfilm Publication M 1064 (J 351 CB 1866), Records of the Appointment, Commission, and Personal Branch ca. 1775–1917, Letters Received 1863–94, National Archives.

154. Stinson, "The Invalid Corps," 27. John William De Forest (1826–1903) was already an acclaimed writer when he mustered in as a captain of the 12th Connecticut Volunteers on New Year's Day 1862. His *History of the Indians of Connecticut from the Earliest Known Period to 1850,* the first study of its kind, was published in 1851. During the war he wrote, "The First Time Under Fire" (often cited as Stephen Crane's inspiration for *The Red Badge of Courage*) for *Harper's New Monthly Magazine.* De Forest was commissioned as a captain in the VRC in February 1865. His final report on the corps, in the *Official Records,* is the only extensive general history of the corps ever written. In May 1866, he was assigned to the Freedmen's Bureau, where he remained until mustering out on January 1, 1868, serving as a bureau major in Greenville, South Carolina.

During this period, De Forest wrote *Miss Ravenel's Conversion from Secession to Loyalty,* the first "realist" novel to come out of the Civil War, which was published in 1867 and received with critical praise but popular apathy. By this time the public seemed no longer interested in realistic accounts of combat and its bloody aftermath, nor did it favor his exploration of racism and classism in occupied New Orleans. For a discussion of De Forest and his work, see James F. Light, *John William De Forest* (New York: Twayne, 1965); and Reid Mitchell, *The Vacant Chair: The Northern Soldier Leaves Home* (New York: Oxford University Press, 1993), 127–30.

155. Charles F. Johnson to Secretary of War Stanton, August 13, 1866, National Archives Microfilm Publication M 1064 (J 351 CB 1866), Records of the Appointment, Commission, and Personal Branch ca. 1775–1917, Letters Received 1863–94, National Archives.

156. A.A.A. General V.R.C. to Major General O. O. Howard, March 9, 1866, March 28, 1866, April 25, 1866, Letters Sent, General Records, Correspondence, May 1863–Sept. 1866, vol. 5, Records of Office Subdivisions, 1862–1866, Veteran Reserve Corps Branch, entry 290, Provost Marshal General's Bureau, RG 110, National Archives.

157. The peak figure of 764 officers was reached on October 1, 1864 (*Official Records,* series 3, vol. 5, 681). Howard, in his autobiography, put the total number of "the whole Bureau force" in late 1865 at "upward of 2,000 officers, agents and other employees." Howard, *Autobiography of Oliver Otis Howard,* vol. 2, 217.

158. H. Horton to Provost Major General Fisk, July 25, 1866, Registered Letters Received, National Archives Microfilm Publication M 999, roll 10, frames 0714–15, Records of the Asst. Commissioner for the State of Tennessee, Bureau of Refugees, Freedmen and Abandoned Lands, RG 105, National Archives.

159. F. W. Gilbreth to Maj. Gen. O. O. Howard, "Report of an investigation of

the cause, origin, and results, of the late riots in the city of Memphis, made by Col. Charles F. Johnson, Inspector General States of Ky. & Tennessee and Major F. W. Gilbreth, A.D.C. to Maj. Genl. Howard, Commissioner Bureau of R.F. & A. Lands," Records Relating to Outrages (National Archives Microfim Publication M 999, roll 34, frames 0672–83, Records of the Assistant Commissioner for the State of Tennessee, Bureau of Refugees, Freedmen, and Abandoned Lands, 1865–1869, RG 105, National Archives). Charles F. Johnson is misidentified as "Chas F. Jackson" in the cover letter to the report.

160. *The Reports of the Committees of the House of Representatives, Made during the First Session of the Thirty-ninth Congress, 1865–66.* Report No. 101, Memphis Riots and Massacres (Washington, D.C.: 1866), 61–62, quoted in *Mass Violence in America: Memphis Riots and Massacres,* ed. Robert M. Fogelson and Richard E. Rubenstein. (New York: Arno Press / New York Times, 1969).

161. See note 159 above.

162. Johnson was by no means unique in his role as former VRC officer turned Freedmen's Bureau official. This marks perhaps the first time that a substantial number of whites with disabilities found themselves connected, *as people with disabilities,* with the struggles of people of color. One of the central tenets of the disability rights movement of the 1970s was that the place assigned by American society to people with disabilities was analogous to that of people of color and other oppressed minorities. For example, until the 1970s, children with disabilities were routinely enrolled in segregated "special" schools and classes (if not denied a public education altogether), and people with severe disabilities were almost uniformly excluded from public transit, prohibited from voting, and discriminated against in housing and employment. See Frank Bowe, *Handicapping America: Barriers to Disabled People* (New York: Harper & Row, 1978). This central analogy of what would become "the last civil rights movement" was perhaps first explicitly stated in Leonard Kriegel's seminal essay, "Uncle Tom and Tiny Tim: Some Reflections on the Cripple as Negro," *American Scholar* 38 (summer 1969): 412–30. That people with disabilities and people of color had shared a public arena fully a century earlier is an aspect of American social history that has remained entirely unexplored. For a discussion of the relationship between racism and ableism, see Baynton, "Disability and the Justification of Inequality," 33–57.

163. Charles F. Johnson to U. E. Johns, October 1, 1866, Letters Sent July 1866–June 1868, Bowling Green, Ky., entry 1101, Records of the Bureau of Refugees, Freedmen, and Abandoned Lands, RG 105, National Archives.

164. Johnson himself forcefully argued against "miscegeny"—that is, interracial sexual relations, telling Mary that some of his men in the 18th VRC had taken black women as lovers, "so low does a bad Soldier sink himself—I intend, the first one that I catch to trot them out before the Command at Dress Parade and make an example of him." Letter, November 21, 1864.

165. Charles F. Johnson to Chief Supt. State of Ky., March 9, 1867, Letters Sent July 1866–June 1868, Bowling Green, Ky., entry 1101, Records of the Bureau of Refugees, Freedmen, and Abandoned Lands, RG 105, National Archives.

166. Charles F. Johnson to Chief Supt. State of Ky., March 18, 1867, Letters Sent July 1866–June 1868, Bowling Green, Ky., entry 1101, Records of the Bureau of Refugees, Freedmen, and Abandoned Lands, RG 105, National Archives.

167. Charles F. Johnson to Supt. Martin, October 27, 1866, Letters Sent July 1866–June 1868, Bowling Green, Ky., entry 1101, Records of the Bureau of Refugees, Freedmen, and Abandoned Lands, RG 105, National Archives.

168. For example: Charles F. Johnson to Chief Supt. State of Ky., March 19, 1867, Letters Sent July 1866–June 1868, Bowling Green, Ky., entry 1101, Records of the Bureau of Refugees, Freedmen, and Abandoned Lands, RG 105, National Archives.

169. Charles F. Johnson, December 24, 1866, Letters Sent July 1866–June 1868, Bowling Green, Ky., entry 1101, Records of the Bureau of Refugees, Freedmen, and Abandoned Lands, RG 105, National Archives.

170. Col. Chas. F. Johnson, Monthly Report, September 1866, Kentucky Assistant Commissioner, Letters Received, vol. 1–9, box 4, entry 1068, Records of the Bureau of Refugees, Freedmen, and Abandoned Lands, RG 105, National Archives. Here again Samuel Craig's diary provides confirmation of Johnson's impressions and testimony. Like Johnson, he was appointed as assistant commissioner for the bureau, first in Indiana, then in Texas, where he soon ran afoul of the local whites. "Texas was as yet, very much un-reconstructed," he wrote, "and its [white] citizens very bitter." His account includes details of assaults on bureau officials and the terrorizing and murder of blacks. Craig, *Memoirs of Civil War and Reconstruction,* 78. See also Donald G. Nieman, ed., *The Freedmen's Bureau and Black Freedom* (New York: Garland, 1994); Leon F. Litwack, *Been in the Storm So Long: The Aftermath of Slavery* (New York: Alfred A. Knopf, 1979).

171. Charles F. Johnson to Prov. Brig. Genl. Bureau of R.F. & A.L., Bowling Green, June 30, 1867, Letters Sent July 1866–June 1868, Bowling Green, Ky., entry 1101, Records of the Bureau of Refugees, Freedmen, and Abandoned Lands, RG 105, National Archives.

172. The cause of death is listed on Mary Johnson's pension application for Clara, filed in Des Moines on February 18, 1869, Johnson Papers. Johnson's obituary is quoted in Lynch, *From Whence We Came,* 99.

173. Stuart McConnell, *Glorious Contentment: The Grand Army of the Republic, 1865–1900* (Chapel Hill: University of North Carolina Press, 1992), 128–29.

174. Douglas C. McMurtrie, *The Disabled Soldier* (New York, Macmillan, 1919), 24.

175. Glasson, *Federal Military Pensions in the United States,* 129–43; Skocpol, *Protecting Soldiers and Mothers,* 102–51; Amy E. Holmes, "'Such is the Price We Pay': American Widows and the Civil War Pension System," in *Toward a Social History of the American Civil War,* ed. Maris A. Vinovskis. (Cambridge: Cambridge University Press, 1990), 171–95.

176. McConnell, *Glorious Contentment,* 155.

177. Mary R. Dearing, *Veterans in Politics: The Story of the G.A.R.* (Baton Rouge: Louisiana State University Press, 1952), 394–95.

178. Peter Blanck and Chen Song, "Civil War Attorneys and Disability Politics," *University of Michigan Journal of Law Reform* 35, nos. 1, 2 (fall 2001–winter 2002), 3, 7.

179. Skocpol, *Protecting Soldiers and Mothers,* viii.

180. "The Naval Hospital Establishment," *United States Service Magazine* (Sept. 1864): 256. Women have often worked as personal-care providers for disabled veterans, then and now. The organizers of the Sanitary Commission Fair in New York City in 1864, for instance, assigned "a colored woman" to assist the severely disabled veterans in attendance. Dannett, *Noble Women of the North,* 274.

There is a substantial and growing literature on the links between gender and disability as social constructs. For example, Susan Wendell notes that people with disabilities and women with and without disabilities have been traditionally defined "primarily as symbolic of something else—usually, but not always, something we reject and fear and project onto them" (Wendell, *The Rejected Body: Feminist Philosophical Reflections on Disability* [New York: Routledge, 1996], 60). The social role of women has often been dictated by their ability to bear children, a circumstance that is analogous to the way that people with physical disabilities have been relegated to social roles dictated by their "defective bodies." Menstruation and pregnancy in the modern era have been "medicalized" and approached in much the same way that diseases and disability have been, women and people with disabilities both being patronized by the medical establishment in similar ways. See, for example, the discussion of the medicalization of pregnancy and childbirth in Boston Women's Health Book Collective, *The New Our Bodies, Ourselves* (New York: Simon & Schuster, 1984), 328; Nancy Krieger and Elizabeth Fee, "Man-Made Medicine and Women's Heath: The Biopolitics of Sex/Gender and Race/Ethnicity," in *Man-Made Medicine: Women's Health, Public Policy, and Reform,* ed. Kary L. Moss. (Durham: Duke University Press, 1996), 16–18; Abby L. Wilkerson, *Diagnosis: Difference—The Moral Authority of Medicine* (Ithaca: Cornell University Press, 1998), 13–42.

181. David W. Blight, *Race and Reunion: The Civil War in American Memory* (Cambridge: Harvard University Press, 2001). See also Taylor Branch, *Parting the Waters: America in the King Years, 1954–63* (New York: Simon & Schuster, 1988), 54–55.

182. Leslie Fieldler, *Freaks: Myths and Images of the Secret Self* (New York: Simon & Schuster, 1978), 135.

183. Thomson, *Extraordinary Bodies,* 65.

184. Mark Van Doren, ed., *The Portable Walt Whitman* (1945; reprint, New York: Viking, 1973), 469.

185. Sometimes even the mainstream volunteer regiments remained unchronicled. The veterans of the 81st Pennsylvania, for example, never produced a regimental history, perhaps because so many of those involved in the regiment's formation—Colonels Miller and Johnson among them—were killed in the war or died soon thereafter. The history of war may not always be written by the winners—Thucydides being an early case in point—but post-war memoirs can be written only by those who survive.

186. Peter David Blanck and Michael Millender, "Before Disability Civil Rights: Civil War Pensions and the Politics of Disability in America," *Alabama Law Review* 52, no. 1 (fall 2000): 33.

187. This dynamic (disabled veterans energizing the larger disability rights movement) can be seen in other nations as well. The movement in Zimbabwe, for example, was invigorated by an influx of newly disabled men (and bona-fide revolutionaries) after the conclusion of that nation's struggle for independence. See Fred Pelka, "Disability Rights in Zimbabwe," *Mainstream: Magazine of the Able-Disabled* 14, no. 3 (October 1989): 21–23.

188. Lynch, *From Whence We Came,* 32.

189. Ibid., 33–34.

190. Ibid., 42.

191. Ibid., 37.

Chapter One

1. The 81st remained at Camp Washington until it was moved to Washington, D.C., on October 10, 1861. Dyer, *Compendium of the War of the Rebellion,* 1600.

2. Dr. William Dixon, assistant surgeon. The regimental books of the 81st list Dixon as "not mustered in." 81st Pennsylvania Infantry, Regimental Descriptive Book, vol. 1, Book Records of Volunteer Union Organizations, RG 94, National Archives.

3. Clara Adelia Johnson was born September 24, 1858. The Johnsons' twin sons Joseph Hufty Johnson and William Ewing Wiley Johnson were born November 7, 1850. Lynch, *From Whence We Came,* 32.

4. "Remember Thee?" from *Irish Melodies and Sacred Songs* by Thomas Moore (1779–1853). The poem refers not to an absent loved one but to Ireland. "thy chains as they rankle, thy blood as it runs, / But make thee more painfully dear to thy sons." A. D. Godley, ed., *The Poetical Works of Thomas Moore* (London: Oxford University Press, 1910), 213.

5. Colonel James Miller, a Mexican War veteran, was the principal organizer of the 81st. Miller was killed at the battle of Fair Oaks, Virginia, on June 1, 1862. Lindbuchler, *History of the 81st P.V.I.,* 5.

6. Captain John Alexander, appointed August 6, 1861, resigned from the regiment November 14, 1862, owing to dropsy. 81st Pennsylvania Infantry, Regimental Descriptive Book, vol. 1, Book Records of Volunteer Union Organizations, RG 94, National Archives. Officers with means, North and South, often relied on black servants, sometimes slaves, to manage such chores as laundry, shopping, and cooking.

7. George Deal was Johnson's close friend, and the quartermaster sergeant of the 81st Pennsylvania (Janet B. Hewett, *The Roster of Union Soldiers: 1861–1865:* Pennsylvania, vol. 1 [Wilmington, N. C.: Broadfoot, 1998], 372). His daughter Harriet would eventually marry Johnson's son William (Lynch, *From Whence We Came,* 79). In 1864, Deal joined Johnson at his post in Washington, D.C., to become sutler to the 18th Regiment of the Veteran Reserve Corps. In May 1868, following Johnson's death, Deal filed an affidavit in support of Mary Johnson's request for a widow's compensation, swearing that he "has known the said Charles F. Johnson for the last 14 years and that he was a Sound and healthy man prior to entering" the army. Charles F. Johnson, Federal Pension Application, Min. C 141775, National Archives.

8. Johnson was thirty-four years old.

9. This was probably George Deal.

10. This was perhaps John M. Dutton. Dutton was appointed quartermaster to the 81st on September 14, 1861, and is listed as having "died of heart disease, April 26, 1862 at Camp Winfield Scott" (81st Pennsylvania Infantry, Regimental Descriptive Book, vol. 1, Book Records of Volunteer Union Organizations, RG 94, National Archives). It was then that George Deal was apparently appointed in his place.

11. The Wissahickon River runs "through Landsdale, North Wales, Upper and Lower Gwynedd Townships, Whitpain Township, the town of Penllyn (an early African American settlement and stop on the Underground Railroad), Ambler, Fort Washington, Flourtown, and then into Philadelphia's Fairmount Park and on down to the Schuylkill River." Robert Adams, correspondence of September 2, 2003, Wissahickon Valley Watershed Association.

12. Johnson, in this and other letters, shows an empathy for his men often lacking among commissioned officers. In a letter home in April 1862, Sergeant Sidney Hawk wrote: "Our field officers are the best selected men in the Army of the Potomac. Colonel Miller is the right man in the right place and Lt. Col. Johnson is a gentleman and a soldier in every respect." Lindbuchler, *History of the 81st P.V.I.*, 5.

13. Food and clothing for newly organized regiments were generally provided by individual state governments and private citizens until the regiments were mustered into federal service. Desertion was often a problem, in both Union and Confederate armies, when such provisions failed to arrive.

14. The 81st Pennsylvania began its move south to join the Army of the Potomac in its camps around Washington on October 10, 1861. There it was attached to Casey's brigade, Richardson's division, until March 1862. Dyer, *Compendium of the War of the Rebellion,* 1600.

15. Charles Johnson's father Henry was married to George W. Hufty's sister Mariah, born in 1804. George Hufty served as a quartermaster for a New Jersey regiment (Letters, July 2, 1863). Mariah Hufty died in Camden on January 25, 1866. Baldwin Hufty, often referred to by Johnson as "Bald. Hufty," was the son of Samuel Hufty, Mariah's oldest brother, and the younger brother of William G. Hufty (Lynch, *From Whence We Came,* 121–22). Samuel would win fame as captain of Company D of the 4th New Jersey, and then as commander of the New Jersey Brigade (4th New Jersey Regimental Descriptive Book, vol. 1, Book Records of Volunteer Union Organizations, RG 94, National Archives). He returned to Camden after the war, where he resided until his death (Lynch, 214). William P. Hufty, son of George W., was listed in 1901 as a resident of the Soldiers and Sailors Home in Erie, Pennsylvania (Lynch, 123).

16. Kendell Green might well have been the field in Washington named after Amos Kendell, one of the founders, in 1856, of the Columbia Institution for Deaf and Blind Children, which became the core of the campus of Gallaudet University, the world's first liberal arts university for Deaf people. The school's charter was signed by Abraham Lincoln in 1864.

17. William Wilson, appointed first lieutenant on August 10, 1861, and then captain of Company B, 81st Pennsylvania, on December 9, 1861. He was wounded in action on June 30, 1862 (81st Pennsylvania Infantry, Regimental Descriptive Book, vol. 1, Record Books of Volunteer Union Organizations, RG 94, National Archives). Wilson was eventually commissioned a colonel and after the war became an inspector of customs in the Philadelphia Customs House until 1871, when he resumed his trade as a carriage painter. He died in Camden, New Jersey, in 1894. *Review of Camden, New Jersey,* September 19, 1894.

18. Daniel Lambert was known as "the Jolly Gaoeler of Leicester," one of England's "famous Fat Men," whose top weight was reported at 739 pounds. He died in 1809, but apparently his fame persisted in nineteenth-century America. Fiedler, *Freaks,* 128.

19. This is the first of many references to the Johnsons' financial woes, which were often exacerbated by the army's inability to pay its officers and enlisted men on a regular basis.

20. Colonel and U.S. Senator from Oregon, Edward D. Baker, close friend to

President Lincoln, was killed at the debacle at Balls Bluff on October 21, 1861. His funeral was held in Washington on October 24 and was attended by the president and other dignitaries. Denney, *Civil War Years,* 89.

21. This is probably Mary's older brother, William Blackiston Davis, who lived in Maryland near Washington, D.C.

22. Johnson, like many Northerners, believed that white Southerners were lazy and ignorant as a consequence of living with slavery. McPherson, *Battle Cry of Freedom,* 198–200.

23. Brigadier General Daniel Edgar Sickles, a Tammany Hall politician who had won fame before the war as the first man to be found not guilty of murder due to temporary insanity Geoffrey C. Ward, *The Civil War: An Illustrated History* (New York: Alfred A. Knopf, 1990), 218.

24. Oliver Otis Howard (1830–1909). A graduate of West Point and a mathematics teacher before the war, Howard lost an arm during the battle of Fair Oaks on June 1, 1862. He was appointed a major general of volunteers in November 1862 and held several important commands, including that of a corps at Gettysburg. After the war he was appointed commissioner of the Bureau of Refugees, Freedmen, and Abandoned Lands. Heitman, *Historical Register of the United States Army,* 546–47.

25. The 81st Pennsylvania was originally formed as the 36th; the designation was eventually changed.

26. An article in the November 20, 1861, Philadelphia *Inquirer* reported how the regiment was ordered on November 5 "to different places, to protect the Union voters at the election to be held on the 6th. Company K, Captain FOSTER, and Company E, Captain HACKER, were ordered to Queen Anne, in Prince George's County nine miles from Upper Marlborough."

27. "Our Quartermaster's department very frequently gives cause for dissatisfaction among our men. When we receive molasses but once in eight days, potatoes twice a week, and bean soup with about three beans for every tin cupfull, there is naturally some complaint. Still, there is less murmuring now than there was during the first four weeks we were at Easton, when we received *no* potatoes or molasses, and only about two-thirds of a loaf of bread each day. Perhaps this matter will appear clearer to you when I state that our Quartermaster is John M. Dutton" (Alma, "From Col. Miller's Thirty-sixth Regiment Pennsylvania Volunteers," *Philadelphia Sunday Dispatch,* November 3, 1861). Johnson will make several comments on these "Alma" letters, written by an anonymous soldier and printed from time to time in the *Dispatch.*

28. Charles E. Foster, commissioned October 27, 1861, resignation owing to illness accepted July 9, 1862. 81st Pennsylvania Infantry, Regimental Descriptive Book, vol. 1, Book Records of Volunteer Union Organizations, RG 94, National Archives.

29. Captain William Hacker, "mustered out by examining board Dec. 9, 1861"; Captain Charles R. Robbins, assigned September 24, 1861, "mustered out by examining board Dec. 9, 1861"; Lieutenants William P. Prickett and John Brooker of Co. A, appointed August 6, 1861, "mustered out by examining board Dec. 9, 1861." 81st Pennsylvania Infantry, Regimental Descriptive Book, vol. 1, Book Records of Volunteer Union Organizations, RG 94, National Archives.

30. Colonel E. E. Cross, 5th New Hampshire Volunteer Infantry, was a Mexican

War veteran and former newspaper editor. Bruce Catton, *Mr. Lincoln's Army* (Garden City, N.J.: Doubleday, 1951), 128.

31. Lieutenant Joseph R. Smith of Company E, 81st Pennsylvania, was appointed on September 20, 1861. His resignation was accepted on January 28, 1863. 81st Pennsylvania Infantry, Regimental Descriptive Book, vol. 1, Book Records of Volunteer Union Organizations, RG 94, National Archives.

32. Dr. Charles S. Tripler, medical director of the Army of the Potomac. Stephen Sears describes him as "at heart a spinner of bureaucratic red tape," an officer of the regular army who was to be completely overwhelmed by the coming casualties. Sears, *To the Gates of Richmond,* 147.

33. This is a reference to the examining committee, appointed by General McClellan, to weed out obviously incompetent officers.

34. Johnson was a member of the Improved Order of Red Men, one of the many fraternal societies that flourished at the time. For a discussion of the significance of fraternal societies in nineteenth-century American social life, see Mary Ann Clawson, *Constructing Brotherhood: Class, Gender, and Fraternalism* (Princeton, N.J.: Princeton University Press, 1989).

35. General Edwin Vose "Bull" Sumner, born in 1797 and first commissioned as a 2nd lieutenant in 1819, was known as a strict disciplinarian. The engagement Johnson alludes to might be the encounter at Springfield Station, Virginia, on October 2 and 3, described by Denney as "cavalry skirmishing" (*Civil War Years,* 83–84), in which case Johnson was right to be skeptical of newspaper reports, because the 81st (or the 36th) was still in Pennsylvania at the time. The skirmish at Annandale occurred on December 2 but did not involve the 81st. E. B. Long, *The Civil War Day by Day: An Almanac 1861–1865* (Garden City, N.Y.: Doubleday, 1971), 123, 146.

36. Colonel Elmer Ellsworth, the 24-year-old commander of the 11th New York and personal friend of Abraham Lincoln, was one of the first Union officers to enter Alexandria during the Northern advance of May 24, 1861. Seeing a Confederate flag flying from the Marshal House, he entered the hotel and pulled it down, whereupon he was shot by a rebel sympathizer, who was himself killed by a Union soldier. Ellsworth, already something of a celebrity, thus became a Northern hero and martyr. Long, *Civil War Day by Day,* 75–76. There is a George W. Chambers, proprietor of a "varieties store" at 919 North 2nd Street, listed in *McElroy's Philadelphia City Directory for 1860,* 23rd ed. (Philadelphia: E. C. & J. Biddle, 1860).

37. Johnson is perhaps referring to the Apprentices' Library in Philadelphia, which opened in 1820 on "Chestnut Street above Third." As a "Chestnut Street clerk," Johnson may well have had an opportunity to visit the library and borrow some of its volumes. J. Thomas Scharf and Thompson Westcott, *History of Philadelphia 1609–1884,* vol. 2 (Philadelphia: L. H. Everts & Co., 1884), 1208.

38. This was Lieutenant Thomas R. Grapewine, first lieutenant of Company H of the 4th New Jersey, appointed on August 17, 1861. 4th New Jersey Regimental Descriptive Book, vol. 1, Book Records of Volunteer Union Organizations, RG 94, National Archives.

39. See note 35 above.

40. "Of Anticipation" by Martin Farquhar Tupper, *Proverbial Philosophy: A Book of Thoughts and Arguments Originally Treated* (Boston: Phillips, Sampson and Company, 1851), 8–9.

41. This could be a reference to Brigadier General John Sedgwick, at that time commander of the Second Division, II Corps. Sears, *To the Gates of Richmond,* 359.

42. There is no Captain "Schafles" listed as being in the 81st at this time. Johnson might have been referring to Captain Philip N. Schuyler, appointed on August 28, 1861, and listed as "killed in action at Antietam, Sept. 17, 1862." 81st Pennsylvania Infantry, Regimental Descriptive Book, vol. 1, Book Records of Volunteer Union Organizations, RG 94, National Archives.

43. This would probably be Brigadier General Louis Blenker, whose division was transferred from the Army of the Potomac to the Mountain Department (in Virginia) under General John Charles Fremont in late March 1862. Sears, *To the Gates of Richmond,* 32.

44. It is typical of the amateur nature of the American military at that time that Johnson, a lieutenant colonel in a frontline regiment, would have to send home for a map of his theater of operations. Generally speaking, few officers, North or South, had detailed maps of what would become the battlefields of the Civil War, and so Confederate General Thomas Jackson's detailed topographical map of the Shenandoah Valley would give him a marked advantage over his opponents.

45. Newspapers of the time commonly printed letters from soldiers, often under pseudonyms, containing news of the regiments and criticism of officers and army life in general. One such correspondent was "Alma," apparently an enlisted man in the 81st Pennsylvania, who wrote home to the Philadelphia papers.

46. Captain Amos Stiles, appointed August 10, 1861, did indeed pass inspection by the board, but was "dishonorably dismissed June 30, 1862, for cowardice." 81st Pennsylvania Infantry, Regimental Descriptive Book, vol. 1, Book Records of Volunteer Union Organizations, RG 94, National Archives. As for Hacker, Robbins, Prickett, and Brooker, see note 29 above.

47. "Anna" is perhaps a reference to Johnson's older sister Anna B. Johnson. Johnson here and elsewhere refers to "Harry." This is possibly his older brother, Henry Johnson Jr., birth date unknown, who died January 10, 1901, and whose first wife, Josephine Ottenger, died of tuberculosis ca. 1867. It could also be that the various references to "Harry" are to someone else, perhaps one of several different friends or relations of the Johnsons. Lynch, *From Whence We Came,* 31.

48. Tupper, "Of Writing," in *Proverbial Philosophy,* 89.

49. Martin Farquhar Tupper, "Never Give Up," in *Tupper's Complete Poetical Works* (Boston: Phillips, Sampson and Company, 1851), 262. This poem was one of Tupper's most famous, but Johnson misquotes one phrase, "Providence kindly has mingled the cup . . ."

50. See note 17 above.

51. Johnson's relationship with General Howard continued after the war, when Howard became commissioner of the Bureau of Refugees, Freedmen, and Abandoned Lands. In his autobiography, Howard does not mention this altercation with Colonel Miller.

52. This presumably was J. P. Kimball, who in turn resigned on January 30, 1862. 81st Pennsylvania Infantry, Regimental Descriptive Book, vol. 1, Book Records of Volunteer Union Organizations, RG 94, National Archives.

53. A leading citizen after whom, presumably, Camp Scitz was named.

Chapter Two

1. Johnson is referring to the resolution of the "*Trent* affair." On November 8, 1861, sailors of the U.S.S. *San Jacinto* boarded the British mail packet *Trent* and arrested James M. Mason and John Slidell, who were on their way to Europe to act as Confederate commissioners in Great Britain and France. Mason and Slidell were taken to Union Fort Monroe. The British government protested, demanding their release. The controversy had the potential to seriously damage relations between the United States and Great Britain, with some on both sides of the Atlantic threatening open war. Lincoln and his cabinet decided to release Mason and Slidell on December 26, thus ending the crisis. Long, *Civil War Day by Day*, 137, 151.

2. The first two lines are from Byron and are often quoted by Johnson: "A change came o'er the spirit of my dream." Byron, "The Dream," in *The Poetical Works of Lord Byron* (New York: R. Martin, 1855), 484–86. The last four are from Shakespeare, *Hamlet* 1.5.17–20: "Make thy two eyes like stars start from their spheres, / Thy knotted and combined locks to part, / And each particular hair to stand on end / Like quills upon the fearful porpentine."

3. A combined naval/army force under Brigadier General Ambrose E. Burnside sailed for the coast of North Carolina on January 11. It captured Roanoke Island on February 8 and moved to gain control of the strategic Pamlico Sound. Long, *Civil War Day by Day*, 159, 168.

4. The Olden Legion was a group of volunteer regiments, named after New Jersey Governor Charles S. Olden, recruited from the Trenton area in 1861.

5. The officer is unidentified, but this again illustrates Johnson's concern for his men.

6. Captain William J. Conner, assigned October 15, 1861, and Captain Thomas Harkness, assigned September 18, 1861, both wounded with Johnson at Charles City Crossroads, June 30, 1862. 81st Pennsylvania Infantry, Regimental Descriptive Book, vol. 1, Book Records of Volunteer Union Organizations, RG 94, National Archives.

7. Brigadier General Samuel Peter Heintzelman, West Point graduate (in 1826), brevetted major for gallantry during the Mexican War, appointed brigadier general of volunteers in May 1861. Ezra J. Warner, *Generals in Blue: Lives of the Union Commanders* (Baton Rouge: Louisiana State University Press, 1964), 227–28.

8. John M. Dutton would die in camp, of "heart disease," on April 26. 81st Pennsylvania Infantry, Regimental Descriptive Book, vol. 1, Book Records of Volunteer Union Organizations, RG 94, National Archives.

9. Johnson was not always so light hearted when it came to Mary showing affection to other men, dentists or otherwise (see especially his letter of December 11, 1864), nor is this the last time he will be concerned with Mary's health and spirits. He often urges her to "take it easy" for the sake of her physical and mental well-being.

10. There are several John Cunninghams listed in Hewett. Perhaps the most likely candidate, although he was a three-month volunteer, is Captain John R. Cunningham of Company G, 4th New Jersey Infantry. Hewett, *Roster of Union Soldiers: New Jersey*, 69.

11. See page 297, note 29.

12. The 81st continued under Howard's command through the siege of York-

town and the battle of Seven Pines, after which the First Brigade was assigned to Brigadier General John C. Caldwell. Sears, *To the Gates of Richmond,* 377.

13. Second Lieutenant John Davis, appointed October 27, 1861, "resigned & accepted July 9, 1862." 81st Pennsylvania Infantry, Regimental Descriptive Book, vol. 1, RG 94, National Archives.

14. Like many middle-class men of his era, Johnson believed that a respectably married woman should not work for wages, though of course women, Mary included, were expected to perform all of the work necessary to keep a household running. As in other aspects of American life, the Civil War led to marked changes in the role of women, in the field of nursing, for instance: "One of the astonishing facets of this astonishing war was the widespread and apparently spontaneous belief that women should, for the first time in history, carry the burden of wartime nursing in hospitals and camps." Agatha Young, *The Women and the Crisis: Women of the North in the Civil War* (New York: McDowell, Obolensky, 1959), 61. See also Judith Ann Giesberg, *Civil War Sisterhood: The U.S. Sanitary Commission and Women's Politics in Transition* (Boston: Northeastern University Press, 2000).

15. "Dreams," in Tupper, *Tupper's Complete Poetical Works,* 395.

16. William A. Gardiner was appointed regimental surgeon on September 19, 1861. In an earlier letter, Johnson had written that "Dr. Gardiner is, I am sorry to say worse than ever, and the prospect is that he will be 'dishonorably discharged from the service' as his conduct is such that he has lost every friend he ever had among the officers, myself included." Gardiner apparently was an alcoholic, and his resignation was accepted on August 5, 1862. Letters, October 27, 1861; 81st Pennsylvania Infantry, Regimental Descriptive Book, vol. 1, RG 94, National Archives.

17. Pennsylvania Congressman Galusha Grow was the Speaker of the U.S. House of Representatives from 1860 to 1862, when he was defeated in his bid for reelection.

18. This was probably another reference to "Alma," whose anonymous letters regularly appeared in the *Philadelphia Dispatch.* Other soldiers wrote to other papers, for instance, the *Philadelphia Inquirer,* providing another set of eyewitness accounts of the history of the 81st.

19. Johnson frequently enclosed articles or other papers for Mary; most often, as in this case, they have not been preserved.

20. "The staple" was most likely a metal hoop used to secure chains, and thus slaves, to the wall of the pen.

21. William Blackiston Davis, Mary Johnson's older brother, who lived near Laurel, Maryland. Johnson was not on the best of terms with this part of his wife's family, as will be seen in subsequent letters.

22. Dorothea Dix, noted reformer and advocate for the improved care of people with mental disabilities, at this time was the superintendent of women nurses in Union hospitals.

23. A reference, perhaps, to a chamber pot.

24. Major Eli. F. Conner, appointed October 1, 1861, commissioned as lieutenant colonel June 1, 1862, killed in action July 1, 1862; Adjutant H. Boyd McKeen, appointed October 27, 1861, commissioned as major, June 1, 1862. Such "legions" and "clubs" were common, as a way of ensuring that a soldier would get a decent burial and, perhaps more important, so that his family would know the circumstances of his death and the location of his grave.

25. "From the Chippewa Regiment," in the *Philadelphia Inquirer* of January 18, 1862, reported the 81st to be "at present in camp at 'Cloud's Mill,' under the guns of Fort Worth, and are the advance of our division. We are at present with our pioneer corps making the road and building bridges from here to Edsell's Hill, where in a few days they will commence the erection of a new fort." Discussing the regiment's officers, the correspondent described Colonel James Miller, "of New York, but formerly of Easton, Pa., a thorough-going man and a brave soldier. . . . Our Lieutenant-Colonel Charles Johnson, of Philadelphia, is a kind, humane soldier, and we privates know little of him but to admire."

26. In his letter of October 17, 1861, Johnson had expressed the hope that the officers of the regiment would be paid by the army from the time of their enlistment, rather than from their federal mustering some two months later. Secretary of War Simon Cameron resigned on January 11, after allegations of corruption in the granting of military contracts, and Lincoln appointed Edwin M. Stanton as his replacement. Because Cameron was a politician from Pennsylvania, Johnson perhaps assumed that he would be more sympathetic to the claims of Pennsylvania soldiers than Ohio attorney Stanton. McPherson, *Battle Cry of Freedom,* 324.

27. Johnson here demonstrates his skill in military politics. Over the next five years, he would serve under a variety of officers in a variety of posts, and manage, with perhaps one exception, to avoid the squabbling that often bedeviled both Union and Confederate commands.

28. "There is one objectionable feature, however, in the treatment of our sick, which I hope our Colonel will abolish. In the morning, when the 'sick-call' is beaten, the sick march up to the front of our Surgeon's quarters. . . . No matter how stormy the weather, or how wet and muddy the ground, there the poor fellows must stand. . . . Week before last one very sick private stood in the mud until he seemed almost overcome with weakness and three or four days afterwards he died. I hope our Lieutenant Colonel, whose humanity is as great as his courage, will have some arrangement made by which our sick will be protected from the rain and mud while waiting to be examined by our Surgeon." Alma, "From Col. Miller's Mauch Chunk Regiment (Late Thirty-sixth)," *Philadelphia Sunday Dispatch,* February 16, 1862.

29. Johnson evidently trusts Gardiner's medical judgement, despite the doctor's apparent alcoholism.

30. This "rumor" of impending action may have been a response to President Lincoln's General Order No. 1, issued January 27, which called for "the 22nd day of February 1862, [to] be the day for a general movement of the Land and Naval forces of the United States against the insurgent forces." Lincoln, frustrated with the slow pace of McClellan and his other generals, and believing that only coordinated military action along the whole front could end the war, simply ordered all of his generals and admirals to move forward on the same day. The order was ignored, however, McClellan arguing instead for an amphibious thrust by the Army of the Potomac toward Richmond via the Virginia peninsula. Roy P. Basler, ed., *The Collected Works of Abraham Lincoln,* vol. 5 (New Brunswick, N.J.: Rutgers University Press, 1953), 111; Stephen B. Oates, *Abraham Lincoln: The Man Behind the Myths* (New York: Harper & Row, 1984), 129.

31. There is no Jim or James Hufty listed in Lynch. Henry Little might have been the husband of Josephine Hufty, daughter of Samuel (Lynch, *From Whence We Came,*

123). In Hewett there is a Henry D. Little listed as belonging to Company F of the 29th New Jersey Infantry. Hewett, *Roster of Union Soldiers: New Jersey*, 175.

32. Captain Robert M. Lee Jr., of Company F, appointed October 10, 1861, wounded at Fair Oaks June 1, 1862, and promoted to major. His brother, Lieutenant Horace M. Lee, was killed at the same battle. Captain Lee was promoted to lieutenant colonel in November 1862 but resigned shortly thereafter because of his wounds (81st Pennsylvania Infantry, Regimental Descriptive Book, vol. 1, Book Records of Volunteer Union Organizations, RG 94, National Archives). He died on September 21, 1863. Taylor, *Philadelphia in the Civil War*, 284.

33. The inscription on the sword read: "Presented to Lieut. Col. Johnson by the Officers and Privates of the 81st Reg. Pa. V. as a token of Respect and Esteem as an officer and soldier." It was dated 1861 and manufactured by Tiffany & Co. in New York City. Johnson's sword was kept in the Johnson family long after his death but was destroyed in a fire at the home of his great grandson, Harry Melville Johnson II, in Grand Rapids, Minnesota. Bob Oftehe, "Family traces ancestors back over 50 generations," *Grand Rapids Mich. Herald Review*, February 28, 1988, 20.

34. Confederate General Joseph E. Johnston, fearing that his forces would be overwhelmed by the much larger federal army, retreated from his advanced positions in northern Virginia. McClellan cautiously followed, finding empty fortifications and "Quaker guns"—wooden cannons, which he had supposed to be real. Long, *Civil War Day by Day*, 180.

35. General Nathaniel Prentiss Banks, whose troops were chasing Confederate General Thomas Jackson's "Stonewall Brigade" up the Shenandoah Valley.

36. Johnson, in this and subsequent letters, shares with Mary not only past military events but also future plans and orders, though the upcoming federal move on Yorktown was hardly a secret, given the need to prepare the naval transport of more than 100,000 troops.

37. General Pierre Gustave Toutant Beauregard, Confederate commander during the attack on Fort Sumter in April 1861 and the battle of First Bull Run in July 1861. In March 1862, Beauregard was in western Tennessee, so Johnson probably means the Confederate command post during First Bull Run, in which case he has "expropriated" his fine portrait of Washington from a private home.

38. Johnson probably meant General James Ewell Brown ("Jeb") Stuart, Confederate cavalry leader soon to be famous for his ride around McClellan's army.

39. This was the beginning of McClellan's attempt to outflank the rebel army by landing on the Virginia peninsula, east of Richmond, which would culminate in the Seven Days Battles and the emergence of Robert E. Lee as one of the major figures in American military history.

40. Second Lieutenant William H. Booker of Company D, assigned September 24, 1861, "appt. 1st Lieut. Co. D. June 16th 1862." 81st Pennsylvania Infantry, Regimental Descriptive Book, vol. 1, Book Records of Volunteer Union Organizations, RG 94, National Archives.

41. McClellan sought to wage a limited war in which Southerners' property rights—even their right to hold slaves—was respected. Johnson's attitude from the beginning seems to have been less forgiving, and it would harden in the coming years.

42. There are several Captains "Moore" listed in the New Jersey regiments,

including Timothy C. Moore, Company K of the 6th Infantry, and William Henry Moore, Company D, 12th Infantry (Hewett, *Roster of Union Soldiers: New Jersey,* 206). Sergeant Edmund Carles of the 6th New Jersey, and William C. Figner, Company I, 6th New Jersey (Hewett, 46, 97).

43. Johnson's estimate of the rebel forces at Yorktown, like McClellan's, was vastly inflated.

44. The hospital steward for the 81st at this time was Spencer Bonsall. Bonsall kept a journal of this experiences with the 81st, which is now held at the Lister Hill Library of the Health Services at the University of Alabama at Birmingham.

45. Assuming the date on Johnson's letter is correct, he appears to have heard the news of Norfolk's fall a day before it happened. Confederate forces evacuated this important naval base in Virginia on May 9, 1862, and Federal troops moved in to occupy the base and nearby town on May 10. Long, *Civil War Day by Day,* 209–10.

46. This could be either Captain Edmund G. Jackson, Company C of the 4th New Jersey Infantry, or more likely Captain Edward S. Jackson, Company E of the 6th. Captain Richard H. Lee, company I, 6th New Jersey Infantry. Hewett, *Roster of Union Soldiers: New Jersey,* 148, 172.

47. Johnson's preference for "volunteer surgeons" was typical among the army. "Professional" surgeons, that is, those civilian physicians contracted by the military, were perceived by many soldiers to be motivated entirely by greed and, hence, incompetent: "Incompetence was even more prevalent among the contract physicians who were hired as occasion required to supplement the regularly commissioned medical staff." Bell Irvin Wiley, *The Common Soldier in the Civil War* (New York: Grosset & Dunlap, 1952), 130.

48. Johnson often refers to Clara's lisping speech. In this instance the phrase is no doubt Clara's attempt to pronounce "Sunday school."

49. There are several Campions listed in the Camden directory in 1863, all living at 218 North 3rd Street. Harrison was a cabinetmaker, Richard a salesman, while S. B. and William H. Campion are listed with no occupation. *Camden City Directory of 1863,* 29.

50. The Chickahominy River, which was to play an important role when General Joseph E. Johnston, in command of the Confederate army, attacked the Army of the Potomac on May 31, 1862. In that engagement Johnston took advantage of how the river, swollen with spring rains, had divided the Union army in two, choosing to focus his assault on the portion to the south. Long, *Civil War Day by Day,* 218–20, 234.

51. Johnson's illness, which he correctly diagnosed as jaundice, could have had several causes. Sanitation at civil war camps was notoriously bad, and those of the Army of the Potomac in the swamplands of the Virginia Peninsula in 1862 were among the worst.

52. "Baxter's Zuoaves" was the 77th Pennsylvania Volunteer Infantry.

53. Colonel Miller had been killed in combat on June 1, 1862. Johnson, as lieutenant colonel, had then taken command of the regiment. Apparently there had been something of a division within the regiment between those soldiers and officers from Philadelphia proper and those from the surrounding suburbs and countryside. Colonel Johnson, coming from New Jersey, apparently felt himself to be above these regional factions.

According to Union witnesses, Miller was shot and killed by Confederate troops who had identified themselves as Federals. "The loss of our Colonel," wrote one correspondent to the *Philadelphia Inquirer,* "and the deception practiced on us, created a terrible consternation for the time. Lieutenant-Colonel Chas. F. Johnson, deeming it advisable, ordered the right wing to fall back some three or four hundred feet, and formed again." "The Eighty-first Penna. Regiment," *Philadelphia Inquirer,* June 14, 1862. Johnson's letters describing the battle, assuming he wrote any, are no longer with the rest of his papers.

54. Carrying logs and sandbags for hours at a time was a standard civil war punishment for wayward enlisted men.

55. This may have been Mary's uncle, Joseph Blackiston, born February 16, 1760, died January 29, 1850, in Kent County, Maryland. Lynch, *From Whence We Came,* 12.

56. Samuel Shurlock had been appointed Captain on December 9, 1861. He is listed in the regimental record as killed in action, while on picket duty, on June 25, 1862. The Quartermaster Johnson refers to is most likely John Brelford, enlisted November 5, 1861, who is listed as "wounded in the attack on White House, Va." (81st Pennsylvania Infantry, Regimental Descriptive Book, vol. 1., Book Records of Volunteer Union Organizations, RG 94, National Archives). A "Chunker" refers to Capt. Shurlock being from Mauch Chunk in Carbon County, Pennsylvania, making him one of those Colonel Miller might have favored.

57. This is apparently Joseph R. Smith, appointed lieutenant on Sept. 20, 1861. He later resigned his commission. 81st Pennsylvania Infantry, Regimental Descriptive Book, vol. 1, Book Records of Volunteer Union Organizations, RG 94, National Archives.

58. Major General Joseph F. Hooker, known as "Fighting Joe" Hooker, would eventually command the Army of the Potomac at the disasterous Union defeat at Chancellorsville, Virginia, in early May 1863.

59. "Grape" is grapeshot, an artillery projectile "assembled with iron plates and rings and holding a cluster of shot together," more or less resembling a bunch of grapes. Canister, also fired from a cannon, was a metal container filled with metal balls and sawdust. Both weapons were meant to lacerate infantry, much like modern shrapnel, as opposed to destroying fortifications or enemy artillery. Garrison, *Civil War Usage,* 44, 98.

60. Major General Israel Bush Richardson, born in 1815, was wounded at Antietam on September 17, 1862, and died of his wounds on November 3, 1862.

61. George McLaughlin might be related to Captain John G. McLaughlin of the 81st, appointed September 18, 1861. There appears to be no listing for a George McLaughlin in Baldwin Hufty's regiment, the 4th New Jersey Volunteer Infantry.

Chapter Three

1. Dyer, *Compendium of the War of the Rebellion,* 1601.

2. The fact that the War Department was unaware of the location of a Union regiment, and only vaguely aware of where the commander of its largest army might be, is indicative of the chaos prevailing at the time. After forcing McClellan to retreat from the outskirts of Richmond, the Confederate army struck to the north, defeating

Union General John F. Pope at the battle of Second Bull Run, prepatory to launching an offensive into Maryland that would culminate in the battle of Antietam on September 17, 1862.

3. The 81st arrived on the field too late to participate in the battle of Second Bull Run but was a part of the general retreat afterward.

4. Brigadier General John Curtis Caldwell. Caldwell commanded the brigade of which the 81st was a part at the battles of Antietam and Fredericksburg. Lindbuchler, *History of the 81st P.V.I.*, 9–11.

5. Tom McKeen may be related to Colonel Harold Boyd McKeen, who took command of the 81st after Johnson had been wounded.

6. General Robert E. Lee had in fact by this time already moved through Frederick. Johnson was quite correct in his supposition that Mary's brother William, in Laurel, Maryland, was in no danger.

7. "Our Harry" is probably a reference to Colonel McKeen.

8. General Winfield Scott Hancock, a Pennsylvania native and West Point graduate, best known for his quick thinking in saving the Union position during the first day of the battle of Gettysburg. Disabled while in command of the II Corps of the Army of the Potomac during the battle's third day, Hancock convalesced for almost year before returning to command the Corps at the battles of the Wilderness, Spotsylvania, and Cold Harbor. Suffering a humiliating defeat at Ream's Station and bothered by his Gettysburg wound, he was shifted to a post behind the lines as the commander of the 1st Veteran Volunteer Corps. Warner, *Generals in Blue,* 202–4.

9. Assistant surgeon J. B. Beshler was appointed on June 14, 1862. 81st Pennsylvania Infantry, Regimental Descriptive Book, vol. 1, Book Records of Volunteer Union Organizations, RG 94, National Archives.

10. Captain Thomas G. Harkness, mustered into service in September 1861 and wounded in action with Colonel Johnson on June 30, 1862. Thomas Morton, appointed as second lieutenant September 18, 1861, promoted to first lieutenant September 17, 1862. Norton Reiber, appointed second lieutenant on January 1, 1862. 81st Pennsylvania Infantry, Regimental Descriptive Book, vol. 1, Book Records of Volunteer Union Organizations, RG 94, National Archives. For Captain Lee, see chapter 2, note 32.

11. Captain Alexander (see chapter 1, note 6) was not the only officer suffering from illness or wounds. In his letter of October 25, 1862, Johnson tells Mary how "The Lieut. Col. arrived here yesterday and brought the two suspension belts which arrived very opportunily as my testicle had become like—well, what? like a full blown peach—ram-like; I put it on immediately and now feel 'bully[.]'"

12. Like "Alma," "Chunk" appears to have been an anonymous correspondent, writing letters about the regiment to his hometown paper.

13. "Harry" is probably Colonel Harold McKeen, "Swain" is Clinton Swain, second lieutenant appointed regimental adjutant June 16, 1862. 81st Pennsylvania Infantry, Regimental Descriptive Book, vol. 1. "Lees," the aspiring sutler mentioned two paragraphs later, is otherwise unidentified.

14. William B. Franklin graduated the U.S. Military Academy in 1843, served during the Mexican War, and taught at West Point. He was appointed a brigadier general in May 1861. General Ambrose Everett Burnside had twice turned down command of the Army of the Potomac before finally assuming command on November 9. His

short tenure in this post would end in the disaster at Fredericksburg, where he ordered waves of his troops to attack Confederates in a virtually impregnable position, resulting in 1,284 Federals killed, 9,600 wounded, and 1,769 missing, compared to Lee's casualties of 595 killed, 4,061 wounded, and 653 missing. His subsequent attempt to outmaneuver Lee was also spectacularly unsuccessful and ended in the famous "Mud March" of January 1863, during which the entire Army of the Potomac became mired in the Virginia mud. Lincoln relieved Burnside of command on January 25. Burnside served in various capacities until the end of the war. Long, *Civil War Day by Day,* 286, 295–96, 313–15.

15. From *Julius Caesar,* 3. s2.194–96: "Oh, what a fall was there, my countrymen! / Then I, and you, and all of us fell down, / Whilst bloody treason flourished over us."

16. Lincoln, weary of McClellan's excuses during the Peninsula campaign and the general's unwillingness to follow up the partial victory at Antietam, relieved McClellan of his command on November 7, 1862. Many of his soldiers, however, like Johnson, continued to worship him, and there was some concern in Washington that the Army of the Potomac would itself rebel and "change front" or march on Washington. This never happened, of course, but McClellan did run as a presidential candidate against Lincoln in 1864. Long, *Civil War Day by Day,* 285; Catton, *Mr. Lincoln's Army,* 335–37.

17. Johnson obviously misdated this section of his letter, no doubt meaning to write November rather than October.

18. This was probably the battery commanded by Captain Rufus D. Pettit, of the 1st New York Light Artillery, stationed at Fort Richardson on the Peninsula, near where the 81st was located at this time.

Chapter Four

1. Lynch, *From Whence We Came,* 75.

2. Ibid., 103.

3. Colonel E. A. Parrott, assistant adjutant at the Provost Marshal's Office in Columbus, Ohio, and commander of the 1st Ohio Volunteers. Johnson hints in his letter of October 7, 1863, that Colonel Parrott is something of a "rake," or womanizer.

4. Johnson apparently found blacks in Ohio, a free state, to be less docile than Abraham, his servant while stationed in Virginia and the District of Columbia.

5. There is a Francis Fitzgerald listed as a private in Company C, 4th New Jersey Infantry (Hewett, *Roster of Union Soldiers: New Jersey,* 99). A George House is listed as a "weaver" in the *The Camden and Gloucester Directory for 1850.*

6. "Hooker" is General Joseph Hooker, now the commander of the Army of the Potomac. Johnson is referring in this letter to Lee's expedition north, his second in less than a year, which would culminate in the battle of Gettysburg. This same day the commander of Invalid Corps detachments stationed at Harrisburg was ordered to have them ready "for service in another part of the state. Special orders in relation thereto will be sent you so soon as you report them ready." Two thousand rifles, two thousand uniforms, and 120 thousand rounds of ammunition were to be made available to these companies, in the event that they were needed to help stop Lee. Provost Marshal General's Office to Col. Chas. M. Prevost, 118th Pa. vols., June 12,

1863, June 16, 1863, Records of the Office Subdivisions, 1862–66, Veteran Reserve Corps Branch, General Records, Issuances, entry 306, vol. 1, RG 110, National Archives.

7. There is no Edward C. Johnson listed in Lynch, nor does Samuel Luchess appear in any other context in the Johnson papers.

8. "Can such things be, / And overcome us like a summer's cloud, / Without our special wonder?" *Macbeth,* 3.4.110–12.

9. There is a First Lieutenant Alexander A. Black listed in Company A of the 147th Pennsylvania Volunteer Infantry. Hewett, *Roster of Union Soldiers: Pennsylvania, vol. 1,* 125.

10. William Cooper, "On the Receipt of My Mother's Picture," in *The Poetical Works of William Cooper* (Boston: Little, Brown, 1859), 252. The second line is a misquote for "the meek intelligence of those dear eyes."

11. Johnson was evidently a Mason, as well as a member of the Improved Order of Red Men.

12. Major Lucius V. Bierce, a member of the regular army. Heitman, *Historical Register of the United States Army,* 217.

13. Ohio Governor David F. Tod. Unfortunately, the "epistle" is not among Johnson's papers.

14. Vicksburg, Mississippi, fell to forces under the command of General Ulysses S. Grant on July 4, 1863. This crucial victory opened up the entire Mississippi River to Union navigation and divided the Confederacy in two. Together with the federal victory at Gettysburg, July 1–3, it marked the turning point of the Civil War.

15. Rioting broke out in New York City on July 13, 1863, in response to the drawing of names for the first draft. Over the next days, white mobs murdered and beat many blacks, and burned down a black church and orphanage. Federal troops, some of whom had just fought at Gettysburg, were brought in to quell the violence (Long, *Civil War Day by Day,* 384). By the time the violence ended, approximately one thousand people had been killed or injured. Bruce Catton, *Reflections on the Civil War* (New York: Berkley Books, 1981), 58.

16. Johnson seems to have felt no contradiction when praising the patriotism of those answering Governor Tod's call for militia and expressing sympathy for a friend seeking to avoid service by paying a "substitute" to take his place in the draft.

17. George Deal's occupation was listed in the *Camden City Directory of 1864* (40), which presumably was compiled in 1863, as "police" and his address as 212 North Fifth Street.

18. Charles Welch was the husband of Adaline Hufty, Maria Hufty Johnson's older sister. Lynch, *From Whence We Came,* 121.

19. The disruption of civil war led to a breakdown in law and order through vast sections of the North and South, however distant from the front. For instance, Jane Keeler, writing to her husband Elnathan in the Veteran Reserve Corps in June 1865, reports an attempted abduction and rape, apparently in broad daylight, on the streets of St. Johnsville, New York. Klass, *Portrait of Elnathan Keeler,* 79.

20. In his letter of July 30, 1863 (not included here), Charles had written, in reply to Mary's comment that "Clara wants a baby" brother or sister, that he "just now . . . could go to my death to satisfy her." While willing to joke about sex from time to time, Johnson's embarrassment at expressing his sexual feelings for Mary is in marked

contrast to enlisted man Elnathan Keeler, who wrote quite openly of his desire for his wife Jane. See, for example, Klass, *Portrait of Elnathan Keeler,* 21, 26.

Chapter Five

1. Colonel Edmund Brooke Alexander, Acting Assistant Provost Marshall for Missouri. In the "regular army," he was the commander of the 10th U.S. Infantry and had earned a brevet promotion for gallantry and meritorious conduct in the Mexican War. In October 1865, he was promoted to brigadier general for "meritorious service in recruitment of the armies of the U.S." Heitman, *Historical Register of the United States Army,* 156.

2. Alva Stites was the son of John K. F. Stites, who filed an affidavit on December 14, 1869, to the effect that he had known Charles and Mary Johnson, and had "occupied the adjoining house to them" during Clara Johnson's infancy (Charles F. Johnson, Federal Pension File, Min. C 141775, National Archives). The elder Stites lived at 412 Hamilton Street; his occupation is not listed. *Camden and Gloucester Directory of 1863–1864,* 122.

3. "The boys" were most likely visiting with relatives.

4. This Mary Davis, judging from subsequent letters, would seem to be not Mary Johnson's mother but rather a younger and probably unrelated woman with whom Alva Stites was romantically involved.

5. The Meeting of Resigned Officers in Philadelphia, along with the Union League of Philadelphia, advocated the creation of a national Invalid Corps. Lynch, *From Whence We Came,* 103.

6. The men mentioned were perhaps Captain Robert Hicks of the 77th Pennsylvania (Hewett, *Roster of Union Soldiers: Pennsylvania, vol. 1,* 206); Captain James H. Rice and Captain Charles Russell, of the 7th Veteran Reserve Corps, who in April 1863 served at the St. Louis headquarters of the Provost Marshal General's Office of Missouri. Charles Russell, Affidavit, Missouri Acting Assistant Provost Marshal General, Letters Received 1862–64, entry 4167, box 1, RG 110, National Archives.

7. Much of Missouri was in a state of turmoil, and the scene of a vicious guerilla war, which Johnson goes on to describe in some detail.

8. This may be Major Ambrose A. Stevens from Michigan rather than from Wisconsin. See also note 15 below.

9. Brigadier General McCormick, identified as one of "nearly an hundred citizens of Pilot Knob and Ironton" who defended Missouri against Price's raid of August–September 1864. *Official Records,* series 1, vol. 41, no. 1, 445.

10. John Sappington Marmaduke and Sterling "Pap" Price, Confederate commanders in Missouri.

11. This expression of extreme racism is all the more chilling when one considers that "George" is probably George Deal, at that time a Camden policeman. Within three years Johnson, as an official with the Freedmen's Bureau, will order the arrest of whites accused of shooting and committing other acts of terrorism and intimidation against newly emancipated slaves.

12. As in note 4 above, Mary Davis in this instance would appear to be Alva's former sweetheart and not Charles Johnson's mother-in-law. The Stites family apparently became relatives of the Johnsons, after Charles's death, when one of the twins

(William) married Hariet Stites Sewel Deal, the daughter of Johnson's close friend George Deal. Lynch, *From Whence We Came,* 41.

13. See Letter, July 23, 1863.

14. A picayune was worth five cents.

15. A member of the regular army, Ambrose A. Stevens had commanded the 21st Michigan Infantry before resigning his commission for medical reasons on February 3, 1863. He entered the Invalid Corps as a major in July and was appointed colonel of the 5th Veteran Reserve Corps on September 25, 1863. Regimental Descriptive, Letter, Endorsement, Order and Detail Book, 5th Veteran Reserve Corps, vol. 1, Book Records of Volunteer Union Organizations, RG 94, National Archives; and Heitman, *Historical Register of the United States Army,* 922.

16. This is the "Captain Comingo" Johnson praised in his report to Colonel Alexander; see introduction, p. 17.

17. Captain William J. Conner of the 81st Pennsylvania. See chapter 2, note 6.

18. In his letter of July 26, 1863, Johnson asked Mary, "What Reed is it that the boys go with, is it the Reed that cleans the Schools?" There are eight Reeds listed in the Camden directory of 1864, but none as a custodian. Several, however, have no occupation listed.

19. Although he never explicitly names it, it is obvious from this and subsequent letters that some form of sexual contact or abuse had occurred. At the time, Joseph and William Johnson were twelve years old.

20. Assignments were made to the First or Second Battalion of the Invalid Corps based on the level of the soldier's disability. See introduction, p. 11–12.

21. Captain Edward Geer Bush, of the 10th US Infantry, had been brevetted as major for gallantry and meritorious service in the battle of Gettysburg. Heitman, *Historical Register of the United States Army,* 268.

22. This could be Dr. Samuel Carels, listed on page 29 of the Camden Directory of 1863, or Dr. Samuel Cauls, who filed an affidavit in Camden on May 6, 1868, describing himself as "a practicing physician of 13 years . . . acquainted with Col. Charles F. Johnson, deceased" and "the physician of the said Col. Johnson." Charles F. Johnson, Federal Pension Application, Min. C 141775, National Archives.

23. Presumably, the book was one of a multitude of works published on "the evils" of masturbation and homosexuality; for example, Leopold Deslandes, *Manhood: The Cause of Its Premature Decline, with directions for its perfect restoration; addressed to those suffering from the destructive effects of excessive indulgence, solitary habits, etc.,* trans. from the French, with many additions, by an American physician (Boston: Otis Broaders), 1843.

24. *Dutch,* meaning "German," an American corruption of the German word *Deutsch.* Support for the Union cause and for abolition was strong among German-Americans in Missouri, with its large immigrant population in St. Louis, while many of Missouri's native born supported the rebellion. McPherson, *Battle Cry of Freedom,* 290–91.

25. William P. Hufty and his father, Mary's "Uncle George" W. Hufty. See chapter 1, note 15 above.

26. Captain W. Spencer, from Carlisle, Pennsylvania, appointed to the Invalid Corps on August 17, 1863. Records of Office Subdivisions, Veteran Reserve Corps

Branch, General Records, Issuances, vol. 1, entry 306, Records of the Provost Marshal General's Bureau, RG 110, National Archives.

27. Timothy Middleton, mayor of Camden 1863 to 1864. It seems likely, from Johnson's comments, that Mary brought some sort of legal action against Reed for his assault on their children.

28. Captain Samuel K. Brown, assigned first lieutenant in the 81st Pennsylvania on September 12, 1861, "appointed Capt. Co. D June 16th, 1862 . . . wounded at Antietam Sept. 17, 1862." 81st Pennsylvania Volunteer Infantry, Regimental Books, vol. 1, Book Records of Volunteer Union Organizations, RG 94, National Archives.

29. William Moore, Johnson's brother-in-law, was drafted in July. Maria, with their children George and Anne Marie, presumably was either visiting or living with Henry (Harry) Johnson.

30. A character in the popular play, *The Toodles: A Domestic Drama in Two Acts,* by Richard J. Raymond, circa 1853.

31. Johnson's writing here is difficult to make out; this might also be "Herminica, Mo."

32. The Office of the Provost Marshal was in charge of military discipline as well as law enforcement in areas under martial law; the Invalid Corps was also used to enforce martial law. This is Johnson's first reference to his work tracking down and arresting people suspected of disloyalty. For another perspective on the Invalid Corps as military police, see William W. Hummel, "The Military Occupation of Columbia County," *Pennsylvania Magazine of History and Biography,* 80, no. 3 (July 1956).

33. These items are no longer with the Johnson letters.

34. "True, I talk of dreams, / Which are the children of an idle brain, / Begot of nothing but vain fantasy." *Romeo and Juliet,* 1.4.97–99.

35. George W. Ford, attorney in Philadelphia. On April 13, 1866, Ford wrote to Johnson, "I have this day received a check for your state pay amounting to $255, out of which I have retained $105 for Mr. Chambers, payable by your order and fees and expenses of $25. and enclosed I send you a check for the balance $125, marked good by the 1st Nat. Bank of Phila. for which you will please acknowledge the receipt and oblige." A note in Johnson's handwriting reads, "Acknowledged April 14 = 1866." Johnson Papers, 1866.

36. The references to "Lillies safes" are unclear. Evidently, the Johnsons had experienced financial problems before the war, probably related to Charles's work as an engraver.

37. Colonel James Barnet Fry began his service in the regular army as an artillery officer but spent the Civil War in the Provost Marshal General's Office, becoming a brigadier general on April 21, 1864. Heitman, *Historical Register of the United States Army,* 439.

38. That is, cheeses.

39. For more on the significance of the Invalid Corps uniform, see introduction, pp. 14–15.

40. The 38th Congress began consideration of a bill to organize "the invalid corps of the Army" during its first session in March 1864. The bill was referred back to the Committee on Military Affairs and Militia, and although it came up for some additional discussion, there is no record of further congressional action on the

Invalid Corps until after the war. Most likely, the various general orders of the War Department were considered sufficient. *Congressional Globe,* 38th Cong., 1st sess. March 7–April 29, 1864, 34, pt. 2: 1130, 1207.

41. This was not the first incident of the harassment of women in the streets of Camden that Mary had reported to Charles. See Letter, July 23, 1863. Johnson's victim blaming is typical of his, and perhaps our own, era's view of sexual harassment. This might be seen as yet another facet of the "just world" theory described in the introduction, in which bad things only happen to bad people.

42. Enclosed in the letter was a "notarized contract" giving Johnson possession and use of the jug. The contract gives the address of his boarding house as "No. 146 Pine Street, City of St. Louis."

43. Provost Marshal General Fry's order for such examinations was issued on November 6, 1863, and called for them to "commence as soon after the 1st of January, 1864 as practicable. [Officers] will be examined as to their acquaintance with the Regulations of the United States Army and its tactics, (so far as they bear upon the duties of Regimental officers,) and in regard to their qualifications as officers, their fitness for their positions, and for promotion." *Orders, Letters, Circulars Concerning the Invalid Corps, 1863,* Research Collection, Boston Public Library.

Johnson's irritation at this process is understandable. Officers applying for positions in the corps had already been required to file "satisfactory recommendations from his superiors in the field as to good character and behavior in active service" (*Official Records,* series 3, vol. 5, 680), and Johnson had already passed another such examination during his service with the 81st Pennsylvania. A medical examination was also required of aspiring Invalid Corps officers, to "determine the question of disability."

44. Fort Laramie, Wyoming. Johnson was no doubt anticipating taking his own leave, once Captain Bush had returned from his.

45. Mary's mother, Mary Davis, born circa 1793 in Maryland, died on December 6, 1863, in Camden, New Jersey. Her death certificate lists the cause of death as typhoid fever. Lynch, *From Whence We Came,* 30.

Chapter Six

1. Johnson dated this letter "December 6, 1864" and in the text below dated the second portion "Dec. 7." In December 1864 however, he was, stationed in Washington, D.C. It is also unlikely that the letter was written in December 1863, because Johnson was obviously just returning to St. Louis from Camden. The word *December* is crossed out and the word *January* written in its place but in a hand different from Johnson's. This would date the letter at the point of Johnson's return from his Christmas furlough of December 1863, and because this seems to make the most sense, I have dated the letter January 6, 1864.

2. Probably Crestline, Ohio.

3. "There are more things in heaven and earth, Horatio, / Than are dreamt of in your philosophy." *Hamlet,* 1.5.166–67.

4. Randolph Barnes Marcy was in fact a brigadier general. Heitman, *Historical Register of the United States Army,* 689.

5. Lieutenant Colonel Newton T. Colby, listed in 1865 as "aged 34, from State of

New York, entered volunteer service April 1861, as first Lieutenant; took active part in the battles of Ball's Cross Roads, Antietam, Chancellorsville, and South Mountain; was disabled by typhus fever. Entered the Veteran Reserve Corps December, 1863" (*Field Record of the Officers of the U.S. Army Veteran Reserve Corps,* 3). Lieutenant Colonel Colby was transferred to the 19th Regiment VRC on May 5, 1864. The list of commissioned officers in the Regimental Descriptive Book of the 18th VRC gives the date of Major Martin Flood's appointment as December 4, 1864, but this no doubt was intended as 1863. He was promoted to lieutenant colonel on June 20, 1864, and then assigned to the 15th Regiment VRC on August 12, 1864. He is not listed in the *Field Record.* 18th Veteran Reserve Corps, Regimental Descriptive Book, vol. 1, Book Records of Volunteer Union Organizations, RG 94, National Archives.

6. Camp Morton, located on the grounds of the Indiana State Fair, was first established as a training camp, but by the time of Johnson's arrival it had been used as a prisoner-of-war camp for more than a year: "[F]ew if any other facilities of this sort equaled the exemplary record of this prison. Soon after the war, Col. Richard Owen became the only former prison commandant to be honored with a monument erected by grateful former inmates" (Webb Garrison and Cheryl Garrison, *The Encyclopedia of Civil War Usage* [Nashville: Cumberland House, 2001], 43). In 1864, on any given day, Camp Morton contained an average of four thousand prisoners (*Official Records,* series 3, vol. 5, 561).

7. This is Colonel A. A. Stevens, commander of Burnside Barracks.

8. The 5th Regiment Invalid or Veteran Reserve Corps served all its duty in the west, with its headquarters at Indianapolis, mostly guarding prisoners and federal property. The 17th would remain in Indianapolis for the remainder of the war, but the 18th under Johnson would soon be moved to the Washington, D.C., area. Companies of the 23rd would see duty in Wisconsin, Minnesota, Missouri, Kentucky, and Iowa. *Official Records,* series 3, vol. 5, 560–65.

9. Colonel Richard H. Rush, formerly of the 6th Pennsylvania Cavalry and the first commander of the Invalid Corps.

10. An apparent slur against the Irish.

11. Colonel Baker had written to Washington asking that Johnson be transferred to his office as his adjutant general. Letter, February 3, 1864.

12. This is most likely Major Martin Flood, who had orginally enlisted in the 3rd Wisconsin. See note 5 above.

13. Colonel A. J. Warner, commander of the 17th Regiment of the Invalid Corps.

14. Governor Oliver P. Morton, for whom Camp Morton was named.

15. Johnson did not make a very good impression with the board (see introduction, pp. 24–25), but despite this he would be retained in the corps.

16. "Copperheads" were opposed to the war and the Lincoln administration. The holiday Johnson is referring to is Washington's birthday, which received renewed attention during the Civil War. The Indianapolis *Daily State Sentinel* of February 23, 1864, described the military parade through the city that day, noting that the Invalid Corps marched "with thorough discipline, and to the admiration of everybody. They numbered, we supposed, about three thousand." The February 23 issue of the Indianapolis *Daily Gazette* described the "4,000" men of the Invalid Corps as "a splendid body of men," whose "soldierly bearing and scrupulous neatness won the admiration of the interested crowd," while the Indianapolis *Daily Journal* noted that "but for the

wounds or concealed feebleness that would make marching difficult or dangerous, it would be hard to imagine a worse misnomer than their name. But sometimes a halting stop after several squares of marching, and a gun swinging a little out of its exact line, told the explanation of the title. And the officers, as they poised their swords, to steady a wheeling platoon, upon a stump of an arm, told only too plainly where they had earned their name. . . . It was a wonderful body, that Invalid Corps, and we heard many a compliment as it passed on its soldierly bearing and appearance." Newspaper Section, Indiana State Library, Indianapolis, Indiana.

17. This was Lieutenant Colonel Newton Colby, who was transferred out of the regiment in May.

18. This may have been First Lieutenant Frank R. Rice of the 17th VRC. Johnson and others often addressed officers by the rank they had attained in their regiment of origin; thus, those in Johnson's office seem often to have addressed him as "Colonel," though he was first a major and then a lieutenant colonel in the Invalid Corps. The *Field Record of the Officers of the U.S. Army Veteran Reserve Corps* refers to Frank R. Rice as "Aged 22, from the State of Michigan, entered the volunteer service in April, 1861; took part in the battles of Bull Run, Mechanicsville, Gaines' Mill, Malvern, 2nd Bull Run, Antietam, Sharpsburg, Shepherdstown, and Fredericksburg; was shot in the groin, and entered the Vet. Res. Corps in February, 1864" (*Field Record,* 20). Major John H. Gardiner was appointed to the 5th VRC on October 28, 1863, and was promoted to lieutenant colonel "by the President to rank from 30 March 1864 and transferred to the 17th Regt. V.R.C." 5th Veteran Reserve Corps, Regimental Descriptive, Letter, Endorsement, Order, and Detail Book, vol. 1, RG 94, National Archives.

19. This was Captain Gustave Mauer, appointed as a captain in the Invalid Corps September 23, 1863, assigned to the 18th regiment on January 16, 1864, and "Dismissed [from] the service of [the] U.S. per S.O.A.G.O. no. 78 dated February 22, 1864." 18th Regiment Veteran Reserve Corps, Regimental Descriptive Book, vol. 1, RG 94, National Archives.

20. Pennsylvania Governor Andrew G. Curtin. Johnson's charge that political pressure determined which officers passed examination for a post in the Veteran Reserve Corps probably had some validity, for commissions in both the regular and volunteer armies were often granted for political, as well as, and sometimes in spite of, military ability. It was because of the poor performance of such "political officers" that review boards were established. It is unclear why Johnson believed Secretary of War Stanton was so ill disposed toward him, but whether or not this was the case Johnson was passed by the examining board and given a commission.

21. Johnson's prediction that the corps would become a political "shuttlecock" seems not to have come to pass, for appointments to the corps seem not to have been any more (or less) "political" than appointments to the regular and volunteer armies. In any case, no brigadier generals were commissioned to serve with the Invalid Corps.

22. This good reputation enjoyed by the officers of the Invalid Corps seems very much in contrast to the poor reputation the corps suffered among many, particularly enlisted men, in the mainstream army.

23. For the significance of first vs. second battalion of the Invalid Corps/Veteran Reserve Corps, see introduction, p. 12.

24. A prisoner-of-war camp like Camp Morton, Johnson's Island was opened near

Sandusky, Ohio, in February 1862. Built to accommodate one thousand prisoners, by the end of the war it held some three thousand. Garrison, *The Encyclopedia of Civil War Usage,* 129.

25. Actually, this was Brigadier General Samuel Peter Heintzelman, West Point Graduate, and corps commander under McClellan during the Peninsula campaign. After Second Bull Run he was assigned to the military district of Washington, D.C. (Warner, *Generals in Blue,* 227–28). General Order 111, Adjutant General's Office, issued March 18, 1864, turned the Invalid Corps into the Veteran Reserve Corps. For the significance of this order, see introduction, p. 24.

26. In a previous letter, not included here, Mary had informed Charles that Clara had taken to using the word *nosed* to describe items such as her new hat.

27. Johnson apparently believed the injury to his testicles made him sterile, and he seems to imply here that he is also impotent, although comments in other letters seem to belie this. For example, see chapter 3, note 20.

28. "The battery" refers to the use of electricity and magnetism as "remedies" for various medical problems. Such "galvanic treatments" were very popular well into the twentieth century. Margaret Rowbottom and Charles Susskind, *Electricity and Medicine, History of Their Interaction* (San Francisco: San Francisco Press, 1984).

29. For the significance of this change in uniform, see introduction, pp. 14–15, 19.

30. Probably Generals Howard and Sumner, both of whom Johnson knew personally.

31. There are no letters from Charles to Mary dated between April 26 and this of May 5. In the interim, Mary and the children had probably visited him in Indianapolis, after which he was summoned to Washington. For Briggs, see chapter 7, note 1.

Chapter Seven

1. Brigadier General Henry Shaw Briggs, enlisted as a captain with the 8th Massachusetts militia in April 1861 and was promoted to colonel of the 10th Massachusetts Infantry in June 1861 and to brigadier general in July 1862. Heitman, *Historical Register of the United States Army,* 244.

2. Aquia Creek. This letter was written one day after the battle of Spotsylvania, in which the Army of the Potomac under Grant attacked entrenched positions held by the Army of Northern Virginia under Lee. The battle came after a week of fighting and maneuvering, during which Grant tried to edge around Lee's flank, while Lee withdrew to the south and east to prevent Grant's progress. McPherson, *Battle Cry of Freedom,* 727.

3. Brigadier General John Joseph Abercrombie, regular army, Mexican War veteran, brevetted a major in Florida in 1837 for gallantry and meritorious service. (F. B. Heitman, *Historical Register and Dictionary of the U.S. Army,* vol. 1: Washington, D.C.: GPO, 1903), 217.

4. The U.S. Sanitary Commission.

5. General Jeb Stuart was mortally wounded, not captured, at the battle of Yellow Tavern, Virginia, on May 11 (Long, *Civil War Day by Day,* 498). There were several Confederate General Johnsons, but none of these is mentioned in the records of the 18th VRC. A volunteer nurse serving in the area, however, noted in her diary entry March 9, 1864, that "All the 'Invalid Corps' from our hospital who marched off that day are

down here guarding prisoners: Generals Stuart and Bradley Johnson among them." Dannett, *Noble Women of the North,* 288.

6. Colonel William Hoffman had charge of all Union prisoner-of-war camps. Cited for gallantry and meritorious conduct during the Mexican War, his record as commissary general of prisoners is controversial at best, and he has been held at least partially responsible for the terrible conditions prevailing at camps such as Elmira, New York, and Fort Delaware. Heitman, *Historical Register of the United States Army,* 535.

7. As Johnson explained, he dated this letter twice and wrote two separate headings, apparently because he was distracted by official business.

8. Captain Frederick W. Thibaut, "Aged 30, from the State of New York, entered the volunteer service in April, 1861; took part in the battles of Big Bethel, Newport News, Fair Oaks, Savage Station, Malvern Hill, Antietam, and Fredericksburg; he received a gun shot wound in the left leg (compound fracture of the left thigh bone), lost a finger of the left hand, wounded in the right shoulder and side by minie ball. He entered the Vet. Res. Corps in October, 1863" (*Field Record,* 15). He was assigned to the 18th VRC on May 3, 1864. 18th Regiment Veteran Reserve Corps, Regimental Descriptive Book, vol. 1, RG 94, National Archives.

9. Johnson's old friend George Deal would eventually become the sutler for the 18th VRC.

10. Johnson doesn't explain what he means by "the companionship of Nancy," and there are no references to this elsewhere in his correspondence.

11. John Singleton Mosby, leader of the Confederate partisan group "Mosby's Raiders." Guerillas were a constant threat to Union troops in eastern Virginia, as will be seen in Johnson's letters of the next several weeks.

12. Aquia Creek.

13. Johnson's letter of May 17th is not among his collected papers.

14. A "Contraband," or escaped slave.

15. An example of one of the "pledges of the Government in reference to the Corps" can be found early on in the official correspondence of the corps. A circular from the Provost Marshal General's Office in Washington, dated June 20, 1863, reported difficulties in recruiting for the corps "in consequence of a prevalent opinion having got abroad that the Invalid Corps is only intended as a 'Catch,' a sort of 'Trick' to raise troops, and that when once enlisted, the men will be diverted from the purpose to which they were enlisted, and sent on field campaigns." The circular therefore urged recruiters to "disabuse the minds of discharged soldiers in a calm and decided manner and to assure them that the Government is sincere in its desire to create a Corps of Honor, to be employed in Home service &c &c . . ." Provost Marshal General's Office to Romford, June 20, 1863, Records of Office Subdivisions 1862–66, Veteran Reserve Corps Branch, vol. 1, entry 306, Orders and Circulars of the Provost Marshal General, RG 110, National Archives.

16. J. W. De Forest's final report on the VRC includes an account of this march of the 18th VRC: "The six companies [of the 18th] were assigned to Colonel Johnson on the 7th of May. Four days afterward he received an order to embark at 6 on the following morning for Belle Plain, Va., then a depot of stores and prisoners in the rear of the Army of the Potomac. The regiment numbered 10 officers and 514 men present for duty, and 10 men present sick. The first five days at Belle Plain were passed in a continual rain, without tents, without rubber blankets, without medical

stores, without even a surgeon. Until May 24 the regiment guarded the rebel prisoners at the post and escorted detachments of them northward, transmitting in this manner 2,996, with a loss of two escaped and one killed in the attempt. As General Grant advanced toward Petersburg it became necessary to move the base of supplies southward, and on the 23rd of May a medical examination was made of the Eighteenth to decide what men could go to Port Royal, a distance of about twenty-five miles by land. The surgeons reported that of the 474 present 166 could march without knapsacks, and that the rest were not able to march at all. The officers all refused to be examined, or represented themselves as fit for the field. While the mass of the regiment, 308 men, were put on a transport and sent by water to their destination, Colonel Johnson with his select band, still miserably provided for active service, set out as part of the marching column. The first field night of this forlorn hope of invalids was passed in a furious storm of rain and hail, without tents or other cover, the men wrapping themselves in their wet blankets and finding what shelter they could in the corners of rail-fences.

"Next morning Colonel Johnson requested that his command might be left to make its own way and take care of itself in its own time.

"It could not advance, he said, above a mile an hour; if attacked by guerrillas it could not run away and it would fight; it did not fear any force which was not superior in numbers; its greatest enemy was rapidity of movement. All that day he and his officers coaxed the men on; ordered, pleaded, persuaded, reasoned with the poor fellows who dropped by the roadside; halted those who could walk, to enable those who could only limp to catch up; marched fifteen minutes at a time and then rested ten; accomplished in thirteen hours only twelve miles. On the morning after the conclusion of the journey but 42 of the 166 were able to fall in for roll-call. Then the surgeon who had been assigned to the regiment was ordered to Washington. Colonel Johnson himself attended to the sick; that is, he administered to the lighter cases such medicine as he understood and had; but the graver maladies, the old wounds which had reopened, the limbs which were warped by injuries or helpless with rheumatism, were necessarily neglected. At Port Royal the regiment, now reunited, received its shelter tents." *Official Records,* series 3, vol. 5, 554.

17. Johnson was correct to the extent that the front did continue to shift southward, with the 18th Regiment and other units under Johnson's command at White House Landing within two weeks. Grant, however, ended up farther south than McClellan and settled into a siege of Petersburg that would last almost to the end of the war.

18. Point Lookout, Maryland, was the site of another federal prisoner-of-war camp.

19. Colonel Harold Boyd McKeen (listed as "Henry Boyd" or "H. Boyd" in Hewett, *Roster of Union Soldiers: Pennsylvania, vol. 1,* 59) began his military career as the adjutant with the 81st Pennsylvania. He was promoted to major after Colonel Miller was killed at Fair Oaks on June 1, 1862, promoted to lieutenant colonel after the death of Lieutenant Colonel Eli T. Conner at Malvern Hill on July 1st. McKeen was promoted again, to colonel, and took command of the 81st after Johnson's resignation in November 1862. McKeen was killed at Cold Harbor, Virginia, on June 3, 1864.

20. See note 25 below.

21. In a report submitted on June 10, 1864, Inspector-General Schriver described the conditions at White House Landing as of June 8. There were, he said, 225 officers

and 5,343 men, "of whom 35 officers and 1,341 men are reported as constituting the 'permanent garrison.' These last were inspected by me to ascertain their character and condition. The detachments of the Veteran Reserve Corps are not fit for duty in the field, being entirely unable to march or perform any fatiguing work. This statement of the commanding officer [Johnson] is confirmed by their appearance, &c.; they are well supplied in every respect. . . . The provost guard is composed of some 60 regular infantry and a detachment of Veteran Reserves, whom I did not inspect. . . .

"The field works are completed. . . . I think any attempt the enemy can make on the depot might be easily resisted with the present arrangement. . . . Officers were attentive to their duties, and order is everywhere observed." *Official Records,* series 1, vol. 36, pt. 3, 722–23.

22. Schriver's report (see note 21 above) described the three-year volunteer regiments and veteran volunteer regiments as generally "in good condition." The high-numbered Ohio regiments, by contrast, were National Guard or "100-days' men." Schriver concluded, "Troops more unfit for the field I never saw." *Official Records,* series 1, vol. 36, pt. 3, 723.

23. General Benjamin F. Butler from Massachusetts. It was Butler, while commander in 1861 of Fort Monroe, who coined the phrase "contraband of war" to justify the army's use of escaped slaves. After serving as military governor of New Orleans in 1862, Butler now commanded Union troops on the Bermuda Hundred, a peninsula between the James and Appomattox River southeast of Richmond.

24. Colonel M. N. Wisewell, formerly commander of the 6th Regiment of the Veteran Reserve Corps, took command of the entire organization on November 9, 1863. *Official Records,* series 3, vol. 5, 550.

25. Colonel William Wilson, who took command of the 81st Pennsylvania after the death of McKeen. It might be Wilson to whom Johnson was referring in a previous letter. See Letters, June 6, 1864.

26. Neither the *North American* of June 8, 1864, nor the *Philadelphia North American Review* of that date contain any mention of Colonel Johnson or the Veteran Reserve Corps. Mary may have mistaken the title for any of the dozens of papers published in the Philadelphia/Camden area at that time.

27. The 28th U.S. Colored Troops, under the command of Lieutenant Colonel C. S. Russell (*Official Records,* series 1, vol. 40, 724). The use of black troops was highly controversial to white Northerners and an anathema to white Southerners. It was doubted among many whites that African Americans, particularly freed slaves, would fight, while Southern commands killed or sold back into slavery any blacks taken prisoner in uniform. The refusal to exchange black prisoners was the primary reason for the breakdown of the exchange cartel. The massacre of black prisoners after the capture of Fort Pillow on April 12, 1864, by troops under the command of General Nathan Bedford Forrest, is generally acknowledged as one of the worst atrocities of the war. After their performance at Fort Wagner, South Carolina, and many other posts and battlefields, black soldiers earned a grudging respect from many white Northerners. McPherson, *Battle Cry of Freedom,* 564, 565–66, 634, 686–87, 792–96.

28. Earlier in the war, Major General David Hunter had drawn Lincoln's ire by announcing, without the president's approval, the immediate emancipation of all slaves in his military district. In June 1864 Hunter was the commander of Union forces in the Shenandoah Valley, but his incompetence there would give Confeder-

ate General Jubal Early an opportunity to make his famous lunge at Washington, and Hunter would be replaced by General Philip Sheridan. Catton, *Stillness at Appomattox,* 257–59.

29. For the significance of the name change, from "Invalid Corps" to "Veteran Reserve Corps" see introduction, pp. 13–14, 24.

30. Major General Philip Henry Sheridan, commander of cavalry in the Army of the Potomac and soon-to-be-named commander of Union forces in the Shenandoah Valley.

31. On June 10, 1864, Major General Henry W. Halleck, army chief of staff, ordered that "No more troops be sent to White House. All re-enforcements and others for Army of the Potomac will be sent to Bermuda Hundred." *Official Records,* series 1, vol. 36, pt. 3, 738.

32. On June 12, 1864, Grant ordered that Abercrombie be relieved from his command at the White House, and "proceed to Washington D.C. . . . for orders." Brigadier General George W. Getty was assigned to take his place. *Official Records,* series 1, vol. 36, pt. 3, 758.

33. Johnson wrote this postscript in the margin on the first page of the letter.

34. Confederate partisan commander Wade Hampton. Johnson's estimate of the number of men under his command is no doubt exaggerated.

35. The regimental books of the 25th New York Cavalry list First Lieutenant C. N. Howard as having been "killed at White House landing June 12, 1864." The date could be erroneous; in any event Lieutenant Howard is the only officer listed as killed at White House Landing from this regiment. 25th New York Cavalry, Regimental Record Book, vol. 1, Book Records of Volunteer Union Organizations, RG 94, National Archives.

36. On June 20 Abercrombie sent a message to General Halleck, which was received at 8:30 P.M., stating, "We were attacked this morning by rebel cavalry and artillery; the firing still continues. I think we shall be able to hold our position until General Sheridan arrives. . . . I have crossed the supply train to the north side of the river to avoid the enemy's shells, which have been falling in the midst of it. The firing has abated and distant artillery can be heard above us on the river. I will hold this place to the last." A message from Abercrombie received at 4 P.M. at the headquarters of the Army of the Potomac reported, "This place was attacked at 7 a.m. this day by Hampton's division of cavalry and artillery. So far I have foiled all their attempts to get into the depot. About one hour ago one of their caissons exploded. There has been no firing from them since. The head of General Sheridan's column is in sight. But 2 or 3 wounded in my command. General Getty has just arrived."

These messages apparently crossed with Grant's, who ordered Abercrombie to "Hold out at all hazards. Two gun-boats were sent from here yesterday, and must now be at White House. General Sheridan is also near you, if not yet arrived" (*Official Records,* series 1, vol. 36, pt. 3, 785). Johnson's implied charge of cowardice against General Abercrombie is not repeated in any other account, and Abercrombie was given an honorable discharge from the volunteer army on June 24, 1864. Heitman, *Historical Register and Dictionary of the U.S. Army,* vol. 1, 150.

37. "The undersigned hereby relinquishes the command of the troops at this station to Brigadier-General Getty. In doing so, he avails himself of this opportunity of expressing his high appreciation of the services of his staff in their respective

positions, tendering his sincere thanks to Captain Babcock and the officers of the navy for their very efficient aid and support to the land forces in the persistent attack on the post of the day, by the enemy." General Orders no. 10, June 20, 1864, J. J. Abercrombie, Brigadier-General. *Official Records,* series 1, vol. 36, pt. 3, 786.

38. Headquarters of the Army of the Potomac,
June 20, 1864.

Brigadier-General Getty,
Commanding, White House:

General: Major-General Sheridan has been ordered to join the Army of the Potomac. So soon as he has left you will break up the depot at White House and, sending your Veteran Reserves to Washington, bring the balance of your command and all public property to City Point. . . .

Geo. G. Meade
Major-General, Commanding

Official Records, series 1, vol. 36, pt. 3, 786.

Chapter Eight

1. Colonel "Geo. A. Woodward—Aged 31, from the State of Pennsylvania, entered the volunteer service in May 1861; took part in the battles of Mechanicsville, Gaines' Mills, Glendale, and Gettysburg; received a gun shot wound in the right foot, and another in the left leg, and entered the Vet. Res. Corps in August, 1863." *Field Record,* 2.

2. George W. Woodward, state supreme court judge in Pennsylvania, Democratic gubernatorial candidate for that state in 1863. He opposed making war to preserve the Union and ruled that the national conscription act was unconstitutional. McPherson, *Battle Cry of Freedom,* 684–85.

3. This seems to contradict Johnson's idea that Stanton was prejudiced against him.

4. Confederate Major General Fitzhugh Lee, nephew of Robert E. Lee, became a famous cavalry commander in his own right. Ezra J. Warner, *Generals in Gray: Lives of the Confederate Commanders* (Baton Rouge: Louisiana State University Press, 1959), 178.

5. Commissions made by the president had to be confirmed by the U.S. Senate.

6. Johnson was referring to the battle of the Monocacy, Maryland, where forces under the command of Confederate General Jubal Early attacked federal troops attempting to keep the rebel raiders from advancing on Washington.

7. The forces under Early were now advancing on Washington from the north, having swung completely around the capitol. Panic erupted. Although the fortress line surrounding Washington was likely the strongest on earth at the time, most of its garrison had gone south with the Army of the Potomac. Urgent telegrams were sent to Grant, who dispatched reinforcements by boat. In the meantime, all that stood in the way of Early's capture of Washington were "hundred day" militia men, hastily armed government clerks, and several regiments of the Veteran Reserve Corps.

8. Since Johnson's letter of July 10th, the defenses of Washington had come under attack by Early's forces, with members of the VRC (but not Johnson's regiment) rushing into the rifle pits in an attempt to convince Early that the forts around the capitol were well defended. Encountering resistance, Early hesitated long enough on July 11 for Grant's reinforcements to arrive, allowing VRC soldiers such as Alfred Bel-

lard to claim that they had saved the Union (Long, *Civil War Day by Day,* 537–38). Early began his withdrawal on July 12.

Alfred Bellard, a private with what was originally designated "as the 97th company of the 1st Battalion of Invalids, (or as the boys called us Condemned Yanks)" wrote an eyewitness account of the battle in front of Fort Stevens, in which he participated (Donald, *Gone for a Soldier,* 270–76). Another, hitherto unpublished account of the defense of Washington was written by Lieutenant Colonel Robert E. Johnston, commander of the 9th Regiment of the Veteran Reserve Corps, and is contained in his report to Colonel Wisewell of October 1, 1864:

"We left Camp Fry on the evening of July 10th at 4 o'clock in light marching order and arrived at Crystal Springs at about 8 o'clock P.M. and bivouacked for the night. About 1 A.M. 11th inst. we received orders from Major Gen.l McCook to form line of battle immediately and await further orders. We remained in line until about 7 o'clock A.M., at which time we received orders to take position near Battery Stevens in the Rifle Pits.

"About 4 o'clock P.M. the enemy advanced a heavy line of skirmishers and drove our skirmish line some distance back and took up their position so close to Fort Stevens, that they became quite annoying to the gunners, killing and wounding a number in the fort. The regiment was ordered to advance and relieve the 25th N.Y. Cavalry (dismounted) and if possible, to dislodge the enemy from the position they had taken up. The regiment was at once moved forward from the line of rifle pits and ordered to advance, and as they advanced they were deployed, when within about 300 yards of the enemy's position they were ordered to charge. The charge was made in good order—driving the enemy at several points for some distance. A continuous fire was kept up until we were relieved by the advance of the 6th Corps at which time seven companies of the regiment were relieved. Three companies remaining on the line during the night—who were in turn relieved by three companies of the regiment the following morning at 7 o'clock.

"Our loss on the skirmish line was One (1) killed, four (4) mortally wounded (since died) and (7) seven severely wounded.

"The conduct of the Officers and the men of the regiment was all that could have been desired. They knew their duties and performed them to my entire satisfaction." R. E. Johnston, to Colonel M. N. Wisewell, October 1, 1864, Veteran Reserve Corps Letters Received, box 28, entry 297, Provost Marshal General's Bureau, RG 110, National Archives.

Charles Johnson's regiment in the meantime had been shifted north into Maryland, where to judge from his account there was also much confusion and panic.

9. William Blackiston Davis, Mary's older brother, who was married to Mary Frances Roy. Lynch, *From Whence We Came,* 11.

10. Johnson again identifies "the upper crust" with the rebels, while noting that working and middle-class Marylanders side with the Union. As for the attempt to ambush his command, see Letter, July 19, 1864.

11. This would have been either Mary or Alice Davis. Lynch, *From Whence We Came,* 11.

12. William Cowper, "The Time Piece," in *The Complete Poetical Works of William Cowper* (New York: D. Appleton & Co., 1856), 244.

13. Josiah Gilbert Holland, *Bittersweet: A poem* (New York: C. Scribner, 1863).

14. Thomas Moore, "And Doth Not a Meeting Like This," in *The Poetical Works of Thomas Moore,* ed. William Michael Rossetti (London: Ward, Lock, 1911), 298–99.

15. This is most likely Philip James Bailey (1816–1902), Romantic poet who most famous work was "Festus," a blank-verse version of Goethe's *Faust,* published in 1839. Adam Roberts, *Romantic and Victorian Long Poems: A Guide* (Brookfield, Vt.: Ashgate, 1999), 87–90.

16. William Carleton (1794–1869), Irish poet and novelist.

17. George Gordon Byron, "From Anacreon," in *Poetical Works of Byron* (Boston: Houghton Mifflin, 1975). The line should read: "Her car half round yon sable heaven . . ."

18. "The better part of valor is discretion." *King Henry IV,* Part 1, 5.4.120.

19. Johnson's "parchment" is dated December 7, 1863. "You are hereby informed that the President of the United States has appointed you Colonel in the Invalid Corps" as of December 4. It is signed by Secretary of War Edwin M. Stanton. Johnson Papers.

20. Thomas Moore, "Lalla Rookh," in Godley, *Poetical Works of Thomas Moore* (London: Oxford University Press, 1910), 340–437.

21. Fort Pulaski, near Savannah, Georgia, was seized by Southern forces in January 1861 and retaken by federal troops in April 1862.

22. "Mary and Charly" are Mary E. Johnson, Charles Johnson's older sister, and her husband, Charles Redding. The conflicting loyalties of civil war tore many families apart, and even President Lincoln had in-laws fighting on the rebel side.

23. Major General Christopher Columbus Augur, commander of the department of Washington, D.C., since October 14, 1863. Long, *Civil War Day by Day,* 422.

24. Savage, Maryland.

25. Out for a ride, Johnson's horse had stumbled and "it was a race to see who would get over the horse's head first, the saddle or me—I beat it!" Johnson slammed head first into a tree stump, suffering a gashed head and what was probably a concussion. Letters, September 2, 1864.

26. "I had rather be a toad / And live upon the vapor of a dungeon." *Othello,* 3.3.269–70.

27. These "flights of fancy" may be the long philosophical essay, not published with this collection but included with Johnson's collected papers and dating from this period. The essay is a meditation on the harshness and fleetingness of life, which can only be redeemed through duty to family and country, and made more or less tolerable, in its worst moments, by dwelling on the memory of better times (Johnson Papers, September 2, 1864). A more concise rendition can be found in Letter, October 9, 1866.

Chapter Nine

1. Charles F. Johnson, April 20, 1865, 18th VRC, Regimental Letter and Order Book, vol. 4, RG 94, National Archives.

2. Built at the corner of First and A streets in 1800 as a tavern and boardinghouse, the three-story brick building was used by congress from 1814 until 1819, until the new (present) Capitol building was occupied. In 1861 the building was com-

mandeered by the military for use as a prison. Together with the adjacent Carroll Prison, the facility had capacity sufficient to house more than fifteen hundred prisoners at any one time. Among its more celebrated prisoners were Confederate spies Rose O'Neal Greenhow and Belle Boyd, and (in 1865) several members of the Lincoln assassination conspiracy. Garrison, *Encyclopedia of Civil War Usage,* 178–79.

3. The upcoming presidential election pitted Abraham Lincoln against Johnson's old commanding officer, Major General George B. McClellan. A third party candidate, Charles Fremont, had dropped out of the race to ensure that the pro-emancipation vote was not split. It is uncertain which candidate Johnson supported, but given his high regard for the general, it most likely was McClellan. The army vote, however, went overwhelmingly to Lincoln, however some of the officers of the Army of the Potomac were still "McClellanized." In any case, Mary's opinion hardly mattered because women had not yet won the right to vote.

4. Byron, *The Giaour.* The line should read, "It was Eternity to Thought."

5. In a letter dated November 23, 1864, Colonel George W. Gile informed headquarters that "the commissioned officers of the 18th Regiment V.R.C. . . . selected George Deal of Camden, N.J. as sutler of the . . . regiment." National Archives Microfilm Publication M 1064, roll 86, frame 0779 D 645, Records of the Appointment, Commission, and Personal Branch ca. 1775–1917, Letters Received 1864–94, National Archives. Gile had entered the volunteer army as a private from New Hampshire in 1861, participated in the battles of Cedar Mountain, Second Bull Run, Chantilly, and South Mountain, and was disabled at Antietam. He entered the Invalid Corps in May 1863. Field Record, 2. Johnson later refers to Gile (as "Giles"), on page 269.

6. "Mounted scouts and patrols" were eventually formed within the 11th Regiment of the Veteran Reserve Corps. *Official Records,* series 3, vol. 5, 562.

7. Johnson evidently enrolled his sons in the Georgetown College. A report card from the school, dated March 1865, shows that William Ewing Wiley Johnson, aged 14, received grades of "very good," "high" and "excellent." Lynch, *From Whence We Came,* 36.

8. Johnson's aversion to interracial sexual relations was shared by many white Americans. Indeed, the Democratic Party, in its 1864 race against Lincoln, tried to make "miscegenation" or "race-mixing" a campaign issue. McPherson, *Battle Cry of Freedom,* 789–90.

9. Lieutenant Colonel Newton F. Colby. There is no other reference in Johnson's letters to his "case," nor is there any indication of whether the rapist mentioned earlier in the letter was apprehended.

10. Disabled during the third day of the battle of Gettysburg, General Winfield Scott Hancock convalesced for almost a year before returning to command the II Corps at the battles of the Wilderness, Spotsylvania, and Cold Harbor. Suffering defeat at Ream's Station, and bothered by his Gettysburg wound, Hancock was shifted to a post behind the lines as the commander of the 1st Veteran Volunteer Corps (Warner, *Generals in Blue,* 202–4). Established in 1864, the Veteran Volunteer Corps consisted of able-bodied men who had already completed a full term of service (usually three years) but wished to re-enlist. Such men, unlike members of the VRC, were offered substantial bounties on re-enlisting. Garrison, *Encyclopedia of Civil War Usage,* 256.

11. Adaline Hufty was Johnson's aunt, older sister to his mother Maria Hufty Johnson.

12. See Letter, August 19, 1863.

13. This letter was transcribed, apparently by or at the request of Grace Johnson Lynch. The original letter, however, was no longer in her possession.

Bibliography

Adams, George Worthington. *Doctors in Blue: The Medical History of the Union Army in the Civil War.* New York: Henry Shulman, 1952.

Adams, Robert, Wissahickon Valley Watershed Association, to Fred Pelka, September 2, 2003.

Alma [an anonymous correspondent]. "From Col. Miller's Mauch Chunk Regiment (Late Thirty-sixth)." *Philadelphia Sunday Dispatch,* February 16, 1862.

———. "From Col. Miller's Thirty-sixth Regiment Pennsylvania Volunteers." *Philadelphia Sunday Dispatch,* November 3, 1861.

———. "From the Same Regiment." *Philadelphia Sunday Dispatch,* 17 November, 1861.

Basler, Roy P., ed. *The Collected Works of Abraham Lincoln.* New Brunswick, N.J.: Rutgers University Press, 1953.

Baynton, Douglas C. "Disability and the Justification of Inequality in American History." In *The New Disability History: American Perspectives,* edited by Paul K. Longmore and Lauri Umansky, 33–57. New York: New York University Press, 2001.

Blanck, Peter, and Chen Song. "Civil War Pension Attorneys and Disability Politics." *University of Michigan Journal of Law Reform* 35, nos. 1, 2 (fall 2001–winter 2002): 137–217.

Blanck, Peter David, and Michael Millender. "Before Disability Civil Rights: Civil War Pensions and the Politics of Disability in America." *Alabama Law Review* 52, no. 1. (fall 2000): 1–50.

Blight, David W. *Race and Reunion: The Civil War in American Memory.* Cambridge: Harvard University Press, 2001.

Book Records of Volunteer Union Organizations, Records of the Adjutant General, RG 94, National Archives.

Boston Women's Health Book Collective. *The New Our Bodies, Ourselves.* New York: Simon & Schuster, 1984.

Bowe, Frank. *Handicapping America: Barriers to Disabled People.* New York: Harper & Row, 1978.

Boyden, Anna L. *Echoes from Hospital and White House: A Record of Mrs. Rebecca R. Pomeroy's Experience in War-Times.* Boston: D. Lothrop, 1884.

Branch, Taylor. *Parting the Waters: America in the King Years, 1954–63.* New York: Simon & Schuster, 1988.

Brooks, Stewart. *Civil War Medicine.* Springfield, Ill.: Charles C. Thomas, 1966.

Byron, George Gordon. *The Poetical Works of Byron.* Boston: Houghton Mifflin, 1975.

———. *The Poetical Works of Lord Byron.* New York: R. Martin, 1855.

The Camden and Gloucester Directory of 1863–1864: Containing the Names of the Inhabitants, Their Occupations, and Dwelling Houses: A List of the Streets, Lanes, and Alleys, the City Offices, Public Institutions &c. Camden, N.J.: O. Durang, W. Hindman, H. Curts, 1864.

Catton, Bruce. *Glory Road.* Garden City, N.Y.: Doubleday, 1952.

———. *Mr. Lincoln's Army.* Garden City, N.Y.: Doubleday, 1951.

———. *Reflections on the Civil War.* New York: Berkley Books, 1981.

———. *A Stillness at Appomattox.* Garden City, N.Y.: Doubleday, 1953.

Clawson, Mary Ann. *Constructing Brotherhood: Class, Gender, and Fraternalism.* Princeton, N.J.: Princeton University Press, 1989.

Congressional Globe. 39th Cong. 1st sess., 1866. Vol. 36, pt. 1.

Cooper, William. *The Poetical Works of William Cooper.* Boston: Little, Brown, 1859.

Covey, Herbert C. *Social Perceptions of People with Disabilities in History.* Springfield, Ill.: Charles C. Thomas, 1998.

Cowper, William. *The Complete Poetical Works of William Cowper.* New York: D. Appleton, 1856.

Craig, Samuel A. *Memoirs of Civil War and Reconstruction.* Type cript. at Civil War Times Illustrated Collection. Carlisle, Pa.: United States Army Military History Institute.

Crowell, Joseph E. *The Young Volunteer: The Everyday Experiences of a Soldier Boy in the Civil War.* New York: G.W. Dillingham, 1906.

Dannett, Sylvia G. L., ed. *Noble Women of the North.* New York: Thomas Yoseloff, 1959.

Dearing, Mary R. *Veterans in Politics: The Story of the G.A.R.* Baton Rouge: Louisiana State University Press, 1952.

De Forest, John W. *Miss Ravenel's Conversion from Secession to Loyalty.* New York: Harper & Brothers, 1939.

Denney, Robert E. *The Civil War Years: A Day-By-Day Chronicle of the Life of a Nation.* New York: Sterling, 1992.

Donald, David Herbert, ed. *Gone for a Soldier: The Civil War Memoirs of Private Alfred Bellard.* Boston: Little, Brown, 1975.

D.S.L. "From the Thirty-sixth Regiment." *Philadelphia Inquirer,* November 20, 1861.

Dyer, Frederick H. *A Compendium of the War of the Rebellion.* Wilmington, N.C.: Broadfoot, 1994.

Eckhart, Thomas D. *The History of Carbon County.* Leighton, Pa.: Thomas Eckhart and the Carbon County History Project, 1992.

"The Eighty-first Penna. Regiment." *Philadelphia Inquirer,* June 14, 1862.

Fellman, Michael. *Inside War: The Guerilla Conflict in Missouri during the American Civil War.* New York: Oxford University Press, 1989.

Fiedler, Leslie. *Freaks: Myths and Images of the Secret Self.* New York: Simon & Schuster, 1978.

Field Record of the Officers of the U.S. Army Veteran Reserve Corps, From the Commencement to the Close of the Rebellion. Washington, D.C.: Scriver & Swing, 1865.

Fitzpatrick, John C. "The Invalid Regiment and Its Colonel." *Daughters of the American Revolution Magazine* (November 1919): 649–53.

Fogelson, Robert M., and Rubenstein, Richard E., eds. *Mass Violence in America: Memphis Riots and Massacres.* New York: Arno Press / New York Times, 1969.

"From the Chippewa Regiment: Correspondence of the Inquirer." *Philadelphia Inquirer,* January 18, 1862.

Gamache, Peter. "The Civil War Experiences of Sergeant Peter Gamache." Manuscript. Civil War Miscellaneous Collection. Carlisle, Pa.: United States Army Military History Institute.

Gardner, Harrison. *Diary of Harrison Gardner.* Manuscript. Civil War Miscellaneous Collection. United States Army Military History Institute, Carlisle, Pa.

Garland, Robert. *The Eye of the Beholder: Deformity and Disability in the Graeco-Roman World.* Ithaca, N.Y.: Cornell University Press, 1995.

Garrison, Webb, and Cheryl Garrison. *The Encyclopedia of Civil War Usage.* Nashville: Cumberland House, 2001.

Giesberg, Judith Ann. *Civil War Sisterhood: The U.S. Sanitary Commission and Women's Politics in Transition.* Boston: Northeastern University Press, 2000.

Glasson, William H. *Federal Military Pensions in the United States.* New York: Oxford University Press, 1918.

Hansel, Sarah. *Soldier's Heart: Survivors' Views of Combat Trauma.* Lutherville, Md.: Sidron Press, 1995.

Hardin, Martin D. "The Defense of Washington against Early's Attack in July, 1864." In *Military Essays and Recollections: Papers Read before the Commandery of the State of Illinois, Military Order of the Loyal Legion of the United States,* vol. 2, 121–44. Wilmington, N.C.: Broadfoot, 1992.

Heitman, Francis B. *Historical Register and Dictionary of the U.S. Army.* Washington, D.C.: Government Printing Office, 1903.

———. *Historical Register of the United States Army from Its Organization: September 29, 1789, to September 29, 1889.* Washington, D.C.: National Tribune, 1890.

Hemingway, Ernest. "Soldier's Home." In *In Our Time,* 87–101. 1925. Reprint, New York: Charles Scribner's Sons, 1958.

Herman, Judith Lewis. *Trauma and Recovery.* New York: Basic Books, 1992.

Hewett, Janet B. *The Roster of Union Soldiers: 1861–1865.* Wilmington, N.C.: Broadfoot, 1998.

Hickel, K. Walter. "Medicine, Bureaucracy, and Social Welfare: The Politics of Disability Compensation for American Veterans of World War I." In *The New Disability History: American Perspectives,* edited by Paul K. Longmore and Lauri Umansky, 236–67. New York: New York University Press, 2001.

Holland, Josiah Gilbert. *Bittersweet: A poem.* New York: C. Scribner, 1863.

Holmes, Amy E. "'Such is the Price We Pay': American Widows and the Civil War Pension System." In *Toward a Social History of the American Civil War: Exporatory Essays,* edited by Maris A. Vinovskis, 171–95. Cambridge: Cambridge University Press, 1990.

"Homes for Discharged Invalid Soldiers." *United States Service Magazine* (September 1864): 489–93.

Howard, Oliver Otis. *The Autobiography of Oliver Otis Howard, Major General United States Army.* New York: Baker & Taylor, 1908.

Hummel, William W. "The Military Occupation of Columbia County." *Pennsylvania Magazine of History and Biography* 80, no. 3 (July 1956).

"The Invalids." *United States Service Magazine* (September 1864): 235–39.

Johnson, Charles F. Letters and Documents. Bancroft Library, University of California at Berkeley.

Klass, Helen, ed. *Portrait of Elnathan Keeler: A Union Soldier.* Wappinger Falls, N.Y.: Goldleif Productions, 1977.

Kriegel, Leonard. "Uncle Tom and Tiny Tim: Some Reflections on the Cripple as Negro." *The American Scholar* 38 (summer 1969): 412–30.

Lathrop, George Parsons. *History of the Union League of Philadelphia.* Philadelphia: J.B. Lippincott, 1884.

Leech, Margaret. *Reveille in Washington: 1860–1865*. New York: Harper & Brothers, 1941.

Lerner, Melvin J. *The Belief in a Just World: A Fundamental Delusion.* New York: Plenum, 1980.

Light, James F. *John William De Forest.* New York: Twayne, 1965.

Lindbuchler, Ryan. *History of the 81st P.V.I., "The Fighting Chippewas": The Story of the 81st Pennsylvania Volunteer Infantry Regiment in the American Civil War.* 81st Pennsylvania Infantry Regiment, Company K Civil War Reenactment Unit, 1992. Available at http://www.angelfire.com/pa3/81stpennsylvania/.

Linderman, Gerald F. *Embattled Courage: The Experience of Combat in the American Civil War.* New York: Macmillan, 1987.

Litwack, Leon F. *Been in the Storm So Long: The Aftermath of Slavery.* New York: Alfred A. Knopf, 1979.

Long, E. B. *The Civil War Day by Day: An Almanac 1861–1865.* Garden City, N.Y.: Doubleday, 1971.

Longmore, Paul K., and Lauri Umansky. "Disability History: From the Margins to the Mainstream." In *The New Disability History: American Perspectives,* edited by Paul K. Longmore and Lauri Umansky, 1–29. New York: New York University Press, 2001.

Lynch, Grace Johnson. *From Whence We Came.* Hibbing, Minn.: Self-Published, 1985.

Manning, Lynn. "The Magic Wand." In *Staring Back: The Disability Experience from the Inside Out,* edited by Kenny Fries, 165. New York: Plume, 1997.

McConnell, Stuart. *Glorious Contentment: The Grand Army of the Republic, 1865–1900.* Chapel Hill: University of North Carolina Press, 1992.

McElroy's Philadelphia City Directory for 1860: Names of the Inhabitants of the Consolidated City, Their Occupations, Places of Business, and Dwelling Houses: A Business Directory: A List of the Streets, Lanes, Alleys, the City Offices, Public Institutions, Banks &c, also the Names of the Housekeepers &c in Camden, New Jersey. Twenty-Third Edition. Philadelphia: E.C. & J. Biddle, 1860.

McMurtrie, Douglas C. *The Disabled Soldier.* New York: Macmillan, 1919.

McPherson, James M. *The Battle Cry of Freedom: The Civil War Era.* New York: Ballantine Books, 1989.

Mitchell, Reid. *The Vacant Chair: The Northern Soldier Leaves Home.* New York: Oxford University Press, 1993.

Moore, Thomas. *The Poetical Works of Thomas Moore.* Edited by A. D. Godley. London: Oxford University Press, 1910.

———. *The Poetical Works of Thomas Moore.* Edited by William Michael Rossetti, London: Ward, Lock, 1911.

Moss, Kary L., ed. *Man-Made Medicine: Women's Health, Public Policy, and Reform.* Durham: Duke University Press, 1996.

National Archives. Records of the Adjutant General's Office. RG 94.

———. Records of the Asst. Commissioner for the State of Tennessee, Bureau of Refugees, Freedmen and Abandoned Lands, Registered Letters Received, RG 105.

———. Records of the Appointment, Commission, and Personal Branch ca. 1775–1917, Letters Received 1863–94.

———. Records of the Bureau of Refugees, Freedmen, and Abandoned Lands. RG 105.

———. Records of the Provost Marshal General's Bureau (Civil War). RG 110.

"The Naval Hospital Establishment." *United States Service Magazine* (September 1864): 261–62.

Nieman, Donald G., ed. *The Freedman's Bureau and Black Freedom.* New York: Garland, 1994.

Norden, Martin F. *The Cinema of Isolation: A History of Physical Disability in the Movies.* New Brunswick, N.J.: Rutgers University Press, 1994.

Oates, Stephen B. *Abraham Lincoln: The Man Behind the Myths.* New York: Harper & Row, 1984.

Orders, Letters, Circulars Concerning the Invalid Corps, 1863. Research Collection. Boston Public Library.

Patterson, Gerard A. *Debris of Battle: The Wounded of Gettysburg.* Mechanicsburg, Pa.: Stackpole Books, 1997.

Paulsen, Gary. *Soldier's Heart: Being the Story of the Enlistment and Due Service of the Boy Charley Goddard in the First Minnesota Volunteers.* New York: Delacorte, 1998.

Pelka, Fred. "Disability Rights in Zimbabwe." *Mainstream: Magazine of the Able-Disabled* 14, no. 3 (October 1989): 21–23.

Roberts, Adam. *Romantic and Victorian Long Poems: A Guide.* Brookfield, Vt.: Ashgate, 1999.

Rowbottom, Margaret, and Charles Susskind. *Electricity and Medicine, History of Their Interaction.* San Francisco: San Francisco Press, 1984.

Scharf, J. Thomas, and Thompson Westcott. *History of Philadelphia 1609–1884.* Philadelphia: L. H. Everts & Co., 1884.

Sears, Stephen W. *To the Gates of Richmond: The Peninsula Campaign.* New York: Ticknor & Fields, 1992.

Shakespeare, William. *Shakespeare: The Complete Works.* Edited by G. B. Harrison. New York: Harcourt, Brace & World, 1968.

Skocpol, Theda. *Protecting Soldiers and Mothers: The Political Origins of Social Policy in the United States.* Cambridge: Harvard University Press, 1992.

Stiker, Henri-Jacques. *A History of Disability.* Ann Arbor: University of Michigan Press, 1997.

Stinson, Byron. "The Invalid Corps." *Civil War Times Illustrated* (May 1971): 20–31.

Taylor, Frank H. *Philadelphia in the Civil War.* Philadelphia: Dunlap, 1913.

Thomson, Rosemarie Garland. *Extraordinary Bodies: Figuring Physical Disability in American Culture and Literature.* New York: Columbia University Press, 1997.

T.R. "Letters from the Soldiers: From Colonel James Miller's Thirty-sixth Regiment PA. Volunteers." *Philadelphia Sunday Dispatch,* November 17, 1861.

Tupper, Martin Farquhar. *Proverbial Philosophy: A Book of Thoughts and Arguments Originally Treated.* Boston: Phillips, Sampson and Company, 1851.

———. *Tupper's Complete Poetical Works.* Boston: Phillips, Sampson and Company, 1851.

U.S. War Department. *The War of the Rebellion: A Compilation of the Official Records of the Union and Confederate Armies.* Washington, D.C.: U.S. Government Printing Office, 1902.

Van Doren, Mark, ed. *The Portable Walt Whitman.* 1945. Reprint, New York: Viking, 1973.

Ward, Geoffrey C. *The Civil War: An Illustrated History.* New York: Alfred A. Knopf, 1990.

Warner, Ezra J. *Generals in Blue: Lives of the Union Commanders.* Baton Rouge: Louisiana State University Press, 1964.

Warner, Ezra J. *Generals in Gray: Lives of Confederate Commanders.* Baton Rouge: Louisiana State University Press, 1959.

Wendell, Susan. *The Rejected Body: Feminist Philosophical Reflections on Disability.* New York: Routledge, 1996.

Wiley, Bell Irvin. *The Common Soldier in the Civil War.* New York: Grosset & Dunlap, 1958.

———. *The Life of Billy Yank: The Common Soldier of the Union.* Indianapolis: Bobbs-Merill, 1952.

Wilkerson, Abby L. *Diagnosis: Difference—The Moral Authority of Medicine.* Ithaca: Cornell University Press, 1998.

Young, Agatha. *The Women and the Crisis: Women of the North in the Civil War.* New York: McDowell, Obolensky, 1959.

Index

References to illustrations are given as *illus.*

FRED PELKA is a freelance writer and researcher based in Northampton, Massachusetts. He has written articles on legislation, health care, disability rights, and many other issues and was a contributor to *Mainstream,* a national monthly newsmagazine for people with disabilities, from 1984 to 1999. He is the author of the *ABC-CLIO Companion to the Disability Rights Movement* and a 2004 Guggenheim Fellow.